I0867774

Praise for *American Defense Reform*

"Oliver and Toprani have brilliantly written about a proven model to transform our military for the twenty-first century, and specifically to succeed in the peer competition with China. Deeply insightful and underpinned by matchless historical analysis, herein lies a strategic path ahead vastly different from the normal weapons system by weapons system assessment to which we typically revert. Every serious national security expert should be informed by this extraordinary book." —**Adm. Mike Mullen**, USN (Ret.), former chief of naval operations, former chairman of the Joint Chiefs of Staff

"The United States is due for a fundamental national defense rethink to confront the challenges of the twenty-first century. Dave Oliver and Anand Toprani skillfully use history to illuminate a way for our civilian and military leaders to rebalance the Pentagon." —**Maj. Gen. Robert Kimmit**, USAR (Ret.), former ambassador to Germany

"Dave Oliver and Anand Toprani well describe the forces that have complicated defense management over the years. Their discussion considers the roles played by Congress, industry, and the numerous internal actors within the Pentagon. Finding a way to better coordinate and integrate these often-opposing groups is essential for dealing with the threat posed by rising powers such as China." —**Maj. Gen. Arnold Punaro**, USMCR (Ret.), author of *On War and Politics: The Battlefield Inside Washington's Beltway*

"With the end of 20 years of war in Afghanistan, the United States is turning to confront the challenges of China and climate change, requiring a material reordering of US defense priorities. Admiral Oliver's unique decades-long experience at the highest levels of Washington power enables an extraordinary collection of insights. Oliver details the paths to achieve the close collaboration among a wide group of civilian and military leaders necessary for success. Every secretary of defense needs to have a blueprint to follow and Dave Oliver and Anand Toprani's is a terrific offering." —**Michael A. Bayer**, advisor for the Defense Science and Defense Business Boards

"Oliver and Toprani address a fundamental question: Burdened by equipment, processes, incentives, and mindsets shaped by past wars and intensely pressed by today's contingencies, how do leaders build civilian and military coalitions to prepare for tomorrow's wars? The authors harvest personal experience and extensive historical analysis to illuminate ways of achieving cooperation that can break the bonds of the past and present to create a better future." —**Richard Danzig**, former secretary of the Navy, trustee of the RAND Corporation, member of the President's Intelligence Advisory Board

"It would have been most helpful to have learned of the knowledge and experience diffused throughout this book before facing the challenges of reducing the Navy's force structure and Marine Corps forces and cutting the Defense Department's budget from $106 billion to $78 billion. This is a must read for anyone aspiring to meet similar future challenges, because they are coming!" —**H. Lawrence Garrett III**, former secretary of the Navy and general counsel for the secretary of defense

"As Washington works to accelerate cultural, technological, and operational change to better deter China, Dave Oliver and Anand Toprani have performed an invaluable service at an important time by producing a thoughtful 'how-to guide' to drive lasting change drawn from the US Navy's post-World War II history." —**Vago Muradian**, editor, *Defense & Aerospace Report*

"This in-depth national security analysis provides rich historical context from the US Navy's perspective. A must read on the essential but often stormy interrelationship among the nation's top military and civilian leaders. Oliver and Toprani's insights vividly illustrate why civilian control of the military—a sacred cornerstone of American democracy—cannot function optimally unless it cohesively incorporates military experience." —**Joe R. Reeder**, former undersecretary of the US Army and former chairman of the Panama Canal Commission

"Dave Oliver and Anand Toprani have written a superb examination of our naval history, drawing on those past experiences to guide a reshaping of our military to meet twenty-first century challenges." —**Gen. Anthony C. Zinni**, former commander in chief of US Central Command

"Modeled after a method used by a former chief of naval operations, *American Defense Reform* combines both leadership and persuasion in equal parts. Dave Oliver and Anand Toprani bring a fresh and spirited approach to the problem now facing the Biden administration." —**Irv Blickstein**, SES 18, former senior Navy programmer, senior engineer at the RAND Corporation

"This book is a cutting-edge recipe for impending defense strategies." —**Mike Wynne**, former undersecretary of defense for acquisition and former secretary of the Air Force

"Retired Admiral David Oliver and Naval War College strategist and historian Anand Toprani offer a valuable critique of the current state of the national security community. Their policy prescriptions should be required reading for all who are concerned about America's ability to maintain the military advantage that has underpinned its longtime leadership of the Free World." —**Dov Zakheim**, former defense official under President Ronald Reagan and former undersecretary of defense under President George W. Bush

AMERICAN DEFENSE REFORM

AMERICAN DEFENSE REFORM

LESSONS FROM FAILURE AND SUCCESS IN NAVY HISTORY

REAR ADM. DAVE OLIVER, USN (RET.)
AND ANAND TOPRANI

FOREWORD BY ADM. BILL OWENS, USN (RET.)

Georgetown University Press / Washington, DC

Library of Congress Cataloging-in-Publication Data

Names: Oliver, Dave, 1941– author. | Toprani, Anand, author.
Title: American defense reform: lessons from failure and success in Navy history / Dave Oliver and Anand Toprani.
Description: Washington, D.C.: Georgetown University Press, [2022] | Includes bibliographical references and index.
Identifiers: LCCN 2021058307 (print) | LCCN 2021058308 (ebook) | ISBN 9781647122768 (paperback) | ISBN 9781647122751 (hardback) | ISBN 9781647122775 (ebook)
Subjects: LCSH: United States. Department of Defense. | United States—History, Naval—20th century. | United States—Military policy. | United States—Defenses.
Classification: LCC VA58 .O45 2022 (print) | LCC VA58 (ebook) | DDC 359.00973—dc23/eng/20211220
LC record available at https://lccn.loc.gov/2021058307
LC ebook record available at https://lccn.loc.gov/2021058308

♾ This paper meets the requirements of ANSI/NISO Z39.48-1992 (Permanence of Paper).

23 22 9 8 7 6 5 4 3 2 First printing

Printed in the United States of America

Cover design by Jeremy John Parker
Interior design by BookComp, Inc.

The views expressed in this publication are those of the authors and do not necessarily reflect the official policy or position of the Department of Defense or of the US government.

CONTENTS

ILLUSTRATIONS

FIGURES

TABLES

FOREWORD

I am very pleased to endorse this fine book. I lived much of my life following and instigating change in the Department of Defense. Sometimes these were more rudimentary, year-to-year budget changes, and occasionally they were changes to major strategies and procurements. These strategies included the Maritime Strategy of the 1980s and the technically driven strategies of the 1990s associated with the "revolution in military affairs," the effort to fund game-changing technologies that would bring together the four services and their various capabilities to make for a successful "joint force."

What Dave Oliver and Anand Toprani have done in this book is to point out the enormous complexity of this effort of "national security procurement." This is the most complicated business in the world—larger than any other, more complex and difficult to understand, and certainly more challenging to drive real results and implement them through the congressional process than anyone would ever forecast.

Dramatic changes in our defense budget are very difficult to implement. Even though changes are necessary at times such as the end of the Cold War (with the need for large budget reductions) or the beginning of a technical revolution, the services typically don't react with great vision. Neither is it possible for civilian leaders to react with great vision without having the complete and sincere help of the four services' leaders, with their knowledge of operational requirements. Today we face a vastly changing world—from Europe, the Middle East and Central Asia (from which we have essentially withdrawn), to an emerging China—with all of the various challenges that entails, including dramatic technologies both in our hands and in those of potential challengers, as well as real budget challenges as we consider post-COVID economic realities. Arguably, again, we need to apply serious thought to a new broad-based national security review, including our defense budget.

Oliver and Toprani have discussed in this book many of those challenges, such as the need for innovative civilian leaders, an understanding Congress, and military leaders who are willing to cooperate and provide true and long-term strategic advice.

It's my pleasure to have known Dave Oliver as a fellow admiral in the Navy, working side by side and trying to do the best we could (sometimes against overwhelming bureaucratic forces) and making serious and major changes in the defense budget with the great help of senior leadership in the Navy and the Department of Defense.

Later I came to realize the great value of "jointness" through my time as the vice chairman of the Joint Chiefs of Staff, a job that Congress established primarily to bring together the joint forces' strategy and programming to ensure that the budgets of the four services and several agencies were aligned with the needs of the nation, as defined by civilian leadership and Congress.

The complex "business" of national defense can change—we have seen that. But it takes patience, it takes real planning, and it cannot happen as part of a budget cycle or as part of a congressional committee's activities. It takes deep thought, long-term strategy, and deep expertise about how to spend the nation's treasury wisely.

This book is a genuine contribution to understanding this complex problem, with many concepts and ideas about how it might be improved and the imperative of doing it correctly. It will be an important reference for many of those who have not been exposed to the challenges of this most complex and difficult "business"—one that has much more importance to our country than most realize.

—Adm. Bill Owens, USN (Ret.),
former vice chairman of the US Joint Chiefs of Staff

PREFACE

This book is a how-to guide for reshaping the Department of Defense. There have been several attempts to do so, some more successful than others. To understand why, we explore the experience of the US Navy during several key periods since 1945: the years immediately following the end of World War II, the beginning and winding down of the Vietnam War, and the denouement of the Cold War. In addition to our own research and personal recollections, our analysis leverages insights from unpublished interviews with three former chiefs of naval operations—Arleigh Burke, George Anderson, and David McDonald—as well as James Russell, who served as the vice chief for Burke and Anderson.

The book also uses historical events to appreciate the interactions of civilian officials with a military whose culture, norms, and practices they may not have fully understood. Such misapprehensions resulted in some very public disputes, such as the "Revolt of the Admirals" in 1949 and, fourteen years later, Anderson's firing during the scuffle over designing a plane intended for joint Navy and Air Force use. After Adm. Elmo Zumwalt yanked the Navy into the twentieth century by forcefully tackling racial discrimination in the ranks, Adm. Frank Kelso proactively met the challenges of the post–Cold War world. He succeeded in steering the Navy to a new course while simultaneously avoiding many of the mistakes of his Navy predecessors as well as his peers in the Army and Air Force.

Our historical research helps explain why the Navy found it challenging to overcome its service culture and embrace change. Armed with this knowledge, this book also examines why political appointees find it so difficult to force change on the Department of Defense, how Congress is ill-suited for the demanding task of reshaping defense, and why private industry provides so few answers. Our analysis also demonstrates why there is no substitute for close collaboration among a wide group of people, civilian and military, and in our conclusion we outline one proven process that leverages each group's particular strengths for the common good.

ACKNOWLEDGMENTS

This book would have been impossible without insights from a legion of friends and colleagues, active and retired, military and civilian, scholars and practitioners. First, we wish to thank Donald Jacobs of Georgetown University Press, who was an enthusiastic proponent of this project from the moment we submitted our book proposal. We are also obliged to our two anonymous peer reviewers. Besides offering extensive feedback, they were tolerant of our occasional missteps and offered constructive suggestions for improvement.

Our list of acknowledgments is far too long for us to provide an individualized message of thanks to every person who assisted us. Suffice it to say, all of the people listed below were generous with their time and expertise. We are especially grateful to those people who read all or part of the manuscript while in draft.

Dave Oliver wishes to acknowledge, in particular, the contributions of Jim and Liz Bailey, Irv Blickstein, John Briquelet, Mike Conners, Jay Davis, John Douglas, Joe Dyer, Eric Labs, John Lockhart, Riley Mixson, Vago Muradian, Charles Nemfakos, Tim Oliver, Ron O'Rourke, Whit Peters, Joe Reeder, Jim Roche, Joe Sestak, Harlan Ullman, Charles Williams, Mike Wynne, and Ann Zumwalt.

Anand Toprani is grateful to Michael Dennis, Peter Dombrowski, Jim FitzSimonds, Benjamin Fordham, Chas Freeman, Phil Haun, Jim Holmes, Colin Jackson, Rick Moss, Nick Murray, Chris Nelson, Matt Noland, David Painter, Sally Paine, Michael Riordan, David Rosenberg, Kristian Smith, Craig Symonds, and Evan Wilson. He is also indebted to Dave Oliver for his mentorship, patience, and frankness about military, political, and corporate life.

We dedicate this book to the women who chose us as their life partners: Linda Bithell Oliver and Maria Toprani. Our journeys together began well before this book, and we hope they will continue long afterward.

NATIONAL SECURITY LEADERS FROM 1945 TO 2001

Chief of Naval Operations	Secretary of the Navy	Secretary of Defense	President	Years
Chester Nimitz (1945–47)	James Forrestal (1944–47)		Harry Truman	1945–53
Louis Denfeld (1947–49)	John Sullivan (1947–49)	James Forrestal (1947–49)		
Forrest Sherman (1949–51)	Francis Matthews (1949–51)	Louis Johnson (1949–50)		
William Fechteler (1951–53)	Dan Kimball (1951–53)	George Marshall (1950–51)		
		Robert Lovett (1951–53)		
Robert Carney (1953–55)	Robert Anderson (1953–54)	Charles Wilson (1957–57)	Dwight Eisenhower	1953–61
	Charles Thomas (1954–57)	Neil McElroy (1957–59)		
Arleigh Burke (1955–61)	Thomas Gates (1957–59)			
	William Franke (1959–61)	Thomas Gates (1959–61)		
George Anderson (1961–63)	John Connally (1961)	Robert McNamara (1961–68)	John Kennedy	1961–63
	Fred Korth (1962–63)			
David McDonald (1963–67)	Paul Nitze (1963–67)		Lyndon Johnson	1963–69

Chief of Naval Operations	**Secretary of the Navy**	**Secretary of Defense**	**President**	**Years**
Thomas Moorer (1967–70)	Paul Ignatius (1967–69)	Clark Clifford (1968–69)		
Elmo Zumwalt (1970–74)	John Chafee (1969–72)	Melvin Laird (1969–73)	Richard Nixon	1969–74
	John Warner (1972–74)	Elliot Richardson (1973)		
	William Middendorf (1974–77)	James Schlesinger (1973–75)		
James Holloway (1974–78)		Donald Rumsfeld (1975–77)	Gerald Ford	1974–77
	Graham Claytor (1977–79)	Harold Brown (1977–81)	Jimmy Carter	1977–81
Thomas Hayward (1978–82)	Edward Hidalgo (1979–81)			
James Watkins (1982–86)	John Lehman (1981–87)	Caspar Weinberger (1981–87)	Ronald Reagan	1981–89
Carlisle Trost (1986–90)	James Webb (1987–88)	Frank Carlucci (1987–89)		
		William Ball (1988–89)		
Frank B. Kelso (1990–94)	Henry Garrett (1989–92)	Dick Cheney (1989–93)	George H. W. Bush	1989–93
	Sean O'Keefe (1992–93)			
	John Dalton (1993–98)	Les Aspin (1993–94)	Bill Clinton	1993–2001
		William Perry (1994–97)		

Note: We have not included officials who served on an acting basis.

INTRODUCTION

The United States has several pillars of its national power. Although often the most visible, the US military is only one of them. Americans have come to take their dominance within the conventional realms of war for granted, but many defense analysts warn that the United States has been resting on its laurels for too long. US forces have been stretched thin by decades of conflicts in the Middle East and South Asia as well as a demanding operations tempo around the globe, and the rest of the world has not stood still. A rival that achieves some form of overmatch, perhaps in the emerging cyber and space domains, might well leapfrog a distracted or complacent United States.[1]

Confrontations with rival powers, technological advances, and unexpected challenges such as pandemics and natural disasters promise to become regular occurrences. Unlike past decades, there is a fear that the United States no longer can rely on an overwhelming power position that compensates for its occasional missteps. Hovering over all of these immediate threats, moreover, is the specter of anthropogenic climate change, whose effects are unknown but may dwarf all other concerns.

The entire United States must prepare itself to confront these challenges, and the military must also be prepared to reconsider its existing assumptions, norms, and operating procedures.

The question this book seeks to answer is, How best can we encourage the US military, specifically the services that it comprises, to respond to new circumstances at home or abroad? The US military, like all complex bureaucracies, resists changes that contradicts its historical experience, ethos, and prevailing organization.[2] Two subsidiary questions flow from this fact. First, who will guide or correct it? Should it be the executive branch? Or will it be Congress through the power of the purse? Will it be the services themselves, selecting which weapon systems or concepts will survive or be jettisoned? Or is it private industry, with its ethos of efficiency and profit maximization? Addressing this "who" question requires an awareness of each institution's fitness to direct national defense.

Second, how change will happen is at least as important as who will be the driver. Each of the services and the wider Department of Defense—which, for the sake of convenience, we synonymously refer to as the Pentagon, its headquarters—are complex organizations. No policy prescription is viable if it does not account for political exigencies and bureaucratic obstacles, and any leader—civilian or military—who hopes to reshape defense will need many allies, not the least within the military itself.

Sometimes, frustrated critics will conclude that the US military—indeed, any military—is incapable of reinvention. Many scholars have tackled the subject of why and how militaries adjust to changes in their operating environment. One popular framework they have established is to distinguish between those changes that occur in peacetime versus wartime. They associate innovation with the former because peacetime affords innovators "time to form, test, and evaluate . . . [their] ideas and perceptions." Conversely, adaptations occur during wartime because of the interaction with the enemy, shortened time horizons, and vicissitudes of chance, "fog," and friction. A proclivity for the former is supposedly a predictor of success for the latter.[3] Other scholars have further sliced and diced by adding a third category—technological innovation—as opposed to doctrinal changes that occur in peace and war (i.e., *what* people fight with versus *how* they fight).[4]

Other analysts reject the rigid dichotomy between adaptation and innovation, preferring instead to situate them along a spectrum of changes and instead study how change occurs, with emphasis on military cultures and educational or learning systems.[5] The former seems wise since the notion that one can separate technological innovation from the doctrinal variety is questionable, as new technologies must be integrated into a service (a process of socialization), often resulting in significant bureaucratic churn or even outright opposition.

In contrast to many studies of military innovation, we reject the peacetime-innovation-versus-wartime-adaptation dichotomy because it does not apply today to the United States. Components of the US military have been continuously engaged in high-tempo operations, both "hot" and "cold" wars, since the end of World War II. Some of these conflicts obviously were higher profile than others. Moreover, the burden of such fighting wars has, since World War II, fallen disproportionately on specific services or service components. In the case of the wars in Korea, Vietnam, Iraq, and Afghanistan, the most-affected services were the Army and the Marine Corps, while in the Navy and the Air Force, the burden fell largely on naval aviation and tactical air forces, respectively.

The misperception that there is sharp difference between "peace" and "war" in the United States arises, in part, because even in the US military, many people (including senior leaders) are unaware of what the rest of the military beyond their service or component is doing. For example, after the fall of Saigon in 1975, Army and Marine leaders (as well as most Air Force and the Navy aviators) may have thought the United States was at peace. This was a grave misconception. Leave aside the fact that the State Department and the Intelligence Community (much of the latter is funded from the Department of Defense) were busy fighting the Cold War with (usually) nonviolent means of coercion. Within the US military, Air Force and Navy elements, such as the strategic missile and bomber forces and the submarine community, saw increases in their operating tempo as the Cold War turned hotter.

Accordingly, for the US military the notion of a lazy, docile "peacetime" in which to innovate is a mirage. Expecting services to adapt when "the shooting starts" is but another in the litany of rationales that the military advances to justify why "now" is never the right moment for change.

Furthermore, demarcating periods of war from peace distorts how the US defense enterprise functions. With the reforms of the Goldwater-Nichols Department of Defense Reorganization Act of 1986, the task of fighting wars has fallen to field commanders, either at the regional (combatant command) or theater-specific levels (e.g., Military Assistance Command, Vietnam, and the International Security Assistance Force in Afghanistan). These leaders and institutions are *consumers* of national resources, and they are laser-focused, quite naturally, on short-term considerations. Their tactical and operational considerations do not include the long-term, national implications of resource allocation. For example, the lifespan of specific weapons platforms is typically measured in decades, which often exceeds the careers of the senior military leaders who will use them.

Resource production for theater-level consumers is the responsibility of the Department of Defense, most important the Office of the Secretary of Defense (OSD) and the military services. (The Joint Chiefs of Staff—JCS—and most of its subsidiaries are venues for developing joint war plans.) Contrary to popular perception, the Pentagon is never entirely focused on the current war but must think about future conflicts and the potential demands of waging or deterring them. To critics such as former secretary of defense Robert Gates, this "peacetime" obsession with long-term planning and budgeting reflected an almost criminal indifference to the plight of US service members then engaged in combat in Iraq and Afghanistan.[6]

What Gates may not have fully appreciated was that because the military operates in a world of finite resources (however arbitrary their demarcation may be at times), it must always balance the long-term demands of "winning the peace" or "preparing for the next war" with the short-term imperative of bringing ongoing conflicts to a satisfactory conclusion.[7] Every dollar, bullet, or person devoted to the latter cannot easily be redirected (if at all) to the former, and vice versa. Sometimes leaders' decisions must come at the expense of those on the "sharp end of the spear," as future national requirements may well transcend those of specific, ongoing conflicts.

The failure to heed change undoubtedly explains some past military failures. One scholar of military "incompetence" argued that such failures stem from the hierarchical nature of military organizations, which enforces conformity, venerates tradition, and sometimes denigrates intellectualism.[8] Even officers with long track records of success were not immune from the institutional pressures that created catastrophic failure. Conversely, some of those officers who chafed under peacetime constraints proved to be excellent wartime commanders, and vice versa.[9]

While these may seem to be abstract, academic matters, they are in fact deeply relevant to the US military today. Consider the example of the US Navy, which has enjoyed unchallenged command of the seas since World War II. This luxury may well prove to be a mixed blessing. One British scholar observed that the "long calm lee of Trafalgar" hobbled the Royal Navy after its great triumph over Napoleonic France because it discouraged innovative thinking and individual initiative in warfighting by British naval officers.[10] Today's US Navy may well find itself in the "long calm lee of Leyte"—the Battle of Leyte Gulf in 1944 being the last major fleet engagement of the US Navy. It has long operated on the assumption of overwhelming tactical, operational, and technological superiority, which may no longer be justified. Not surprisingly, this scholar's book found a place on the professional reading list of the chief of naval operations (CNO).

It is plausible that prolonged periods of conventional military dominance and the rigid hierarchies of military organizations together can inhibit necessary changes—whether they be social, doctrinal, or technological. It is not surprising, therefore, that sometimes officials—civilian leaders and even some military officers—have felt it necessary to enforce innovation over the objections of a recalcitrant military leadership.

This belief is, however, misguided. Top-down changes mandated by civilian leaders are often difficult to enforce because bureaucratic and institutional factors stifle evolution.[11] In the United States, no organization is larger or more complex than the Department of Defense. In the past, critics believed that the services resisted new ideas because they resented the loss of status or budgets. This is only partially accurate and reflects a shortsighted perspective because it ignores service cultures and doctrine. Outsiders who have disregarded these factors and pursued radical change of the US defense enterprise have unwittingly undermined the effectiveness of their efforts. Because these outsiders did not understand the Department of Defense, they engendered unnecessary resistance from the military, its allies in Congress, the defense industry, and the media and sometimes overlooked the most significant, as opposed to the most pressing, issues.

To succeed, those who press for change need the support of those who best understand the institutions being changed—that is, the leadership of the US military services. This requires recognizing the expertise of military leaders in areas that outsiders cannot match. Accordingly, one central challenge confronting anyone tasked with managing US national defense is how to strike the correct balance between bold reform and prudent compromise that avoids unnecessary resistance.

This is easier said than done, but it is essential. If it is any consolation, this is not a new challenge. Decades ago, Gen. Matthew Ridgway, who rescued the United Nations' war effort in Korea in 1950–51, put his finger on this challenge. The demands of "limited" war—which moderated the use of violence to achieve political aims short of the complete defeat the adversary—required a reevaluation of how Americans thought about national policy and military strategy. As he put it,

> [neither] civilian statesmen nor military professionals, working in separate compartments, could by themselves lay down the lines that would give direction to our intercourse with other sovereignties. It is clear now . . . that best results flow from intimate day-to-day collaboration among military and civilian leaders, wherein the civilian leaders propose the *ends* that must be achieved and the military leaders supply their estimate of how much can be attained by military *means* and how those means may be best employed.[12]

So far, so good—but Ridgway went further perhaps than many would accept today:

> Such collaboration is possible only when civil and military authorities seek and earnestly consider each other's point of view. Sound decisions will not be reached through automatic overruling of the preponderant recommendations of the nation's senior military advisers by their civilian superiors. The civilian authority, under our Constitution, of course remains supreme. But a failure to seek, hear, and weigh the counsel of our experienced military advisers is to court disaster.

We embrace Ridgway's recommendations, even if the general sometimes fell short of the lofty expectations he set for others.[13] Effective national security depends on active and continuous collaboration among the various groups responsible for formulating, executing, and evaluating national strategy.

This applies equally to pushing the US military to adapt when necessary. Ridgway and other professional soldiers professed to be the best judges of the challenges their services confronted, but the historical record suggests otherwise. Their participation in the process is necessary but insufficient.

French premier Georges Clemenceau once remarked, perhaps uncharitably, "War is too serious a matter to be left to military leaders."[14] This observation stemmed from Clemenceau's frustration with the quality of French generalship during World War I and his suspicion of the reactionary and anti-Semitic French officer corps.[15] That said, his dictum should not serve as the guiding principle of civil-military relations. A close reading of the famous Prussian theorist of war Carl von Clausewitz requires that we modify Clemenceau's admonition.

War, Clausewitz implied, is too *complex* to be handled by military officers alone. Again, this has nothing to do with any lack of intelligence on the part of the military. The skills necessary to conduct even simple tactical exercises, much less those demanding operational planning, require extensive training and innate abilities. Clausewitz's greatest insight was that war is a political act whose outcome is at the mercy of the vicissitudes of chance.[16] Because of its sheer complexity and inherent uncertainty, it is beyond the mental horizons of any single leader or even a small group to master all of its intricacies.

Similarly, reshaping a complex, sprawling, and proud institution such as the US military so that it copes with major changes in the geopolitical, social, or technological environment is not something that is possible through top-down directives by civilian leaders, as the complex histories of Secretary of Defense Robert McNamara and others demonstrate. Just as we cannot expect military leaders to master all of the nonmilitary aspects of conflict, so too we cannot expect civilians unfamiliar with the norms and practices of the military to choreograph the scope and pace of change within it.

Successful innovations, be they embracing breakthrough technologies, rearranging existing hierarchies, or adapting to new political realities, can take root only if there is appropriate buy-in from the participants—the military or at least some of its senior leadership. Our thesis builds upon the work of previous generations of theorists of military innovation/adaptation but also diverges in certain respects.[17] Many political scientists have concluded that innovation occurs because of top-down, vertical processes, although they disagree as to the sources of that change. Some argue that it is the result of external pressure from civilians. Others contend it arises from inter- or intraservice feuding, with senior military officers acting as the decisive change agents.[18] Historians have offered a necessary clarification by demonstrating that innovation sometimes results from a bottom-up process that filters horizontally throughout a service.[19]

Both explanations may well be correct, depending on the level of analysis or context. Horizontal/bottom-up learning applies to the tactical and operational levels of war.[20] From the perspective of changes arising from choices about force design/structure, acquisition, procurement, and budgeting, however, the vertical process seems more appropriate. Our analysis does not take sides over whether the impetus for change comes from beyond the military or through inter- and intraservice politics. Instead, we see elements of all three approaches at work, usually simultaneously. We do, however, emphatically agree with those theorists who concluded that change is invariably "the outcome of a well-managed political process" that depends on the support of actors within and outside of the military.[21]

Specifically, our analysis suggests that successful and lasting change requires three preconditions:

1. Some shock that challenges existing assumptions and budgets. Such shocks may be external (e.g., the beginning or end of the Cold War) or internal to the United States (e.g., the social and racial tensions after the Vietnam War).
2. Military leaders within the services who are flexible, open to new ideas, and willing to share their esoteric knowledge.
3. Clear guidance from civilian leaders, who can serve as disinterested arbiters among the services and their components and whose approval is essential for the services to justify their plans, capabilities, and budgets.[22]

Of course, the military's response will vary depending on the nature of the shock, but we are more interested in explaining why successful change happens and describing processes to encourage it. Moreover, while external or domestic shocks are a necessary ingredient, change occurs and is enforced during the budget process when civilian and military leaders make decisions regarding the short- and long-term resource allocation, including considerations of possible gains, risks, and trade-offs.[23] Military leaders may speak in the language of "requirements" or "capabilities," but neither can meaningfully exist without adequate resourcing. As one deputy secretary of defense put it, "we do what we fund."[24]

Such funding occurs in a three-stage defense acquisition system: requirements (what is needed), acquisitions (what is bought), and budgeting (how to pay for it). For sake of clarity, we use the term "budgetary process" as shorthand for the entire system, although we shall devote some attention to the acquisition process in chapter 7.[25]

We must disabuse ourselves of the notion that budgets are merely accounting devices that express spending plans. Rather, they are profoundly *moral* documents that reflect an individual's or an institution's values, priorities, and expectations. Because resources are always finite, even in wartime, budgets are also a necessary forcing function to distinguish needs from wants. As the head of systems analysis during the Jimmy Carter administration put it, "making a better defense program at a higher budget level is child's play. Any damn fool can do that." The difficulty arises, as we alluded to earlier, in deciding *what* the optimal allocation of resources is and, equally important, *who* makes that decision.[26]

In the context of national defense, budgets are not simply products of objective analysis of the external threat environment. They must also include considerations of domestic policy (the competing demands for government resources) and public finance (ideas regarding the ideal level of public spending, taxation, and borrowing). Sometimes individuals or institutions attempt to break free of their fiscal constraints by arguing that the existing allocation does not align with the changes in the external or internal environment, as the Navy has attempted to do since the US government identified the People's Republic of China as its primary geopolitical threat.[27]

USING THE US NAVY AS A FRAMEWORK FOR ANALYSIS

The Department of Defense is a mammoth organization—far too large to analyze comprehensively in any one book. Our analysis focuses on a single service, the US Navy, and we intend to extrapolate our findings where relevant to the rest of the defense enterprise. There are certain risks to this approach, given the differing histories and cultures of the various military services, but there are also certain arguments in favor.

We chose the Navy not only because it is the service with which we are most familiar but also because its tasks are of virtually equal importance in wartime and peacetime, as it is the only service integrally involved in protecting the flow of maritime trade. As the "most catholic" of the services, the Department of the Navy, which includes the Marines, operates in all the major domains of contemporary warfare, fulfills the greatest variety of missions, and presents important differences from the other services.[28] Arguably, intraservice politics (e.g., among surface-warfare officers, aviators, and submariners—not to mention the Marines) are more complicated in the Navy than in the other services. Yet the Navy also grapples with many of the same sorts of choices and trade-offs as the other services, albeit on a smaller level, such as the proper role of airpower, the size of ground forces, and juggling current operations with future procurements. How the Navy and Marines resolve their differences and collaborate effectively is not self-evident and deserves clarification.

Prior to the establishment of the Space Force in the Department of the Air Force in 2019, the Department of the Navy was unique in that the Navy and Marines, two separate services, reported to a single civilian secretary. To avoid duplication of effort and waste, the two services worked out a complicated set of living arrangements. Consequently, the Navy Department has been "joint" for much longer than the rest of the US military. For example, there are no Marine medics on a battlefield. Instead, the Navy trains and provides corpsmen for both services. The Navy also buys the Marines their airplanes by providing the money and the necessary contracting officers. Furthermore, naval officers command the ships that deliver the Marines ashore. There are literally hundreds of these symbiotic arrangements that enable both services to function. Consequently, whether or not it is included on their recruiting materials, the Navy and the Marines are linked in what they can accomplish. They are therefore engaged in constant discussions about their future and the best uses of their finite resources.

The Navy has faced a number of major challenges since the end of World War II. For the purposes of our analysis, the most important has been adapting from a world of large fleet engagements against other maritime powers to secure "command of the high seas" to one of achieving limited "sea control" or circumventing "sea denial" while integrating naval, land, and air power against continental powers not easily defeated by blockade—namely, the Soviet Union after 1945 and China today. The former concept originated in the work of Alfred Thayer Mahan, who was arguably the most influential American strategic thinker in history. The latter flows from the work of Julian Corbett, a British civilian strategist who modified Mahan's theories to apply them to Britain's peculiar circumstances. Both men agreed that the primary purpose of naval power was to support a nation's foreign economic interests, which in turn created the material conditions for a large navy.[29]

Another struggle—one not limited to the Navy—has arisen due to changing social norms, specifically the demand for the equitable integration of minorities and women. This is an even more urgent problem today than during the Cold War, with the subsequent entrenchment of the all-volunteer force and the growing need for highly educated, technologically savvy people capable of dominating the cyber domain of warfare and mastering the myriad uses of artificial intelligence.[30]

The first half of our book consists of historical case studies of the Navy since 1945. Each chapter examines why change was necessary and how the Pentagon and naval leadership addressed (or ignored) the key issues.

The post–World War II period (1945 to 1950) featured the absence of any compelling naval threat, political pressure to curtail defense spending, and extravagant claims by the fledgling Air Force about the effectiveness of "strategic bombing." For the US Navy, this cocktail of developments produced a disaster in civil-military relations: the Revolt of the Admirals.

During the 1960s, the Navy confronted Robert McNamara's insistence on securing a greater role for the civilians on his staff in shaping strategic and budgetary choices. McNamara was more effective than his predecessors not only because of his intellect and his strong personality but also because he used new techniques of scientific management such as systems analysis to exercise a dominant role in the budgetary process. He confronted hostility from all the military services, but perhaps none was more intractable than the Navy. Like his predecessor during the Revolt of the Admirals, McNamara chose to fire his CNO.

Future CNOs learned to work more productively with their political bosses, but they firmly resisted changing the culture of the Navy, even as the rest of the country was undergoing profound social upheaval. It would not be until near the end of the Vietnam War that the Navy finally found a leader willing to confront the new realities. Elmo Zumwalt tackled long-standing social, racial, and gender inequities that were crippling the Navy and made more progress than any of his predecessors or successors. But in so doing, he became a pariah to many within the Navy.

The final period we examine is the early 1990s. The CNO then, Frank Kelso, alone among senior military leaders, understood that the military would no longer be able to count on large budgets to sustain an outdated force structure. By directing the Navy to undertake a rigorous process of determining those capabilities that were truly essential for the postwar world (all the while including the Marines), he avoided many of his predecessors' mistakes.

Navy leaders during the aforementioned periods had very different approaches to managing their relationships with civilian leadership. Scholars have spent gallons of ink writing about the importance of civilian control over the US military. Too often they narrowly framed the discussion around the questions of when and how to use force and preserving the independence of the military from political meddling.[31] Establishing how civilians and the military should actually cooperate in matters of war, peace, and politics is, however, considerably more complicated.[32]

Every new secretary of defense faces a choice when deciding how they will approach their job. Will they direct the military as did McNamara and later Donald Rumsfeld, or will they cooperate like Melvin Laird, whom many consider the template for how modern secretaries should run the Pentagon?[33] Put another way, is energetic civilian leadership a recipe for disaster because civilians misunderstand the application of force—as the wars in Vietnam or Iraq might suggest—or is the problem, instead, a profound unfamiliarity with the military as a social institution? Our analysis of political appointees, Congress, and private industry (chapters 5 through 7) shows that, whatever good intentions or ideas these groups might possess, without collaboration with military leaders, they are unsuited to reshape the defense enterprise.

So that we might not lose hope that nothing can change, chapter 8 demonstrates how strong direction from civilian and military leaders, coupled with an awareness of bureaucratic politics, can overcome traditional military reluctance to embrace new ways of analyzing and conducting war. This chapter and the ones that precede it form the basis of our conclusions on how to move forward in an era of geopolitical upheaval abroad and social unrest at home.

The Nobel Prize–winning economist Thomas Schelling once remarked, "You can sit in your armchair and try to predict how people will behave by asking how you would behave if you had your wits around you. You get, free of charge, a lot of vicarious, empirical behavior."[34] We disagree. As a work of history and public policy, this book relies on the perspectives of countless managers who participated in the events we describe. We are fortunate, therefore, to have the use of two remarkable sources of information. The first is a series of unpublished interviews that Dave Oliver conducted in 1974 with three CNOs—Arleigh Burke, George Anderson, and David McDonald—and one vice CNO, James Russell. Each of them grappled in his own way with the challenges of the Cold War, the nuclear-power revolution, and the first truly strong secretary of defense, McNamara.

The second source is Rear Adm. Dave Oliver's decades of military, corporate, and political experience. During his six tours in the Pentagon, he observed firsthand how the highest levels of the US government grappled with a variety of challenges, from the Cold War to the 9/11 terrorist attacks. His position on Zumwalt's personal staff afforded him a ringside seat as the admiral rebuilt the Navy during and after the Vietnam War while fighting the institutional racism that had disfigured the service for decades—all the while feuding with "the father of the nuclear Navy," Adm. Hyman Rickover.

Oliver subsequently directed the submarines of the US Seventh Fleet against the Soviet Union and worked for Secretary of the Navy John Lehman, which provided him an invaluable perspective on the famous Maritime Strategy of the 1980s. He then helped Admiral Kelso reorganize the Navy after the Cold War before serving as an executive in the defense industry and holding political appointments in the Pentagon under presidents of both parties. Few public servants have enjoyed such a diverse career, and even fewer have shared their insights in a book such as this.

NOTES

1. See, e.g., National Defense Strategy Commission, *Providing for the Common Defense: The Assessment and Recommendations of the National Defense Strategy Commission* (Washington, DC: United States Institute of Peace, 2018), https://www.usip.org/sites/default/files/2018-11/providing-for-the-common-defense.pdf.
2. See, e.g., Barry Posen, *The Sources of Military Doctrine: France, Britain, and Germany between the World Wars* (Ithaca, NY: Cornell University Press, 1984), 29–34, 41–59, 222–28; Stephen Peter Rosen, *Winning the Next War: Innovation and the Modern Military* (Ithaca, NY: Cornell University Press, 1991), 2–5.
3. Williamson Murray, *Military Adaptation in War: With Fear of Change* (Cambridge: Cambridge University Press, 1996), 308ff. (quotation from p. 309); David Barno and Nora Bensahel, *Adaptation under Fire: How Militaries Change in Wartime* (Oxford: Oxford University Press, 2020), 17ff.
4. Rosen, *Winning*, 8, 39ff., 183ff.
5. Frank Hoffman, *Mars Adapting: Military Change during War* (Annapolis, MD: Naval Institute Press, 2021), chap. 1.
6. Robert Gates, *Duty: Memoirs of a Secretary at War* (New York: Knopf, 2014), 115ff., 311ff.
7. Christian Brose, *The Kill Chain: Defending America in the Future of High-Tech Warfare* (New York: Hachette, 2020), introduction, chap. 1.
8. Norman Dixon, *On the Psychology of Military Incompetence* (New York: Basic Books, 2016). Dixon's work focused on the British Army before World War II. For a similar study of the US military since 1945, see Tim Bakken, *The Cost of Loyalty: Dishonesty, Hubris, and Failure in the U.S. Military* (New York: Bloomsbury, 2020).
9. This was especially the case among US field commanders during World War II. Jörg Muth, *Command Culture: Officer Education in the U.S. Army and the German Armed Forces, 1901–1940, and the Consequences for World War II* (Denton: University of North Texas Press, 2013).
10. Andrew Gordon, *The Rules of the Game: Jutland and British Naval Command* (London: Penguin, 2015).
11. Rosen, *Winning*, 9ff., 255–57.
12. Matthew Ridgway, *The Korean War* (Garden City, NY: Doubleday, 1967), vii. Emphasis in the original. We are grateful to Michael Riordan for drawing our attention to this quote.

13. A. J. Bacevich, "The Paradox of Professionalism: Eisenhower, Ridgway, and the Challenge to Civilian Control," *Journal of Military History* 61, no. 2 (1997): 303–33.
14. "La guerre! C'est une chose trop grave pour la confier à des militaires."
15. Clemenceau was a key participant in the Dreyfus Affair of the 1890s, when French officers fabricated evidence of treason by a Jewish officer. For more on Clemenceau's wartime leadership, see Eliot Cohen, *Supreme Command: Soldiers, Statesmen and Leadership in Wartime* (New York: Free Press, 2002), 52–94.
16. Alan Beyerchen, "Clausewitz, Nonlinearity and the Unpredictability of War," *International Security* 17, no. 3 (1992): 59–90.
17. There is an excellent summary of the different schools of thought in Hoffman, *Mars Adapting*, chap. 2.
18. For a theoretical overview, see Owen Cote, "The Politics of Innovative Military Doctrine: The U.S. Navy and Fleet Ballistic Missiles" (PhD diss., Massachusetts Institute of Technology, 1996), 10ff.
19. Robert Foley, "Learning War's Lessons: The German Army and the Battle of the Somme 1916," *Journal of Military History* 75, no. 2 (2011): 471–504; Robert Foley, "A Case Study in Horizontal Military Innovation: The German Army, 1916–1918," *Journal of Strategic Studies* 35, no. 6 (2012): 799–827.
20. See, again, Barno and Bensahel, *Adaptation*, which focuses on the US Army with particular emphasis after 2001 and dismisses the air and naval domains of war as rarely "decisive" (p. 5).
21. Harvey Sapolsky, "On the Theory of Military Innovation," *Breakthroughs* 9, no. 1 (2000): 35–40 (quotation from p. 37).
22. This tracks with but differs slightly from the formula Christian Brose (echoing Barry Posen) identified in *The Kill Chain* in chapter 5: clear threats, specific operational problems, and strong civilian and military leadership.
23. Arnold Kanter, *Defense Politics: A Budgetary Perspective* (Chicago: University of Chicago Press, 1979), 3ff.
24. Gates, *Duty*, 146.
25. Irv Blickstein, *Navy Planning, Programming, Budgeting, and Execution: A Reference Guide for Senior Leaders, Managers and Action Officers* (Santa Monica, CA: RAND Corp., 2016), 5ff. See also Brose, *Kill Chain*, chap. 11.
26. Stephen Rosen, "Systems Analysis and the Quest for Rational Defense," *Public Interest* 76, no. 3 (1984): 12.
27. Mark Gunzinger, "The US Navy's So-Called Budget Salvo Demands Too Much," *Defense News*, January 16, 2020, https://www.defensenews.com/opinion/commentary/2020/01/16/the-us-navys-so-called-budget-salvo-demands-too-much/.
28. B. H. Friedman, "The Navy after the Cold War: Progress without Revolution," in *US Military Innovation since the Cold War: Creation without Destruction*, ed. Harvey M. Sapolsky, Benjamin H. Friedman, and Brendan Rittenhouse Green (London: Routledge, 2009), 75–77.
29. A. T. Mahan, *The Influence of Sea Power upon History* (New York: Dover, 1987); Julian Corbett, *Some Principles of Maritime Strategy* (Annapolis, MD: Naval Institute Press, 1988). The differences between the two theorists are summarized in James Holmes, *A Brief Guide to Maritime Strategy* (Annapolis, MD: Naval Institute Press, 2019); and Kevin McCranie, *Mahan, Corbett, and the Foundations of Naval Strategic Thought* (Annapolis, MD: Naval Institute Press, 2021). For a recent statement of naval strategy along

Corbettian lines, see US Marine Corps, US Navy, and US Coast Guard, *Advantage at Sea: Prevailing with Integrated All-Domain Naval Power* (December 2020), https://media.defense.gov/2020/Dec/16/2002553074/-1/-1/0/TRISERVICESTRATEGY.PDF.

30. Alec Ross, "The Pentagon's Army of Nerds," *The Atlantic*, September 12, 2001, https://www.theatlantic.com/ideas/archive/2021/09/pentagon-army-of-nerds/620042/.
31. Risa Brooks, "Paradoxes of Professionalism: Rethinking Civil-Military Relations in the United States," *International Security* 44, no. 4 (2020): 7–44.
32. Risa Brooks, "The Real Threat to Civilian Control of the Military: The Officer Corps Can No Longer Simply Ignore Politics," *Foreign Affairs*, January 18, 2021, https://www.foreignaffairs.com/articles/united-states/2021-01-18/real-threat-civilian-control-military; Risa Brooks, Jim Golby, and Heidi Urban, "Crisis of Command: America's Broken Civil-Military Relationship Imperils National Security," *Foreign Affairs*, May/June 2021, https://www.foreignaffairs.com/articles/united-states/2021-04-09/national-security-crisis-command.
33. See chap. 3.
34. Thomas Schelling, *Arms and Influence* (New Haven, CT: Yale University Press, 1966), 150.

PART I

WHAT HAPPENED?

CHAPTER 1

1940s

The Revolt of the Admirals

After World War II, the US military struggled with massive postwar budget cuts. The Navy, specifically, lost roughly 90 percent of its budget within two years of the war's end.[1] President Harry Truman demanded these savings as part of his wider program of restoring fiscal balance. After his first secretary of defense, James Forrestal, failed to implement these cuts to the president's satisfaction, Truman replaced him with Louis Johnson. Relying on the judgment of the Air Force and Army, Johnson canceled the Navy's prized supercarrier and redirected much of the savings to the Air Force, which promised that its concept of "strategic bombing" would serve as an effective first line of defense in peacetime. Many in the Navy found this claim preposterous, but unfortunately they were unable to make a persuasive argument for retaining a large postwar fleet and instead chose to compete with the Air Force for a share of the strategic bombing mission via carrier-launched aircraft.[2]

Ironically, this warfighting and political misstep by the Navy made it easier for Johnson and his allies to argue that the Navy was engaging in duplication of effort, which was the secretary of defense's reason for canceling the supercarrier. Even before Johnson took this step, however, the Navy decided to challenge civilian authority in a series of events that became known as the "Revolt of the Admirals." The results were predictable and costly for many of the participants on both sides. Although the outbreak of the Korean War ended the postwar budgetary constraints, the Navy did not subsequently reconsider its antipathy toward the newly established position of secretary of defense. Although few remember its specifics today, the "revolt" was a warning of the possible consequences when a service and its political bosses work at cross purposes.

Table 1.1 US Navy Budgets following World War II

Year	Budget ($ billions)
1945	29.2
1946	24.2
1947	4.6
1948	3.7

THE US NAVY IN A CHANGING WORLD

The US Navy had come a long way by 1945.[3] After the American Revolution, Congress rebuilt the Navy to deal with commerce protection against Britain and France as well as the "Barbary pirates" of North Africa.[4] The Navy shrank again following the War of 1812, but the US Merchant Marine grew rapidly in the years before the Civil War. Once that conflict began, the Navy swelled to implement the Anaconda Strategy of blockading the Confederacy, thus depriving the South of the ability to use its rivers to move troops or deep-water ports to export cotton for military supplies (and ultimately diplomatic recognition) from Europe, while Union armies methodically hacked away the South's extremities.[5]

After the Civil War, both the Navy and the Merchant Marine fell on hard times. In 1850, while US overseas merchant ship tonnage was only half that of Britain's, the quality of American sailing ships was actually superior to that of the British. Trouble arose, however, following the advent of steam power and the emergence of petroleum, which devastated the American whaling industry, a major source of innovation in American shipbuilding. The death blow came during the Civil War through the predations of Confederate commerce raiders. Many of the ships not sunk were sold to foreign owners (775,000 tons), while the total fleet was smaller by 443,000 tons. By the early 1880s, American merchant ships carried only 17 percent of US foreign trade (imports and exports) compared to almost 80 percent in the 1850s, and both the tonnage of US merchant ships and the value of the goods they transported declined by almost half.[6] Meanwhile, for two decades the Navy was starved of funds by an inward-looking government focused on westward expansion. By the 1880s, the once mighty US Navy that strangled the Confederacy had become an international laughing stock. When one of Oscar Wilde's American characters remarked that the United States had no ruins or curiosities to compare with Europe, another retorted, "No ruins! No curiosities! You have your Navy and your manners."[7]

Consequently, for a generation after the Civil War, Britain continued to enjoy its supremacy on the oceans while the United States devoted its attention to western landward expansion.[8] The Navy began to grow in the 1880s, but it served a very different purpose than today's force or the Royal Navy before 1914.[9] Starting in the 1890s, thanks in part to thinkers such as Alfred Thayer Mahan (whose work was devoured by contemporary policymakers such as Theodore Roosevelt), the United States made the Monroe Doctrine a reality by exerting its economic and political predominance over the entire Western Hemisphere.[10] That said, until World War II, US naval strategy was strategically defensive. The country still relied on the Atlantic and Pacific Oceans as its first lines of defense against external threats. The long distances from Europe or Japan would afford the US Navy enough time to sortie, establish sea control after destroying the enemy fleet, and, if necessary, blockade its most likely naval adversary (Japan).[11]

This defensive approach was also politically very attractive, especially after World War I. It was fiscally conservative at a time when the Republican administrations running Washington wanted to cut spending, particularly on armaments; pay off the debts incurred during the war; and limit the United States' foreign political commitments.[12] Another benefit of a blue-water navy was that it would confront and destroy its adversaries far from American shores. It thus obviated the need for a large, expensive standing army.[13]

One of the first priorities of the Warren Harding administration in 1921 was promoting disarmament, multilateral in the case of the Navy and unilateral for the Army. While the 1922 Washington Naval Treaty forbade the Navy from building up to the limits authorized by the Naval Act of 1916, the naval service was still better off than the Army. The Navy's ranks shrank by 80 percent from their wartime peak, but at their postwar nadir they were still twice as large as the prewar force. The Army, meanwhile, lost 95 percent of its wartime peak and was only a third larger than the prewar force. Naval spending meanwhile dropped from $2 billion to roughly $300 million, which was still three times greater than before the war. Postwar Army expenditures were only slightly higher than the Navy's (from a wartime peak of over $9 billion), but they were only double the prewar level.[14]

As a result, the Army's plans for retaining a significant peacetime force after the war went nowhere. It had to settle for the 1920 National Defense Act, which professionalized the National Guard and reserves and enhanced the Army's capabilities for long-term and mobilization planning.[15] The Army never forgot its failure, and when the next world war came, it was determined to shape the postwar planning effort.[16]

A defensive national strategy was possible because the likeliest adversary in the 1920s or early 1930s, Japan, would have to operate far from its established bases of supply, while the United States enjoyed (then and now) forward-projection capability in the Pacific through a string of bases, particularly in Hawaii, Guam, and the Philippines, linking California (and its oilfields) to East Asia.[17] The completion of the Panama Canal in 1914 also allowed the United States to transfer forces relatively quickly between the Atlantic and Pacific Oceans.

Still, despite the acquisition of a colonial empire in the Philippines and the Caribbean during the Spanish-American War, the US Navy was not an expeditionary force capable of inserting and sustaining American military power anywhere in the world.[18] It was a defensive navy whose purpose was consistent with the US national experience to that point. This was still a nation that feared foreign invasion, and both times an enemy army had shown up with evil intent (in 1776 and 1812), it had come from the sea.

A threat to the Navy's position as the most favored service arose from the Army Air Service (the Army Air Corps after 1926). Its assistant chief, Brig. Gen. Billy Mitchell, claimed that land-based bombers could defend the country more efficiently (i.e., less expensively) than battleships.[19] His famous experimental sinking of a stationary battleship in 1921 and subsequent very public exercises during the 1930s when long-range bombers successfully intercepted moving ships on the high seas (quite a feat in the days before radar) portended a transformation of US strategy—but that was still in the future.[20] Before World War II, the Navy fended off the assaults by airpower apostles thanks to the patronage of powerful officials such as President Franklin Roosevelt, who had served as assistant secretary of the Navy during World War I, and Rep. Carl Vinson, the longtime chairman of the House Naval Affairs Committee (after 1947 the House Armed Services Committee). The Navy also displayed some impressive political acumen. As early as the 1930s, the Navy recognized the value of selling its needs to Congress by dispersing construction across the nation and emphasizing that naval procurement created civilian employment.[21]

Whatever faith remained in US geographic security evaporated following the attack on Pearl Harbor. This hurt the Navy by validating the case for an independent Air Force. Just as bad from the Navy's perspective, thanks to influence of generals such as George Marshall and Dwight Eisenhower, the Army had become the predominant service in national affairs. It had no intention of returning to its second-class status. The Army and its allies also viewed money spent for maintaining a huge fleet, as well as for a "second army" in the Marine Corps, as costly distractions that served no useful purpose and jeopardized the health of the US economy. These views found a receptive audience in the White House. President Truman was a fiscal conservative who, within days of Japan's surrender, began cutting billions from the defense budget.[22]

At the same time, the Air Corps was discontented with its role within the Army. Army aviators wanted the autonomy that existed within naval aviation. Since 1921, the Navy's Bureau of Aeronautics controlled the development of naval-aviation doctrine and aviation-related procurement. It also had a significant degree of influence over the training, billeting, and promotion of aviators.[23] Four years later, the president's Aircraft Board lent its approval by recommending that naval aviation report to a dedicated assistant secretary for air (which was established the following year). It also insisted that only aviators fill positions supervising significant flight operations and urged the Navy to ensure that aviators had adequate opportunities to promotion and higher command.[24] These policies may explain why there was never any strong desire among naval aviators to join their Army counterparts in an independent air force.[25]

The United States emerged from World War II with the most powerful fleet in history. Like the Army, the Navy had benefited from the United States having the world's premier industrial economy as well as the security afforded by capable allies and favorable geography. While the United States was still unprepared for war in December 1941, it could rely on the Red Army to bleed the Wehrmacht on the Eastern Front while the Royal Navy thinned the German U-boat force.

US allies paid dearly for their successes. The Soviet Union never recovered from the human and economic costs necessary to defeat Nazi Germany.[26] World War II also marked the end of Britain's status as a global power. Despite being the world's largest navy at the start of the war and peaking at 553 ships by its end, the Royal Navy could no longer match the US Navy as the world's dominant naval force.[27] By the end of the war in the Pacific, the US Navy had swelled to over 6,800 ships (compared to just under 400 in 1939), including ninety-nine fleet and escort carriers.[28]

At the end of World War II, United States accounted for roughly *half* of global economic activity, and its economy was at least four times larger than that of the other "superpower," the Soviet Union. Furthermore, the United States dominated global oil production beyond the Soviet Union, which meant that other navies could operate at sea only with the consent of the United States.[29] When the Korean War started in 1950, the Navy had only 634 ships, including fifteen carriers.[30]

For many people, this was still far too large. Despite a 90 percent reduction in ship levels since World War II, the US Navy was still 50 percent larger than before the war and even larger when combined with the Royal Navy. With the Japanese and German fleets at the bottom of the sea and Britain now a supplicant, many people in Washington wondered why the United States still needed a large navy. Such critics did not reject the need for a navy, but they believed it should focus on the traditional mission of protecting sea lines of communication. The Soviet submarine challenge was theoretically complex thanks to the lethal German Type XXI U-boats, some of which fell into Soviet hands and influenced the design of the *Zulu*, *Whiskey*, and *Romeo* classes of submarines. The exact nature of this threat was a matter of debate for much of the Cold War. US Navy leaders claimed publicly that the Soviet Navy was an aggressive blue-water force that aimed to sever US supply lines in the event of a war against the Soviet Union. Conversely, some intelligence analysts argued that the Navy was exaggerating Soviet capabilities and intentions to justify the Navy's force structure and budget.[31]

The Navy's desire to retain a considerable postwar fleet was not entirely self-serving.[32] Critics of large naval expenditures perhaps overlooked the degree to which navies were multipurpose instruments. In wartime, the Navy was how the United States projected power ashore across Eurasia in areas without US bases, either by launching air and missile strikes or protecting amphibious operations.[33] In peacetime, Navy ships could establish a US presence in the world's hot spots, protect commerce, preserve ties with allies, maintain deterrence, and generally keep trouble at arm's length from American shores.

There was still much discontent across the oceans. Even with the Axis in ruins, national-security experts believed that the United States could not afford to disengage militarily from the rest of the world as it had after World War I. The experience of the 1930s had taught US leaders that capable military threats could emerge suddenly—Germany had needed only six years to expand its army and even less to create a first-class air force before going to war. Long-range airpower posed both a risk and an opportunity. On one hand, it afforded the United States immense leverage when it forward-deployed its forces. On the other, the consequences for failing to perceive developing threats could be catastrophic in the atomic age.[34]

The challenge for the US government was to defend its postwar order as cheaply as possible. Eliminating duplication of effort among the services was therefore one of the key objectives of the 1947 National Security Act, which "unified" the War and Navy Departments into a single National Military Establishment—the Department of Defense after 1949. Congress had already merged the House and Senate committees for military and naval affairs into unified armed services committees the year before.[35]

Unification simplified organization charts, but it did not answer the question of which service's capabilities should be sacrificed in the interest of efficiency—a situation not improved by the absence of a powerful military chief of staff and the existence of a statutorily weak secretary of defense. The inaugural holder of that unhappy office was Forrestal. Ironically, in his previous job as secretary of the Navy, he had led a campaign arguing against creating either a powerful secretary of defense or a chief of staff.[36]

THE REVOLT OF THE ADMIRALS BEGINS

While disappointing in many respects, the 1947 legislation fulfilled the aspirations of airpower enthusiasts to create an independent air force. But the airpower advocates were not yet satisfied. As a new service, the Air Force needed to establish itself, which meant creating a clear set of "roles" and "functions" that would justify future appropriations.[37] Air Force leaders believed that strategic bombing was the solution to their problems and those of the nation, both in terms of security and economics. They claimed that a standing force of seventy groups (each comprising several squadrons with up to two dozen aircraft each), spearheaded by long-range bombers, could deter aggression in Europe and, if necessary, either launch a preemptive attack on the Soviet Union or firebomb it with conventional munitions and the still tiny atomic arsenal after a war began.[38] The fact that the Air Force was the first of the services to take up the challenge of desegregation, had acquitted itself well during the Berlin Blockade of 1948–49, and skillfully pursued its interests on Capitol Hill only added to the service's luster.[39]

The Air Force had essentially appropriated the theories of Alfred Thayer Mahan to argue that the great prize of modern warfare was command of the new "commons"—the air domain—and that it was the only service capable of doing so.[40] The Navy realized the danger too late. During the war, the reluctance of naval leaders to publicize their service's exploits had exasperated Forrestal to no end.[41] Now it belatedly retorted that it could fulfill a larger set of functions—not just tactical air support or amphibious operations but also presence missions that reassured allies and deterred adversaries, such as when USS *Missouri* visited Greece and Turkey in 1946 at the height of the Soviet-American dispute over the Turkish Straits. Businessmen also understood that unlike airplanes and tanks that could roll off assemble lines within months, warships took years to build. Finally, there were questions about the effectiveness of precision bombing during World War II and its appropriateness in future conflicts.

Nevertheless, most Americans were eager to move on from the war. They wished to leave large bills for defense—along with the accompanying taxes—far behind them. At first glance, all the technologies from that conflict seemed to favor the Army and the new Air Force. The new atomic bombs being built were too big and heavy to be carried by any current Navy plane launched from the existing large aircraft carriers (the *Essex* and *Midway* classes). To compete in strategic bombing, the Navy needed both a new airplane and a carrier with longer flight deck. These requirements gave birth to a design for a "supercarrier"—CVA-58—that would eventually be christened USS *United States*.[42] The Air Force, however, wanted to use the same money the Navy would need for its carrier (along with supporting ships and aircraft) to pay for its seventy groups, including new B-36 Peacemaker intercontinental bombers that could carry conventional or nuclear weapons on missions extending several thousand miles.

If the Navy was to keep pace, it could not let the Air Force monopolize the delivery of nuclear weapons. During the early Cold War, attaching the word "nuclear" was the best way to get a concept, no matter how foolish, funded in the Department of Defense. During the 1950s and 1960s, for example, the Army produced 2,100 Davy Crockett tactical nuclear weapon launchers, whose range was barely greater than that of the radioactive fallout of the weapons they fired.[43] The Navy was guilty of its own share of irrationality by developing and deploying a nuclear magnetic mine to be attached to the sides of ships by frogmen.[44] The Air Force, meanwhile, was building a nuclear-tipped surface-to-air missile, the Nike Hercules, whose fallout would drift back down over the firing site. Additionally, at a remote site in Idaho, it was even developing a nuclear pulse-jet aircraft engine to explore space.[45] Not all of the money spent on nuclear-weapons projects was wasted, but no nuclear project was ever cheap. Today, the projected cost from 2021 to 2030 of developing and fielding a new generation of US nuclear weapons is over $600 billion.[46]

During the Cold War, the Air Force spent roughly $8 billion (in 1965 dollars) developing the first generation of intercontinental ballistic missiles (ICBMs)—the Atlas.[47] The Navy had its own successes. In San Diego, Lt. Cmdr. Eugene Wilkinson, who eventually became the first commanding officer of the first nuclear-powered submarine, was experimenting with captured German cruise missiles—the V-1 "buzz bombs" that had terrorized London—firing them off the deck of his diesel submarine. Farther to the east, at that same Idaho site where the Air Force's nuclear jet engine predictably failed, in 1950, a Navy captain by the name of Hyman Rickover was building the world's first reactor capable of generating controlled nuclear power. Not only was Rickover determined to make history, but he was also determined to fit his revolutionary reactor into a submarine hull.[48]

Meanwhile, back at the Pentagon, all the services agreed that controlling the air domain was critical. They concurred on the importance of the quick delivery of supplies by air and the use of air assets for obtaining intelligence. The Army, Marine Corps, and Navy also believed that direct firepower from the air in support of ground troops was a critical wartime mission. The main point of disagreement was again over the relative value of strategic bombing. Today the adjective "strategic" refers to nuclear weapons, but back then it meant targeting an enemy's civilian and economic centers ("countervalue" in nuclear-weapons parlance). Essentially, the Air Force believed that precision bombing within the enemy's heartland would bring about the collapse of its war effort without the need for large and expensive ground forces to defeat the enemy's armed forces and occupy its territory.

The Marines believed from experience in the Pacific that intelligence and close air support were the key capabilities that airplanes provided. Aircraft were enablers and force multipliers for troops in the field. Back then, soldiers carried "only" eighty pounds of weight on their backs into battle—only twenty pounds of which, or two hundred rounds, was ammunition.[49] When a platoon engaged the enemy, that two hundred rounds could go very fast. If that happened, the Marines did not want US aircraft hours away trying to bomb the factories manufacturing the enemy's ammunition. Field commanders wanted air assets at their beck and call, and they wanted them to reload and return quickly when they had emptied their magazines—not six hours from now or tomorrow.

The Air Force, by contrast, has never valued the close-air-support mission. At the same time, it has refused to relinquish that mission lest the Army retrieve it along with the necessary budgetary resources, which would come at the expense of the Air Force. Accordingly, the Air Force has retained the close-air-support mission but only at the lowest possible cost. Until the development of the A-10 Warthog, for example, the Air Force had never developed a dedicated ground-attack plane during the Cold War and used only obsolete planes or aircraft provided by the other services for close air support.[50] Their origins notwithstanding, some of these cast-off aircraft proved most effective. An aircraft like the AD-1 Skyraider—nicknamed the "Spad"—over Korea or Vietnam could keep an entire platoon alive all by itself. It had four 20mm cannons, each firing two hundred rounds a minute, and carried eight thousand pounds of ordnance.[51]

Unlike the Air Force, the Marines insisted their aviators understood that the primary mission of airpower was to provide support for ground forces.

To emphasize that point, the commandant of the Marine Corps (until very recently) always came from the infantry and never from aviation, which was a supporting community. Again, until recently, Marine expeditionary strike groups were built around amphibious-assault ships equipped with helicopters and vertical and/or short takeoff and landing (V/STOL) planes that provided mobility and fire support for Marines going ashore.[52]

The Navy was, however, conflicted. Naval aviators had convinced everyone that battleships were now sitting ducks for aircraft launching either bombs or torpedoes. The actual experience from World War II, however, contradicted such a sweeping generalization. Innovations such as advanced fire-control systems and radar-guided proximity fuzes allowed battleships, under the right circumstances, to be deadly to attacking aircraft.[53] Those nuances were lost in the scramble for dollars. The aviators won their case in the court of public opinion, and since there was no disputing the fact that airplanes could sink ships at greater ranges than guns, the Navy transferred the responsibility for providing long-range fire support from surface combatants to planes launched from carriers. The shift was so sudden that by the end of World War II, 40 percent of the Navy's officers were aviators.[54]

The Navy, then and now, makes its selections for promotion based on the percentage of officers in the different communities, so the aviators were destined for prominence (in this case, at least 40 percent of those selected for senior or flag rank). They were also the dominant community within the naval leadership in Washington because of the prestige they had accrued during the war and the patronage of Forrestal, who considered the younger, more aggressive pilots allies against a conservative naval bureaucracy.[55] In the Navy's feud with the Air Force, naval aviators sometimes displayed more loyalty to their community than to their service. This meant the Navy often fought battles over strategic bombing on the Air Force's conceptual ground.

To preserve naval aviation, after World War II the Navy pushed for a supercarrier and new airplanes capable of carrying atomic payloads thousands of miles. The Navy was thus competing with the Air Force to accomplish a variant of the strategic-bombing mission. Whereas the Air Force was still committed to striking the economic and administrative hubs of an adversary to induce strategic paralysis, many in the Navy were focused on achieving effects at the operational level by hitting logistical hubs and bases to derail enemy offensives.[56] Both approaches differed from (and largely ignored) the tactically orientated mission of close air support, which aided friendly forces in direct contact with the enemy.

Although the Air Force and Navy's conceptions of aerial warfare technically operated at different levels of warfare—the strategic and operational—

we have referred to both as strategic bombing because the two services embraced the term "strategic air warfare" at the time, as codified in two agreements Forrestal negotiated among the squabbling services in 1948.[57] These agreements carefully delineated each service's primary and collateral functions. They are the reason why, for instance, the Army generally cannot procure fixed-wing aircraft except for administrative purposes and relies instead on helicopters and the Air Force for close air support and airlift over land (as a result of the Johnson-McConnell Agreement of 1966), while the Navy provides the same service over water and relies instead on helicopters and the Air Force for close air support and airlift over land, while the Navy provides the same service over water.[58] Despite debacles such as the Vietnam War, which demonstrated that helicopters were vulnerable in the close-air-support role, and the failed rescue of the hostages from the US embassy in Iran in 1980, the 1948 division of labor survived the reforms of the 1986 Goldwater-Nichols Act and has essentially remained in place to the present day.[59]

For the purposes of our narrative, the reader should note that while the Air Force received primary responsibility for strategic air warfare, Forrestal granted the Navy a supporting role, which it then used to justify the construction of large aircraft carriers to launch long-range strikes using atomic weapons. Although the Navy had less ambitious aims than the Air Force, naval officers did not accept that it was still cheaper to perform long-range aerial strike from land bases than carriers.[60] Instead of questioning the efficacy of strategic bombing and offering alternatives, the Navy had essentially doubled down on a flawed concept.

By the 1960s, strategic bombing had morphed into "deep interdiction." Defenders of the Air Force have argued that the service was not obsessed with strategic bombing before or after World War II and did not neglect its tactical or logistical duties.[61] While deep-interdiction missions were closer to the battlefield, they were not a substitute for close air support and had many of the same drawbacks as strategic bombing. As one of the fathers of systems analysis, Alain Enthoven, explained, "Historically speaking, the case for the deep-interdiction mission is poor. . . . Moreover, deep-interdiction missions are very expensive . . . [and] not worthwhile particularly when compared with the advantages of expenditures for direct combat capabilities such as close air support and maneuver forces."[62]

Future CNO Arleigh Burke was an active participant in the Navy–Air Force feud from his perch in a secretive Navy office in the Pentagon called OP-23. Boasting the innocuous title of Organizational Research and Policy Unit, the office had been established by Secretary of the Navy James Forrestal in 1945 (under a slightly different name) to lead the fight against unification. The office went dormant after the 1947 National Act passed, but the Navy resurrected once rumors surfaced that the Navy's rivals wanted to pass amendments strengthening the act. Burke did not mince words when he reflected on these events years later. He expressed the view of many in the Navy when he claimed that the "Air Force was pushing airpower" and "did not have the wisdom nor the integrity, one or the other, to realize that was not the whole answer."[63]

Integrity is everything in the US military. Burke was not saying that the men serving in the Air Force were stupid. The officer community is, in fact, one of the best-educated segments of US society.[64] What Burke meant, rather, was that Air Force officers knew privately that precision bombing did not work. That they argued otherwise publicly therefore meant they were being deceptive.[65]

This emotion, held strongly by Burke and his peers, was destructive to interservice comity. For one thing, it overlooked the fact that there were many aviators in the Navy who believed in their own variant of strategic bombing. Many Navy pilots, for example, would risk their lives during the Korean and Vietnam Wars flying deep-interdiction missions that struck population and economic centers as well as logistical hubs. Anger over a perceived lack of integrity among Air Force officers and their own internal dissonance made naval leaders both deaf to valid criticisms and prone to see conspiracies all around them. The Navy even turned on its erstwhile champion, Forrestal, for advocating for an increase in his power as secretary of defense and the unification of the Navy's air-transport divisions with those of the Army.[66] Bereft of leadership and political or strategic acumen, the Navy would instead plunge, again and again, into the brick wall of public opinion that the Air Force had carefully reinforced.[67]

Secretary of War Henry Stimson famously lampooned the Navy's old guard during World War II for living in a "dim religious world in which Neptune was God, Mahan his prophet, and the United States Navy the only true church."[68] The war had broken the stranglehold of this particular group. The new vanguard was composed of naval aviators who had covered themselves in glory in the war against Japan. After the war, however, the aviators and their allies failed to provide the American people with a convincing rationale for preserving a large fleet built around expensive aircraft carriers in the absence of any naval threat. As one senior admiral lamented, the Navy had plenty of skilled operators and administrators, "but very few of us . . . were able to reason with the Congress or present our case convincingly to the people so our own service should be saved from comparative oblivion.

Our understanding and our exposition of the indispensable character of our profession and the undiminished and vital nature of Sea Power have been dangerously superficial and elementary."[69]

Instead, postwar Navy officers assumed that the case of naval power as they defined it was self-evident and that anyone who failed to grasp that truth was, by definition, either a fool or a knave, as Burke insinuated. This assumption would lead to decades of problems for the Navy.

At the end of World War II, there were few political leaders in Washington willing to indulge the admirals' (or Forrestal's) plans for a large postwar Navy or interested in hearing the Navy's (or the Army's) complaints about the frantic pace of demobilization.[70] At its peak, the United States had spent almost 40 percent of its gross domestic product (GDP) on the war effort.[71] If postwar defense spending was too high, officials feared it would spark inflation and undermine prosperity. At the same time, airpower advocates were extolling the successes of strategic bombing in Europe and Japan.

Airpower had made vital contributions to the defeat of the Axis, primarily through the disruption of war production and its distribution, but it had failed to bring either Germany or Japan to their knees independently.[72] Wars are not decided by any one factor. Even in World War II, despite the Allies' immense economic and manpower advantages, their path to victory could have been much rockier without some fortuitous breaks.[73] If Allied scientists and codebreakers had not figured out how to hunt German submarines efficiently, Allied maritime losses would have complicated efforts to concentrate a preponderance of land forces to invade Axis Europe.[74] At the same time, without the Red Army inflicting the bulk of casualties on the Wehrmacht, the United States and Britain would have had to put more workers in uniform, which might have eroded their industrial output. Without Lend-Lease, the Soviet Union might have collapsed and it certainly would not have driven the Germans back to Berlin.[75]

Victory over the Axis was therefore a collective effort among allies and various military services. That was not the lesson the Air Force was proclaiming afterward. It was offering a relatively inexpensive way to defend the country—relative not because the planes were cheap (they are luxuries only rich countries can afford in quantity) but because they promised to make large armies and navies obsolete.

How was the Navy to best respond? Probably not as it did.

Mahan had warned his fellow citizens the century before not to be dazzled by panaceas, particularly those "presented in the fascinating garb of cheapness."[76] There were, superficially speaking, plenty of reasons to like precision bombing: it preserved the fiction of an antiseptic war and allowed the United States to exploit its comparative advantage in the economic, industrial, and technological domains of conflict. Additionally, strategic bombing ensured that future wars would be fought away from American soil. This was a major selling point for a country traumatized by Pearl Harbor and terrified by the destructiveness of modern warfare. Finally, an Air Force was supposedly less expensive to maintain in peacetime than a large Army and Navy.

In the late 1940s, this last attribute was appealing. The United States was transitioning to a peacetime economy, and politicians wanted to reduce the national debt and cut spending. Ordinary people wanted lower taxes and higher production of civilian goods on which to spend the money they had earned during the war. It was easy to fall in love with an expansive yet inexpensive military concept.

At the end of the war, many in Congress were predisposed toward the Air Force solution. One example was the chairman of the House Appropriations Committee, Clarence Cannon. He was known for his interest in a balanced budget along with his criticism of the Navy's carrier program. In his opinion, the United States should put its "money in the only place that counts, and this is on long-range land-based bombers."[77] Cannon (like many others) assumed that a third world war would be short. That would place a premium on weapons that could be deployed quickly with maximum effect.[78] Perhaps coincidentally, the McDonnell Air Corporation (today part of Boeing) was also based in Cannon's home state of Missouri, although it built planes for both the Air Force and Navy.

Cannon's hostility was a real problem for the Navy because all money bills originate in the House of Representatives, and before the creation of the authorization process in 1959, the Appropriations Committee exercised almost complete control over the defense budget. Cannon was such an unrelenting enemy of the Navy's carrier program that people searched for any reason, no matter how fanciful, for his hostility. The *Saturday Evening Post* speculated in March 1950, "Cannon himself has not taken a junket since his trip to Europe in the fall of 1947, when he came down with a ferocious toothache in Athens. He hunted up a United States Navy dentist, but in the excitement the luckless medic nervously pulled the wrong tooth. Cannon has taken a dim view of the Navy ever since."[79]

Such anecdotes are colorful, but they obscure the larger picture. After World War II, US leaders had developed a new, expansive conception of national security. The country had to undertake a role of global leadership, they believed, without wrecking the domestic economy. It was therefore up to civilian and military leaders, starting with the president, to make hard choices about how to allocate scarce resources. Perhaps a victim of its earlier successes within the corridors of power, the Navy was unprepared to compete in the court of public opinion. One Gallup poll in October 1949 had the Navy's popularity at 4 percent versus 76 percent for the Air Force.[80] When it became obvious that change benefiting the Air Force was inevitable, rather than continuing to put forward constructive alternatives and tempering their criticism of unification, the "revolting" admirals—a group that included many heroes from World War II, including Ernest King, Raymond Spruance, and William Halsey—escalated the Navy's opposition by taking their criticism public.

During the war years, the Navy had been shielded from the Army by President Franklin Roosevelt and Adm. William Leahy, Roosevelt's de facto military chief of staff. Last but not least, there was the legal separation between the War and Navy Departments. While the Army had forceful men such as Marshall and Eisenhower, the Navy had an even more ruthless operator in King, not to mention the urbane Forrestal as secretary.[81] The National Security Act, as well as various deaths and retirements, wrecked this happy arrangement for the Navy.

After 1947, with the split of the Air Force from the Army, there were now two votes against one within the new Joint Chiefs of Staff (JCS); the Marine Corps did not yet have a separate vote. Things quickly got even worse from the Navy's perspective. In January 1949 Truman fired Forrestal. Rumors had abounded across Washington about Forrestal's deteriorating mental health, and the president suspected Forrestal of disloyalty during the 1948 election.[82] Truman had never warmed to Forrestal and increasingly held him in contempt for not standing up to the military when the White House demanded fiscal discipline. After winning reelection, Truman seized the opportunity to cashier Forrestal and sped up his removal when he appeared on the verge of a nervous breakdown.

Truman replaced Forrestal with the chief fundraiser for his 1948 reelection campaign, Louis Johnson. Contrary to what the Navy and his critics thought, Johnson was qualified for the job.[83] An Army veteran of World War I, he had risen to leadership of the American Legion during the 1930s and served as the assistant secretary of war from 1937 to 1940. Johnson had studied what happened to Forrestal and was determined to avoid a similar fate. The best way to retain Truman's favor was enforcing the White House's spending cuts and furthering unification by eliminating duplication of effort. To that end, Johnson tried to curtail the role of the Marines, accepting the Army's argument that amphibious landings were impossible in the atomic age (although he changed his mind when an admiral made a compelling argument refuting the Army).[84] Johnson's focus was, however, on the

Navy—specifically naval aviation, which was a tempting target for budget cuts since it theoretically duplicated the Air Force's roles.

Only a month after the Navy laid down the keel for its new supercarrier, after briefly soliciting input from the JCS, Johnson announced the carrier's cancellation (as well as the other ships the Navy had sacrificed to pay for the carrier). The Navy claimed that Johnson had made only a pro forma consultation, but the secretary had been careful to keep the president and Congress informed. While the Air Force did not escape cuts to its budget either, Johnson's approach to budgeting in effect validated both the centrality of strategic bombing and the Air Force's preeminent role in waging war (as opposed to dividing responsibility with the Navy).

According to legend, Johnson's cancellation of the Navy's supercarrier was the spark for the Revolt of the Admirals, a catchy if misleading moniker. In fact, as one naval officer later recalled, "it wasn't a revolt and it wasn't just the admirals. The whole Navy was questioning what the future held, what were the policies, why?"[85]

In fact, it was the Navy rather than Johnson that struck first. Even before the supercarrier was canceled, a Navy Department civilian (perhaps with Burke's help) manufactured a study that supposedly proved the B-36 was selected despite its known flaws because its manufacturer had contributed to Truman's reelection and kept Johnson—a high-powered Washington lawyer—on retainer. The House Armed Services Committee (HASC) convened hearings in August to investigate the charges and quickly cleared Johnson of any wrongdoing.

Some in the Navy, and definitely the HASC chairman, Vinson, were desperate to let sleeping dogs lie. Unfortunately, a naval officer attached to the Joint Staff leaked internal Navy memorandums critical of Johnson and Francis Matthews, the new secretary of the Navy (the previous one had resigned over the cancellation of the supercarrier). The resulting furor forced the HASC to reconvene in October, and the Navy got another chance to make its case before the nation.

As an example of the extraordinary efforts that were made, Adm. James Russell (later vice CNO under Burke) subsequently claimed he had borrowed the only assembled nuclear weapon in the US arsenal from his classmate who ran the weapons depot in San Diego, welded the weapon with angle iron to the bomb-bay of his airplane (nuclear security was less restrictive in those days), and flew it from California to Andrews Air Force Base. He then took a car to a Senate hearing room to report that Navy aircraft could also deliver a nuclear weapon three thousand miles.[86]

This unique—some might say reckless—act had no effect because the Navy could not resolve the essential conundrum confronting it. Should it discredit strategic bombing and make a positive case for tactical naval carrier power? Or should it claim that it was more capable than the Air Force of delivering atomic weapons? The former was intellectually honest but did not lend itself to snappy sound bites and went against the trend in public and congressional opinion. The latter allowed the Air Force to frame the terms of the debate. There is no record that anyone looked for a third option.

In the end, the Navy fell between two stools and convinced no one. The president and defense secretary's decisions were affirmed, and the CNO was forced to resign, along with several other senior officers. Burke's career was saved only when the president's naval aide personally intervened after Johnson removed Burke from the slate for promotion to rear admiral.[87]

The event might be more accurately labeled a "rout" rather than a "revolt" of the admirals. The Navy had found out the hard way that fighting city hall was a long, tough slog. The Air Force concept of strategic bombing had moved the national-defense goalposts. It appeared to satisfy existing political and fiscal demands. Instead of addressing the flaws with strategic bombing, the Navy fell back on attacking whether the political leadership had the right to make decisions that contradicted service prerogatives. It was a losing proposition. The Navy would not resolve its internal fissures concerning strategic bombing for another fifty years.

FORTUNE SMILES ON THE NAVY

In 1950 North Korean forces crossed the thirty-eighth parallel, driving South Korean and US Army forces southward nearly into the Sea of Japan. As the United States was now at war, money was no longer an issue. What mattered was creating the circumstances for the application of the United States' immense power. The United States could crush any foe in conventional warfare, but it would take some time to remobilize the economy. In the meantime, what forces were immediately available to stave off disaster on the Korean Peninsula?

Because the Air Force had invested in carrying out strategic bombing, when its planes deployed from Japan, they proved inadequate in certain respects. The postwar Air Force had poured its resources into developing its strategic capacity and had allowed any close-air-support skills from World War II to atrophy. Air Force commanders also preferred to keep tight control over their assets rather than delegate them to field commanders from the other services. Because Air Force planes could not communicate with Army and Marine ground troops in Korea, they could not initially provide effective close air support. Air Force planes also lacked the endurance to loiter over the Korean Peninsula and establish persistent command of the skies. Fortunately, Navy carriers arrived within a week of the North Korean invasion, and their planes helped to establish aerial supremacy.[88]

The Air Force eventually adapted to conditions in Korea, but it never changed its preference for deep-interdiction missions focused on enemy logistics and industry. By the end of the war, the Air Force had devoted almost two hundred thousand of its seven hundred thousand total sorties to interdiction missions (and the overwhelming preponderance of combat missions), compared to only fifty-eight thousand for close air support.[89] These missions struck at targets whose destruction affected the battlefield over the days, weeks, and months to come but were of little help to US Army and Marine forces that were already under fire and needed immediate close air support.

Besides providing such air support, the Navy had to get troops onto the Korean Peninsula. Originally the Navy relied on transport ships provided by allies to ferry troops to Korea, but eventually it and the Marines scraped together sufficient assets to stage an amphibious operation at Inchon in September 1950 (Operation Chromite). The driving force for the landing came from Army general Douglas MacArthur, who had become a convert to joint operations during the war against Japan.[90] The CNO, Forrest Sherman, had opposed Chromite and implored the deputy chief of staff for naval operations in the Far East, Burke, to quash the operation. To Sherman's chagrin, Burke was a strong supporter of MacArthur. The landing at Inchon helped turn the tide of the war and became one of the Navy's proudest moments.[91] The Navy further demonstrated its value in December 1950, when it evacuated tens of thousands of troops and refugees from North Korea following China's intervention.[92]

Louis Johnson did not last long enough to witness any of this—he was fired shortly before Inchon as a scapegoat for US unpreparedness.[93] This was hardly fair since he was only implementing the president's explicit instructions to cut spending and enforce unification, but as the saying goes, "politics ain't beanbag."[94]

The Air Force continued to soak up a disproportionate share of defense dollars until the early 1960s, when its buildup was complete. That said, starting in 1951 the Navy did receive enough funding to retain and then expand its carrier-aviation program by launching the *Forrestal* class of supercarriers. Around the same time Congress authorized the building of these carriers, with much less fanfare, it also authorized a number of experimental nuclear submarines to follow up on the successful USS *Nautilus*. The fact that both services got what they wanted did not, however, resolve the underlying hostility between the Navy and the Air Force so much as obfuscate it. Nor did these events induce any doubts among the participants in the "revolt" as to whether the Navy's defiance of civilian leadership was the wisest approach. Was this arrogance a cultural aversion in the Navy to change, or was it something else? Whatever the reason, the Navy's inability to adapt to new political realties would soon return to haunt it.

SUMMARY

Despite the Navy's undeniable successes during World War II, following that conflict its leadership stumbled badly. Its first mistake was to oppose the drive for unification, which had the strong support of the Army and Air Force, many in Congress, and the president, who was desperate to control government spending. The second mistake was, in effect, to embrace strategic bombing (albeit from carriers rather than land-based bombers as the Air Force wanted) rather than expose its limitations. The instigators and participants in the Revolt of the Admirals believed they were acting in the national interest, but they had already lost the argument both within policymaking circles and within the general public. Although their brief "revolt" became a rout, subsequent events would validate the substance of their argument for a powerful postwar Navy capable of both controlling sea lines of communication and projecting power ashore. Unfortunately, this reversal of fortune would also engender a sense of overconfidence, even arrogance, which in turn left the Navy unprepared to deal with a civilian leader determined to exercise the full prerogatives of the secretary of defense.

NOTES

1. "Budget of the US Navy: 1794 to 2014," Naval History and Heritage Command (NHHC), August 23, 2017, https://www.history.navy.mil/research/library/online-reading-room/title-list-alphabetically/b/budget-of-the-us-navy-1794-to-2004.html.
2. Besides the sources cited below, there is an excellent overview in Steven Rearden, *The Formative Years, 1947–1950* (Washington, DC: Historical Office, Office of the Secretary of Defense, 1984), esp. 11ff., 309ff., 521ff.
3. The following summary draws from Craig Symonds, *The U.S. Navy: A Concise History* (Oxford: Oxford University Press, 2016), 1–64; Harold Sprout and Margaret Sprout,

The Rise of American Naval Power, 1776–1918 (Princeton, NJ: Princeton University Press, 1967), 24ff.; and Kenneth Hagan, *This People's Navy: The Making of American Sea Power* (New York: Free Press, 1991), 21ff.

4. James Sofka, "The Jeffersonian Idea of National Security: Commerce, the Atlantic Balance of Power, and the Barbary War, 1786–1805," *Diplomatic History* 21, no. 4 (1997): 519–44.
5. Russell Weigley, *The American Way of War: A History of United States Military Strategy and Policy* (Bloomington: Indiana University Press, 1973), 93, 98, 128–29; Herman Hattaway and Archer Jones, *How the North Won: A Military History of the Civil War* (Urbana: University of Illinois Press, 1991), 35ff. and passim; Andrew Smith, *Starving the South: How the North Won the Civil War* (New York: St. Martin's, 2011), 11–13; Williamson Murray and Wayne Wei-Siang Hsieh, *A Savage War: A Military History of the Civil War* (Princeton, NJ: Princeton University Press, 2016), 77–78, 119ff.; Jay Sexton, *Debtor Diplomacy: Finance and American Foreign Relations in the Civil War Era, 1837–1873* (Oxford: Clarendon, 2005); Lance Davis and Stanley Engerman, *Naval Blockades in Peace and War: An Economic History since 1750* (Cambridge: Cambridge University Press, 2006), 109–58.
6. F. E. Chadwick and C. G. Calkins, "Our Merchant Marine: The Causes of Its Decline, and the Means to Be Taken for Its Revival," *Proceedings* 8, no. 1 (January 1882), https://www.usni.org/magazines/proceedings/1882/january/our-merchant-marine-causes-its-decline-and-means-be-taken-its-0 and https://www.usni.org/magazines/proceedings/1882/january/our-merchant-marine-causes-its-decline-and-means-be-taken-its-1; *Merchant Marine for Trade and Defense* (Washington, DC: US Maritime Commission, 1946); Christopher McMahon, "The U.S. Merchant Marine: Back to the Future," *Naval War College Review* 69, no. 1 (2016): 87–108; Tim Johnson, "Dwindling Merchant Marine Fleet Crimps U.S. Ability to Wage War," McClatchy Washington Bureau, May 14, 2018, https://www.mcclatchydc.com/news/nation-world/national/national-security/article210623279.html; Peter Hugill, *Transition in Power: Technological "Warfare" and the Shift from British to American Hegemony since 1919* (Lanham, MD: Lexington, 2018), chaps. 1–2.
7. Symonds, *U.S. Navy*, 58.
8. Robert Beisner, *From the Old Diplomacy to the New, 1865–1900* (Arlington Heights, IL: Harlan Davidson, 1986); Walter LaFeber, *The Cambridge History of American Foreign Relations*, vol. 2, *The American Search for Opportunity, 1865–1913* (Cambridge: Cambridge University Press, 1993); George Herring, *From Colony to Superpower: U.S. Foreign Relations since 1776* (Oxford: Oxford University Press, 2008), 224ff.
9. Peter Trubowitz, *Defining the National Interest: Conflict and Change in American Foreign Policy* (Chicago: University of Chicago Press, 1998), 31–95; Dirk Bönker, *Militarism in a Global Age: Naval Ambitions in Germany and the United States* (Ithaca, NY: Cornell University Press, 2012).
10. Walter LaFeber, *The New Empire: An Interpretation of American Expansion, 1860–1898* (Ithaca, NY: Cornell University Press, 1998), esp. 1–196. See also Walter LaFeber, "A Note on the 'Mercantilistic Imperialism' of Alfred Thayer Mahan," *Mississippi Valley Historical Review* 48, no. 4 (1962): 674–85.
11. Weigley, *Way of War*, 242ff.; Edward Miller, *War Plan Orange: The U.S. Strategy to Defeat Japan, 1897–1945* (Annapolis, MD: Naval Institute Press, 2007).
12. Robert Boyce, *The Great Interwar Crisis and the Collapse of Globalization* (Basingstoke, UK: Palgrave, 2009).

13. "The term is colloquial rather than doctrinal and most sea-going states differ on its specifics. Broadly speaking, a blue-water navy is capable of prolonged and sustained operations across the open oceans, and has a capacity to project 'credible power' in the distant seas." Abhijit Singh, "'Blue-Water' Navies in the Indian Ocean Region," *The Diplomat*, January 21, 2015, https://thediplomat.com/2015/01/blue-water-navies-in-the-indian-ocean-region/.
14. US Department of Commerce, *Historical Statistics of the United States: Colonial Times to 1970, Part 2* (Washington, DC: Bureau of the Census, 1975), 1114, 1141.
15. John Garry Clifford, *Citizen Soldiers: The Plattsburg Training Camp Movement, 1913–1920* (Lexington: University Press of Kentucky, 2015), 262ff.; Michael Carew, *Becoming the Arsenal: The American Industrial Mobilization for World War II, 1938–1942* (Lanham, MD: University Press of America, 2010), 142ff.; David Johnson, *Fast Tanks and Heavy Bombers: Innovation the U.S. Army, 1917–1945* (Ithaca, NY: Cornell University Press, 1998), 28–29, 67, 71, 95; Matthew Muehlbauer and David Ulbrich, *Ways of War: American Military History from the Colonial Era to the Twenty-First Century* (New York: Routledge, 2014), 317ff.
16. Michael Sherry, *Preparing for the Next War: American Plans for Postwar Defense, 1941–1945* (New Haven, CT: Yale University Press, 1977).
17. John Maurer, "Fuel and the Battle Fleet: Coal, Oil, and American Naval Strategy, 1898–1925," *Naval War College Review* 34, no. 6 (1981): 60–77.
18. Thomas Mahnken, "Forward Presence in the Modern Navy: From the Cold War to a Future Tailored Force," NHHC, August 16, 2017, https://www.history.navy.mil/research/library/online-reading-room/title-list-alphabetically/n/needs-opportunities-modern-history-us-navy/forward-presence-modern-navy-cold-war-future-tailored-force.html.
19. Thomas Wildenberg, "Billy Mitchell Takes on the Navy," *Proceedings*, September 2013, https://www.usni.org/magazines/naval-history-magazine/2013/september/billy-mitchell-takes-navy; Thomas Wildenberg, *Billy Mitchell's War with the Navy: The Interwar Rivalry over Air Power* (Annapolis, MD: Naval Institute Press, 2013); John Correll, "The Billy Mitchell Court-Martial," *Air Force Magazine*, August 1, 2012, https://www.airforcemag.com/article/0812mitchell/; Rebecca Grant "The Billy Mitchell Syndrome," *Air Force Magazine*, December 1, 2006, https://www.airforcemag.com/article/1206syndrome/.
20. Blake Stilwell, "Air Force Legend Curtis LeMay Once Bombed the Navy to Prove a Point," Military.com, 2020, https://www.military.com/off-duty/air-force-legend-curtis-lemay-once-bombed-navy-prove-point.html.
21. Anand Toprani, "'Our Efforts Have Degenerated into a Competition for Dollars': The 'Revolt of the Admirals,' NSC-68, and the Political Economy of the Cold War," *Diplomacy & Statecraft* 30, no. 4 (2019): 683.
22. Michael Hogan, *Cross of Iron: Harry S. Truman and the Origins of the National Security State, 1945–1954* (Cambridge: Cambridge University Press, 2000), 69ff., 159ff.; Jonathan House, *A Military History of the Cold War, 1944–1962* (Norman: University of Oklahoma Press, 2012), 76ff.; Anand Toprani, "Budgets and Strategy: The Enduring Legacy of the Revolt of the Admirals," *Political Science Quarterly* 134, no. 1 (2019): 121ff.; Toprani, "'Our Efforts Have Degenerated,'" 682ff.; Thomas Hone and Curtis Utz, *History of the Office of the Chief of Naval Operations, 1915–2015* (Washington, DC: NHHC, 2015), 187ff. (hereafter cited as *OPNAV*).
23. Hone, *OPNAV*, 66–67, 75–76, 262; "Navy Air Leadership: Rear Admiral William A. Moffett as Chief of the Bureau of Aeronautics," in *Air Leadership*, ed. Wayne Thompson

(Washington, DC: Office of Air Force History), 83–117; Mark Jelonek, *Toward an Air and Space Force: Naval Aviation and the Implications for Space Power* (Maxwell Air Force Base [AFB], AL: Air University Press, 1999), 13–37.

24. *Report of the President's Aircraft Board* (Washington, DC: Government Printing Office, 1925), 22–26.
25. For an excellent discussion on the differences between the two services following World War II, see Vincent Davis, *The Admirals Lobby* (Chapel Hill: University of North Carolina Press, 1967), 60–100.
26. Mark Harrison, "Industrial Mobilization for World War II: A German Comparison," in *The Soviet Defence Industry Complex from Stalin to Khrushchev*, ed. John Barber and Mark Harrison (Basingstoke, UK: Macmillan, 2000), 99–117.
27. "The Royal Navy's Size throughout History," Historic UK, n.d., https://www.historic-uk.com/Blog/British-Navy-Size-Over-Time/; "British and Commonwealth Navies at the Beginning and End of World War 2," Naval-History.net, July 8, 2011, https://www.naval-history.net/WW2CampaignRoyalNavy.htm.
28. "US Ship Force Levels," NHHC, November 17, 2017, https://www.history.navy.mil/research/histories/ship-histories/us-ship-force-levels.html.
29. Anand Toprani, *Oil and the Great Powers: Britain and Germany* (Oxford: Oxford University Press, 2019).
30. "US Ship Force Levels"; George Hodermarsky, *Postwar Naval Force Reductions, 1945–1950: Impact on the Next War* (Newport, RI: Naval War College, 1990), https://apps.dtic.mil/dtic/tr/fulltext/u2/a227251.pdf.
31. Robert Herrick, *Soviet Naval Strategy: Fifty Years of Theory and Practice* (Annapolis, MD: Naval Institute Press, 1968), esp. 143ff.; Dmitry Filipoff, "Brad Dismukes on the Soviet Navy and Attacking Ballistic Missile Submarines," Center for International Maritime Security, March 24, 2021, https://cimsec.org/brad-dismukes-on-the-soviet-navy-and-attacking-ballistic-missile-nuclear-submarines/; Gregory Vistica, *Fall from Glory: The Men Who Sank the U.S. Navy* (New York: Simon & Schuster, 1995), 49ff.
32. David Rosenberg and Floyd Kennedy, *U.S. Aircraft Carriers in the Strategic Role* (Falls Church, VA: Lulejian & Associates, 1975).
33. Samuel Huntington, "National Policy and the Transoceanic Navy," *Proceedings*, May 1954, https://blog.usni.org/posts/2009/03/09/from-our-archive-national-policy-and-the-transoceanic-navy-by-samuel-p-huntington.
34. Melvyn Leffler, *A Preponderance of Power: National Security, the Truman Administration, and the Cold War* (Stanford, CA: Stanford University Press, 1992); Michael Sherry, *The Rise of American Air Power: The Creation of Armageddon* (New Haven, CT: Yale University Press, 1987).
35. Until the Legislative Reorganization Act of 1946, the House and Senate had separate committees for military and naval affairs. Thereafter, they were merged into armed services committees, presaging the "unification" of the War and Navy departments into a single National Military Establishment (later renamed the Department of Defense) in 1947. George Galloway, "The Operation of the Legislative Reorganization Act of 1946," *American Political Science Review* 45, no. 1 (1951): 41–68; Frank Trager, "The National Security Act of 1947: Its Thirtieth Anniversary," *Air University Review* 29, no. 1 (1977): 2–15; Hone, *OPNAV*, 193.
36. Demetrious Caraley, *The Politics of Military Unification: A Study in Conflict* (New York: Columbia University Press, 1966); Townsend Hoopes and Douglas Brinkley, *Driven*

Patriot: The Life and Times of James Forrestal (Annapolis, MD: Naval Institute Press, 1992), 319ff.

37. "Roles" refer to the basic purpose of each component of the Department of Defense. "Functions" are the broad objectives each service is supposed to achieve. "Missions" refer to specific tasks to assist combatant commanders. Daniel Kuehl and Charles Miller, "Roles, Missions, and Functions: Terms of Debate," *Joint Force Quarterly* (Summer 1994): 103–5. The current breakdown of functions within the Department of Defense is listed in Department of Defense, "Functions of the Department of Defense and Its Major Components," December 21, 2010, https://www.esd.whs.mil/Portals/54/Documents/DD/issuances/dodd/510001p.pdf.
38. Herman S. Wolk, "The Battle of the B-36," *Air Force Magazine*, July 1, 1996, https://www.airforcemag.com/article/0796battle/; Herman S. Wolk, "The Revolt of the Admirals," *Air Force Magazine*, May 1, 1998, https://www.airforcemag.com/article/0588revolt/; Herman S. Wolk, *Planning and Organizing the Postwar Air Force* (Washington, DC: US Air Force, 1984); *The Struggle for Air Force Independence* (Washington, DC: Air Force History and Museums Program, 1997); Herman S. Wolk, *Fulcrum of Power: Essays on the United States Air Force and National Security* (Washington, DC: Air Force History and Museums Program, 2003); Lynn Eden, "Capitalist Conflict and the State: The Making of United States Military Policy in 1948," in *Statemaking and Social Movements, Essays in History and Theory*, ed. Charles Bright and Susan Harding (Ann Arbor: University of Michigan Press, 1984), 233–61.
39. Herman S. Wolk, "The First Five Years of the First 50," *Air Force Magazine*, September 1, 1997, https://www.airforcemag.com/article/0997first/.
40. George Baer, "U.S. Naval Strategy, 1890–1945," *Naval War College Review* 44, no. 1 (1991): 26–27.
41. Hoopes and Brinkley, *Driven Patriot*, 190–94.
42. Thomas Hone, Norman Friedman, and Mark Mandeles, "The Development of the Angled-Deck Aircraft Carrier: Innovation and Adaptation," *Naval War College Review* 64, no. 2 (2011): 63–78; Hone, *OPNAV*, 197.
43. "Meet the Army's Davy Crockett Rocket That Fired Tactical 'Mini' Nukes," *National Interest*, February 27, 2020, https://nationalinterest.org/blog/buzz/meet-armys-davy-crockett-rocket-fired-tactical-mini-nukes-125776?page=0%2C1.
44. Dave Oliver saw one such device while deployed aboard USS *Trumpetfish* in September 1963. The weapon had a maximum timer of forty minutes, which meant the frogmen had to swim at a speed of three knots to escape.
45. William Corliss and Francis Schwenk, *Nuclear Propulsion for Space* (Washington, DC: US Atomic Energy Commission, 1971), https://www.osti.gov/includes/opennet/includes/Understanding%20the%20Atom/Nuclear%20Propulsion%20for%20Space%20V.2.pdf.
46. Congressional Budget Office, "Projected Costs of U.S. Nuclear Forces, 2021–2030," May 2021, https://www.cbo.gov/system/files/2021-05/57130-Nuclear-Forces.pdf.
47. "Atlas," Encyclopedia Aeronautica, n.d., http://www.astronautix.com/a/atlas.html.
48. Westinghouse provided technical support for the reactor while Electric Boat would design the submarine to carry it. E. E. Kintner, "Admiral Rickover's Gamble: The Landlocked Submarine," *The Atlantic*, January 1959, https://www.theatlantic.com/magazine/archive/1959/01/admiral-rickovers-gamble/308436/; Theodore Rockwell, *The Rickover Effect: How One Man Made a Difference* (Lincoln, NE: iUniverse, 2002), 51ff.

49. Lauren Fish and Paul Scharre, "The Soldier's Heavy Load," Center for a New American Security, September 26, 2018, https://www.cnas.org/publications/reports/the-soldiers-heavy-load-1.
50. Robert Coram, *Boyd: The Fighter Pilot Who Changed the Art of War* (Boston: Little, Brown, 2002), 232–37.
51. Don Holloway, "How the Low, Slow A-1 Skyraider Earned Its Place in Our Hearts in Vietnam," *Military Times*, December 15, 2017, https://www.militarytimes.com/off-duty/2017/12/15/how-the-low-slow-a-1-skyraider-earned-its-place-in-the-hearts-of-us-troops-in-vietnam/.
52. Bryan McGrath, "More than Just a Fire: The Implications of the *Bonhomme Richard* Catastrophe," War on the Rocks, July 16, 2020, https://warontherocks.com/2020/07/more-than-just-a-fire-the-implications-of-the-bonhomme-richard-catastrophe/.
53. James R. FitzSimonds, "Aircraft Carriers versus Battleships in War and Myth: Demythologizing Carrier Air Dominance at Sea," *Journal of Military History* 84, no. 3 (July 2020): 843–65.
54. Vincent Davis, *Postwar Defense Policy and the U.S. Navy, 1943–1946* (Chapel Hill: University of North Carolina Press, 1966), 127.
55. Robert Ablion and Robert Connery, *Forrestal and the Navy* (New York: Columbia University Press, 1966); Hone, *OPNAV*, 190–93.
56. Compare Melvin Deaile, "The SAC Mentality: The Origins of Strategic Air Command's Organizational Culture, 1948–1951," *Air & Space Power Journal* (March/April 2015): 48–73; Toprani, "Budgets and Strategy," 124–25.
57. See documents 7–8 in *The United States Air Force: Basic Documents on Roles and Missions*, ed. Richard Wolf (Washington, DC: Office of Air Force History, 1987).
58. Mike Pietrucha, "Slaying the Unicorn: The Army and the Fixed-Wing Attack," War on the Rocks, December 9, 2019, https://warontherocks.com/2019/12/slaying-the-unicorn-the-army-and-fixed-wing-attack/.
59. Morton Halperin and David Halperin, "The Key West Key," *Foreign Policy* 53 (Winter 1983–84): 114–30.
60. Rosenberg and Kennedy, *Carriers*, 108ff.
61. Phillip Meilinger, *Airpower Myths and Facts* (Maxwell AFB, AL: Air University Press, 2003).
62. Alain Enthoven, *How Much Is Enough? Shaping the Defense Program, 1961–1969* (Santa Monica, CA: RAND Corp., 2005), 221.
63. Appendix A, Burke interview.
64. "Today's Military: A Well-Educated Force," Face the Facts USA, May 26, 2013, https://facethefactsusa.org/facts/tanks-and-humvees-caps-and-gowns/. Moreover, until the Air Force Academy graduated its first class in 1964, the Air Force drew a significant number of its pilots from the Naval Academy's graduates. Dana Born, Andrew Phillips, and Timothy Trainor, "America's Service Academies, Your Service Academies," *Liberal Education* 98, no. 1 (2012).
65. This perception of radically different service cultures is widespread. It is sometimes referred to as the "Three D Culture": "The Air Force is slick and devious: they will lie. The Navy is defiant and will ignore you: damn the torpedoes, full speed ahead. The Army is dumb: they will talk when they should keep their mouths shut." Stephen Scroggs, *Army Relations with Congress: Thick Armor, Dull Sword, Slow Horse* (Westport, CT: Praeger, 2000), 57.
66. Hone, *OPNAV*, 201.

67. George Baer, *One Hundred Years of Sea Power: The U.S. Navy, 1890–1990* (Stanford, CA: Stanford University Press, 1993), 275ff., esp. 278–79.
68. Henry Stimson and McGeorge Bundy, *On Active Service in Peace and War* (New York: Harper, 1948), 506.
69. Richard Conolly to Forrest Sherman, May 1, 1950, quoted in Joseph Wyle, *Military Strategy: A General Theory of Military Control* (Annapolis, MD: Naval Institute, 1989), xii.
70. The latter was code-named Operation Magic Carpet. See R. Alton Lee, "The Army 'Mutiny' of 1946," *Journal of American History* 53, no. 3 (1966): 555–71.
71. Christopher Tassava, "The American Economy during World War II," EH.met Encyclopedia, February 10, 2008, https://eh.net/encyclopedia/the-american-economy-during-world-war-ii/.
72. Phillips Payson O'Brien, *How the War Was Won* (Cambridge: Cambridge University Press, 2015). The United States Strategic Bombing Survey, done at the end of World War II, concluded that airpower in its broadest sense had played a role during the conflict and even used the word "decisive" but was also remarkably candid about the limitations of strategic bombing. The survey had little to no effect on the argument (in public at least) but proved prophetic on the future limitations of "strategic bombing" in such diverse conflicts and environments as Korea, Vietnam, and Kosovo. *The United States Strategic Bombing Surveys (European War) (Pacific War)* (Maxwell AFB, AL: Air University Press, 1987), https://www.airuniversity.af.edu/Portals/10/AUPress/Books/B_0020_SPANGRUD_STRATEGIC_BOMBING_SURVEYS.pdf; David MacIsaac, *Strategic Bombing in World War Two: The Story of the Strategic Bombing Survey* (New York: Garland, 1976); Gian Gentile, *How Effective Is Strategic Bombing? Lessons from World War II to Kosovo* (New York: New York University Press, 2001); Rebecca Grant, "The Long Arm of the US Strategic Bombing Survey," *Air Force Magazine*, February 1, 2008, https://www.airforcemag.com/article/0208bombing/.
73. Besides O'Brien, *How the War Was Won*. See also Richard Overy, *Why the Allies Won* (New York: Norton, 1995).
74. Alan Levine, "Was World War II a Near-Run Thing?," *Journal of Strategic Studies* 8, no. 1 (1985): 46–50.
75. Boris Sokolov, "The Role of Lend-Lease in Soviet Military Efforts," *Journal of Slavic Military Studies* 7, no. 3 (1994): 567–86.
76. A. T. Mahan, *The Influence of Sea Power upon History* (New York: Dover, 1987), 539.
77. *Congressional Record* 105, no. 12 (August 4, 1959): 15105–6. Cannon, a Democratic representative from Missouri, served as chair of the House Appropriations Committee from 1941 to 1964 except for the four years the Republican Party held the majority. Cannon had long been an opponent of Navy carriers. Dave Oliver, "Secretary McNamara, The Navy and the CVA-67 Controversy" (master's thesis, American University, 1974), n. 39.
78. Edward Kolodziej. *The Uncommon Defense and Congress, 1945–1963* (Columbus: Ohio State University Press, 1966), 103.
79. Paul Healy, "Nobody Loves Clarence," *Saturday Evening Post*, March 25, 1959, 132.
80. Paul Schratz, "The Admirals' Revolt," *Proceedings* 112 (February 1986): 68.
81. For King, see Hoopes and Brinkley, *Driven Patriot*, 169ff.; and Alan Rems, "I Neglected to Consult the President," *Naval History*, August 2018, https://www.usni.org/magazines/naval-history-magazine/2018/august/i-neglected-consult-president.
82. Forrestal's most relentless critic was the muckraking columnist Drew Pearson. See Toprani, "'Our Efforts Have Degenerated,'" 689n91.

83. For a sympathetic biography, see Keith McFarland and David Roll, *Louis Johnson and the Arming of America: The Roosevelt and Truman Years* (Bloomington: Indiana University Press, 2005).
84. The Marines loathed Johnson. Aaron O'Connell, *Underdogs: The Making of the Modern Marine Corps* (Cambridge, MA: Harvard University Press, 2012), 126ff. For Johnson's views on amphibious operations, see Paolo Coletta, *United States Navy and Defense Unification, 1947–1953* (Newark: University of Delaware Press, 1981), 213.
85. Robert Dennison oral history, November 2, 1971, Harry S. Truman Library. For additional background information, see Paul Hammond, "Super Carriers and B-36 Bombers: Appropriations, Strategy and Politics," in *American Civil Military Decisions*, ed. Harold Stein (Birmingham: University of Alabama Press, 1963), 465–567; and Jeffrey Barlow, *The Revolt of the Admiral: The Fight for Naval Aviation* (Washington, DC: Naval Historical Center, 1994).
86. Appendix B, Russell interview.
87. Dennison oral history, November 2, 1971.
88. James Field, *History of United States Naval Operations Korea* (Washington: Government Printing Office [GPO], 1962); Richard Hallion, "Naval Air Operations in Korea," in *A Revolutionary War: Korea and the Transformation of the Postwar World*, ed. William Williams (Chicago: Imprint, 1973), 129–48; Roger Kropf, *The US Air Force in Korea: Problems Which Hindered the Effectiveness of Airpower*, report no. 89-14301989 (Maxwell AFB, AL: Air Command and Staff College, (1989), https://apps.dtic.mil/dtic/tr/fulltext/u2/a208027.pdf. The authors are grateful to Sally Paine for identifying these sources.
89. Frank Hoffman, *Mars Adapting: Military Change during War* (Annapolis, MD: Naval Institute Press, 2021), chap. 4.
90. Clark Reynolds, "MacArthur as Maritime Strategist," *Naval War College Review* 33, no. 2 (1980): 79–91.
91. Samuel Cox, "H-054-1: Inchon Landing and Naval Action in the Korean War, September–October 1950," Naval Heritage and History Command, September 2020, https://www.history.navy.mil/about-us/leadership/director/directors-corner/h-grams/h-gram-054/h-054-1.html.
92. Michael Pearlman, *Truman and MacArthur: Policy, Politics, and the Hunger for Renown* (Bloomington: Indiana University Press, 2008), 86–107.
93. McFarland and Roll, *Johnson and Arming*, 188ff. See also *Congressional Record* 96, no. 16 (July 26, 1950): A5411–A5413.
94. Chuck McCutcheon and David Mark, "Politics Ain't Beanbag," *CS Monitor*, November 14, 2014, https://www.csmonitor.com/USA/Politics/Politics-Voices/2014/1114/Politics-ain-t-beanbag.

CHAPTER 2

1960s

The McNamara Revolution

Following its successes during World War II, the Navy floundered in the postwar US political environment. By failing to offer alternatives to the Air Force's strategic bombing strategy that satisfied the overarching pressure for unification and reduced defense spending, the Navy did not carry its weight in the nation's strategic discourse. After its unsuccessful "revolt" against civilian authority in 1949, the Navy recovered during the Korean War, recouping some its earlier losses, most notably by getting the supercarriers of the *Forrestal* class.

Over the course of the 1950s, new challenges emerged. Despite extraordinary peacetime defense budgets after the Korean War, many civilians and even some military officers believed that the US military had become overly reliant on nuclear weapons and was strategically ineffective.[1] This sense of unease set the stage for the "McNamara Revolution."[2]

Robert Strange McNamara would become the longest-serving and strongest secretary of defense in history. After Secretary of Defense Louis Johnson's ouster in 1950, the balance of power between the OSD and the military shifted to the services. McNamara was determined to reverse this trend. His actions shifted power to the OSD and literally transformed how the Pentagon operated. None of the services went along with these changes willingly, least of all the Navy, whose leadership was as confident of its abilities as McNamara was of his.

In 1955 Arleigh Burke became the CNO over ninety-two of his more senior peers.[3] A surface-warfare officer by trade, Burke achieved fame during World War II as a destroyer captain and chief of staff to Adm. Marc Mitscher, who commanded the fast carrier task force that overran the Central Pacific in 1944 and 1945.[4] Perhaps even more remarkable than his war record was Burke's openness to new technologies such as the Polaris submarine-launched ballistic missile (SLBM) and novel warfighting concepts such as finite deterrence (the minimum number of nuclear weapons necessary to deter aggression).[5] Unlike virtually all of his predecessors, he took long-term planning seriously, recognizing that the growing cost and complexity of weapon systems meant that the Navy could no longer simply wait until a crisis began and then react. Crucially, he linked planning efforts to budgeting, which ensured that the Office of the Chief of Naval Operations (OPNAV), rather than other major Navy commands and bureaus, would remain the dominant player when it came to force-structure questions.

Unfortunately, Burke displayed less political acumen, which is a problem considering that the head of a military service, like it or not, is a political position as much as a military one. Burke had witnessed, many say participated in, the Revolt of the Admirals. No matter what his actual level of involvement, there is no doubt that the fight against unification scarred him. As the memos he wrote in OP-23 during the dispute make clear, Burke believed that the Navy was the victim of a conspiracy by the Pentagon and the other services to strip it of its independence.[6] Not surprisingly, he was intellectually and emotionally unprepared to deal constructively with the power of the new secretary of defense or the new Air Force after he became CNO. He, like his Navy colleagues, perpetuated the blood feuds of the late 1940s, albeit less publicly.

RECONSIDERING INTERSERVICE RIVALRY

While it may seem counterintuitive to some observers, interservice rivalry actually has much to commend it. Just as competition drives innovation in the private sector, interservice rivalry can and does encourage positive development at the technological and doctrinal levels.[7] Although interservice cooperation is often essential at the operational level, the same uniformity is not necessary or even desirable every day in the Pentagon. In fact, interservice harmony often stifles innovation and promotes waste through "logrolling." This occurs when key players such as service chiefs agree not to interfere with each other's prized projects. It creates the mirage of interservice harmony but concurrently fosters inefficiencies, while making the military less susceptible to external review or control.[8]

While interservice rivalry does result in the occasional embarrassing headline and may perpetuate some duplication of effort ("redundancy" in business-speak), in the American context—an immense economy that can sustain a huge military establishment, a relatively benign security environment, and strong culture of military subordination to civilian control—we should not overlook the positive outcomes for national security.[9] For example, Army-Navy competition before World War II allowed the country to develop both a strategic-bombing force and a naval-air arm as well as amphibious infantry forces. During the Cold War, competition was a hallmark of the various ballistic missile programs. The key factor, some scholars argue, behind successful competition is agreement over strategic aims or at least ensuring they are not contradictory.[10]

Interservice rivalry also provides another contribution to defense: it is vital to the preservation of effective civilian control over the military—something that Burke recognized in 1947.[11] When disagreements occur, there is an opportunity for civilians to learn from the dispute and even gain relative advantage during civil-military disputes (especially over budgets). It is only when interservice disputes erupt that outsiders get a glimpse of important issues. How else does a political appointee or elected official gain insight into, say, the relative value of strategic bombing versus close air support? The balance of armor versus speed in land engagements? The value of different systems in antisubmarine warfare? The use of high-energy lasers? The control of surveillance assets? When no issue boils over into public view, it does not mean there is no dirty laundry. To the cognoscenti, it signifies that everything is being hustled out of the Pentagon at night in an unmarked van and laundered in some windowless building in Washington. To put it more formally, the services are resolving their disputes privately by creating a "negotiated environment" that preserves the equities of key military stakeholders.[12]

Burke was a firm believer in interservice competition, and it guided his thinking as CNO. Burke had the utmost faith in himself, but the same attributes that served him so well in wartime arguably failed him in Washington. His number two, Vice Adm. James Russell, recollected that Burke was stubborn and refused to alter course even after the rout of the admirals: "Burke . . . wasn't a particularly good politician. He didn't like to use politics or use systems analysis to try to muddy up the waters. . . . He was not at all inhibited by the events of 1949. I served with him in the Pacific during the war. He didn't change."[13]

When Burke became CNO, his views regarding unification had not changed since his last Washington tour six years before. Some officers, such as the JCS chairman, Arthur Radford, one of the leaders of the Revolt of the Admirals, had trimmed their sails and learned to live with strategic bombing to get along with the cost-conscious President Dwight Eisenhower and his "New Look" strategy.[14] Eisenhower, like Truman before him, was terrified that high peacetime defense budgets would undermine domestic prosperity and impinge on civil liberties. Upon ending the Korean War, Eisenhower was determined to avoid future protracted conflicts by maintaining a credible yet cost-effective peacetime deterrent.[15] The only way to square the circle was to adopt a military strategy that enabled the United States to use overwhelming military force—including nuclear weapons—at the beginning of any conflict.[16]

How did any of this affect the Navy? Besides hard limits on the size of the defense budget, in the short run Eisenhower's strategy benefited the Air Force. This was during the same period the Navy was scrambling to find sufficient funds to build its new fleet of forty-one Polaris-armed submarines. Eisenhower also continued to support unification to enhance efficiency, while Burke remained a staunch opponent of any policies that threatened the Navy's independence, whether it was centralizing power in the JCS or enhancing the stature of the secretary of defense.

Eisenhower had long been a supporter of greater unification and wanted the JCS to be a vehicle for generating consensus among the services. When he appointed Burke as CNO, Burke recalled that Eisenhower "insisted, I guess he told me half a dozen times in two or three meetings that my big job was not to head the Navy, my big job was my job as a member of the Joint Chiefs of Staff." Burke considered such a belief to be misguided. The chiefs simply could not achieve consensus on issues regarding "an allocation of money to the services, or missions of the services" because each of them was raised within their peculiar service culture and naturally believed that their service was best suited to achieve national objectives. Rather than enforcing "unity" at the expense of military judgment, which would either stifle dissent or encourage "back scratching" that impaired military effectiveness, it was the job of the chiefs to *encourage* disagreements and present the president with the tools to make an informed decision. It was up to the president to resolve military disagreements because national leaders should not view such problems in isolation: "You cannot separate military, economic, political affairs. They're all mixed up together, and somebody, and only the President can do it, has to make the decisions as to what shall be done, how much of each kind of power there shall be and what the capabilities of that kind of power shall be and how it will be used."[17]

This appears an enlightened perspective at first glance, but it reflects a curious myopia on Burke's part. A president simply could not devote complete attention to military affairs, because they were responsible for the entire executive branch. Presidents therefore had to delegate some of their authority—otherwise national policy would become constipated. This had been the rationale for creating a secretary of defense who could oversee defense policy on behalf of the president.

Burke never accepted the authority of the secretary of defense to make decisions that contradicted his preferences as CNO. Before the passage of the National Security Act of 1947, CNOs had only one civilian between them and the president—the secretary of the Navy, who enjoyed cabinet rank. The act added an additional layer, the secretary of defense, while the secretary of the Navy (and the secretary of the Army) lost both their cabinet status in 1949 and their nominal place in the chain of command in 1958.

Burke was not reluctant to bypass (or at least threaten to bypass) the secretary of the Navy or the secretary of defense to appeal directly to the president, Congress, or the media over issues ranging from continuing the draft, to whether the Navy should retain Pacific Command, to resisting Air Force control over the Navy's nuclear assets.[18] The case of retaining the draft is illustrative because Burke had just taken office and challenged a decision made by his predecessor (Adm. Robert Carney) and both the secretaries of defense and the Navy. He brought his misgivings directly to Eisenhower's attention because he knew the president could not afford the embarrassment of firing Burke or allowing him to resign. Burke also subverted 1953 legislation eliminating the CNO's power to issue operational orders by sending out informal "anticipatory orders."[19]

The Navy was not the only unruly service during the Eisenhower administration—the president sacked *two* Army chiefs of staff for challenging government policy (Matthew Ridgway and Maxwell Taylor). One student of the Pentagon budgetary process called Eisenhower's JCS "the most colorful, controversial, independent, outspoken, and least cooperative collection in American military history."[20] There was no end to their squabbling. Eugene Zuckert, one of the founding leaders of the Air Force after the passage of the National Security Act, later complained, "I sometimes think that the Joint Chiefs in my time was the most terrible organization I ever observed. I used to think, 'Aren't we fortunate that, through dumb luck, the production of nuclear weapons were taken out of the military?' Because, if it had been under the military . . . we wouldn't ever have produced, for example, the tactical nuclear weapons, because of the roles-and-missions types of fight."[21]

Things got so bad that, by the time the Kennedy administration took over, the different services were not even pretending to develop joint war plans. As Alain Enthoven (deputy assistant secretary and then assistant secretary of defense for systems analysis from 1961 to 1969) observed, the Navy gave a very skillful presentation in 1961 regarding how many Polaris missiles and submarines it would require to destroy its targets in the Soviet Union: "It was a very neat analysis . . . a very nice job, but never once did it mention the existence of the United States Air Force or any of its weapon systems, even though at that time the air force commanded the majority of the strategic nuclear weapons."[22]

Not surprisingly, the most vicious fights were those over budgets. Eisenhower had told Burke and the other chiefs that if they expected him to resolve differences, the chiefs should reciprocate by supporting whatever decision he made, even if they did not like the result. He told Burke, "Once I approve a budget I don't want you people going up there and undercutting my budget."

The chiefs, in turn, wiggled their way out this restriction through some impressive semantic gymnastics: officially, the chiefs would "support" the president's budget, but if Congress asked for their personal judgment, they were obligated to share any criticism they had. Eisenhower insisted, "You'd . . . better not plant it either," but as Burke knew full well, such a question did not "have to be planted, it's always asked."[23]

Of course, the only way to ensure the chiefs would not vent their spleen on Capitol Hill was busting whatever budget limits the White House imposed. Eisenhower tried to convince the JCS to keep its budget request under his administration's "topline" (the extent of the Pentagon's budget), including hosting "stag dinners" for the chiefs where he cajoled them to cooperate. The chiefs proved immune to Eisenhower's charms, and the president gave up on working with them as a group, preferring to act through the chairman of the JCS or the secretary of defense to implement the requirements of the New Look.[24] The latter's powers were expanded under legislation passed in 1953 and 1958, while the chiefs were effectively sidelined as an advisory body for the president.[25]

At one point Eisenhower called the chiefs' defiance of his budget preferences "damn near treason." According to Russell, the events of the Eisenhower period poisoned relations among senior military and civilian defense officials even before McNamara took office: "[Thomas] Gates [McNamara's predecessor] was pretty mad at us, and he told McNamara he had to watch those admirals and generals, or they'd run over him. For a man of McNamara's personality, that was all he needed."[26]

McNamara was, in 1960, one of the brightest minds in the country. During World War II, he left the faculty of Harvard Business School to serve with the Army Air Corps as a statistical control officer with the Twentieth Air Force, most notably assisting the then major general Curtis LeMay with the firebombing of Japan in 1944–45.[27] After the war, he and a team of fellow Air Corps officers (the original "Whiz Kids") joined the Ford Motor Company. They proposed to run the venerable company using a new science developed during the war based on mathematics, analysis, and statistics and that relied on early computers—what is known as management information systems today. The Whiz Kids revolutionized Ford's antiquated business practices and restored the company to profitability but achieved mixed results in terms of automotive design and production (although McNamara's insistence on safety and building more fuel-efficient and environmentally friendly automobiles was ahead of its time). Irrespective of their actual accomplishments at Ford, the Whiz Kids' greatest success was burnishing McNamara's reputation as a visionary leader, which resulted in his appointment as Ford's first president from outside the Ford family.[28]

McNamara barely had time to settle into his new job before the quintessential "wise man," Robert Lovett (Truman's last secretary of defense and Marshall's closest confidant), brought the young executive to the attention of president-elect John F. Kennedy.[29] Kennedy offered McNamara the job of secretary of the treasury, presumably because appointing one of the country's best-known executives would placate the business community, but McNamara pleaded ignorance of monetary affairs. The world would have been a very different place had he not been so modest. Kennedy then offered him the Pentagon, which McNamara again declined until the incoming president insisted.[30] He would subsequently serve as secretary of defense for seven years, transforming the position like no one before or since.[31]

McNamara came into office without any firm ideas about defense but with a supreme confidence in his ability to master any issue he tackled. One aide put it, "I think Mr. McNamara's theory was . . . that if a person was basically capable, had basic intelligence, and a desire to work, that he could master any job in the Pentagon, possibly including his own."[32] This was not the sort of attitude that sat well among military officers who believed their expertise came from a lifetime of experience in peace and war.

By the end of the 1950s, many defense intellectuals, both uniformed and civilian, were critical of the Eisenhower administration's overreliance on nuclear weapons under the New Look. Eisenhower had intended to pursue a more nuanced policy of developing US military capabilities to deter Soviet aggression, but over time the New Look became synonymous with "massive retaliation"—that the United States would privilege the use of nuclear weapons. Burke put the blame for this misconception on the Air Force, which he accused of subverting the New Look to create political support for larger budgets.[33] No matter the cause, critics argued that massive retaliation was a pure bluff because it was unreasonable to expect the United States to resort to nuclear war in every instance of communist aggression, particularly in the colonial world. Instead, they advocated some variant of "flexible response"—upgrading conventional forces to wage limited wars.[34]

McNamara was not involved in any of these debates before he became secretary, and beyond delivering policymakers with a larger portfolio of military options to handle various crises, his concerns had less to do with the substance of military strategy than with the supposedly humdrum world of management.[35] Rather than question how and why the United States would use force, McNamara and his civilian aides focused on the more prosaic questions of "how much" military hardware and what sort of weapons were required to achieve broader political and military needs.[36]

WHAT MCNAMARA WROUGHT

Two of his reforms, in particular, left a mark on the US defense establishment. The first was the introduction of program management into the Pentagon's budgeting process—the Planning, Programming, and Budgeting System (PPBS). Rather than budgeting items individually by service in terms of inputs, McNamara created a unified, multiservice planning and budget process composed of "major programs" that delivered vital outputs (strategic forces, conventional forces, etc.) and costed them out over the next five years.[37] This meant that platforms would be judged on how they contributed to the Pentagon's overall requirements and capabilities. He recognized that there were great advantages to be gained by simply organizing and presenting data more clearly. For example, if everything that delivered firepower—be it a warship or a strike airplane—could be funded in one category, and everything that delivered cargo—be it a cargo ship, airplane, or truck—were in another, people would make better judgments on the relative values of different systems.

If done properly, this process would reduce the duplication of effort, long the bugbear of defense reformers and apostles of unification (or "jointness" in today's parlance). PPBS (in its current incarnation as Planning, Programing, Budgeting and Execution—PPBE) has remained in place largely unchanged to this very day, and despite PPBE's showing its age, there are no viable alternatives on the horizon.[38]

Second, whenever the services did put forward competing systems, the secretary of defense would no longer rely on their subjective evaluations of which option was superior. Instead, the secretary would also consider assessments by their own researchers within the OSD. They would scrutinize the services' justifications and, if necessary, offer their own alternatives using comparative judgments derived through systems analysis.

Although the application of systems analysis can become excruciatingly complex, at its foundation it is simply an attempt to measure the effectiveness—the outputs—of a system by assessing various inputs, with everything expressed in a common system of numbers or in dollars. In other words, it is an attempt to measure "bang for your buck." The aim was not to find the "right" answer so much as the most efficient one—the solution that yielded the largest payoff relative to the smallest investment.[39] Just as sabermetrics sought to reevaluate baseball players by using new sets of statistics that "old-timers" had ignored or undervalued, or as asset managers scrutinize financial disclosures to find hidden value in companies beyond just profits and losses, systems analysis in the Pentagon was the application of usually very simple mathematical models derived from academic economics (especially marginal utility) to build the most effective military at the lowest cost. Enthoven explained, "Our idea is that analysis is not intended to tell you what the best answer is. In fact, in the problems we're dealing with there is no such thing as a best answer. . . . I see our goal as being to try to avoid disaster and gross waste, rather than trying to find the best possible solution."[40]

The systems analysts pored over data to determine which weapons to buy, but they often went further. Their training as economists—conventionally defined as the study of choice under scarcity—also encouraged them to consider the potential trade-offs, opportunity costs, or marginal utility of each decision.[41] For instance, McNamara's team quickly figured out that there were diminishing returns on the size of the US nuclear arsenal. The extra damage the United States could inflict was not commensurate with the cost of acquiring additional warheads and systems.[42]

If the United States did not have to worry about resource scarcity, there would be no reason to fret over efficiency. As we know, however, there are multiple competing demands for resources going to defense, which makes budgetary allocations inherently political decisions. Systems analysis would ideally aid politicians by showing them how to avoid wastage, but it refrained from making claims about policy preferences, which were inherently normative and subjective. As Enthoven was fond of repeating, "analysis is the servant of judgment, not a substitute for judgment."[43]

Systems analysis was a forward-thinking enterprise in a building where there is a temptation to focus on immediate crises or the budget cycle.[44] Perhaps systems analysis's greatest insight came from its demand that budgetary decisions not be made on the basis of individual weapons or units. Rather, each weapon was part of a larger, more complex "system" that made it functional. For instance, no one should make decisions about the cost of an aircraft carrier just on the basis of how much each steel hull costs. They also had to include the costs of research and development (R & D), training the ship's crew, and buying the aircraft, the flight crews, and other ships in the strike group. Most important, systems analysts evaluated the carrier's effectiveness in relation to its possible alternatives, such as land-based aircraft, whose cost also included base construction and maintenance, logistics, security, and so on.[45]

This sort of thinking was invaluable in controlling costs because frequently the money Congress appropriated to buy a system would not cover all of the necessary operating costs.[46] Of course, this "rational" approach could, if pursued relentlessly, lead defense planners astray. As one critic noted, if every system comprises different subsystems or sub-subsystems, it could theoretically result in "the very smallest issues in the Department of Defense, such as the rationalization of the size of ladies exercise bloomers, being seen as a stage in the final end of balancing the global communist threat."[47]

There is another, more fundamental problem with systems analysis. Weapons are used in the field, which is hardly an ideal testing ground. Students of Clausewitz will remember that the "fog of war" and "friction" are the most important factors "that distinguish real war from war on paper." If armies could operate without worrying about either, there would be no reason for physical combat (battle). Rather, nations would simply calculate which side would triumph before every engagement and act accordingly. Clausewitz dismissed this fantasy as "war by algebra," and perhaps the systems analysts should have heeded his warning.[48]

The analysis process develops mathematical models to represent situations and then lets the numbers unemotionally and repetitively manipulate those situations to assist the examiners. At its heart, the system relies on assumptions—mathematical models—and, of course, algorithms to run the models. The challenge is that it is much more difficult to model some battlefields than others (the sea domain, for example, is much more complex than the air). Consequently, there must be more adjustment for the fog of war (or "scatter" in the data) in more chaotic or unfamiliar environments. If someone constructed models that assume clear air, it can become very tedious or even mathematically impossible when moving to models of undersea warfare. Analysts have to account for salinity and pressure changes, along with mundane factors such as the noises produced by marine life. Few mathematicians were terribly interested in discussions about possible flaws in their models, and few naval officers in the McNamara era were capable of or interested in having dispassionate discussions of mathematics and modeling the maritime environment with outside experts.

As radical as this approach to warfare seems, certain elements of it had for decades already influenced budgetary and strategic decision-making, from the design of modern battleships (e.g., evaluating the trade-offs among speed, armor, and firepower) to the selection of bombing targets in World War II.[49] The Navy was not a laggard when it came to mathematical modeling. It had its own system, operational requirements (today called operations research—OR), and had been doing it for two decades before McNamara arrived at the Pentagon.

OR had its origins in Britain during the 1930s, when researchers such as physicists and mathematicians figured out how to use fledgling radar systems to shoot down enemy planes. In the United States, OR arrived during World War II, and the Navy had several such teams.[50] One, led by Ellis Johnson, studied the problems of mine warfare and wrought havoc on Japan.[51] William Shockley, who would later win the Nobel Prize for his work on transistors, led another team, which focused on antisubmarine warfare. Another group, the Operations Research Group (ORG), was attached to the staff of CNO Ernest King. After the war, the Navy signed a contract with an Operations Evaluation Group (OEG).[52] A form of this contract has remained active to this day, and the Navy is still teaching OR at its postgraduate school in Monterey, California.[53]

So, what exactly is OR? One textbook defines it using the language of systems analysis. It is nothing more than the "scientific search for optimal solutions to problems involved in the operations of systems."[54] In other words, OR is the use of mathematical modeling at the tactical and operational levels of warfare, including the optimal allocation of scarce resources, such as the deployment of weapon systems (e.g., the use of aircraft to hunt submarines) and even their production. Consequently, should not the Navy have applauded McNamara's approach to making procurement and budgetary decisions?

Yes—but it did not. Burke believed that OR was a tool for the Navy to control its own future, not for civilians in the Pentagon to tell the Navy what to do. In one oral history, he lauded McNamara's intellect while gently critiquing the secretary's inexperience with running a large organization, which Burke claimed left him prone to make changes for their own sake and without reflecting on their long-term consequences.[55] (Ironically, McNamara believed in the early 1960s that his experience at Ford made him well qualified to run the Pentagon, whose "administrative problems are very similar."[56]) Privately, to another naval officer, Burke was less inhibited—he complained that systems analysis was simply a mask for ignorance and selfishness:

> They [McNamara and his staff] were interested in getting control of the military. . . . They didn't know their ass from a tin cup about the military, strategy, or world problems. . . . They wanted an answer that couldn't be disproved . . . [but] what is needed for defense of the country is only an estimate. It is only a feel that you acquire. You can't analyze or quantify it—it's a feel. . . . The use of analysis is often done cynically. It is done in order to prove something which you have already decided on.[57]

Burke's successor, Adm. George Anderson, felt the same way:

> The Navy had been doing systems analysis for years. We had used the "estimate of the situation" as a basis for reaching a decision.[58] We had the OEG as their evaluation group integrated with fleet operational units, and they were very efficient. McNamara may have called it cost-effectiveness but it was really just the application of operation analysis, and we had operation analysis representatives/teams with all our fleets. We were using cost as an analysis factor.[59]

Systems analysis, Burke and Anderson recognized, is only a tool decision-makers can use to assign a value to things that can be quantified. It complemented but did not supplant decision-making only on the basis of experience and emotions (or "judgment," as the military calls it). An admiral with thirty or more years of experience in a military organization may resent giving up control, but it is important to strike a balance between the tangible and intangible because, as we noted in the introduction, war is simply too complex for any person or small group to master every one of its intricacies.

Burke and Anderson understood what the stakes were in the feud with McNamara. As McNamara later explained, upon taking office, besides the overreliance on nuclear weapons, he was disgusted that during the Eisenhower administration, the only real civilian input into the defense budget came when setting the "top line" for defense spending. The services routinely ignored this limit, along with the guidance provided by the National Security Council's Basic National Security Policy documents. Instead, each service drafted its own requirements independent of the others, and the three budgets were simply added together before being presented to the secretary of defense. This resulted not only in uncontrolled spending (defense requests averaged 15 percent more than the Treasury Department's top line) but also provided only "a façade rather than the reality of military power." McNamara's aim, he explained, was to create the capabilities necessary for "a controlled, flexible response," which he defined as bolstering conventional forces such as infantry divisions or wings of tactical fighters but also improving the readiness and survivability of strategic forces such as bombers.[60]

As astute contemporaries observed, McNamara's overarching goal was to wrest budgetary control away from the services and impose real, as opposed to nominal, civilian leadership: "Gradually, and with a finesse which demands respect, the services are being dismembered and disemboweled, so that the question of their utility is decided continually in decrements."[61]

In contradiction to Burke's vision of how to manage defense, systems analysis required consensus regarding how to measure military effectiveness. Because the systems analysts believed one could make informed judgments about the efficiency of competing systems, they had trouble concealing their disdain for interservice rivalry ("parochialism" was a common slur), which stressed the qualitative or experiential differences among how the services used force based on their peculiar cultures and history. To Enthoven, discussions along these lines detracted from the "public interest," which is why the systems analysts did "not to try to manage the Defense Department by reaching a satisfactory compromise between the different vested local parochial interests . . . but rather to try to think through and define very clearly what is the public interest and to state it explicitly."[62]

Unfortunately, by claiming they were acting in the national interest, McNamara's team insinuated that the military was acting selfishly. When Enthoven floated an Air Force proposal to secure the OSD's support for an additional B-52 Stratofortress wing, Deputy Secretary Roswell Gilpatric retorted, "Alain, no deals. We're going to figure out what the right thing to do is, and then we'll do that. No bargaining. No deals. Never again."[63]

Burke and Anderson did not appreciate this attitude, which may explain their complaints about the "anti-military" attitudes of McNamara's aides.[64] What they missed, perhaps, was that there are many important aspects of military affairs—logistics, medical services, transportation—that are handled much more effectively (and much less expensively) by nonmilitary organizations. There are a limited number of admirals or generals who care about these tasks, so long as they are done well and remain responsive to the changing needs of commanders. McNamara was pushing on an open door so long as he refrained from interfering with military affairs, for which the services claimed he had limited appreciation.

Burke had another problem with McNamara. He knew that an agile mind could make an analysis say nearly anything, and he was convinced that the Air Force and McNamara's staff engaged in improper analysis. This infuriated Burke: "You can't fire people who don't come up with the answers you want.

You have to be able to fight honestly. You can't cheat at analysis, even when you know the other side is cheating, and retain your integrity."[65]

A new group of Whiz Kids followed McNamara to the Pentagon, many from an extraordinary think tank in Santa Monica, California—the RAND Corporation.[66] The RAND analysts were especially interested in questions of nuclear strategy, and they had developed a theory of counterforce to control nuclear escalation during the 1950s. Their Air Force patrons had brushed aside their ideas, suspecting RAND of disloyalty for supporting the Polaris and thereby Burke's concept of finite deterrence, which undermined the basis of the nuclear triad of bombers, ICBMS, and SLBMS.[67] RAND slowly expanded its network of patrons to include the Advanced Research Projects Agency (ARPA), which reported to the OSD, and even the Kennedy presidential campaign. Not surprisingly, many analysts like Enthoven (who was already working at the Pentagon before 1961) seized on McNamara's assent to implement their ideas about nuclear strategy, whose abstract, quantitative nature apparently lent itself to broader questions of strategy and budgeting.[68]

Burke and Anderson refused to establish a Navy systems analysis team at the Pentagon. (The Navy's operational research teams were then located on staffs at the fleet-commander level.) Senior admirals made a concerted effort to humiliate the systems analysts soon after they had taken office. According to Secretary of the Navy Fred Korth, "Admiral Anderson's feeling with reference to the 'bright young men' . . . of the Secretary of Defense's office were these were people who had never fought a war; these were people who had never seen the battle line; never been to sea; never studied military strategy; and, therefore, their concepts, their ideas and their views were groundless and were without foundation and, therefore, should be immediately rejected, irrespective of how sound they might be."[69]

It took two years before the Navy began to adapt. The official story is that the driving force came from Korth, whom the Navy's leadership held in genial contempt.[70] He pushed for the creation of an Office of Program Appraisal (OPA) that would ensure that the Navy and Marines' programs were meeting McNamara's criteria.[71] The first director, Rear Adm. Draper Kauffman, held none of Burke and Anderson's prejudices. He moved to establish good relations with the systems analysts—Enthoven in particular—while ensuring that the OPA, which was located in the Secretariat (the Office of the Secretary of the Navy), did not step on anyone's toes in OPNAV. The latter had its own programming office, led by the OP-090 (director, Navy Program Planning), but it still lacked "direction authority"—the ability to enforce its decisions.[72] That shortcoming was finally rectified by Korth's successor, Paul Nitze, who established OP-96, the first systems analysis office within OPNAV in 1966 and installed his former aide, the then rear admiral Elmo Zumwalt, as its chief.[73]

Why did it take five years for the Navy to adjust to McNamara's management style? The Navy had simply learned the wrong lessons from the Revolt of the Admirals. Its leaders were confident they would get their way in the end. These divergent viewpoints among the old sailors and the young civilians would come to a head during the protracted fight over the TFX (Tactical Fighter Experimental).[74]

THE TFX/F-111 DEBACLE

McNamara was an apostle of jointness before the term existed, and there was indeed ample scope for the services to use the same equipment. The necessity for "commonality" is littered throughout documents of the period. Some of the military's resistance to this concept went beyond petty, as McNamara recounted:

> There were such absurd examples as different belt buckles among the services, different butcher smocks. There was an immensely strong resistance to accepting a common piece of equipment. I don't know whether to this day the Marine Corps and the army have ever agreed on a common belt buckle. It was a relatively minor matter and I didn't spend too much of my time working on a common belt buckle except to note in the back of my mind that it illustrated a frame of mind which we certainly didn't overcome fully while we were there.[75]

An airplane is not the same thing as a belt buckle, but it seems as if McNamara's frustrations about the latter may have clouded his judgment about the former.

The TFX (eventually known as the F-111 Aardvark) was supposed to be a joint airplane. In theory, it was cheaper to design and build a multiservice airplane than have each service make its own specialized aircraft. Theoretically, this would allow for cost savings through economies of scale and avoid duplicative R & D. Whether a properly executed joint airplane program would have provided additional national capabilities more efficiently than airplanes designed by individual services is debatable.[76] What is indisputable is that in the case of the TFX, the execution of the program was a disaster.

There had already been multimission, multiservice airplanes such as the F-4 Phantom and A-7 Corsair, and the TFX was also going to be a fighter-bomber.[77] LeMay had previously not supported joint airplanes but realized that this was the only way to convince McNamara to fund a new tactical air platform. He also convinced Anderson that it was possible to build a plane acceptable to both services.[78]

The problem was that LeMay wanted the Air Force to be in charge and McNamara's acquiescence to LeMay was a mistake—even his own people knew it. Enthoven, who served in the Pentagon throughout the Kennedy and Lyndon Johnson administrations, disclaimed any responsibility for the ensuing train wreck. The decision to build a joint fighter-bomber happened in September 1961, Enthoven observed, before McNamara was able to implement his vision for managing the Pentagon. As a result, systems analysis played no role in developing capabilities and requirements of the TFX. If it had, Enthoven suggested, the OSD would have pushed back more aggressively against the services' excessive and irreconcilable requirements. If McNamara was guilty of misjudgment, Enthoven believed it was for being *too* deferential to the military: "It is typical of the ironies of the defense business that McNamara was severely attacked later for overruling the Services, when, in fact, the troubles that were to beset the F-111 . . . stemmed not from McNamara's decisions but from the unjustifiably demanding performance requirements set by the Services for the aircraft."[79]

Investigative journalists such as I. F. Stone pointed out that many of Enthoven's excuses were nonsense and that even if the systems analysts were not involved in the decision to build the plane, they nonetheless rallied to its defense afterward. Enthoven, in particular, was publicly supporting the F-111 as late as 1967. Stone concluded that the only reasons systems analysis was not involved were political considerations and a fear of offending McNamara on an issue that was near and dear to his heart.[80]

So, if the Whiz Kids did not design the plane, then who did? The TFX was designed the old-fashioned way: at the direction of the service in charge, in this case the Air Force. The Air Force resented that McNamara had canceled its F-105 Thunderchief and had forced it to use the F-4 (a Navy plane).[81] It was therefore desperate to ensure the TFX would be an Air Force plane first and foremost.

McNamara—with Kennedy's explicit backing—had already provoked plenty of other fights with the Air Force, most notably by canceling its prized Mach 3 bomber, the B-70 Valkyrie, along with the Skybolt air-launched ballistic missile, so he likely gave in to the Air Force to avoid further grumbling.[82] The fight over the B-70 had been particularly rancorous. The men who became the Pentagon's first generation of systems analysts had long been critical of the United States' overreliance on manned bombers for "strategic" purposes (nuclear warfighting). These bombers flew from exposed bases, and far too many of them were on the ground at any given time, which meant they were vulnerable to a sneak attack, while the Soviets could shoot down the few that were airborne. The B-70 might have flown higher and faster than the B-52 it was supposed to replace, but it also had many of the same drawbacks of older bombers and cost too much considering the marginal gain in capabilities.[83] Consequently, after he became secretary of defense, McNamara tried to kill the program, preferring instead to channel resources to ICBMs, which could be dispersed, and to Polaris-armed submarines, which could avoid detection altogether.[84]

Eisenhower had a similarly low opinion of the B-70 and tried to cancel it in 1960 but ran out of time after the Air Force went public with its disagreement. Eisenhower could only fume at senior officers' loss of fiscal restraint and willingness to challenge the White House: "Everyone seems to think he has a compulsion to tell in public his personal views."[85] When Kennedy followed through with his predecessor's intent and canceled the B-70 in 1961, LeMay took his case to Congress in defiance of McNamara's attempts to have the OSD coordinate all interactions between the Pentagon and Congress. The Air Force was not shy about taking its case to Congress because, unlike the Army or even the Navy, it knew it would find a receptive audience for its complaints.[86]

Rep. Carl Vinson was particularly furious with the Kennedy administration's decision, as he believed it violated a gentleman's agreement with McNamara to keep bombers as the centerpiece of US nuclear strategy until 1970.[87] The HASC took the unusual step of drafting legislation directing the administration to continue spending the money appropriated for the B-70.[88] Kennedy only averted a minor constitutional crisis by smooth-talking Vinson into amending the legislative language from "direct" to "authorize." Years later, McNamara recollected that there had been "blood on the floor" after the B-70 fight.[89]

Consequently, McNamara ensured that LeMay kept his job as Air Force chief of staff when his first term ended in 1963 despite Kennedy's distaste for the general.[90] McNamara, although he knew it would infuriate the Navy, also gave the Air Force the lead role on the TFX. The implication was that it would make no difference which service was in charge since the same defense companies would be designing the TFX.

Actually, program-management responsibility is the sine qua non to all responsible development. The program manager decides which requirements have primacy. Previous joint airplanes such as the F-4 and A-7 were designed by one service and adapted by others, thereby avoiding the problem of design compromises and irreconcilable requirements. In the case of the TFX, each service had different conceptions of what the plane was supposed to be. The Air Force wanted a long-range bomber to perform "deep interdiction" (today known as "deep penetration," but both are euphemisms for strategic bombing), while the Navy wanted a fighter to provide air cover for its carriers. All the previous airplanes used by more than one service (most notably the F-4 and A-7) had been originally designed to Navy specifications. Those aircraft therefore began their careers constructed with more robust frames and materials to defend against the corrosive sea environment and to support the heavier landing gear necessary for carrier operations.[91] When these aircraft had subsequently been adapted for the Air Force, the modified (and considerably lighter) variant always consequently had a better thrust-to-weight ratio as well as the ability to be able to carry extra fuel and ordnance.

The drama in aircraft design is always in the engineering and the necessary trade-offs among speed, range, armor, and armament. For carrier-launched planes, there is limited time to provide sufficient energy to get them aloft and then a limited area on which to capture them while landing. Aircraft deploying from carriers also have to absorb the extraordinary longitudinal stresses inherent when a large body is accelerated to flight speeds. Catapult strokes (the working length of the catapult) ranged from 200 feet on USS *Coral Sea* to 250 feet on USS *Independence* to 300 feet on USS *Stennis*. Upon landing, the planes were yanked to a stop at comparable distances. For a fifty-thousand-pound-class aircraft like the TFX, the arresting gear "roll out" was typically 300 feet.[92] Since the Air Force had program authority for the TFX, this requirement was not foremost in the engineers' minds. Rather, the Air Force managers designed the TFX assuming more gentle stresses—such as those experienced when landing and taking off while using the long runways standard on Air Force bases. They also neglected the safety margin (extra thicknesses) Navy airframes require to combat corrosion in a seawater environment.[93]

Reducing weight is always *the* major problem for aircraft designers. It dogs every engineer from the day the first numbers go on the paper or into the computer until the day when the plane leaves service. If designers and engineers are not careful, an airplane will gain weight every single day while in development. For a multiservice plane, there is always a temptation to accept greater weight to give the plane more capabilities, with the intention of doing whatever was necessary later to lighten those planes assigned to the Navy. Those later changes are patches, not optimal designs, and patches are invariably heavier than an original design solution.

An aircraft designed to accept stresses from one direction (from being flung from a catapult or being stopped by a wire) does not easily redirect forces into another axis. Experience demonstrated that patched Navy aircraft were always too heavy. On a land runway, a few extra pounds may not always be a problem, as the plane can taxi a few more feet. Aboard a carrier, however, the deck abruptly ends, and each extra pound on an airplane requires generating additional lift to keep it aloft over the water, which also means it has to approach at higher speeds. Higher speeds require quicker pilot-reaction times, more pilot experience, less-challenging weather conditions, and all-around better equipment. Every additional knot of landing speed decreases safety, not simply by a linear multiple but also geometrically until some discontinuity is tripped, at which point the aircraft spirals from the carrier deck off into the water. Finally, a heavier plane would have a reduced flight time, which would in turn decrease the length of air coverage (sortie time) the plane could provide.

To make a long story short, it is much simpler to design a plane for the Navy and Marines and adapt it for Air Force than vice versa. The Air Force's specifications were for a plane that could launch tactical nuclear weapons to defend Europe. Accordingly, additional weight—exacerbated by newfangled swing-wing technology—was not a problem as long as it did not compromise speed, and the Air Force believed that guns were an unnecessary luxury. A heavier plane that relied solely on missiles—what the Air Force wanted—was inadequate in close air combat, as outspoken fighter pilots vainly argued.[94] The Navy was interested in maintaining air superiority around its carriers. As Navy pilots accumulated experience over North Vietnam against agile MiG fighters, they realized that a poor dogfighter like the F-111 would be chewed up by Soviet planes that got close to American ships or aircraft formations.[95]

When the bid for the TFX came up, it was worth about $6 billion (about $55 billion today when adjusted for inflation), and McNamara chose a joint effort by General Dynamics and Grumman over a rival bid by Boeing. In fact, both the Air Force and Navy preferred the Boeing bid, which was essentially two separate planes for each service using titanium for the body. McNamara rejected their preference because Boeing had no experience building fighters, much less ones using titanium rather than steel, unlike Grumman, which had already designed several Navy planes. Grumman was also a leader in the "swing wing" technology essential to the TFX concept. The secretary considered the General Dynamics and Grumman bid to be more realistic, in terms of cost and the development schedule, because its designs for both services' variants were largely identical.[96] This last point was arguably decisive. As one of McNamara's aides later put it, "the essential difference between the Boeing and the General Dynamics proposals was that General Dynamics bet that the Secretary of Defense meant what he said about producing a common Air

Force–Navy airplane, and Boeing bet that the services would persuade the Secretary to forget it. Boeing lost."[97]

The collective reaction of the military was fury. One writer for *Air Force Magazine* fumed that McNamara's decision was "a grab for power that would menace not only our security but our very pattern of government."[98] Anderson, meanwhile, insinuated that McNamara had overruled the Navy because General Dynamics was better connected within the Kennedy administration.[99] Even if there was no fire, there was plenty of smoke. Critics in Congress and the media raised questions about Korth's role in the TFX decision since he was from Fort Worth, Texas (where General Dynamics was based), and served on the board of a bank with large loans to General Dynamics (the company was nearly bankrupt in 1961).[100] Another senior official with questionable ties to General Dynamics was Deputy Secretary Gilpatric, whose law firm provided legal services to the company and who conveniently resigned in 1964.[101]

Whether there was political influence involved in the decision is impossible to say (it is not as though Boeing was a political lightweight), but as we pointed out earlier, the actual builder did not matter as much as the service in charge of the program. McNamara chose the Air Force to manage the program. Even if he selected it for the best of reasons, it was an error, and McNamara could still make terrible choices and found it difficult to admit his mistakes.

As the TFX progressed, just like every airplane ever designed, its weight increased and trade-offs arose. The Air Force was in charge of making those trade-offs, and its decisions collectively made the airplane too heavy (by about 13,500 pounds more than the original Navy specifications) to safely land aboard smaller carriers.[102] The General Dynamics designers accepted that the TFX was overweight. They tried to compensate with additional lift and claimed the plane would be a more efficient weapons-delivery system.[103]

The Navy would subsequently rigorously test its variant, including a week of sea trials Navy aboard USS *Coral Sea* in 1967. These tests revealed over one hundred serious problems, the Navy evaluators concluding the plane was "unfit" for naval service. Both the Air Force and Navy versions of the plane would, in fact, crash during testing. Even worse, despite McNamara's insistence that a joint plane would save money, the costs nonetheless spiraled upward. The naval variant of the TFX (F-111B) would ultimately cost over $9 million per unit, as opposed to the promised $2.8 million.[104] Overall, the program would deliver only five hundred of the promised seventeen hundred planes at a cost of $8 billion.[105]

Defenders of the TFX/F-111 would later claim that the plane performed "adequate" service for the Air Force and that the design work conducted for the Navy variant proved valuable for the development of the F-14 Tomcat (which, perhaps unsurprisingly, initially had some of the same shortcomings as the F-111).[106] Additionally, the lessons of the TFX debacle were a useful guide when developing the F-35.[107] (That plane suffered from a different set of defects as the OSD failed to preserve competition among potential contractors or curb the services' penchant for adding requirements.[108])

Were the modest benefits of the TFX experience worth the cost of alienating a service from its civilian leadership? A decade later, McNamara was still bitter. He conceded in 1975 that "certain programs of the department initiated while I was in charge, although well-conceived, were poorly implemented, poorly executed" but that others were "I would say even sabotaged. The TFX, the F-111, was an illustration of that."[109]

Secretary of the Air Force Zuckert backed up McNamara. While he had been skeptical of any effort to reconcile the Air Force and Navy's requirements in 1961, after two years of close observation he had come around to the TFX's merits. When questioned about the services' failures of the F-111, Zuckert disputed that that plane's track record was noticeably worse than other aircraft, poured cold water on the corruption allegations, and chalked up criticism of the plane to bad publicity.[110] To grasp the emotions the TFX raised, Zuckert later told an interviewer that "one of the wisest people I know in Washington once said, 'If the Navy had wanted the F-111 to work, it would have worked.'"[111]

Zuckert was an experienced public servant, but there was no factual basis to make such an accusation. Alas, there are no clear-cut heroes or villains in the TFX story—everybody believed they were acting on principle, using the best available evidence. Just as the Air Force lined up behind the plane and its chief of staff, the Navy, led by its CNO, was determined to make its voice heard. Anderson was an aviator with a son who was a test pilot, and he had lost two nephews in naval aviation accidents. He therefore was not going to compromise on a matter of safety.

While Anderson let it be known he would not support the TFX, at the same time he claimed that "McNamara put out the word that his decision was to be justified no matter who got hurt if they got in the way."[112] Anderson nevertheless proceeded to testify on April 5, 1963, before the Subcommittee on Investigations of the Senate Committee on Government Operations (the so-called McClellan hearings) about the TFX's inadequacies.[113] He also urged other officers to speak their minds (to the point where Korth felt that his own staff was not supporting him, for fear of offending Anderson). After the Navy resisted him on the airplane, McNamara retaliated by confirming his decision against using a nuclear power plant for the next carrier

(CVA-67—later christened USS *John F. Kennedy*). This prompted the resignation of Secretary Korth, who was already under pressure over the TFX.[114]

Years later, Anderson publicly maintained that his professional relationship with the OSD went swimmingly. This was his "Beltway professionalism" on display for outsiders, but it did not represent his true feelings toward McNamara, whom he privately described as having "two faults": McNamara "considered himself infallible, and his judgment was bad." Anderson also believed that McNamara "told Congress he was going to do one thing at the very time he was doing something exactly opposite."[115]

In the wake of the failure of the Vietnam War, it is easy to overlook the good that McNamara accomplished: implementing the PPBS, using greater quantification where appropriate, taking logistics seriously (the pre-McNamara services had little capacity to support sustained operations), championing major cost savings through measures such as competitive bidding and shedding superfluous infrastructure, and building simpler weapons to be used across the services. These changes produced savings of billions of dollars that were redirected within the Pentagon or channeled to social spending during the War on Poverty.[116] Unfortunately, McNamara also had a propensity to drift dangerously from his own area of expertise into the realm of military operations or even tactics.[117]

Senior military leaders did not respond constructively to his entreaties, dismissing them as meddling. Anderson had that attitude, and although Burke tried to engage with McNamara during the secretary's first year, the admiral's approach was viewed as condescending.[118] There was a constructive alternative that, unfortunately, few chose.

The commandant of the Marine Corps from 1960 to 1963, David Shoup, was infuriated by McNamara's questioning of how the Marines organized their mortar platoons. When the other chiefs refused to confront McNamara, Shoup went in alone and gave the secretary his unvarnished opinion. He was stunned by McNamara's responsiveness and eventually conceded that the secretary had good reason to ask such questions. (McNamara wanted to contrast the Marines' approach with that of the Army to find efficiencies.) Shoup was no lackey—he remained skeptical of the assumptions of "flexible response" and became a critic of the Vietnam War in retirement—but he had served as the Marines' fiscal director and had an eye for numbers, which meant he had the empathy to view the situation from McNamara's perspective.[119] Ultimately, Shoup attributed the chiefs' reticence with McNamara to a lack of "guts," but what he really meant was the absence of the mutual trust and respect that Ridgway had identified as necessary.[120] Unfortunately, Burke and Anderson never established the sort of relationship Shoup advised, with negative consequences for the Navy as a whole.

A decade after the TFX debacle, Anderson remarked,

> I gave it as forthrightly as I could; I pulled no punches although I think that what testimony I gave was constructive and has since been borne out by developments. Nevertheless this testimony infuriated certain people in the civilian side of the Department of Defense. Efforts were made . . . to discredit any of the witnesses who testified against the position taken by the Secretary of Defense. I had told and instructed my people that if they were called upon to testify on the subject of the TFX, they would testify as to facts under their own competence, tell the truth, avoid speculation, and that if they did this, I would back them one hundred per cent.[121]

As these sorts of remarks make clear, intense suspicion stemming from multiple causes hindered civilians and the military from trusting one another. The Navy was correct that the TFX was a poor design, but Anderson's insistence about the consistency of his objections is undermined by Korth's recollections. According to Korth, Anderson and senior naval officers told him privately that there was little difference between the Boeing and the Grumman–General Dynamics bids but testified otherwise before the McClellan committee. This was a serious discrepancy since, following Anderson's briefing of Korth, the three senior civilians—McNamara, Korth, and Zuckert—met to formalize their choice, which left Anderson no way to influence the decision until *after* the civilians had made it.[122] Whether or not Korth's accusations about Anderson's "personal disloyalty" are accurate, one thing is certain: Anderson's relationship with his civilian bosses was damaged beyond repair.[123]

On Easter in 1963, a week after Anderson had testified, Korth and Gilpatric came to the Naval Observatory (then the CNO's personal residence) to tell Anderson he would not be nominated for a second two-year term. He was instead offered the ambassadorship to Portugal, which Anderson accepted against the "furious" advice of Burke.[124]

This episode was essentially a second Revolt of the Admirals against civilian authority. This time, however, Anderson stayed in his lane. He made the issue not one of government policy or strategy but of warfighting—the Navy was convinced the TFX/F-111 would have been a terrible plane to fly from aircraft carriers. Nevertheless, the admiral was still fired. Does this mean that there is no place for principled military objections in areas where military leaders' expertise eclipses that of civilians? If that is the case, then there is little prospect of establishing fruitful civil-military cooperation between military and civilian authorities. Instead, we should expect only a never-ending struggle for power and suboptimal strategic outcomes.

In reality, Anderson had probably wrecked his relationship with McNamara long before the TFX fracas. As noted before, the admiral did not hide his contempt for the systems analysts in the Pentagon. When Lyman Lemnitzer was eased out as JCS chairman in September 1962, Anderson expected he would get the job because it was the Navy's turn. In a classic case of counting his chickens before they hatched, Anderson started interviewing officers to serve on his staff and must have felt humiliated when the chairmanship went to White House favorite Maxwell Taylor.[125] This probably explains Anderson's behavior during the Cuban Missile Crisis the following month, when the CNO refused to control his fury over civilian "micromanagement." According to Gilpatric, Anderson lashed out at McNamara's prodding regarding the conduct of the quarantine on Cuba: "This is none of your goddamn business . . . ! We've been doing this since the days of John Paul Jones, and if you'll just go back to your quarters, Mr. Secretary, we'll take care of this."[126]

McNamara swore to Gilpatric that this was the moment when Anderson lost his confidence, even if the admiral always insisted that it was the TFX fracas that had cost him his job.[127] Whatever the reasons for his dismissal, Anderson's public opposition ensured the Navy did not have to buy the TFX/F-111.

That said, the TFX incident was also proof that the Navy had not yet found a way short of direct confrontation to resolve differences with an administration. As with the Revolt of the Admirals, even if the Navy was ultimately proven right about the issue at stake, its conduct appeared disingenuous. In 1949 the Navy openly challenged civilian control of the military over an aircraft carrier designed to conduct "strategic bombing." With the TFX, the Navy justified its need for a new fighter—which eventually became the F-14—to defend its carriers against a Soviet nuclear-armed bomber threat that did not then exist and never would. According to their doctrine, the Soviets intended to fight the US Navy primarily with submarines and missile boats.[128]

Even if its requirements were unnecessary, buying or not buying the TFX as designed for the Navy was essentially an issue of safety of flight in the sea domain. The Navy owned the "sea domain"—that was its area of expertise. The Navy was therefore solely responsible for the issue of safety of flight from carriers at sea. So, it had two areas of expertise in which neither the Air Force nor the OSD had any equivalent knowledge. If the Navy had been more adroit about how it applied its technical expertise to the development of the TFX, could the issue with McNamara have been defused? We will never know because Anderson and his confederates railed about civilian meddling in defense affairs from the moment McNamara became secretary rather than seeking to draw hard lines around areas that were solely their responsibility.[129] Despite his selection as CNO and his subsequent service as an ambassador and chairman of the President's Foreign Intelligence Advisory Board, Anderson lacked a politicians' gift for negotiation and compromise.

The entire Navy, and not just Anderson, suffered as a result. The more problems arose with the TFX, the more determined McNamara seemed not to ask Congress for what the Navy most desired—additional carriers. In the big picture, therefore, the 1963 clash had the same results as the 1949 fight, even if this time only one admiral was fired. This was hardly progress.

TEACHING POLITICS TO THE NAVY

When Adm. David McDonald followed Anderson into office, the new CNO inherited a Navy underfunded relative to its commitments abroad.[130] President Johnson desired to deter communist expansion in Asia but did not want to raise taxes to pay for the war in Vietnam he had inherited. It might have worked if the conflict had been a short war—but it was not, with tragic consequences for the United States and Vietnam. In the former, the war created political and social divisions that persist to this very day, and the Johnson administration's mishandling of war finances accelerated the collapse of the Bretton Woods monetary system, potentially undermining US leadership of the world economy.[131]

Fighting wars always involves many unforeseen and extraordinary expenses. Absent proper funding from Congress, the military paid for Vietnam by scrimping and saving, denuding Europe of forces, and stripping the reserves.[132] These actions reduced inventories of spare parts, increased accidents, and reduced the effectiveness of allied forces. To make matters worse, the Pentagon's financial juggling during the war aroused the suspicion of Congress and probably exacerbated the cutting of the defense budget after 1968 (cuts between FY 1968 and FY 1979 averaged 5 to 9 percent).[133] All of these factors conspired to create the "hollow force" of the 1970s and early 1980s.[134]

While the Navy was arguably better off than the Army, to sustain naval operations the sea service devoted nearly every available dollar to keeping the machinery running and planes flying. As a result, there was little left over to take care of sailors.[135] Before Vietnam, even under the best of circumstances, the working and berthing conditions aboard ship belowdecks had been uncomfortable. After the war began, some ships let these areas slide even further. These deteriorating conditions exacerbated the racial tensions that were tearing apart the country and increasingly affecting the military.

There were other problems. At the conceptual level, the Navy had yet to sort out how its delivery of airpower was any different from what the Air Force was offering. The Navy was also still balking at the use of systems analysis at the service-headquarters level. In other words, the Navy leadership remained committed to "fighting city hall" rather than seeking accommodation when disputes arose with the OSD. This is where the new CNO made his most significant contributions.

McDonald's career had been much like Anderson's—they were both aviators.[136] McDonald did, however, have a much more accommodating approach and extraordinary political instincts. McDonald's ties on Capitol Hill were deep, and he used them to great effect. Very little of his political expertise made it into his official reminiscences, but as he confessed privately, "Dick Russell . . . [chairman of the Senate Armed Services Committee] and I were from the [same] small town in Georgia [Winder], probably about six thousand people total."[137] If that were not enough, "John Connally [briefly the secretary of the Navy and a close friend of President Johnson] is probably the best friend I ever had in the world. He and I were shipmates during the war [World War II]" aboard USS *Essex*.[138]

While McDonald did not have anything like the new vision for the Navy that Elmo Zumwalt would display, he understood, unlike all of his predecessors other than Forrest Sherman (with whom he shares some similarities), that the two previous revolts against civilian authority had been two too many.[139] McDonald knew exactly why he had the nice office on the fourth floor of the Pentagon's E-Ring looking out over the Potomac River: "I looked at my job as one of pouring oil on troubled waters. The Navy and the secretary of defense had gotten so far apart the Navy was not going to get anything. All communications had broken down. I know many people felt I was kowtowing, and they were right. I would have kissed McNamara's ass at high noon if I thought it would help to smooth things over, and there were many times I felt I had."[140]

To achieve this end, McDonald ruthlessly subordinated any personal misgivings to what he considered to be the interests of the Navy. He once remarked, "You know about the fellow who says, 'I'd rather be right than be President,' he was never President." McDonald accomplished his primary goal—he convinced McNamara of the Navy's loyalty, which got McDonald what he wanted: additional carriers to fulfill the Navy's core mission of command of the seas. Compared to that, in his mind, squabbling with Johnson or McNamara over Vietnam was a distraction.[141]

McNamara had overruled his military and many of his civilian leaders in 1963 by rejecting the use of nuclear power for CVA-67, which entered service in 1968.[142] He also sidestepped the Navy's ploy to defer construction of the carrier in the hope that it could reverse the secretary's decision.[143] Although the Navy had launched its first nuclear-powered carrier, USS *Enterprise* (CVN-65), in 1961, McNamara's staff determined that the greater costs of nuclear power outweighed the operational benefits that the Navy claimed. The OSD analysts concluded it was more efficient to apply the cost savings from conventional propulsion to purchasing more oil-powered ships.[144]

Instead of publicly arguing against McNamara's decision, as his predecessors did, McDonald gave the secretary of defense a "soft landing." While other admirals fumed over McNamara's decision for the carrier to be oil-fired, McDonald remained neutral. He maintained he was only interested in acquiring another carrier.[145] This gave him an advantage because the question of authorizing a carrier reoccurs about every four years in Washington as the Norfolk shipyard that builds these ships nears completion of the last one. McDonald therefore accepted the oil-fired solution at the beginning of his four-year tour because he knew there would be time to revisit the issue.

In late 1965, halfway through McDonald's tour, he prepared a budget for FY 1967 calling for the construction of three nuclear-powered carriers (the *Nimitz* class) over five years.[146] This proposal found a more receptive audience in the OSD. In the absence of overt pressure from the Navy, McNamara had devised a face-saving explanation for his volte-face—the new *Nimitz*-class carriers required only two reactors as opposed to eight for the *Enterprise* and the proposed four for CVA-67. McNamara could therefore plausibly claim in public that the delay in constructing a nuclear-powered carrier had allowed the Navy to perfect a two-reactor power plant, which obviated some of McNamara's previous complaints about costs.[147] In fact, the key intervention had come from President Johnson himself, who privately assured McDonald in December 1965 the Navy would get its nuclear-powered carrier despite the escalating cost of the war in Vietnam.[148]

McDonald was clearly unusual among naval officers when it came to his political sensibility. He understood Washington and how to work with the different personalities on the Hill. He had been groomed for high office while serving as an aide to Dan Kimball from 1949 to 1951. Kimball held a variety of jobs with the Navy Department under Truman, eventually rising to secretary in 1951, and McDonald's service with him overlapped with the Revolt of the Admirals.[149] Kimball had previously worked as a lobbyist, and he introduced McDonald to a number of congressmen.[150] Not surprisingly, when McDonald became CNO, he well remembered the lessons of his internship with Kimball:

> I was the first CNO to invite visiting CNOs [from abroad] to stay at my house rather than at a hotel. And a few weeks after relieving [Anderson], I noticed that a congressman had played football at Michigan, so I called him up and invited him to go with me to the Navy-Michigan football game. . . . Then Jerry Ford and I went out [to the game], and within a couple of months he and his wife were guests at my house. We always had some congressmen as guests at all our social occasions, when just a few friends sat around and talked.[151]

Armed with this exceptional political background, McDonald called for a cease-fire in the running fight between the Navy and McNamara so that he could focus on rebuilding the Navy's credibility. That entailed not undercutting McNamara every time the Navy did not get its way, as Anderson had done over the TFX. Accordingly, McDonald directed his aide, Capt. Isaac Kidd, to stop leaking information critical of McNamara to Congress.[152]

The new CNO had another priority for Kidd—to keep a close eye on the people McDonald considered the real threats to the Navy: the ambitious secretary of the Navy, Nitze, and his former naval aide, Zumwalt. While McDonald had relished running the Navy when he had been Kimball's aide, he did not appreciate other people undercutting him once he was the CNO. McDonald thought that Nitze and Zumwalt were undermining his authority.[153] McDonald neither forgave nor forgot. A decade after he retired, McDonald confessed, "I have never been happier with Barry Goldwater" than when the Arizona senator vetoed Nitze's appointment to the Nixon administration in 1975.[154]

The Navy had not welcomed Nitze's appointment back in 1963, viewing him (inaccurately) as a McNamara clone. Granted, Nitze was not the sort of man to be satisfied with a purely ceremonial role. As mentioned previously, he created the Navy's first systems analysis office (OP-96). He also supported the elimination of the Navy's venerable bureaus in 1966 and their replacement with various systems commands that reported directly to him and the CNO through the new Naval Material Command.[155] Nevertheless, Nitze immersed himself in the technical details of his job and won over some of his critics in the Navy.[156]

McDonald, however, remained skeptical. One area of contention between him and Nitze was over the role of OP-96. Both men wanted to use that office to enforce their policy preferences, but Nitze had the upper hand thanks to Zumwalt. After the latter's promotion to flag rank and a short sea tour out of San Diego, Zumwalt had returned to the Pentagon in 1966 to lead OP-96. This office was composed of more than just number crunchers ("green-eyeshade people" in Pentagonspeak).[157] Rather, OP-96 used analysis to tackle questions about the future of the Navy, such as the characteristics of the next class of destroyers (*Spruance*) and rather belatedly the TFX.[158]

During its short history (less than twenty years), Navy leaders identified OP-96 as a posting for their best officers.[159] Unfortunately, Ronald Reagan's secretary of the Navy, John Lehman, suspected OP-96 of opposing his plan to construct a "600-ship" Navy and forced CNO James Watkins to abolish it in 1983.[160] Lehman's actions merely confirmed the old Navy prejudice against systems analysis dating back to McNamara's tenure—that it was a tool for validating predetermined decisions rather than an impartial decision-making tool.

Despite his association with Nitze and McDonald's suspicion, Zumwalt received a third star in the Far East as the commander of Naval Forces Vietnam. He would impress Melvin Laird, the incoming secretary of defense for President Richard Nixon, by his understanding of the seriousness of the personnel issues the Navy faced.[161] When Nixon tapped CNO Thomas Moorer (McDonald's replacement) to become his chairman of the JCS in 1970, Laird recommended Zumwalt as the youngest CNO in history, even though McDonald, like the majority of his peers, opposed Zumwalt's selection.[162]

These men wrote Zumwalt off as a toady who had risen through the ranks only because of Nitze's patronage.[163] The two had met during Zumwalt's year at the Naval War College in 1961–62, when Nitze gave a guest lecture as assistant secretary of defense for international security affairs. After Zumwalt joined Nitze's staff, his family even lived on the Nitze estate.[164] McDonald's hostility arose from more than just envy or resentment. Outsiders might assume there is little difference among officers who achieve such rank—that they share a common mentality and career path—but that would be a serious misconception. The services can, in fact, produce quite different people at the very top—even some iconoclasts.

We can draw an illuminating contrast between McDonald and Zumwalt using their own words. Here is a quote from McDonald's reminiscences:

> I'm a white, Anglo-Saxon Protestant [WASP] male. I make no bones about that. I'm also a capitalist. I was born white. I was born an Anglo-Saxon. I was born a male. I selected to be a Protestant, and I like capitalism. If it's a question of Protestants or Catholics, it's going to be

> Protestant. If it be male or female, it's going to be male. If it's to be black or white, it's going to be white. No bones about it. . . . I think my record in the Navy shows that nobody ever treated minority groups nicer, but hell, that doesn't mean that I like them as well as I do my own people.[165]

McDonald's views were probably not so different from many of the other White Anglo-Saxon Protestant men who joined the Navy as officers. They made up the bulk of the incoming class at the US Naval Academy in Annapolis, Maryland, every year, and little they learned there contradicted their prior social beliefs.[166] Anyone who studies the writings of Alfred Thayer Mahan, for instance, will detect a hint of anti-Catholicism in his disparagement of the French, Spanish, and Portuguese, despite his Irish Catholic lineage on his paternal side.[167] Mahan was simply echoing the prejudices of the WASP elite, who were raised on a steady diet of the "Black Legend" of Spanish cruelty and barbarism.[168]

McDonald may have been a personal laggard on race, but the Georgian had certainly moved the Navy forward in how it worked with its civilian leaders. We take it for granted today that four-star officers are skilled political operators, but this was not always so. In his time, McDonald was extraordinary for understanding how to get things done in Washington. He was the first CNO since Sherman to secure a draw in the war of Air Force wings versus Navy carriers. Since World War II, the Navy had gone from ninety-nine carriers to fifteen on the eve of the Korean War. By the time McDonald replaced Anderson, it had increased to twenty-four, and he held that number almost steady at twenty-three until he left office in 1967.[169]

So how are we to judge McDonald's leadership of the Navy? It turns out he left an ambiguous legacy. The Navy got the *Nimitz* class, the backbone of the Navy's carrier fleet well into the twenty-first century. McNamara also ensured that the Navy retained control of Pacific Command. The political price was steep—as McDonald admitted, "I always felt indebted to McNamara, on Vietnam and other issues."[170] Years later in retirement, McDonald lamented that he had not resigned when the Johnson administration failed to call up the reserves or ask for sufficient funds during the Vietnam War.[171] He was unlikely to have taken such extreme measures while on active duty. It should be clear by now that stirring the pot simply was not McDonald's style, especially if such actions compromised his wider priorities. McDonald got what he wanted, but every year the Vietnam War continued without proper appropriations to pay for it, the conditions aboard ships worsened. Despite his success at making peace with McNamara and stabilizing the number of carriers, when McDonald retired the Navy was in serious trouble.

SUMMARY

Robert McNamara demonstrated that managerial competence did not also guarantee a mastery of the full breadth of military affairs. His strategic acumen was sometimes questionable (as demonstrated during the Vietnam War), as was his grasp of technical matters such as airplane design (as proven by the TFX fiasco). It is a matter of record that McNamara's efforts to induce revolutionary changes into the military, however well-intentioned, inspired intransigence and civil-military competition rather than cooperation.

The Navy's hostility to McNamara appeared on the surface to be nothing more than resistance to systems analysis—but appearances are deceiving. In fact, Navy leaders questioned whether McNamara was using analysis as an impartial decision-making tool. It seemed to them rather more of a fig leaf for the accumulation of power in the OSD. Admirals Burke, Anderson, and Russell simply did not trust McNamara—a judgment confirmed by the secretary's poor handling of the TFX. Whether or not he agreed with his predecessors, upon becoming CNO McDonald decided this attitude was shortsighted. He had the skills and contacts to reach an accommodation and left office having achieved his primary aims. There are, however, always trade-offs in politics. To return to McNamara's "good graces," the Navy had squelched its concerns about how the Vietnam War was impairing the long-term readiness of the Navy. Another CNO would have to pick up McDonald's tab.

NOTES

1. The most famous critique came from Maxwell Taylor, *The Uncertain Trumpet* (New York: Harper, 1960).
2. Alain Enthoven, *How Much Is Enough? Shaping the Defense Program, 1961–1969* (Santa Monica, CA: RAND Corp., 2005), 1–30; William Kaufman, *The McNamara Strategy* (New York: Harper, 1964); Paul Hammond, "A Functional Analysis of Defense Department Decision-Making in the McNamara Administration," *American Political Science Review* 62, no. 1 (1968): 57–69.
3. The following discussion draws from Thomas Hone and Curtis Utz, *History of the Office of the Chief of Naval Operations, 1915–2015* (Washington, DC: NHHC, 2015), 222–41.
4. For further details, see E. B. Potter, *Admiral Arleigh Burke* (New York: Random House, 1990); David Alan Rosenberg, "Arleigh Burke: The Last CNO," NHHC, September 2, 2020, https://www.history.navy.mil/research/library/online-reading-room/title-list-alphabetically/a/arleigh-burke-the-last-cno.html.
5. William Burr, "'How Much Is Enough?': The U.S. Navy and 'Finite Deterrence,'" National Security Archive (NSA), Electronic Briefing Book 779, October 14, 2021, https://nsarchive.gwu.edu/briefing-book/nuclear-vault/2021-10-14/how-much-enough-us-navy-and-finite-deterrence.

6. Hone, *OPNAV*, 202–5.
7. Harvey Sapolsky, "Interservice Competition: The Solution, Not the Problem," *Joint Force Quarterly* 15 (Spring 1997): 50–53.
8. Owen Cote, "The Politics of Innovative Military Doctrine: The U.S. Navy and Fleet Ballistic Missiles" (PhD diss., Massachusetts Institute of Technology, 1996), 24–28, 36–37, 339–54, 377–84, 391–95. For the argument that interservice *cooperation* can promote innovation under specific conditions, see Phil Haun, "Peacetime Military Innovation through Inter-Service Cooperation: The Unique Case of the U.S. Air Force and Battlefield Air Interdiction," *Journal of Strategic Studies* 43, no. 5 (2020): 710–36.
9. Imperial Japan is a case study for truly destructive interservice competition. For example, Japan's navy did not let the army, much less civilian politicians, know that it planned to strike Pearl Harbor in December 1941. See S. C. M. Paine, *The Wars in Asia: 1911–1949* (Cambridge: Cambridge University Press, 2012), 45–46, 147, 184; and Michael Barnhart, "Domestic Politics, Interservice Impasse, and Japan's Decisions for War," in *History and Neorealism*, ed. Ernest R. May, Richard N. Rosecrance, and Zara S. Steiner (Cambridge: Cambridge University Press, 2010), 185–200.
10. Stephen Rosen, "Service Redundancy: Waste or Hidden Capability," *Joint Force Quarterly* 1 (Summer 1993): 36–39.
11. Hone, *OPNAV*, 202.
12. Barry Posen, *The Sources of Military Doctrine: France, Britain, and Germany between the World Wars* (Ithaca, NY: Cornell University Press, 1984), 46, 54, 227. See also Arnold Kanter, *Defense Politics: A Budgetary Perspective* (Chicago: University of Chicago Press, 1979), 24ff.
13. Appendix B, Russell interview.
14. "Adm. Arthur Radford, 77, Ex-Joint Chief Head, Dies," *New York Times*, August 18, 1973. Burke complained that, as chairman, Radford "did not want to be a naval officer and stay with the Navy, so he was very careful always, if there was any doubt, the Navy lost." Arleigh Burke oral history, Columbia University Center for Oral History.
15. Douglas Kinnard, "Eisenhower and the Defense Budget," *Journal of Politics* 39, no. 3 (1977): 596–623.
16. For the genesis of the New Look, see Michael Hogan, *Cross of Iron: Harry S. Truman and the Origins of the National Security State, 1945–1954* (Cambridge: Cambridge University Press, 2000), 366ff.; William McClenahan and William Becker, *Eisenhower and the Cold War Economy* (Baltimore: Johns Hopkins University Press, 2011), 24ff.; and Gerald Clarfield, *Security with Solvency: Dwight Eisenhower and the Shaping of the American Military Establishment* (Westport, CT: Praeger, 1999), 121ff.
17. Burke oral history, Columbia.
18. Burke feared (correctly as it turned out) that Strategic Air Command would effectively seize control of the Navy's Polaris missile through the Joint Strategic Target Planning Staff. "They're Smart and Ruthless [...]," document 17 in Burr, "'How Much Is Enough?'" See also appendix B, Russell interview; and Rosenberg, "Burke."
19. Burke oral history, Columbia.
20. Lawrence Korb, "The Secretary of Defense and the Joint Chiefs of Staff: Conflict in the Budgetary Process, 1947–1971," *Naval War College Review* 24, no. 10 (1971): 21–38 (quotation from p. 27).
21. Eugene Zuckert oral history, Lyndon Baines Johnson Library (LBJL).
22. Alain Enthoven oral history, LBJL. Today Enthoven's position is held by the director of the Office of Cost Assessment and Program Evaluation (CAPE).

23. Burke oral history, Columbia.
24. Alan Donald Carter, "Eisenhower versus the Generals," *Journal of Military History* 71, no. 4 (2007): 1169–99; Kanter, *Defense Politics*, 62ff.
25. Douglas Stuart, *Creating the National Security State: A History of the Law That Transformed America* (Princeton, NJ: Princeton University Press, 2012), 180ff.
26. Appendix B, Russell interview. See also Matthew Moten, *Presidents and Their Generals: An American History of Command in War* (Cambridge, MA: Harvard University Press, 2014), 273–76.
27. George Watson and Herman Wolk, "'Whiz Kid': Robert S. McNamara's World War II Service," *Air Power History* 50, no. 4 (2003): 4–15.
28. Besides John Byrne, *The Whiz Kids: The Founding Fathers of American Business—and the Legacy They Left Us* (New York: Doubleday, 1993), and David Halberstam, *The Reckoning* (New York: William Morrow, 1986), 204–23, 236–60, see Thomas Bonsall, *Disaster in Dearborn: The Story of the Edsel* (Stanford, CA: Stanford University Press, 2002), 55ff., 71ff., 135ff., passim; Phil Rosenzweig, "Robert S. McNamara and the Evolution of Modern Management," *Harvard Business Review*, December 2010, https://hbr.org/2010/12/robert-s-mcnamara-and-the-evolution-of-modern-management; Angus MacKenzie, "Robert McNamara: Before Vietnam, There Was Ford," *Motor Trend*, July 7, 2009, https://www.motortrend.com/news/robert-mcnamara-before-vietnam-there-was-ford-2366/; Richard Johnson, "The Bean Counter Who Could Have Changed Auto History," *Automotive News*, June 6, 2016, https://www.autonews.com/article/20160606/OEM02/160609934/the-bean-counter-who-could-have-changed-auto-history; Phil Patton, "McNamara: The Father of the Ford Falcon," *New York Times*, July 7, 2009; Jim Donnelly, "Robert S. McNamara," *Hemmings Classic Car*, October 2009, https://www.hemmings.com/stories/article/robert-s-mcnamara; Ronald Ahrens, "The Whiz Kids," *DBusiness*, February 4, 2014, https://www.dbusiness.com/from-the-magazine/the-whiz-kids/; and Tristan Gaston-Breton, "How Robert McNamara and the Whiz Kids Invented Big Data," *Worldcrunch*, September 13, 2016, https://worldcrunch.com/business-finance/how-robert-mcnamara-and-the-whiz-kids-invented-big-data.
29. Adam Yarmolinsky oral history no. 1, John F. Kennedy Library (JFKL).
30. Robert McNamara, *In Retrospect: The Tragedy and Lessons of Vietnam* (New York: Vintage, 1996), 3ff.; McNamara oral history, JFKL.
31. We lack a complete biography of McNamara using declassified sources from the Pentagon and World Bank. One must tie together the various strands of McNamara's life by reading a variety of sources, including Deborah Shapley, *Promise and Power: The Life and Times of Robert McNamara* (Boston: Little, Brown, 1993); Lawrence Kaplan, Ronald Landa, and Edward Drea, *The McNamara Ascendancy, 1961–1965* (Washington, DC: OSD Historical Office, 2006); Edward Drea, *McNamara, Clifford, and the Burdens of Vietnam, 1965–1969* (Washington, DC: OSD Historical Office, 2011); Aurélie Basha i Novosejt, *I Made Mistakes: Robert McNamara's Vietnam War Policy, 1960–1968* (Cambridge: Cambridge University Press, 2019); and Patrick Sharma, *Robert McNamara's Other War: The World Bank and International Development* (Philadelphia: University of Pennsylvania Press, 2017). Errol Morris's documentary *The Fog of War: Eleven Lessons from the Life of Robert S. McNamara* (2003) is invaluable because of its revealing interviews with McNamara, who was famously reluctant to discuss his personal life or thoughts with outsiders.
32. Normal Paul oral history, LBJL.
33. Burke oral history, Columbia.

34. Kaplan, Landa, and Drea, *McNamara Ascendancy*, 293ff.; Walter Poole, *The Joint Chiefs of Staff and National Policy*, vol. 8, *1961–1964* (Washington, DC: Office of Joint History, 2011), 1–15; Lawrence Freedman, *Kennedy's Wars: Berlin, Cuba, Laos, and Vietnam* (Oxford: Oxford University Press, 2000), 18ff.
35. Cote, "Politics," 357–59, 364–68.
36. Enthoven oral history, LBJL.
37. McNamara called this the Five Year Defense Plan, but today it is known as the Future Years Defense Plan (FYDP). The future cost projections quickly turned out to be nothing more than educated guesses. Kanter, *Defense Politics*, 72–74.
38. Although hope, as ever, springs eternal. See William Greenwalt and Dan Pratt, *Competing in Time: Ensuring Capability Advantage and Mission Success through Adaptable Resource Allocation* (Washington, DC: Hudson Institute, 2021), https://www.hudson.org/research/16717-competing-in-time-ensuring-capability-advantage-and-mission-success-through-adaptable-resource-allocation.
39. Enthoven oral history, LBJL.
40. "The economic theory we are using is the theory most of us learned as sophomores. The reason Ph.D.'s are required is that many economists do not believe what they have learned until they have gone through graduate school." Alain Enthoven, "Economic Analysis in the Department of Defense," *American Economic Review* 53, no. 2 (1963): 413–23 (quotation from p. 422).
41. Enthoven oral history, LBJL.
42. Enthoven, *How Much*, 207–10; Hone, *OPNAV*, 246–48, 266–68.
43. Enthoven oral history, JFKL.
44. Enthoven oral history, LBJL.
45. The classic description of systems analysis and defense is Enthoven, *How Much*, 31–116.
46. Enthoven oral history, JFKL.
47. Gregory Palmer, *The McNamara Strategy and the Vietnam War: Program Budgeting in the Pentagon, 1960–1968* (Westport, CT: Greenwood, 1978), 5. See also Stephanie Young, "Power and the Purse: Defense Budgeting and American Politics, 1947–1972" (PhD diss., University of California, Berkeley, 2009); and Albert Beveridge, "Private Business to Public Service: Robert McNamara's Management Techniques and Their Limits in Peace and War" (PhD diss., Johns Hopkins University, 2014).
48. Clausewitz, *On War* (Princeton, NJ: Princeton University Press, 1976), 100ff. (quotations from pp. 119, 76).
49. Stephen Rosen, "Systems Analysis and the Quest for Rational Defense," *Public Interest* 76, no. 3 (1984): 4–7.
50. M. Fortun and S. S. Schweber, "Scientists and the Legacy of World War II: The Case of Operations Research (OR)," *Social Studies of Science* 23 (1993): 600ff.
51. Ellis Johnson and David Katcher, *Mines against Japan* (Silver Spring, MD: Naval Ordnance Laboratory, 1973).
52. The OEG is the direct antecedent to the Center for Naval Analyses (CNA), established in 1962, which is the Navy's primary source of analysis. Don Boroughs, *The Story of CNA: Civilian Scientists in War and Peace* (Arlington, VA: CNA, 2017).
53. Wayne Hughes, "Navy Operations Research," *Operations Research* 50, no. 1 (2002): 103–4 and passim.
54. Palmer, *McNamara Strategy*, 6.
55. Arleigh Burke oral history, JFKL.

56. McNamara oral history, JFKL.
57. Appendix A, Burke interview. See also Anderson's public statements in his September 1963 speech before the National Press Club, summarized in James Michael Roherty, *Decisions of Robert McNamara: A Study in the Role of the Secretary of Defense* (Coral Gables, FL: University of Miami Press, 1970), 97, 119.
58. Taught at the US Naval War College since before World War I, based on a concept borrowed from the Army. Austin Knight, "The Estimate of the Situation," *Professional Memoirs, Corps of Engineers, United States Army, and Engineer Department at Large* 7, no. 35 (1915): 629–43; US Naval War College, College of Naval Command and Staff, Joint Military Operations Department, *Syllabus and Study Guide for the Joint Maritime Operations Course: Intermediate Level Warfighter's Course*, February 2020.
59. Appendix C, Anderson interview.
60. McNamara oral history, JFKL; Korb, "Secretary of Defense," 27ff. For an alternative perspective that considers the Eisenhower approach as ideal, see Cote, "Politics," 354–57, 368–71, 393–94.
61. Paul Young Hammond, *Organizing for Defense: The American Military Establishment in the Twentieth Century* (Princeton, NJ: Princeton University Press, 1961), 18. See also James Hewes, *From Root to McNamara: Army Organization and Administration* (Washington, DC: Center of Military History, 1975), 296ff.
62. Enthoven oral history, LBJL. See also Enthoven oral history, JFKL: "I am not at all suggesting that there is some alternative to the political process that can make defense decisions without their foundations in value judgments that are politically based. . . . [The] Secretary of Defense, with help from his staff . . . sorts out what alternative objectives we might go after, and tries to define clearly and explicitly what are the things we are trying to do; and then, given those objectives, can . . . with the aid of a good deal of analysis and logic, reasonably derive a set of programs that support those objectives."
63. Enthoven oral history, JFKL.
64. Burke and George Anderson oral histories, JFKL.
65. Appendix A, Burke interview.
66. Established in 1945 as a part of the Douglas Aircraft Company, Project RAND was supposed to create a closer relationship between the Air Corps and scientific researchers. RAND became independent from Douglas in 1948 and, although it was a private nonprofit firm, reported to the Air Force. "Brief History of RAND," RAND, n.d., https://www.rand.org/about/history/a brief history of rand.html. For more on the early history of RAND, see Fred Kaplan, *The Wizards of Armageddon* (New York: Simon & Schuster, 1983). The only full-length history is the highly critical Alex Abella, *The Soldiers of Reason: The RAND Corporation and the Rise of the American Empire* (Orlando, FL: Harcourt, 2008). For a summary, see "The Rand Corporation: The Think Tank That Controls America," Mental Floss, June 30, 2009, https://www.mentalfloss.com/article/22120/rand-corporation-think-tank-controls-america.
67. E. P. Oliver, "Polaris Weapon System," October 28, 1958, document 6 in Burr, "'How Much Is Enough?'"
68. Alain Enthoven, "How Systems Analysis, Cost-Effectiveness Analysis, or Benefit-Cost Analysis First Became Influential in Federal Government Program Decision-Making," *Journal of Benefit-Cost Analysis* 10, no. 2 (2019): 146–55; Andrew David May, "The RAND Corporation and the Dynamics of American Strategic Thought, 1946–1962" (PhD diss., Emory University, 1998), 350ff.

69. Fred Korth oral history, JFKL.
70. According to Anderson, Korth "a) he didn't have the strength of character, and, b) he didn't have the intellectual capability of coping with Secretary McNamara. Furthermore, I always had the distinct impression, backed up by knowledge on certain events, that Korth would say one thing to the Secretary of Defense and another thing to the Chief of Naval Operations or to other people in the Navy." Anderson oral history, JFKL.
71. SECNAVINST 5430.60B, "Office of Program Appraisal; responsibilities of," August 1, 1975.
72. Hone, *OPNAV*, 248–54.
73. An invaluable source on the often confusing setup of OPNAV is Peter Swartz and Michael Markowitz, *Organizing OPNAV (1970–2009)* (Arlington, VA: CNA, 2010), https://www.cna.org/cna_files/pdf/D0020997.A5.pdf. For the creation of OP-96, see pp. 15ff.
74. For a contemporaneous overview (albeit heavily slanted in the services' favor), see US Senate, Committee on Government Operations, Permanent Subcommittee on Investigations, *TFX Contract Investigation*, S. Rep. No. 91-1496, 91st Cong., 2d Sess. (1970). The Senate hearings and report were also summarized in I. F. Stone, "In the Bowels of Behemoth," *New York Review of Books*, March 11, 1971. The key scholarly works on the TFX/F-111 controversy are Robert Art, *The TFX Decision: McNamara and the Military* (Boston: Little, Brown, 1968); and Robert Coulam, *Illusions of Choice: The F-111 and the Problem of Weapons Acquisition Reform* (Princeton, NJ: Princeton University Press, 1973). The Art and Coulam books are the primary sources for the official histories: Kaplan, Landa, and Drea, *McNamara Ascendancy*, 466–73; Drea, *Burdens*, 517–20; and Walter Poole, *Adapting to Flexible Response* (Washington, DC: OSD Historical Office, 2013), 215–48.
75. Robert McNamara oral history I, LBJL.
76. Mark A. Lorell, Michael Kennedy, Robert S. Leonard, Kenneth Munson, Shmuel Abramzon, David L. An, and Robert A. Guffey, *Do Joint Fighter Programs Save Money?* (Santa Monica, CA: RAND Corp., 2013).
77. US Senate, *TFX Contract Investigation: Hearings before the Permanent Subcommittee on Investigations of the Committee on Government Operations, Part* 3, 88th Cong., 1st Sess. (Washington, DC: GPO, 1963), 776–77.
78. Curtis LeMay oral history, LBJL.
79. Enthoven, *How Much*, 262–65; Enthoven oral history, JFKL. See also Adam Yarmolinsky, *The Military Establishment: Its Impacts on American Society* (New York: Harper, 1973), 217–18, 271–72.
80. Stone, "Behemoth" and "Nixon and the Arms Race: The Bomber Boondoggle," *New York Review of Books*, January 2, 1969.
81. Individual Air Force pilots, however, praised the decision. Enthoven oral history, JFKL.
82. I. F. Stone, "The War Machine under Nixon," *New York Review of Books*, June 5, 1969.
83. The B-70 still took too long to reach its target compared to missiles and was just as vulnerable on the ground as older bombers. Luther Carter, "The McNamara Legacy: A Revealing Case History—Death of the B-70," *Science* 159, no. 3817 (February 1968): 859–63; Enthoven, *How Much*, 243–51. Meanwhile, the B-52, albeit with significant upgrades, is still in service six decades later.
84. "Text of McNamara Statement on the B-70 Bomber," *New York Times*, March 16, 1962. See also Enthoven oral history, JFKL.

85. Stephen Ambrose, *Eisenhower: Soldier and President* (New York: Simon & Schuster, 1990), 501–2.
86. Kanter, *Defense Politics*, 37–44.
87. Zachary Matusheski, "Bomber Wars: Curtis LeMay, Robert McNamara and the B-70," *Air Power History* 58, no. 4 (2011): 14–23.
88. Jack Raymond, "House United 'Directs' Production of B-70's," *New York Times*, March 2, 1962.
89. Gordon Sander, "JFK's Forgotten Constitutional Crisis," *Politico*, May 29, 2017, https://www.politico.com/magazine/story/2017/05/29/jfk-xb-70-lemay-constitutional-crisis-215203.
90. H. R. McMaster, *Dereliction of Duty: Lyndon Johnson, Robert McNamara, the Joint Chiefs of Staff, and the Lies That Led to Vietnam* (New York: Harper, 1997), 30–31. See also appendix B, Russell interview.
91. The Air Force "flares" its airplanes, which is defined by the Federal Aviation Administration's *Airplane Flying Handbook* as "a slow smooth transition from a normal approach attitude to a landing attitude, gradually rounding out the flightpath to one that is parallel with and within a very few inches of, the runway." In contrast, because of all the variables involved in a moving flight deck, carrier pilots set a descent rate through touchdown of five hundred feet per minute.
92. The technical data in the preceding paragraphs comes from Vice Adm. Joseph Dyer, USN (Ret.), former commander of Naval Air Command, who provided the information from his personal files.
93. Many years later, when Secretary of Defense William Perry was going to build the next joint airplane, the Joint Strike Fighter (which became the F-35), the Navy was assigned initial program management because of the TFX experience. To keep everyone aboard, management was subsequently rotated between the Navy and the Air Force every two years, with the OSD exercising oversight. James Fallows, "Uncle Sam Buys an Airplane," *Atlantic Monthly*, June 2002, https://www.theatlantic.com/magazine/archive/2002/06/uncle-sam-buys-an-airplane/302509/.
94. Robert Coram, *Boyd: The Fighter Pilot Who Changed the Art of War* (Boston: Little, Brown, 2002), 154–57, 165, 176.
95. Robert Bernier, "Was the Navy's F-111 Really That Bad?," *Air & Space Magazine*, September 2018, https://www.airspacemag.com/military-aviation/13_sep2018-cancelled f111b 1 180969916/.
96. "The TFX Unveiled; McNamara Hails It," *New York Times*, October 16, 1964; Cecil Holland, "Super-Jet Disclosure Intensifies TFX Feud," *Washington Star*, March 1, 1964; *Appendix A: TFX Contract Investigation*, December 1964, CIA Freedom of Information Act Electronic Reading Room, https://www.cia.gov/library/readingroom/docs/CIA-RDP66B00403R000100300005-1.pdf.
97. Yarmolinsky, *Establishment*, 22.
98. Claude Witze, "Is the Stage Being Set for a Political Power Grab in the Pentagon?," *Air Force Magazine*, May 1, 1963, https://www.airforcemag.com/article/0563power/.
99. Paul Nitze oral history no. 3, LBJL; Anderson oral history, JFKL.
100. Tom Wicker, "Korth Quits Post as Head of Navy; Nitze Appointed," *New York Times*, October 15, 1963.
101. I. F. Stone, "Gilpatric and General Dynamics: Some Unanswered Questions," *New York Review of Books*, January 2, 1969; I. F. Stone, "Behemoth," *New York Times*, January 2, 1969.

102. US Senate, *TFX Contract Investigation* (1963), part III, 779.
103. *Congressional Record* 114, no. 6 (March 25, 1968): 7583–84.
104. Peter Davies, *General Dynamics F-111 Aardvark* (London: Osprey, 2014), 37; George Wilson, "Pentagon on the Grill... McNamara, Services Challenged," *Washington Post*, August 7, 1967; George Wilson, "Pentagon, Senate Clash over Releasing TFX Testimony," *Washington Post*, August 10, 1967; Stone, "Nixon and the Arms Race."
105. US Senate, *TFX Contract Investigation* (1970), 92.
106. Nitze oral history no. 3, LBJL; Coram, *Boyd*, 228–31; James Stevenson, *The Pentagon Paradox: The Development of the F-18 Hornet* (Annapolis, MD: Naval Institute Press, 1993), 51–61.
107. Christopher Preble, "Joint Strike Fighter: Can a Multiservice Fighter Program Succeed?," Policy Analysis No. 460, Cato Institute, December 5, 2002, https://www.cato.org/publications/policy-analysis/joint-strike-fighter-can-multiservice-fighter-program-succeed.
108. This is the key finding of Lorell et al., *Money*.
109. McNamara oral history, LBJL.
110. Zuckert oral history, LBJL.
111. Bruce Callander, "Zuckert Remembers," *Air Force Magazine*, June 1, 1998, https://www.airforcemag.com/article/0698zuckert/. See also George Watson, "Man in the Middle: Eugene Zuckert as Secretary of the Air Force," *Air Power History* 36, no. 2 (1989): 20–29.
112. Appendix C, Anderson interview.
113. US Senate, *TFX Contract Investigation* (1963), part III, 772–805.
114. Korth oral history, JFKL.
115. Appendix C, Anderson interview.
116. Enthoven oral history, LBJL.
117. Henry Eccles, "The TFX/F-111 Aircraft: A Perspective in Military Command and Defense Management," *Naval War College Review* 24, no. 9 (1971): 66–87; John Charles Sweeney, "The TFX Program: An Analysis of the McNamara Management and Decision-Making Technique in Major Weapon System Procurement" (MA thesis, College of William and Mary, 1972).
118. Burke oral history, JFKL.
119. McMaster, *Dereliction*, 42–44.
120. Shoup oral history, JFKL.
121. Anderson oral history, JFKL.
122. US Senate, *TFX Contract Investigation* (1963), part III, 793.
123. Korth oral history, JFKL.
124. Appendix B, Russell interview.
125. McMaster, *Dereliction*, 22.
126. Poole, *Chiefs*, 176–77; Brian Vandemark, *Road to Disaster: A New History of America's Descent into Vietnam* (New York: HarperCollins, 2018), 92–94.
127. Anderson oral history, JFKL.
128. Stone, "Nixon and the Arms Race"; Stone, "Behemoth."
129. John Finney, "Anderson Warns of Pentagon Rift; Ex-Navy Chief Says Mutual Civilian-Military Distrust May Imperil Security," *New York Times*, September 5, 1963.
130. David Lamar McDonald, *The Reminiscences of Admiral David Lamar McDonald, U.S. Navy (Retired)* (Annapolis, MD: US Naval Institute, 1976), 382–88.
131. Robert Collins, *More: The Politics of Economic Growth in Postwar America* (Oxford: Oxford University Press, 2000), 68ff.; Hugh Rockoff, *America's Economic Way of War:*

War and the US Economy from the Spanish-American War to the Persian Gulf War (Cambridge: Cambridge University Press, 2012), 276–304; Rosella Cappella Zielinski, *How States Pay for War* (Ithaca, NY: Cornell University Press, 2016), 47–65; Sara Kreps, *Taxing Wars: The American Way of War Finance and the Decline of Democracy* (Oxford: Oxford University Press, 2018), 121–38.

132. Drea, *Burdens*, 130–31, 141, 167, 525ff.
133. Larry Spencer, *The Green Eyeshades of War: An Examination of Financial Management during War* (Maxwell AFB, AL: Air University Press, 2016), 9–24.
134. A description popularized by a former chief of staff of the Army, Gen. Edward Meyer. Andrew Feickert and Stephen Daggett, *A Historical Perspective on "Hollow Forces"* (Washington, DC: Congressional Research Service, 2012).
135. Daniel Cuda, "The Hollow Force That Was," *Air Force Magazine*, April 1, 1994, https://www.airforcemag.com/article/0494hollow/.
136. McDonald, *Reminiscences*, 349–50.
137. Appendix D, McDonald interview. Sen. Richard Russell of Georgia was chairman of the Senate Armed Services Committee from 1951 to 1953 and 1955 to 1969 and a mentor to Lyndon Johnson. Robert Caro, *The Years of Lyndon Johnson: Master of the Senate* (New York: Knopf, 2002), 164ff.
138. Appendix D, McDonald interview. Connally was Lyndon Johnson's factotum and a popular governor of Texas. A lifelong Democrat, he shocked the political world by joining Nixon's cabinet as treasury secretary, where he oversaw the dismantling of the Bretton Woods system, and then joined the Republican Party. A man both Johnson and Nixon considered a possible successor, Connally deserves a thorough biography, but none is imminent because his papers at the LBJL are still unprocessed. See instead John Connally and Mickey Herskowtiz, *In History's Shadow: An American* Odyssey (New York: Hyperion, 1993); and James Reston, *The Lone Star: The Life of John Connally* (New York: Harper, 1989).
139. Sherman was perhaps the Navy's key strategic planner at the end of World War II and a skillful diplomat with the other services. Unfortunately, he has been overlooked by historians—an oversight that will be difficult to correct, considering Sherman's secretive nature and the dearth of personal papers. For hints, see Hone, *OPNAV*, 205–6; David Rosenberg and Floyd Kennedy, *U.S. Aircraft Carriers in the Strategic Role* (Falls Church, VA: Lulejian & Associates, 1975), 165ff.; and Michael Palmer, *Origins of Maritime Strategy: The Development of American Naval Strategy, 1945–1955* (Annapolis, MD: Naval Institute Press, 1990).
140. Appendix D, McDonald interview. To facilitate quick access between the various rooms in the world's largest office building, the Pentagon is arranged in five concentric rings labeled—from the inside out—the A, B, C, D, and E rings. The most senior officials are in the E ring near what is known as the River Entrance. The secretary of defense and their staff occupy much of the third floor. The services are found on the other floors along adjacent corridors.
141. McMaster, *Dereliction*, 44–45.
142. The main opposition to nuclear power for naval propulsion came from the systems analysts. Melvin Price to Harold Brown, January 24, 1977, reprinted in US House of Representatives, Committee on Armed Services, Intelligence and Military Application of Nuclear Energy Subcommittee, *Hearing on H.R. 6566 ERDA Authorization Legislation (National Security Programs) for Fiscal Year 1978*, 95th Cong., 1st Sess. (April 27, 1977), 152–53.

143. Kaplan, Landa, and Drea, *McNamara Ascendancy*, 478.
144. The complicated history is summarized in Peter Tarpgaard, "McNamara and the Rise of Analysis in Defense Planning: A Retrospective," *Naval War College Review* 4, no. 8 (1995): 79–82; Dave Oliver, "Secretary McNamara and the CVA-67 Controversy" (MA thesis, American University, 1974). See also Hans Kristensen, William M. Arkin, and Joshua Handler, *Aircraft Carriers: The Limits of Nuclear Power*, Neptune Papers 7 (June 1994), https://www.nukestrat.com/pubs/nep7.pdf; Quentin Hodgson, *Deciding to Buy: Civil Military Relations and Major Weapons Programs*, Letort Papers (Carlisle, PA: US Army War College, 2010), 3–32.
145. "With respect to the carrier [CVA-67], I felt we needed [another] deck. Also, I had never been a rabid supporter of the need for nuclear power for a carrier." Appendix D, McDonald interview.
146. Drea, *Burdens*, 515–16.
147. Allan Spitz, "Conventional versus Nuclear Power for CVA-67: A Study of Defense Management," *Naval War College Review* 25, no. 4 (1972): 3–14.
148. Appendix D, McDonald interview. See also Drea, *Burdens*, 108.
149. Assistant secretary of the Navy for air (1949–50), undersecretary of the Navy (1950–51), and secretary of the Navy (1951–53).
150. Appendix D, McDonald interview.
151. Appendix D, McDonald interview.
152. Appendix D, McDonald interview.
153. McDonald, *Reminiscences*, 411, described a much more cordial relationship with Nitze than his 1974 interview.
154. Appendix D, McDonald interview. Goldwater opposed Nitze's nomination because he considered him "soft" on defense. Clifton Daniel, "Senate Won't Get Nitze Nomination," *New York Times*, March 27, 1974, https://www.nytimes.com/1974/03/27/archives/senate-wons-get-nitze-nomination-conservatives-oppose-him-for-post.html. For background, see Nicholas Thompson, *The Hawk and Dove: Paul Nitze, George Kennan, and the History of the Cold War* (New York: Picador, 2010), 223–24. Ironically, Nitze, the driving force behind NSC-68, had been a hardliner since the 1940s, opposed détente, and cofounded the second iteration of the Committee on the Present Danger in 1976 along with many of the leading lights of the neoconservative movement. Kaplan, *Wizards*, 377ff.
155. Hone, *OPNAV*, 259–60.
156. Thompson, *Hawk*, 197ff.
157. SECNAV 5250.2A, "Management Studies and Analyses Performed by, or for, the Department of the Navy; Approval of Requests to Contract for," April 19, 1979; Perry Smith and Daniel Gerstein, *Assignment: Pentagon; How to Excel in a Bureaucracy* (Washington, DC: Potomac, 2007), 59.
158. Hone, *OPNAV*, 254; John Darrell Sherwood, *Black Sailor, White Navy: Racial Unrest in the Fleet during the Vietnam War Era* (New York: New York University Press, 2007), 37.
159. Hone, *OPNAV*, 294, 359; Hughes, "Navy," 106ff.
160. Thomas Culora, "Rearranging Deck Chairs: The Near-Normal State for the Navy Staff," *Naval War College Review* 64, no. 1 (2011): 152–53; Hone, *OPNAV*, 339; Swartz, *OPNAV*, 39ff.
161. Elmo Zumwalt, *On Watch: A Memoir* (New York: Quadrangle, 1976), 45, 167.
162. Appendix D, McDonald interview.

163. Hone, *OPNAV*, 284.
164. Zumwalt recalled, "Under the tutelage of Paul Nitze, I earned what I think of as a Ph.D. in political-military affairs." Sherwood, *Black Sailor*, 35–36.
165. McDonald, *Reminiscences*, 238.
166. Peter Karsten, *The Naval Aristocracy: The Golden Age of Annapolis and the Emergence of Modern American Navalism* (New York: Free Press, 1972); David Alan Rosenberg, "Officer Development in the Interwar Navy: Arleigh Burke—The Making of a Naval Professional, 1919–1940," *Pacific Historical Review* 44, no. 4 (1975): 505–9.
167. "If history may be believed, the way in which the Spaniards and their kindred nation, the Portuguese, sought wealth, not only brought a blot upon the national character, but was also fatal to the growth of a healthy commerce; and so to the industries upon which commerce lives, and ultimately to that national wealth which was sought by mistaken paths." A. T. Mahan, *The Influence of Sea Power upon History* (New York: Dover, 1987), 50ff. For Mahan's repression of his Irish Catholic heritage, see William Livezey, *Mahan on Sea Power* (Norman: University of Oklahoma Press, 1981), 5–6.
168. Michael Hunt, *Ideology and U.S. Foreign Policy* (New Haven, CT: Yale University Press, 1987), 58ff.
169. "US Ship Force Levels," NHHC, November 17, 2017, https://www.history.navy.mil/research/histories/ship-histories/us-ship-force-levels.html.
170. "Dereliction of Duty," *Air Force Magazine*, January 1988, https://www.airforcemag.com/article/0198dereliction/.
171. McDonald, *Reminiscences*, 388.

CHAPTER 3

1970s

Unfinished Business

Elmo Zumwalt's years as CNO (1970–74) have received unusual attention for several reasons. Zumwalt, like Burke before him, was relatively junior—he was promoted over every one of the Navy's four-star admirals and nearly all of its three-stars. His political views, which shaped his conduct in office, were idiosyncratic. On national-security issues involving the Soviet Union and Israel, he was more hawkish than President Richard Nixon and National Security Advisor (later secretary of state) Henry Kissinger. At the same time, on the hot-button social issues of the day—the Vietnam War and the scourges of racism and sexism—Zumwalt was much more liberal than either Nixon or Kissinger as well as much of Congress and the Navy's leadership.[1]

Zumwalt inherited a service in crisis—the Navy was literally and figuratively falling apart. Sailors were unhappy with working conditions. Race riots raged aboard ships. As soon as their legal contracts expired, sailors were voting with their feet and leaving the service. The situation was so dire that without significant, immediate change, there soon would be insufficient sailors to put the Navy's aging surface ships to sea. To make his job even more difficult, Zumwalt had to share the stage with another admiral, Hyman Rickover, whose claim to fame as the "father of the nuclear Navy" eclipsed even Zumwalt's reputation with the public and Congress. Rickover was nominally Zumwalt's subordinate, but in practice, like many admirals, he performed his responsibilities relatively independently of the CNO. To add to the drama, these two officers also had contradictory views on the key issue of what ships the country should build.[2]

Every postwar CNO had essentially confronted the same set of bureaucratic challenges. Each had to establish a balance among the Navy's major warfare communities: aviation (including aircraft carriers), surface warfare, and submarine forces. At the same time, the CNO had to defend the Navy's prerogatives (especially its roles and missions) and force structure from the other services, especially the Air Force, which had not yet reconciled itself to its failure to kill off the Navy's carriers following World War II. Finally, Zumwalt had the special problem of refurbishing the Navy, especially its surface forces, after the extraordinary wear and tear of the Vietnam War—all during a period of declining real defense budgets (both because of spending cuts and inflation).

Zumwalt did not begin his tenure as CNO with broad support within either the Navy or the administration, with the exceptions of Secretary of Defense Melvin Laird and Secretary of the Navy John Chafee, who wanted Zumwalt to "bring the Navy into the modern age."[3] Accordingly, Zumwalt relied on a small coterie of officers he knew and trusted, along with some exceptional outside advisers.[4] The advantage of this arrangement was that it enabled Zumwalt to react rapidly to events, outmaneuver his bureaucratic enemies, and quickly institute a number of needed reforms. Unfortunately, the Navy is a large organization with deeply ingrained practices and prejudices. Since Zumwalt did not make sufficient time to educate and convince the entire Navy of his wisdom, much of it remained impervious to Zumwalt's reasoning and resentful of his changes. His opponents would thus chip away at many of his achievements while he was in office and continue after he left, with negative consequences to this day.

RICKOVER AND THE NUCLEAR CHALLENGE

When Zumwalt assumed his office, his most visible challenger was Rickover. Each admiral had his allies in Congress, in the two political parties, and the media. It was also an open secret that the men personally disliked each other. In 1959 Rickover had interviewed Zumwalt to join the nuclear-powered surface fleet. Zumwalt turned Rickover down and subsequently described their interviews in a matter unflattering to Rickover (who had thrown Zumwalt out of his office a record four times).[5] While Zumwalt was CNO, he avoided face-to-face conversations with Rickover, preferring instead to communicate via his aides.

The main bone of contention between the two men was the size of the Navy's nuclear-powered fleet.[6] Zumwalt had reluctantly given in to Rickover's demands for a new class of reactor, which increased the speed of US attack submarines, to get his support for what became the Trident program (the ballistic missile that followed Polaris and Poseidon), but that was as far as Zumwalt was willing to go.[7] Rickover, however, wanted more—he had been pushing for several years for an all-nuclear surface force. He had unusual authority by virtue of the fact that he wore two hats, one military and the other civilian. Since the late 1940s, Rickover had served as head of the nuclear power division at the Bureau of Ships (BUSHIPS) and chief of the Nuclear Reactor Branch at the Atomic Energy Commission.[8] Through his former position, Rickover fought for the right to interview every naval officer applying to join the nuclear program (either submarine or surface ship), an authority that his successors still maintain.[9]

The latter position gave him significant responsibility for the civilian nuclear-power industry.[10] He believed that an all-nuclear Navy would deliver significant benefits to the entire country. Cheaper nuclear energy for US companies would make their products more competitive on world markets, reduce costs for consumers, and help curb the persistent inflation of that era. Large naval contracts would also promote the growth of the civilian nuclear-power industry. Over the long run, so long as oil costs stayed high, investments in nuclear power would allow the Navy to field more advanced vessels at a lower cost. Meanwhile, the Navy's logistics costs would decrease due to the greater endurance and speed of nuclear-powered ships.[11]

There are always costs and trade-offs to embracing any transformative policy.[12] Opponents of Rickover contended that switching entirely to nuclear power would raise ship costs by double-digit percentages across the entire fleet (over 30 percent was a common estimate).[13] Unless the Navy received a massive infusion of cash up front, the expense of transitioning to an all-nuclear force would reduce the size of the fleet in the short run—up to thirty-five fewer cruisers, frigates, and destroyers, according to one Pentagon study.[14] A cash influx to the Navy to pay for converting to nuclear power was unlikely to happen because Congress preferred to cut the defense budget as the Vietnam War wound down. While he was in office, Robert McNamara had relented on nuclear power for aircraft carriers, but he remained opposed to its use for other kinds of surface ships. There was no reason to believe his successors would think any differently.

In addition to the financial concerns over nuclear power, few nonnuclear naval officers were willing to yield further concessions to Rickover, who already had unusually broad powers. Besides interviewing all the individuals who applied for nuclear training, he also enjoyed veto power over any officers the Bureau of Personnel (BUPERS) wished to assign as commanding officers or engineers on nuclear-powered ships or boats. Rickover thereby ensured that his fledgling portion of the fleet would not be starved for intellectual talent and that submarine engineers would not suffer any loss of prestige within the Navy, thereby impairing their promotion prospects, as had occurred during the transition from sail to steam.

Additionally, to guarantee that there was no shortage of young talent, Rickover was determined to transform the education of naval officers at the US Naval Academy. This remains one of his most controversial legacies. Those officers who struggled with mathematics and the physical sciences as midshipmen and resented being forced to work in the sweltering temperatures of an oil-fired engine room were unlikely to support Rickover's agenda. The officers who surmounted those crucibles viewed Rickover differently.

The consequences persisted long after the midshipmen left Annapolis. Critics of the Navy's current fetish of "technicism" still point the finger squarely at Rickover for enabling the atrophy of strategic thinking within the Navy.[15] This is perhaps unfair. Rickover was no philistine—he actually argued that there should be "more emphasis on the liberal arts" at Annapolis at the expense of "purely naval subjects."[16] (Recall that the physical sciences are integral parts of the traditional liberal arts education along with the humanities.) Rickover also deplored the hazing at the academy, which was "the sort of thing which immature boys might enjoy." Most important, he bemoaned Annapolis's lack of academic rigor compared to elite civilian universities. Rickover wanted the academy to turn young people into well-educated professionals rather than mere technicians. The former differed from the latter "by reason of his broad general education, his mastery of a specific area of higher learning and his ability to apply this specialized knowledge to practical problems." He did not want every naval officer to be an engineer but, rather, expected every officer to be properly educated, continue their studies after they graduated, and be capable of critical thinking.[17]

Rickover understood that as a new technology, nuclear reactors would have a future only if they had a safe track record.[18] Accordingly, he forced candidates for the nuclear submarine community to undergo strict screening of their intellectual ability and character. There were a number of senior officers in the Navy who failed to pass one of Rickover's infamous intake interviews yet went on to success elsewhere in the service. Many of these officers later argued that it was better to give most officers a foundation in the humanities, as do their contemporary equivalents.[19]

The unspoken corollary to this argument was that a Navy dominated by traditionally trained officers would keep those with a technical focus in a subordinate role. In a sense, Navy leaders were reprising the old struggle between line and engineering officers that arose in the nineteenth century following the advent of steam propulsion. Back then, the line officers claimed that the engineers were ignorant of naval strategy and the demands of operating in the real world.[20] Perhaps to avoid similar complaints, Rickover and his allies wanted the academy to focus on preparing officers for the kinds of tasks they would perform during their first decade of service.[21] Of these, engineering was the subject that required the longest time to master, which meant that many naval officers deferred their study of politics and strategy until they attended war colleges or graduate programs at civilian universities. Rickover expected that future flag officers would self-identify by their personal postgraduation reading and study choices.[22] Rickover's critics countered that his rigorous training regimen left officers with little time for reflection or intellectual growth.[23]

ZUMWALT'S VISION FOR THE NAVY

In the emotional to-and-fro over nuclear ships, the Navy's old bugaboo, systems analysis, again reared its head. By 1968 congressional frustration with McNamara had reached the boiling point, and the following year the Nixon administration pledged to restore the position of the military in Pentagon decision-making. It seemed the end of the McNamara Revolution, and Alain Enthoven was deeply skeptical of the new secretary of defense, Melvin Laird: "[He] is, in effect, determining what the traffic will bear and then asking for a little more so that he's out in front of his troops and looking good, asking for money. Then, they divide up the pot that they get three ways . . . I think in three equal fractions now, and then the services spend it pretty much the way they want. That alternative has the very serious drawback that it is not systematically related to national need."[24]

Enthoven would have been surprised to learn that Laird resisted calls to abolish the Office of Systems Analysis. He even retained one of McNamara's Whiz Kids, Ivan Selin, as its head for a year. Laird was nonetheless determined to avoid McNamara's mistakes, specifically actions that undermined trust between civilian and military leaders. Later analysts called Laird's management style one of "participatory management," which meant delegating a lot of key decisions regarding force structure and acquisitions back to the services provided that they respected the OSD's or the White House's interests on key issues. Laird also welcomed the military raising their concerns with Congress whenever they disagreed with his decisions. The secretary was no milquetoast—he understood that the only way to deliver the sorts of spending cuts the administration wanted was by letting the services make the tough choices about where to cut. The best way to identify inefficiencies was, of course, through systems analysis, which would, along with the PPBS, remain an invaluable tool in the Pentagon's—and increasingly the services'—arsenal.[25]

As we explained in chapter 2, systems analysis is not an objective science free from bias. As Enthoven argued, it takes careful leadership to ensure that people are not "manipulating the data" to validate a predetermined result.[26] Not every systems analyst is an Enthoven or David Chu (the former's equivalent during the Reagan and George H. W. Bush administrations).[27] When the Navy applied systems analysis to the question of whether to convert all of the Navy's major surface combatants to nuclear power, the results varied wildly depending on the assumptions about the future price of oil, how long ships lasted between nuclear refuelings, and the cost of maintaining a global refueling infrastructure.[28] There were no "right" answers to any of these questions, although some factors were much harder to bound than others. For example, if any naval officer or OSD staffer could confidently predict the future price of oil, they were unlikely to remain in the public sector for long, as their skills would fetch a hefty premium in the oil industry or on Wall Street.

When Zumwalt became the first head of the Navy's own system analysis office (OP-96), he opposed Rickover's push for more nuclear-powered ships. Subsequently, as CNO, he understood how to use analysis to reinforce his arguments. Zumwalt also had a clear idea about what he wanted to accomplish during this tenure—a mix of policies he called "Project Sixty."[29] Some of these were his own ideas; others he adopted from other policymakers, such as the High-Low Mix championed by Deputy Secretary of Defense David Packard.[30] The High-Low Mix was the idea of building a force comprising a large number of less-expensive platforms that were to perform less challenging tasks while operating alongside a smaller number of technologically advanced ships.

Interestingly, Burke had advocated a similar idea as CNO to help control costs, particularly against low-tech adversaries imposing strategies of cost imposition.[31] Zumwalt believed the concept would help the Navy by spurring the development of the command, control, and communications capabilities necessary to coordinate a variety of systems with different capabilities and missions. The overarching aim of these measures would be to shift the Navy away from its Vietnam War focus on power projection back to the traditional task of sea control. Doing so meant the Navy would have to return resources to a long-neglected community, surface warfare.[32]

It was not the most glamorous community, but a healthy surface force was integral to the Navy performing many indispensable, if mundane, tasks. Alas, the surface force had suffered from years of neglect compared to the rest of the Navy. McDonald had demonstrated, using his extraordinary personal network, how to compete politically with the other services, but only naval aviation had benefited from his connections. Rickover, meanwhile, had revolutionized the submarine force, but no one had done the same for the surface-warfare community.

The main challenge for surface forces was finding and killing enemy submarines while protecting themselves (and their screening units) from aircraft or missiles. Zumwalt worried that the United States had overemphasized the use of the Navy for power projection ashore during the Vietnam War. As a result, the fleet was now rundown from years of grueling combat operations, unable to fulfill its sea-control missions, and badly in need of modernization.[33] Zumwalt intended to address the problems his predecessors had ignored.[34]

The tasks of a service chief continually evolve, but essentially they are responsible for managing their service and preserving its cohesion—that is to say, tending to the requirements of its myriad communities (or combat arms, in the Army and Marines). In the case of the Navy, since World War II, the most important communities have been surface warfare, aviation, and submarines. Many CNOs have devoted their personal attention to developing or protecting specific warfighting capabilities.[35] In this vein, Zumwalt spoke constantly of the need to redress the deficiencies in the surface forces. He lamented that "[sea-control] forces—anti-submarine planes and their carriers and ships suitable for patrol and escort duty—were allowed to obsolesce and, finally, retire without replacement," while Rickover's submarines mushroomed thanks to his influence on Capitol Hill.[36]

Zumwalt focused his efforts on the Sea Control Ship (a small aircraft carrier designed primarily to protect convoys), the Surface Effect Ship (a twin-hulled hydrofoil that at high speeds used an air cushion), the FFG-7 (*Perry*-class) frigate, and the DD-963 (*Spruance*-class) destroyer. While Zumwalt was successful in many of the facets of his job as CNO, his track record in bringing a new surface fleet into being was mixed. He did get the frigates into construction, but because of their fragility, they had an uneven record in the fleet.[37] The Sea Control Ship and the Surface Effect Ship attracted little interest after Zumwalt's retirement.[38] His greatest shipbuilding accomplishment was the *Spruance*-class destroyer, which would be the backbone of the Navy until the end of the twentieth century. Zumwalt's mixed legacy is further proof that fielding effective weapons quickly and affordably is a difficult process, even with the best of intentions and senior-level engagement.

Table 3.1 shows the number of Navy surface ships when Zumwalt became CNO and the totals of the same ships four years later when he left.[39]

Laird had tapped Zumwalt as CNO in spite of the latter's well-known affiliation with the previous administration.[40] One of the reasons Zumwalt

Table 3.1 Numbers of Navy Surface Ships, 1970 and 1974

	1970	1974
Total Navy ships	743	587
Surface warships	279	211
Destroyers	155	119
Frigates	47	64

thrived was that he understood how to operate within the Pentagon. He was also successful because he recognized that a key aspect of his role as a service chief was to keep the other services honest. He had sharp elbows and knew how to deal with interservice rivalry, which benefited not only the Navy but also the wider defense community.

INTERSERVICE RIVALRY AND THE TOMAHAWK MISSILE

In Washington, criticism is a blood sport, and even the mildest reproach can sting if it finds a sensitive spot. Each morning, the denizens of the Pentagon thumbed through the daily summary of that day's defense news.[41] One of the many purposes this document served was to fire warning shots across the bows of key actors within the Pentagon. There are certain "red lines" for each service that people cross at their peril. Among them are questioning the platforms or units that allow each service to perform its key roles and missions—for example, the number of Army divisions, Navy carriers, or Air Force wings. Any action that threatens a service's ability to perform the tasks central to its identity will invariably result in canceled dinners, strained friendships, and entire segments of the Pentagon shifting to the highest state of bureaucratic alert. What follows is the story of one Air Force foray that crossed a Navy red line with unexpected consequences.

Zumwalt usually started his day with a small staff meeting. One morning in the spring of 1972, the Navy's representative on the Joint Staff reported that the Air Force had not concurred with the recommended number of aircraft carriers listed in the "buff" copy of the latest policy draft for the secretary of defense. (In this ancient era, the color of major policy documents physically changed as they worked their way through the review process.) The officer reported the Air Force wanted the number of Navy carriers lowered by two before it would agree for the draft to "go green"—that is, be ready for final signature.

The room went silent. Everyone understood what this meant. The Air Force had not merely edged up to a red line—this was a sneak attack, as the Air Force had not laid down the necessary public-relations fire to prepare the battlefield. Some of Zumwalt's staff wondered if this was a feint, but in any case the Navy needed to proceed to "battle stations."

Why in the world had the Air Force launched this particular offensive? The popular view that morning was it was a distraction. It was common knowledge inside the Beltway that the Air Force was having difficulty selling its concept of a new, deep-penetration bomber—what became the B-1 Lancer. The B-1 was hugely expensive at a time when the Nixon administration was determined to trim the defense budget. Was the Air Force attacking the Navy's carriers to find money for its new bomber? Whatever its motives, the Air Force's move was a bureaucratic declaration of war.

Everyone in Zumwalt's office recognized this fight was at best a waste of time and at worst a lose/lose proposition. Once the carrier fight was joined, about a quarter of the CNO's staff would waste the next several weekdays, nights, and weekends fending off challenges from Air Force sympathizers. Consequently, they would ignore or defer other important issues. No one on Zumwalt's staff doubted the Navy would succeed, but in doing so it would have to burn many political chits. The Air Force had, since the 1940s, been waging a protracted campaign against naval aviation. No single engagement would be ever decisive, but over time the costs of such fights would add up in the Air Force's favor. To paraphrase the German strategic commentator Hans Delbrück, the Air Force did not need to win every battle, but through steady attrition it might just win the war by exhaustion.[42]

Having to take time away from real problems annoyed Zumwalt. Did the Air Force perceive the Navy as weak? Was this a personal attack on him? Did the chief of staff of the Air Force think Zumwalt was on shaky political ground? He looked around the room. His eyes were glinting. "Find me a way to screw the Air Force," he ordered. What next occurred was pure serendipity. It was also an example of the underrated benefits of competition among the services and how feuding can serve the wider cause of enabling necessary changes within the Department of Defense.

One of Zumwalt's young aides, Lt. Cmdr. Dave Oliver, left the CNO's office to walk up the two flights of stairs to the confusing maze on the fifth deck of the Pentagon where his own office was located. As he reached the top step, he met a small group of civilians who were lost. One man was carrying a cardboard box, and the other two had the inexpensive, imitation-leather briefcases that often identify men who work with numbers.

"May I help you gentlemen?" Oliver asked.

"You can if you know where the Air Force has its offices," they replied.

"You are on the wrong side of the Pentagon." Getting to the Air Force offices on the top floor of the Pentagon required a several-minute explanation, and there were many potential dead ends. Oliver was not anxious to begin his tasking from Zumwalt. In fact, he had no idea how to start. "I'll guide you over myself."

They set off. Along the way the group fell into conversation and informed their guide that the Air Force had given them a contract several years earlier to compile a terrain map of the Soviet Union. They had used data from the top secret U-2 overflights. The Air Force had originally considered having their B-1 airplane fly near the Soviet Union but at a safe distance (known as "standoff") and fire nuclear-tipped missiles toward targets deep in the Soviet Union. The missiles would have an independent guidance system (yet to be invented) that enabled them to hug the ground in order to avoid the Soviets' air defenses. The group wandering the halls of the Pentagon that morning had succeeded in digitizing all the U-2 data and even built a prototype guidance system. They were calling it a TERCOM (Terrain Contour Matching) system. Unfortunately for their small company, the Air Force had yesterday informed them their contract was canceled.

Oliver began walking more slowly. The previous week, he had learned that the submarine force had a new missile under development. Because the missile was large enough to fit in a submarine's torpedo tube, it could carry sufficient fuel to fly nearly two thousand miles. But there was a hitch—it had no connectivity with other sensors. Thus, the missile could not target anything farther than thirty miles from the submarine. A nuclear submarine could sneak up unseen to anywhere, including the Soviet coast, but continuing the development of the weapon served no rational purpose. No one was interested in putting money into a missile when there were other, less expensive ways to kill a target within thirty miles. On the other hand, people were always looking for a way to get around the Soviets' air-defense systems.

Could this TERCOM system be the answer to that problem?

The leader of the men in suits was still talking. "The missile will fly so low the Soviet radars can't possibly see it, and they won't detect its radar signature. Our system flies out on its own, then looks down, and matches the mountains immediately below it against the terrain [data] we have stored in the TERCOM. It locks onto a profile and then flies straight to the target. The only radar emissions are those directly beneath the missile. No one knows it's there. It can't be electronically fooled."

Oliver began taking the visitors down the wrong corridor. Was this what Zumwalt had been asking for? The B-1 bomber was, at that time, in the Air Force's development phase. There was a very public debate ongoing over whether the strike weapons should be delivered by standoff missiles or by bombs after the pilots had evaded Soviet air defenses. Systems analysis indicated that the former was the more cost-effective option, but the latter was more satisfying to the prevailing Air Force culture, which was shaped by pilots, and bombs would theoretically be cheaper than missiles, assuming aircraft could overfly the target.[43]

As Oliver slowed his steps, he was thinking. If the Air Force had decided to go all out for a deep-penetration bomber that could deliver munitions directly on the target, logic dictated it would be much, much more difficult to sell the program to Congress if an accurate penetrating missile were available. In that case, the Air Force's first step would be to kill the component that made such a missile possible, the TERCOM. Then the Air Force might decide to create a headline-grabbing distraction—like, for example, targeting the Navy's carriers again.

Oliver wondered if the Navy had its own way to use the TERCOM. He steered the technicians into an empty office and asked them a few questions. Would they consider selling their wares to another client? They said they wanted to survive. Oliver immediately took them to Crystal City (the office area to the south of the Pentagon—a warren of buildings shared by defense contractors and government agencies) and introduced them to the Navy's cruise-missile group.

Oliver then returned to the Pentagon and wrote a one-page memo for Zumwalt to send to his friend and boss, Laird. The secretary was then in New York, poised to fly to the Soviet Union for the signing of the first Strategic Arms Limitation Talks agreement (SALT I). Oliver's memo proposed that the Navy begin development of a sea-launched cruise missile (SLCM) that used the TERCOM navigation system to penetrate the Soviet air-defense systems from multiple angles of attack. To avoid offending Kissinger, the memo stressed that the missile would not be covered by the SALT I agreement.[44] (The Carter administration would subsequently offer to give up SLCMs to win a second SALT agreement.[45])

The TERCOM was a godsend for Laird, who was under pressure from hawks for giving up too much under SALT I. Laird had responded to these criticisms by calling for the development of new submarine-launched missiles that were not covered by SALT I. Although the SLCM did not receive as much attention as the proposed Trident SLBM, the cruise missile was bureaucratically even more useful. For one thing, it could be deployed on the smaller Polaris boats that would otherwise have to be retired because they could not launch the Trident missile.[46] Even better, no one in Washington was prepared to challenge the SLCM openly, least of all the Air Force, which did not want to answer any embarrassing questions about why it had paid for the initial research for the navigational system and then dumped the contractor after it was successful.

Within the Navy, the SLCM was not immune from the usual intraservice jockeying that had plagued cruise missiles since World War II. Attack submarines did not want to reduce their torpedo loads, while naval aviators (like their Air Force colleagues) preferred to fly deep-interdiction missions. Nevertheless, the Navy could not ignore the many tactical advantages of the SLCM, known today as the Tomahawk.[47] Beginning with the Gulf War of 1991, the Navy launched hundreds of these missiles from ships and submarines. The Tomahawk proved itself as a cost-effective system that provided troops in the field with a flexible military capability. To avoid being left behind, the Air Force would build its own air-launched cruise missile (ALCM).[48] The ALCM was fired from a B-52 to penetrate the enemy airspace while the firing platform remained standoff. In the end, not only did the Air Force's feint against the carriers fail, but it also had to divert resources to build a competitor to its prized B-1. Zumwalt got his revenge, and the United States obtained an extraordinary weapon for its arsenal.

While this sort of interservice rivalry may appear baffling or even childish to outside observers, these situations can afford opportunities for innovation, much like competition among private firms can promote greater efficiencies. As the aforementioned case suggests, it is unclear whether cruise missiles would have ever been developed in the absence of such rivalry.

Zumwalt was clearly a master at the traditional tasks of CNO, but that capability was insufficient to meet all of his challenges. Because of the indifference, even hostility, of some of his predecessors, Zumwalt had to take responsibility for solving a number of nontraditional challenges. Perhaps the most important was the declining reenlistments due to silly or arbitrary disciplinary requirements, sexism, and racism.

TACKLING SOCIAL AND RACIAL INEQUITIES

While his feud with Rickover received much of the greatest play in the media, Zumwalt had even more difficult, internal problems to address. Amid shrinking budgets and antiwar sentiment, his greatest challenge was improving "personnel retention and motivation."[49] Most admirals and members of Congress had no idea that the Navy was on the cusp of falling apart in 1970. The Navy could always build new ships—but it could not easily replace experienced sailors, who were leaving the service in droves.[50] When Zumwalt became CNO, morale was so poor that reenlistment rates had dropped by almost 75 percent from the norm (from 35 to less than 10 percent).[51] These figures were catastrophic for a service that relied on relatively high-skilled recruits and was transitioning to an all-volunteer force. If Zumwalt did not solve the Navy's social problems, it would not matter how much money Congress subsequently appropriated for ship construction—either there would not have been sufficient sailors remaining in the Navy to cast off the lines and take the ships to sea, or the Navy would have to lower its standards for recruits, with deleterious consequences for the service's effectiveness.

Zumwalt was facing three separate personnel problems. The first was general dissatisfaction, primarily in the ranks of the younger officers and enlisted men, spurred by unnecessary and onerous practices, such as requiring sailors handling dirty at-sea refueling hoses to wear whites, upon which every oily smear instantly showed, when the only audience was seagulls. Because much of the Navy operates out of the sight of immediate supervision while on deployment, there is ample scope for officers to become Captain Queegs.[52] Such martinets created intense resentment among the enlisted toward "chickenshit" (Nixon's word) or "Mickey Mouse" (Zumwalt's term) regulations and practices.[53] During most of the Vietnam War, the sailors had generally repressed their anger, but by the early 1970s, with the conflict winding down, the situation had reached critical mass.

The second major personnel problem facing Zumwalt was perhaps one of the sources of the first problem: entrenched racism. During the first half of the twentieth century, the Navy was the least favorable service to African Americans. Before World War II, only 2 percent of the service was Black (all enlisted), and the vast majority of them served as mess stewards. The Navy abandoned segregation earlier than the other services, in 1945–46, but that did not extend to the ships at sea, as zero Black officers served on either battleships or aircraft carriers.[54] Even by the early 1970s, even after the end of segregation in 1954, Blacks still made up only 5 percent of the service and an even smaller share of the officer corps. The African American community meanwhile shunned the Navy as a preserve of "white America."[55]

Fortunately, some White officers transcended the prejudices of service—Zumwalt especially, as is clear from his obituary in the *Washington Post*: "Zumwalt described in a memoir how he had run into roadblocks at every turn when he helped a Filipino mess steward become an electrician's mate. 'The episode taught me a healthy contempt for the bureaucracy and for the institutional racism in the Navy,' he wrote. Although President Harry S. Truman had ordered the armed services to integrate in 1948, Zumwalt said, 'racism and sexism were still an integral part of the Navy tradition' when he became CNO."[56]

Zumwalt had assumed office to the sound of breaking glass from race riots in American cities and aboard Navy ships. One took place in October 1972 aboard USS *Kitty Hawk* (CVA-63). It was followed very shortly thereafter by incidents aboard USS *Hassayampa* (AO-145) and USS *Constellation* (CVA-64).[57] At the same time, the Marines had charged several Blacks with mutiny in August 1972 after they complained about harassment from White officers and enlisted men aboard USS *Sumter* (LST-1181).[58] In fact, these instances were just the tip of an iceberg of unrest. By the summer of 1972, the Navy was suffering from an epidemic of sabotage by sailors disgruntled with social or racial conditions that was threatening the readiness of the entire fleet.[59] During a mere four months in 1972, the Naval Investigative Service counted ninety-eight criminal cases involving racial issues. Two years later, during a two-month period, the Atlantic Fleet alone counted fifty-seven such incidents.[60]

Zumwalt did not mince words when it came to assigned blame, which he placed squarely on the Navy's all-White leadership.[61] Not surprisingly, Zumwalt's challenge found an icy reception from many of the White senior enlisted and officers.[62] They did not consider racism to be a problem in the Navy, resented Zumwalt's accusation that their service was failing its Black sailors, and worried that his words were undermining good order and discipline. It was up to Zumwalt to break the Navy's racist practices while at the same time placating powerful interest groups with no interest in racial equality and that feared and resisted change, both inside and outside of the Navy.

We should not underestimate how difficult this challenge was. McDonald's disparagement of civil rights and his explicit preference for his own race (quoted in chapter 2) suggested the enormity of the challenge.[63] McDonald's predecessor as CNO, George Anderson, was equally candid during private interviews, with his thinly veiled comment about Jews, when he complained that "the Air Force had supported more of the new 'Harvard people' who are now being appointed to positions of responsibility, and they had supported more of the East European intellectuals who came to prominence after the 1960s. Most of the latter had very shallow roots in America."[64]

The congressional committees that controlled the Navy's money (often dominated by Southerners) agreed with Zumwalt's critics that the problem was not racism but rather Zumwalt.[65] Another notable critic was President Richard Nixon.[66] Nixon rarely spoke about Zumwalt among his aides, but when he did it was usually to disparage the admiral for his misplaced priorities.

On one occasion, Nixon fumed that Zumwalt and Chafee (a former Marine who had served in the Pacific during World War II and in Korea) had undermined discipline by "pandering to . . . the liberals" and "trying to be nice to everybody."[67] Running the Navy as a "social-welfare institution" was counterproductive, according to Nixon. "A military organization has high morale when it's disciplined," he opined. "You don't hear anything in the Marines about riots."[68] Like the army of the United States' feckless South Vietnamese ally, the US military's poor discipline—particularly that of the Navy—was reducing operational effectiveness.[69] Instead of cracking down, as Nixon preferred, Zumwalt "was blaming the Navy for what the goddamn Blacks did."[70]

It never occurred to Nixon or Zumwalt's other critics that the social unrest in the Navy had a longer history and that far from inciting violence, Zumwalt's reforms were a desperate attempt to prevent that violence from crippling the service. Unlike President Lyndon Johnson, who empathized with the poor and downtrodden through his family's poverty and experience teaching underprivileged Hispanic students, Zumwalt had no particular reason to have a progressive view on race relations. The rumor that Zumwalt's mother was Jewish was false. He had few Black friends when he was young. In the dusty farmland of California's Central Valley where he grew up, Zumwalt had even once been arrested with a high school friend for egging hitchhikers.[71] Nor had his career experiences prior to becoming CNO impressed upon him the necessity for racial equity within the Navy.[72]

Yet Zumwalt had no difficulty learning and growing even as an adult. Most important, he was a natural leader and unafraid of courting controversy or expending political capital on issues he considered vital.[73] As a junior officer, Zumwalt almost singlehandedly integrated the wardroom of USS *Wisconsin* in 1953 by insisting to his executive officer that the first Black officer assigned to a battleship have the same treatment as any White officer.[74]

The third personnel issue Zumwalt faced was women. The Navy of that era did not give them nearly the equivalent responsibility it gave men. It did not even admit women to the Naval Academy until after Zumwalt had been retired for several years. For Zumwalt, allowing women to serve in all roles was a demographic necessity—his calculations told him that in two decades the Navy was going to need women in numbers to fill critical billets. He thus invited television cameras into the Pentagon one day and announced his intention to allow women to serve throughout the Navy.[75]

After the interview, the press and their cameras moved down the corridor. As they passed the office of the secretary of the Navy, the occupant, John Warner, emerged and inquired what the gaggle was doing in the Navy's corner of the Pentagon. Several excited voices shouted, "The CNO just announced the Navy is going to put women in all jobs!" The secretary tilted his head, looked directly in the cameras from underneath his bushy eyebrows, and said, "Not in my Navy." He then turned his back on the reporters and returned to his office.[76] Warner knew where the political winds were blowing. (Like Chafee, he eventually ended up in the Senate.) At a meeting with the JCS and National Security Council (NSC) a few months after the announcement, the president said to Zumwalt with a knowing look, "I guess I can put up with this race thing, but don't push so hard for women."[77]

No one can doubt Zumwalt's sincerity about combatting the Navy's sexism, but he found "that it was impossible to discuss the matter rationally with some people. In addition to the folk who feared unisex showers and floating orgies . . . were the folk, many of them high military or civilian officials, from which it was maddeningly difficult to elicit more than locker-room jocularities on the subject."[78] Ultimately, Zumwalt had to choose his battles. No matter how hard he worked, the chances of success if President Nixon, the Senate, and his fellow admirals consistently opposed him were slim. It was simply beyond his capability to solve the problems of poor treatment of the sailors, racism, and sexism simultaneously while rebuilding the fleet after Vietnam. So, Zumwalt focused his energy on the problems that affected the largest number of people—mistreatment of the enlisted and racism.[79] Sadly, sexism slipped from his grasp, and none of his successors took up the challenge until the Tailhook scandal in 1991 forced the Navy to confront the issue.[80]

Zumwalt was frustrated rather than surprised by the issues he confronted as CNO. This was not the first time he had studied these same issues and identified the answers—he had been part of a team that had recommended corrective action several years earlier. Zumwalt was convinced that the only reason why the previous effort had failed was that any naysayer in the chain of command could "slow roll" a change.[81]

Anyone who has ever served or worked in the Pentagon knows that bureaucratic lethargy or obstruction—a refusal to take action—is a difficult problem to overcome. Experienced hands also know that very, very few senior military officers pay more than lip-service attention to enacting new personnel policies. Within the Navy, most senior leaders are focused on "things"—the deployment of ships, planes, and submarines. Congressional interest usually lies in expensive acquisition or infrastructure projects. Zumwalt had to make the Navy focus on people when there was no compelling institutional incentive for its leaders. He therefore decided to take his case to the people who cared the most about personnel issues—the junior officers and enlisted. Accordingly, he began putting out personal messages known as Z-grams. This guidance went out directly to the entire Navy—in Navy parlance, to all the stations and ships afloat—rather than down the chain of command.

An issue soon arose that exemplified the problem Zumwalt was facing. The issue was not about getting money for new ships—it was about treating people decently. Even within the context of a multibillion-dollar enterprise—which is one way of looking at the Navy—it is worth spending time, as Zumwalt did, on what appears to be a trivial issue because it is emblematic of the sorts of difficulties Zumwalt faced.

The issue in question was that of uniforms. For years, enlisted sailors had worn heavy, woolen, two-piece "blues" to work. Those enlisted personnel who worked belowdecks, where the minorities not assigned as stewards and cooks most often served, then changed into dungarees and proceeded to toil all day in a hot and dirty environment. According to the existing regulations, they then had to change back into their blues to cross the ship's or station's "quarterdeck" (a legal or ceremonial spot that marks where the jurisdiction of the ship, station, or base begins or ends) to return to their barracks or home. To make matters worse, blues had a decorative white piping in the cuff and neck areas that was difficult to keep clean under the best conditions. Those uniforms also needed to be dry-cleaned, which was expensive—prohibitively so for junior enlisted sailors, who did not make much money.

At the time, few or no showers were kept operative aboard ships while in port, which reflected the general indifference among senior leaders to conditions for the enlisted. Sailors who did dirty work after shifting to dungarees therefore had no place to clean up before they were required to change back into their blues to go home. Forcing sailors to wear a uniform that was probably going to get dirty and needed to be dry-cleaned for the sake of a sixty-foot walk across the quarterdeck of the ship or station was a burdensome requirement. It applied disproportionately to those who worked in engineering, rather than administrative, tasks. It also (perhaps inadvertently) discriminated predominantly against minorities.

If that were not bad enough, there were commercial shower and locker businesses outside of every Navy base. These businesses made money from junior Black and White sailors washing Navy dirt from Navy bodies. The existence of the showers outside each Navy base were visual statements as to how little the senior leadership of that era cared about their enlisted personnel's welfare. Not surprisingly, the regulation about wearing blues to cross the quarterdeck was despised by the enlisted as well as the young officers responsible for these sailors.

Accordingly, one of Zumwalt's first Z-grams, on July 30, 1970, announced a trial program to assess if there were any problems with sailors wearing civilian clothes to and from ships.[82] Not surprisingly, none arose, and after six months another Z-gram made the new uniform policy permanent.[83]

Zumwalt's decision to bypass the Navy's seniors with Z-grams generated enormous controversy. Many admirals believed he was deliberately subverting the chain of command and undermining the authority of the fleet commanders.[84] The commander of all surface ships in the Atlantic was especially irritated. He asked for an audience with the CNO and let it be known in advance that he was furious with Z-grams in general and specifically with the one on uniform policy. This was not supposed to be some airing of differences among peers—Zumwalt's detractors were secretly promoting this meeting as part of a campaign to convince Nixon not to renominate Zumwalt for a second term as CNO.[85]

The offended admiral brought with him a visual aid.[86] It was a blown-up photograph from the previous week's *Virginian-Pilot* (a newspaper published in Norfolk, Virginia, where a large number of ships of the Atlantic Fleet were based). The picture showed a sailor passed out on the street in front of a bar. The sailor was in dungarees (a work uniform prohibited in public under either the old or new policies). From his waist down, he was lying in a rain puddle. The admiral waved the photograph at Zumwalt, his voice rising: "This is what your Z-grams are doing!"

Zumwalt motioned to be passed the photograph. As it moved down the long table, the room got very quiet. Zumwalt examined it for a second before laying it face down and asking, "Do you think the Navy would be better off if the photo showed the sailor in blues?"

The admiral from Norfolk had not been interested in the sailor or the possible problem of alcoholism in the ranks. He only desired to preserve his own outdated image of the Navy. Zumwalt, meanwhile, was trying to encourage these senior officers to think and grow. He was trying to force the admirals to become real leaders, to seek to adapt their organizations more than preserve them.

By 1973 Zumwalt was isolated bureaucratically. His allies Chafee and Laird had resigned, and the new secretary of the Navy, John Warner, was not a fan. Zumwalt's efforts to correct systemic racism in the Navy had created enormous friction with numerous active-duty and retired admirals, members of Congress, and individuals like President Nixon, who did not consider racism a serious problem in the Navy. This accumulation of political ill will nearly cost Zumwalt his job, but he was saved by events in the fleet—the sailors had again voted with their feet. From 1970 to 1972, reenlistment rates had more than doubled (from 9 to 23 percent). Despite unceasing opposition from across Washington and the Navy, Zumwalt's changes had encouraged reenlistments to rise to a self-sustaining number.[87]

ZUMWALT AS A WASHINGTON OPERATOR

Besides demonstrating his ability to take actions necessary for the Navy's long-term health, Zumwalt also dealt with another area that was traditionally beyond the purview of the CNO—foreign policy. Zumwalt would after his retirement run for a Senate seat in Virginia as a Democrat. Because of his support for minorities and women, Zumwalt was liberal on social issues, but on national security he was very hawkish, much like his political mentor, Paul Nitze.[88]

Zumwalt's intense suspicion of the Soviet Union made him a natural critic of détente, which put him at odds with Nixon's national security advisor and later secretary of state, Henry Kissinger. Zumwalt's autobiography makes clear the admiral disliked Kissinger. The feeling was mutual, although it had not begun that way. In 1970 Laird had recommended Zumwalt to Kissinger as a replacement for Adm. Thomas Moorer.[89] That was apparently enough for Nixon, who did not even bother to mention the admiral in his memoirs.

Zumwalt's early interactions with Kissinger were positive. Kissinger solicited Zumwalt's input on matters such as the 1969 defense management review (the Fitzhugh Report) and supported his personal diplomacy in 1970 with Lee Kuan Yew, the autocratic leader of Singapore, concerning the homeporting by US Navy ships in Singapore and the denial of facilities to the Soviet Navy.[90] Kissinger's opinion of Zumwalt soon soured over the admiral's insistence that USS *Enterprise* conduct a port call in Chile in 1971. Kissinger (and Nixon) disagreed, warning that it would strengthen the socialist government of Salvador Allende, while Zumwalt argued the visit would strengthen ties with the Chilean military and keep Allende "boxed in."[91]

Kissinger then complained that Zumwalt was trying to undercut him over the Navy's budget by going directly to the president. "That won't work in the WH [White House]," he warned Moorer. The chairman had never liked Zumwalt. When Moorer had served as CNO, he had sent Zumwalt to South Vietnam to forestall his future appointment as CNO. Unfortunately for Moorer, Zumwalt's aggressive leadership in Vietnam earned the respect of Gen. Creighton Abrams, the commander of Military Assistance Command, Vietnam. Abrams, in turns, extolled Zumwalt to Secretary of Defense Laird when the latter visited South Vietnam, thereby thwarting Moorer's plan.[92] Moorer's opinion of Zumwalt did not improve after the latter became CNO. "He is bouncing like a rubber ball," Moorer concurred. "I will speak to him."[93]

Thereafter, their relationship remained outwardly cordial but privately poisonous. They still agreed on certain issues, such as their mutual distaste for Rickover.[94] Zumwalt was also careful to flatter the vain Kissinger for his "brilliantly conducted foreign policy."[95] Kissinger reciprocated the insincerity. Whenever Zumwalt made a personnel recommendation, Kissinger gushed, "You have never steered me wrong."[96] And on naval matters, such as the intricacies of the Soviet-American Maritime Agreement of 1972 and naval deployments to Japan, Kissinger was appropriately respectful of Zumwalt's expertise.[97]

Kissinger nonetheless despised Zumwalt as a careerist. "[That] guy is such a whore—he wants to be chairman of the Joint Chiefs," Kissinger explained to Secretary of Commerce Pete Peterson.[98] Kissinger believed that Zumwalt's ambition made him predictable and therefore susceptible to manipulation. "I will handle Zumwalt," Kissinger bragged to a British diplomat. "He has an uncanny sense of where his bread is buttered on."[99] By December 1972 the press was speculating that Kissinger had spoken with Zumwalt about Zumwalt's dismissal due to racial violence within the Navy. (According to Zumwalt's son, Kissinger had insisted the CNO dishonorably discharge all of the sailors who had participated in the recent race riots; Zumwalt had refused.[100]) Kissinger complained to Nixon's press secretary that this was a "total untruth," but his private conversations with Nixon suggest otherwise.[101]

In March 1973 Kissinger urged Nixon to cashier Zumwalt when his second term as CNO expired. When Nixon asked why, Kissinger vented:

Kissinger: Because, first of all, he's a whore a total opportunist [two of Kissinger's favorite slurs]. He was a McNamara man. He was Nitze's aide. He's done everything since he came in purely opportunistically. He talks a tough game. Then he wanted to send an aircraft carrier [the *Enterprise*] to Chile—

Nixon: Yes.

Kissinger: When we stopped that, he leaked it. I think he's let the morale in the Navy go to hell. He's turned it into a social-welfare institution. Moorer is absolutely down on him.

Nixon: Is he?

Kissinger: Oh, yes. And [Deputy Secretary of Defense William] Clements is down on him.

Nixon: Social-welfare institution is right. The way they handled the Black situation there—

Kissinger: It's a disgrace.
Nixon: It's disgusting, disgusting.[102]

Conversely, Zumwalt's antipathy stemmed from mistrust over Kissinger's methods and his motives. Like many in the defense establishment (including Laird and Moorer), Zumwalt mistrusted Kissinger's secretiveness. The Navy, in particular, went to extraordinary lengths to find out what Kissinger was doing. Zumwalt, as he admitted to his daughter, engineered the placement of trusted officers on Kissinger's staff to keep tabs on their boss.[103] His predecessor and nominal superior Moorer even instructed a yeoman to make copies of thousands of sensitive documents Kissinger was not sharing.[104]

Why would Zumwalt go to such extraordinary lengths? It was because he believed that Kissinger was too soft on the Soviet Union. For example, in September 1973 Sen. Stuart Symington complained to Kissinger about the Navy's tactics while pushing for the acquisition of submarines capable of launching the new Trident missile (the *Ohio* class): "[It's] got everybody mad, and the lobbying—I've never seen anything like it. . . . [Admirals] have become as familiar in the corridors of the Senate Office Building as Senate Pages," none more so than Zumwalt, who was telling everyone "'Soviet agents' were on Capitol Hill lobbying against the new submarine."[105] When Zumwalt waged his quixotic Senate campaign in 1976, Kissinger marveled to the governor of Florida that "Zumwalt is trying to run in Virginia to the right of Harry Byrd," by which he meant to the right on foreign policy, since Byrd was an unrepentant segregationist.[106]

Kissinger knew Zumwalt's opinions from firsthand experience. In the early days of Zumwalt's CNO tour, Kissinger was negotiating SALT I with the Soviet Union, which achieved a rough balance of intercontinental nuclear weapons. Zumwalt felt Kissinger was duped on the terms.[107] Whatever the merits of the agreement, there was a technical flaw in Kissinger's approach. The United States (and Kissinger) was relying on satellites and high-flying airplanes to verify the treaty, but US sensors were not appropriately sensitive or sufficiently numerous to continuously and accurately monitor large areas.[108]

On May 26, 1972, Nixon signed the SALT treaty with the Soviet Union. Later that summer, Zumwalt sent Oliver to see Kissinger. A new US satellite with a more sensitive camera had discovered that the Soviets had fabricated a ballistic-missile submarine out of plywood. This allowed them to add twenty-four missile tubes to their official total of launchers, which they could then dismantle as part of a shell game to avoid reducing their actual nuclear weapons stockpile. Oliver had no instructions from Zumwalt other than "Show this photograph to Henry."

Kissinger was working at a standup desk when Oliver arrived. The secretary examined the picture carefully. The plywood had been nicely fitted. The Soviets had used some excellent carpenters—in several places the photo's definition was still insufficient to show the seams. Kissinger did not bother to ask whom Oliver represented—he apparently knew. He did ask if there was another copy of the photo. When Oliver replied in the negative, Kissinger tore the picture in half, placed the pieces in a burn bag beneath his desk, and returned to the paper he had been reading. Oliver returned to the Pentagon. The CNO just nodded when he heard what transpired.[109]

Another difference arose over Israel and the Yom Kippur War of October 1973. Zumwalt believed that Kissinger was not supportive enough of Israel. In his autobiography, Zumwalt referred to Kissinger blaming Secretary of Defense James Schlesinger for late resupply flights to Israel during the war (Operation Nickle Grass). Zumwalt was not fooled: "This tale is just a tale and an extraordinarily disingenuous one at that. It was Henry himself who stalled the aircraft."[110]

Zumwalt later went into some detail about the events in Washington leading up to the war, as well as some of the confusion that reigned after it had started. Nixon was disengaged from events after Vice President Spiro Agnew resigned the vice presidency for taking bribes when he was governor of Maryland. Zumwalt also recalled a meeting with Moorer, who told Zumwalt that the "SECDEF's guidance in general about the way to respond to Israeli requests for supplies is that we are to be overtly niggardly and covertly forthcoming."[111] Zumwalt subsequently pressed Kissinger to increase support for Israel despite the risk of Soviet intervention, but to no effect. In fact, Zumwalt had already taken extraordinary actions that would affect the outcome of the war.

There were a number of warning signs in the Middle East in 1973, but Kissinger insisted they were false. Nixon, one of the United States' ablest presidents in international affairs but also at that time obsessed with the disintegration of his presidency under the weight of the Watergate scandal, deferred to his chief foreign policy adviser. Kissinger subsequently ordered the US government to do nothing that would change the military balance in the Middle East.

The United States had not been a major supplier of arms to Israel during its early years, the Israelis largely relying on exports from France and West Germany. A turning point had come in 1968 with the Johnson administration's decision to sell F-4s to Israel.[112] The Nixon administration had subsequently held up deliveries to induce Israel to reach an accommodation with Egypt over the Suez Canal and Sinai Peninsula and slow the progress of Israel's nuclear weapons program.[113] Meanwhile, the Soviets flooded the

Arab nations with arms.[114] Perhaps to even the odds, and despite instructions to the contrary, in September 1973 Zumwalt secretly directed the transfer of the latest Sidewinder air-to-air missile modifications to Israel. These changes proved critical to Israel a month later when the Yom Kippur War began.[115]

Despite Zumwalt's predictions proving more accurate than those of Kissinger, one might still criticize his covert actions as violating the spirit if not the letter of civilian control of the military.[116] On the other hand, with the Watergate crisis distracting Washington, there was some benefit to having senior military leaders keeping an eye on potential foreign policy crises.

Should there have been better oversight? The US military services have never been easy to manage, the Navy least of all. The Navy's bureaus, with the consent of Congress, effectively ran the service from the 1840s to the 1960s through their control over personnel and acquisition. The Navy secretary and the General Board (a prototypical naval general staff) were largely figureheads.[117] A similar state of affairs existed in the War Department until Elihu Root's reforms at the turn of the twentieth century.[118]

Today we often lament the lack of military experience among public officials, but it has never been a guarantee of success. Veterans have frequently made grievous administrative errors when serving as political appointees. Three of the most criticized secretaries of defense in history—Louis Johnson (Army), Robert McNamara (Air Corps), and Donald Rumsfeld (Navy)—were veterans and had more personal military experience than most civilians who occupied the position.[119] We will explore in chapter 5 the reasons why political appointees are often unsuccessful, but in the meantime note that one of our main contentions is that it is in the public's interest for the services to keep tabs on one another and other national-security agencies. Otherwise, there is a risk of reprising fiascos like the Bay of Pigs, when some have suggested the JCS refused to criticize the CIA's plans because it did not want to create a precedent for external meddling in military affairs.[120]

Zumwalt retired in July 1974. Saigon fell the next year, and the Vietnam War was finally over, at least for the United States. In a period of declining military spending, and despite the objections and interference of many of his peers, Zumwalt had transformed the Navy. The surface force was on a path to launching new ships and capabilities that would last well into the twenty-first century. Zumwalt had also won the High-Low ship-capability argument over the nuclear-power lobby and modernized the strategic force with the deployment of the Trident. Finally, the F-14 (the fleet-defense airplane the Navy built instead of the TFX/F-111) was in production.

The acquisition of new ships and weapons was all well and good, but setting the Navy on a new, post–Vietnam War path and establishing more progressive personnel standards were Zumwalt's greatest contributions. Perhaps someone other than Zumwalt would have fought equally as hard against the systemic racism that was crippling the service in the early 1970s, but that seems unlikely. Zumwalt's predecessors and competitors did not share his personal interest in social justice, as Anderson and McDonald's reminiscences make clear.

After Zumwalt retired, the Navy's commitment to his goals atrophied. Few of his successors or senior Navy flag officers shared his commitment to resolving racial and social tensions (especially gender issues), even if they made admirable progress dealing with other problems such as the rampant drug and alcohol use.[121] Fifty years later, the Navy was still invoking Zumwalt as the standard while admitting it had failed to eliminate racial bias within the service.[122] Zumwalt was a pathbreaker on core social issues in the military, even by today's standards.[123]

We have explored two very different approaches to change in the Navy at the end of a major war. Burke, as a result of his experiences during the Revolt of Admirals, believed he had to restore the Navy from an inferior position relative to the OSD and the Air Force. He empowered some individuals to pursue transformative technologies—for instance, Rickover with nuclear submarines and Adm. William Raborn with the Polaris program—but his adversarial approach alienated potential allies and hardened opposition.[124]

By contrast, Zumwalt planned, attacked, and directed radical change using outside advisers and a small group on his personal staff. He could have met the same fate as his predecessors, but like his mentor Nitze and his predecessor McDonald, Zumwalt was skilled at finding allies among the Pentagon's political leadership from both sides of the aisle. When his tour was ended, the Navy still had problems, but Zumwalt had addressed many of the outstanding issues his peers and predecessors had created or ignored. In doing so, he completed the process of yanking the Navy into the modern era.

SUMMARY

Zumwalt's tenure as CNO completed the Navy's adjustment to the post–World War II environment. Zumwalt was truly a transformational figure for the Navy but in a different fashion from his predecessors, who defined their legacies by battles won or ships constructed. Zumwalt, by contrast, convinced the Navy to accept and operate within the organizational realities of a powerful Air Force and secretary of defense. In yet another departure from his predecessors (with the exception of McDonald, with whom he shares few other similarities), Zumwalt had the sense to only fight city hall over what was vital for the long-term health of the Navy. And because Zumwalt was convinced the war in Vietnam was lost more than a year before American forces abandoned Saigon, he got the Navy a significant jump on the other services in moving to solve their post-Vietnam problems. Finally, Zumwalt almost singlehandedly addressed the pervasive social and racial inequities that were crippling the Navy's ability to recruit and retain good sailors—matters of life and death for the service in the age of the all-volunteer force.

Zumwalt had taken great strides with uneven results, and some of his achievements did not endure long after his departure. Unfortunately, Zumwalt had centralized power within his small personal staff and a group of loyalists primarily drawn from the surface-warfare community. Consequently, when Zumwalt retired, many Navy leaders remained unconvinced of the wisdom of some of Zumwalt's initiatives. Fortunately, two decades later, when it confronted its greatest budgetary crisis since the end of World War II, the Navy would have a leader who had learned from Zumwalt's missteps.

NOTES

1. There is an excellent summary of Zumwalt's tenure as CNO, and the cultural changes he inspired, in John Kuehn, "US Navy Cultural Transformations, 1945–2017: The Jury Is Still Out," in *The Culture of Military Organizations*, ed. Peter Mansoor and Williamson Murray (Cambridge: Cambridge University Press, 2019), 364–71.
2. John Finney, "Zumwalt Scores Rickover in Book," *New York Times*, April 15, 1976; Thomas Hone and Curtis Utz, *History of the Office of the Chief of Naval Operations, 1915–2015* (Washington, DC: NHHC, 2015), 262–63.
3. John Darrell Sherwood, *Black Sailor, White Navy: Racial Unrest in the Fleet during the Vietnam War Era* (New York: New York University Press, 2007), 40.
4. In 1970 Zumwalt established the CNO's Executive Panel (OP-00K), "whose membership . . . should be a mixture of civilian strategic and politico-military analysts, retired flag officers and active duty personnel." Elmo Zumwalt, *On Watch: A Memoir* (New York: Quadrangle, 1976), 285; Hone, *OPNAV*, 283. Capt. Kin McKee, who ran OP-00K and would later relieve Admiral Rickover, managed to recruit some of the nation's most expert minds to participate, volunteer their time, and share their insights. The panel was terminated in 2012. "DOD – 401 – Chief of Naval Operations Panel – Agency Authority," FACADatabase.gov, n.d., https://www.facadatabase.gov/FACA/apex/FACAPublicCommittee?id=a10t0000001h1aaAAA.
5. There is a question as to the accuracy of Zumwalt's description. Two other officers who were present dispute Zumwalt's account. Harold E. Shear, *The Reminiscences of Admiral Harold E. Shear, U.S. Navy (Ret.)* (Annapolis, MD: US Naval Institute, 1997), 159–60; and Raymond E. Peet, *The Reminiscences of Vice Admiral Raymond E. Peet, U.S. Navy (Ret.)* (Annapolis, MD: US Naval Institute, 1984), 163–68. Previously, Rickover

performed these intake interviews without an official recorder. After his experience with Zumwalt, Rickover insisted on having a notetaker present.

6. John Finney, "Zumwalt Scores Rickover in Book," *New York Times*, April 15, 1976.
7. Donald MacKenzie and Graham Spinardi, "The Shaping of Nuclear Weapon System Technology: US Fleet Ballistic Missile Guidance and Navigation: II: 'Going for Broke'—The Path to Trident II," *Social Studies of Science* 18 (1988): 582–84.
8. The Bureau of Ships handled ship design, construction, maintenance, and repair of Navy ships, among other things, from 1940 to 1966. "Records of the Bureau of Ships," National Archives and Records Administration, August 15, 2016, https://www.archives.gov/research/guide-fed-records/groups/019.html.
9. Charles Duncan, *The Reminiscences of Admiral Charles K. Duncan, U.S. Navy (Ret.)* (Annapolis, MD: US Naval Institute, 1978), 839.
10. At the Atomic Energy Commission, Rickover oversaw the development of the first full-scale, commercial nuclear power plant dedicated to peacetime operations.
11. For details, see Francis Duncan, *Rickover and the Nuclear Navy: The Discipline of Technology* (Annapolis, MD: Naval Institute Press, 1990); and Walter Poole, *Adapting to Flexible Response, 1960–1968* (Washington, DC: OSD Historical Office, 2013), 302–8.
12. There are similarities here to John ("Jackie") Fisher and Winston Churchill's determination to convert the Royal Navy from coal to oil after 1912. Daniel Yergin, *The Prize: The Epic Quest for Oil, Money and Power* (New York: Free Press, 2008), 134–48.
13. Zumwalt, *Memoir*, 101.
14. Government Accounting Office, "Nuclear or Conventional Power for Surface Combatant Ships?," PSAD-77-74, March 21, 1977, https://www.gao.gov/assets/120/117947.pdf.
15. See, e.g., William Beasley, "The Rise, Fall, and Early Reawakening of US Naval Professionalism,"' in *Redefining the Modern Military: The Intersection of Profession and Ethics*, ed. Nathan Finney and Tyrell Mayfield (Annapolis, MD: Naval Institute Press, 2018).
16. Today at the academy, two-thirds of the graduates must major in a STEM field (science, technology, engineering, or mathematics). Every midshipman completes a rigorous core curriculum heavily weighted toward math, physical sciences, and naval engineering, and every graduate receives a bachelor of science degree, even if they studied, say, the humanities or social sciences.
17. House Appropriations Committee, *Report on Russia by Vice Admiral Hyman G. Rickover, USN*, 86th Cong., 1st Sess. (Washington, DC: GPO), 67–73. See also Todd Forney, *The Midshipman Culture and Educational Reform: The U.S. Naval Academy, 1946–76* (Newark: University of Delaware Press, 2004), 118–22, 129ff.
18. Hone, *OPNAV*, 286.
19. James Stavridis and Mark Haggerot, "The Heart of an Officer: Joint, Interagency, and International Operations and Navy Career Development," *Naval War College Review* 62, no. 2 (2008): 26–41.
20. William McBride, *Technological Change in the United States Navy, 1865–1945* (Baltimore: Johns Hopkins University Press, 2000), 38–63.
21. Dave Oliver, *Against the Tide: Rickover's Leadership Principles and the Rise of the Nuclear Navy* (Annapolis, MD: Naval Institute Press, 2014), 148n3.
22. Rickover personally expressed this idea to Dave Oliver.
23. John Lehman, *Command of the Seas* (New York: Scribner, 1988), 24–26.
24. Enthoven oral history, JFKL.

25. Lawrence Korb, *The Fall and Rise of the Pentagon: American Defense Policies in the 1970s* (Westport, CT: Greenwood, 1979), 84ff., 116–17; Richard Hunt, *Melvin Laird and the Foundation of the Post-Vietnam Military, 1969–1973* (Washington, DC: OSD Historical Office, 2015), 15–19, 28–29, 252. See also Lawrence Korb, "Remembering Melvin Laird," *Politico*, December 31, 2016, https://www.politico.com/magazine/story/2016/12/melvin-laird-obit-214563; and Hone, *OPNAV*, 268–70.
26. Enthoven oral history, JKFL.
27. David Chu served as director and then assistant secretary of defense for program analysis and evaluation for twelve years beginning in May 1981. From 1978 to 1981, he served as the assistant director for national security and international affairs at the Congressional Budget Office and, after 2001, as the undersecretary of defense for personnel and readiness. Rudi Williams, "David Chu: DoD's Highest-Ranking Asian American Civilian," American Forces Press Service, May 15, 2002. Chu later became the president and CEO of the Institute for Defense Analyses and remains highly regarded in the defense analytic community.
28. See the enormous qualifications attached to Congressional Research Service, "Navy Nuclear-Powered Surface Ships: Background, Issues, and Options for Congress," September 29, 2010, https://fas.org/sgp/crs/weapons/RL33946.pdf; and Congressional Budget Office, *The Cost-Effectiveness of Nuclear Power for Navy Surface Ships*, May 2011, https://www.cbo.gov/sites/default/files/112th-congress-2011-2012/reports/05-12-nuclearpropulsion.pdf.
29. Zumwalt later formalized "Project Sixty" as the CNO Policy and Planning Guidance within OP-96. It would provide strategic guidance for Navy programmers. Hone, *OPNAV*, 282, 288–89.
30. John McLucas, *Reflections of a Technocrat* (Maxwell AFB, AL: Air University Press, 2006), 63ff.; Brian Frederickson, *The Laird-Packard Way: Unpacking Defense Acquisition Policy* (Maxwell AFB, AL: Air University Press, 2020), 46ff.; Scott Bledsoe and Mike Benitez, "Re-thinking the High-Low Mix, Part I: Origins Story," War on the Rocks, January 25, 2017, https://warontherocks.com/2017/01/re-thinking-the-high-low-mix-part-i-origins-story/; Scott Bledsoe and Mike Benitez, "Rethinking the High-Low Mix, Part II: Complexity's Death Spiral," War on the Rocks, March 21, 2017, https://warontherocks.com/2017/03/rethinking-the-high-low-mix-part-ii-complexitys-death-spiral/.
31. Burke oral history, Columbia.
32. "Chief of Naval Operations Zumwalt's Project 60, Part 1," Center for International Maritime Security, August 14, 2019, https://cimsec.org/chief-of-naval-operations-zumwalts-project-60-part-1/.
33. Hone, *OPNAV*, 283.
34. Zumwalt, *Memoir*, 63.
35. Decades later, Zumwalt is still being graded on the weapon systems he helped actualize. Robert Kozloski, "*Project SIXTY: Lessons for Today*," US Naval Institute blog, October 4, 2013, https://blog.usni.org/posts/2013/10/04/project-sixty-lessons-for-today.
36. Zumwalt, *Memoir*, 63.
37. When Vice Adm. Paul McCarthy was the commander of Seventh Fleet, which has responsibility for the Western Pacific, he concluded the *Perry*-class frigates required excessive maintenance relative to their utility. Accordingly he barred them from his fleet.
38. Pete Pagano, "Return of the Sea Control Ship," Center for International Maritime Security, August 29, 2017, http://cimsec.org/return-sea-control-ship/33847; Kyle Mizokami, "When the U.S. Navy Had Tiny Hot Rods That Flew over the Sea," *Popular*

Mechanics, December 23, 2015, https://www.popularmechanics.com/military/navy-ships/a18702/us-navy-pegasus-hydrofoils/.

39. "US Ship Force Levels," NHHC, November 17, 2017, https://www.history.navy.mil/research/histories/ship-histories/us-ship-force-levels.html.
40. Hone, *OPNAV*, 280.
41. This document was initially known as the "Yellow Bird," later the "Early Bird Brief." The Pentagon ceased publication in 2013, but *Defense News* releases its own variant. Claudette Roulo, "Era Ends for Pentagon's 'Early Bird' News Summary," Armed Forces Press Service, November 4, 2013, https://archive.defense.gov/news/newsarticle.aspx?id=121049; Defense News, "Early Bird Brief," https://www.defensenews.com/ebb/.
42. Gordon Craig, "Delbrück: The Military Historian," in *Makers of Modern Strategy: From Machiavelli to the Nuclear Age*, ed. Peter Paret (Princeton, NJ: Princeton University Press, 1986), 326–53.
43. Kenneth Werrell, *The Evolution of the Cruise Missile* (Maxwell AFB, AL: Air University Press, 1985), 146–53.
44. Gregory Engel, "Cruise Missiles and the Tomahawk," in *The Politics of Naval Innovation*, Research Report 4-94, ed. Bradd Hayes and Douglas Smith (Newport, RI: Center for Naval War Studies, US Naval War College, 1994), 20n12.
45. Lehman, *Command*, 164–70.
46. "Harnessing the Missiles," *New York Times*, May 27, 1972; Juan Vasquez, "Laird Discounts Big Arms Savings," *New York Times*, May 27, 1972; Werrell, *Cruise Missile*, 151ff.
47. Kenneth Werrell, "The Weapon the Military Did Not Want: The Modern Strategic Cruise Missile," *Journal of Military History* 53, no. 4 (1989): 419–38 (esp. 425ff.).
48. "[The] USAF reluctantly and, almost, belatedly hurried to 'get on board' to avoid getting 'a torpedo rammed up its bomb bay.'" Werrell, *Cruise Missile*, 156.
49. "Chief of Naval Operations Zumwalt's Project 60, Pt. 3," Center for International Maritime Security, August 27, 2019, https://cimsec.org/chief-of-naval-operations-zumwalts-project-60-pt-3/. See also Oliver, *Tide*, 49–58.
50. The following discussion draws from Hone, *OPNAV*, 292ff.
51. Zumwalt, *Memoir*, 167, appendix E.
52. The unstable commanding officer of the fictional minesweeper USS *Caine* in Herman Wouk's Pulitzer Prize–winning novel *The Caine Mutiny*.
53. Nixon White House Tape 491-11, Richard Nixon Presidential Library, Yorba Linda, CA (hereafter WHT); Zumwalt, *Memoir*, 182. The authors are grateful to Richard Moss and Nixontapes.org for assistance in locating the relevant conversations.
54. Thomas Fleming, "The Navy's Journey from Racial Segregation to Equality," *Navy Times*, July 23, 2019, https://www.navytimes.com/news/your-navy/2019/07/24/the-navys-journey-from-racial-segregation-to-equality/.
55. Morris MacGregor, *Integration of the Armed Forces, 1940–1965* (Washington, DC: Center for Military History, 2001), 58–98, 143–51, 234–52, 331–34, 412–27; Sherwood, *Black Sailor*, 1–15.
56. Y. K. Smith, "Navy Reformer Zumwalt Dies," *Washington Post*, January 3, 2000. See also Sherwood, *Black Sailor*, 30–54.
57. Zumwalt, *Memoir*, 217.
58. The chargers were dropped, but many of the Black Marines involved received less-than-honorable discharges. John Ismay, "The Untold Story of the Black Marines Charged with Mutiny at Sea," *New York Times*, August 19, 2020.

59. Seymour Hersh, "Navy Acts to Halt Racial Violence and Alleged Sabotage on Ships," *New York Times*, November 6, 1972.
60. Sherwood, *Black Sailor*, 193–226.
61. Drew Middleton, "Zumwalt Rebukes Top Navy Leaders on Racial Unrest," *New York Times*, November 11, 1972; "Text of Zumwalt's Remarks to Senior Naval Officers on Causes of Racial Unrest," *New York Times*, November 11, 1972.
62. To give a sense of the racial attitudes of the Navy's rank and file, when the Navy commissioned USS *George Washington Carver* (SSBN 656) in 1966, the first submarine named for a Black man, it made a special effort to crew the boat with equal numbers of Black and White enlisted (there were no Black submarine officers at the time). The boat was at sea during the 1968 election, but the sailors participated in the presidential election while submerged on November 5. George Wallace, the segregationist governor of Alabama, beat Richard Nixon. Hubert Humphrey was a distant third.
63. McDonald, *Reminiscences*, 238.
64. Appendix C, Anderson interview.
65. The key legislators were Richard Russell and John Stennis in the Senate and Carl Vinson, Mendel Rivers, and Edward Hébert in the House. All came from the South and supported segregation. Vinson, despite his retirement, was instrumental in keeping Zumwalt in office when Anderson launched a silent coup against the CNO in 1972 following the incidents on the *Kitty Hawk* and *Constellation*. Hone, *OPNAV*, 293.
66. Zumwalt, *Memoir*, 241.
67. WHT 491-11.
68. WHT 866-4. In fact, there was a race riot at Camp Lejeune, North Carolina, in July 1969 that left one Marine dead.
69. WHT 334-10.
70. WHT 385-30.
71. Leslie Julian Cullen, "Brown Water Admiral: Elmo R. Zumwalt, Jr. and United States Naval Forces Vietnam, 1968–1970" (PhD diss., Texas Tech University, 1998), 28. Zumwalt's daughter insisted the incident was only a youthful prank, with no malicious intent. Ann Zumwalt to Dave Oliver, email, April 7, 2021.
72. Zumwalt, *Memoir*, 197–98.
73. Dave Oliver, *A Navy Admiral's Bronze Rules: Managing Risk and Leadership* (Annapolis, MD: Naval Institute Press, 2021), 11, 54, 61, 127.
74. Linda English, "Nauticus Exhibit Tells Story of First African American Officer aboard USS *Wisconsin*," *Virginian-Pilot*, October 18, 2016, https://www.pilotonline.com/news/article_6c1e4f7c-ad5c-5372-bb80-6b8524c7990a.html.
75. "Navy Opens Way for Women aboard Warships," *Daily Republic*, August 8, 1972, https://www.newspapers.com/clip/1166157/1972-08-08-navy-opens-way-for-women/.
76. Dave Oliver was present at the discussion leading up to this press conference and its aftermath, a major setback that Zumwalt glosses over in his biography.
77. Zumwalt, *Memoir*, 265. The meeting in question took place in the Oval Office on November 30, 1972, but Nixon's taping system did not capture the remark. See "Presidential Daily Diary," 1972, Nixon Library, https://www.nixonlibrary.gov/president/presidential-daily-diary; and WHT 817-5.
78. Zumwalt, *Memoir*, 265.
79. "[The] injustices suffered by the 9,000 or so women in a Navy of half a million men and women, though real enough, and damaging enough to the Navy in the long run, could not be the highest immediate priority." Zumwalt, *Memoir*, 262.

80. The Tailhook Convention was an annual conference in Las Vegas of naval aviators. It had both professional and celebratory aspects, and it enjoyed semiofficial status within the Navy. For some years, there had been concern about the excessive consumption of alcohol at the event. In 1991 at least one aviator, Lt. Paula Coughlin, was assaulted at Tailhook. In the wake of the scandal, the HASC's Personnel and Compensation Subcommittee completed a study comparing the mistreatment of women in the 1990s with the earlier discrimination against Black men. House of Representatives, Military Personnel and Compensation Subcommittee, *Women in the Military: The Tailhook Affair and the Problem of Sexual Harassment*, 102d Cong., 2d Sess. (September 14, 1992).
81. Zumwalt, *Memoir*, 170.
82. Z-gram no. 20, September 9, 1970, https://www.history.navy.mil/research/library/online-reading-room/title-list-alphabetically/z/list-z-grams/z-gram-20.html.
83. Z-gram no. 68, December 23, 1970, https://www.history.navy.mil/research/library/online-reading-room/title-list-alphabetically/z/list-z-grams/z-gram-68.html.
84. Hone, *OPNAV*, 285.
85. Chiefs of each service, as well as the chairman of the JCS, are nominated by the president and confirmed by the Senate for two-year terms. By custom, a chief is renominated for a second term and, very infrequently (like Burke), a third. Only one chairman, Earle Wheeler, has served for longer than four years.
86. At this time, Oliver was assigned to the CNO's staff. Following up on whether senior admirals were following the Z-grams was one of his jobs, so he claimed one of the few remaining seats in the room.
87. Hone, *OPNAV*, 293, 296–97.
88. Anand Toprani, "'Our Efforts Have Degenerated into a Competition for Dollars': The 'Revolt of the Admirals,' NSC-68, and the Political Economy of the Cold War," *Diplomacy & Statecraft* 30, no. 4 (2019): 694ff.; Paul Nitze, *From Hiroshima to Glasnost: At the Center of Decision; A Memoir* (New York: Weidenfeld, 1989); Nicholas Thompson, *The Hawk and Dove: Paul Nitze, George Kennan, and the History of the Cold War* (New York: Picador, 2010), 250ff.
89. Record of telephone conversation (telcon), Laird, March 10, 1970, and March 13, 1970, NSA. All subsequent references to Kissinger's telcons are from the NSA.
90. Telcon, Zumwalt, August 18, 1970, and November 5, 1970. The report, like many before and since, called for personnel reductions at the Pentagon and various headquarters to stem administrative bloat. Hone, *OPNAV*, 281–82; Mark Lowenthal, *Defense Department Reorganization: The Fitzhugh Report, 1969–1970* (Washington, DC: Congressional Research Service, 1976), https://digital.library.unt.edu/ark:/67531/metadc1228816/.
91. Telcon, Zumwalt/Kissinger, February 24, 1971; telcon, Nixon, February 25, 1971. For additional background on the Nixon administration's approach to Allende following his inauguration, see Anand Toprani and Richard Moss, "Filling the Three-Year Gap: Nixon, Allende, and the White House Tapes, 1971–1973," *Passport: Newsletter of the Society of Historians of American Foreign Relations* 41, no. 3 (2011): https://shafr.org/sites/default/files/January11Draft6.pdf.
92. James Gregory Zumwalt II, lecture, US Naval War College, February 11, 2021. See also Sherwood, *Black Sailor*, 36.
93. Telcon, Moorer/Kissinger, August 2, 1971.
94. Telcon, Zumwalt, August 30, 1971.
95. Telcon, Zumwalt/Kissinger, February 10, 1972.

96. Telcon, Zumwalt/Kissinger, March 31, 1972; telcon, Kissinger/Zumwalt, September 6, 1973.
97. WHT 145-17; telcon, Zumwalt/Kissinger, October 2, 1972; telcon, Zumwalt/Kissinger, June 7, 192. See also Jean Gerard, "The U.S.-Soviet Maritime Agreement: A New Plan for Bilateral Cooperation," *Fordham International Law Journal* 1, no. 2 (1977): 22–43; and "Moscow Accepts Sea Freight Rise; Signs U.S. Accord," *New York Times*, October 15, 1972.
98. Telcon, Peterson/Kissinger, September 30, 1972.
99. Telcon, Guy Elwin Millard (deputy chief of mission, UK Embassy, Washington, DC)/ Kissinger, August 9, 1971.
100. Zumwalt lecture.
101. Telcon, Ron Ziegler / Kissinger, December 15, 1972.
102. WHT 866-4.
103. Ann Zumwalt to Dave Oliver, email, April 7, 2021.
104. Seymour Hersh, "Spying in the White House Said to Have Begun in '70," *New York Times*, February 3, 1974; James Rosen, "Nixon and the Chiefs," *The Atlantic*, April 2002, https://www.theatlantic.com/magazine/archive/2002/04/nixon-and-the-chiefs/302473/; James Rosen, "The Men Who Spied on Nixon: New Details Reveal Extent of 'Moorer-Radford Affair,'" Fox News, December 15, 2008, https://www.foxnews.com/politics/the-men-who-spied-on-nixon-new-details-reveal-extent-of-moorer-radford-affair; Hone, *OPNAV*, 295.
105. Telcon, Symington/Kissinger, September 20, 1973.
106. Telcon, Reubin O'Donovan Askew / Kissinger, September 15, 1975.
107. Zumwalt, *Memoir*, 400–406.
108. The lack of a large area sensor would prove to be an intelligence disaster that the Soviets would exploit to circumvent SALT. Oliver, *Bronze Rules*, 3.
109. Forty-two years later, Oliver was shaking hands with Kissinger in a receiving line after a Kissinger speech. "Ever find another copy of that picture?" Kissinger asked. Oliver again responded in the negative. "Good," Kissinger replied, and he turned to the next couple in the line.
110. Zumwalt, *Memoir*, 432.
111. Zumwalt, 434. This was another point of disagreement with Moorer, who blamed Israel for a "deliberate" attack on the intelligence-gathering ship USS *Liberty* in 1967. Thomas Moorer, "Betrayal behind Israeli Attack on U.S. Ship," *Houston Chronicle*, January 11, 2004, https://www.chron.com/opinion/outlook/article/Betrayal-behind-Israeli-attack-on-U-S-ship-1493153.php.
112. David Rodman, "Phantom Fracas: The 1968 American Sale of F-4 Aircraft to Israel," *Middle Eastern Studies* 40, no. 6 (2004): 130–44; Mitchell Bard, "U.S.-Israeli Strategic Cooperation: The 1968 Sale of Phantom Jets to Israel," Jewish Virtual Library, n.d., https://www.jewishvirtuallibrary.org/the-1968-sale-of-phantom-jets-to-israel.
113. William Beecher, "U.S. Said to Agree to Supply Israel 42 Phantom Jets," *New York Times*, February 6, 1972; Avner Cohen, "Israel Crosses Threshold," NSA Electronic Briefing Book 189, April 28, 2006, https://nsarchive2.gwu.edu/NSAEBB/NSAEBB189/index.htm; Noam Kochavi, *Nixon and Israel: Forging a Conservative Partnership* (Albany: State University of New York Press, 2009), 9ff.; Lewis Sorley, *Conventional Arms Transfers and the Nixon Administration: A Policy Analysis* (Lexington: University Press of Kentucky, 1983), 77ff.

114. Andrew Pierre, *Global Politics of Arms Sales* (Princeton, NJ: Princeton University Press, 1982), 138ff.; Robbin Laird and Erik Hoffmann, *Soviet Foreign Policy in a Changing World* (New York: Aldine, 1986), 713ff.; Craig Daigle, *The Limits of Détente: The United States, the Soviet Union, and the Arab-Israeli Conflict, 1969–1973* (New Haven, CT: Yale University Press, 2012); Alexander Bennett, "Arms Transfer as an Instrument of Soviet Policy in the Middle East," *Middle East Journal* 39, no. 4 (1985): 745–74; Robbin Laird, "Soviet Arms Trade with the Noncommunist Third World," *Proceedings of the Academy of Political Science* 35, no. 3 (1984): 196–213.
115. Several weeks before the war, Zumwalt provided Israel with the AIM-9L modification for the Sidewinder air-to-air missile, which increased its potential lethality by a factor of fifteen to twenty. Oliver, *Bronze Rules*, 11.
116. This anecdote supports the thesis of Peter Feaver in *Armed Servants: Agency, Oversight, and Civil-Military Relations* (Cambridge, MA: Harvard University Press, 2003) that the US military is prone to "shirking" in the face of "intrusive" civilian oversight that runs contrary to its preferences.
117. James Bradford, *The Admirals of the New Steel Navy: Makers of the American Naval Tradition, 1880–1930* (Annapolis, MD: Naval Institute Press, 1990), 101; Elliott Converse, *Rearming for the Cold War, 1945–1960* (Washington, DC: OSD Historical Office, 2012), 336ff.; Poole, *Flexible*, 285–89; Manley Irwin, *Silent Strategists: Harding, Denby, and the U.S. Navy's Trans-Pacific Offensive, World War II* (Lanham, MD: University Press of America, 2013), 6–9.
118. James Hewes, *From Root to McNamara: Army Organization and Administration, 1900–1963* (Washington, DC: Center of Military History, 1975), 3ff.; Terrence Gough, "The Root Reforms and Command," n.d., https://history.army.mil/documents/1901/Root-Cmd.htm. For a comparison of the Army and Navy, see James Locher, *Victory on the Potomac: The Goldwater-Nichols Act Unifies the Pentagon* (College Station: Texas A&M University Press, 2002), 16ff.
119. For example, see Tom Ricks, "The Best and Worst Defense Secretaries, as Rated by *Foreign Policy*'s Best Defense," *Foreign Policy*, January 9, 2014, https://foreignpolicy.com/2014/01/09/the-best-and-worst-defense-secretaries-as-rated-by-foreign-policys-best-defense/.
120. Brian Vandemark, *Road to Disaster: A New History of America's Descent into Vietnam* (New York: HarperCollins, 2018), 24–25. According to LeMay, "all they [the CIA] wanted was an answer to a question which beach was best." LeMay oral history, LBJL. See also Burke oral history, Columbia: "The Chiefs themselves did not realize how little the administration knew or how small their capability was for that kind of thing. And we didn't insist upon knowing."
121. Frederick Hartmann, *Naval Renaissance: The U.S. Navy in the 1980s* (Annapolis, MD: Naval Institute Press, 1990), 20ff.
122. Sam LaGrone, "Navy Learning from Past Attempts to Eliminate Bias in the Fleet," *USNI News*, September 23, 2020, https://news.usni.org/2020/09/23/navy-learning-from-past-attempts-to-eliminate-bias-in-the-fleet.
123. Phil Stewart, "Long-Withheld Pentagon Survey Shows Widespread Racial Discrimination, Harassment," Reuters, January 14, 2021, https://www.reuters.com/article/us-usa-military-civilrights-exclusive/exclusive-long-withheld-pentagon-survey-shows-widespread-racial-discrimination-harassment-idUSKBN29J1N1.
124. Raborn led the Office of Special Projects, which developed Polaris. He subsequently served as director of Central Intelligence from 1965 to 1966.

CHAPTER 4

1980s

Preparing for Life after the Cold War

The late 1980s was a complex and confusing period. While it appears obvious in hindsight, very few Americans at the time, including many high-ranking officials, realized until well after 1989 that the Soviet Union was on its last legs even as it continued to churn out military hardware.[1] One of the few who did was Adm. Frank Kelso, the CNO from 1990 to 1994. He used this insight to reshape the organization he led, which meant that for the immediate post–Cold War period, the Navy was easily the best-prepared service—quite a reversal from the situation following World War II.

What did Kelso see that so many of his contemporaries missed? Why him and not someone else? One possible reason was his service in the submarine community. Unlike the rest of the Navy or the other services, the submarine community had not been distracted by Vietnam or the subsequent skirmishes in places such as Iran, Lebanon, Grenada, Libya, and Panama. Kelso had participated in some of these actions after he became an admiral, but for the first two decades of his career, as a submariner, he was focused on the Soviet Union and preserving an edge in the "balance of terror" (assured second-strike capability) between the nuclear-armed superpowers.[2]

Nuclear submarines were key components in the US military strategy against the Soviet Union.[3] Laypeople might think that the primary responsibility of US submarines then (and today) was the same as during World War II—sinking merchant ships. Actually, alone among the Navy's communities, the submarine community abandoned much of its wartime legacy in the 1950s (a shift we will further discuss in chapter 8). US submarines gave up hunting enemy merchant ships. What was the point, after all, when the Soviet Union did not rely on overseas commerce? Instead, US submarines' most important contributions during the Cold War were providing assured nuclear deterrence and gathering intelligence that was otherwise impossible to obtain.[4] To do this, US attack submarines spent years in Soviet backyards. From peering through their periscopes, many submarine officers were as familiar with the skylines of Murmansk, Vladivostok, and Petropavlovsk as those of any American city.[5]

With that background, for submariners, three events in the late 1980s suggested that the foundational assumption of the Cold War was dissolving. The first was a Soviet photo-op in Houston in the fall of 1989. While on an official visit to NASA's Johnson Space Center in Texas, Boris Yeltsin, one of the three men then competing to run the Soviet Union, took a side trip to an unremarkable grocery store in the small town of Clear Lake.[6]

The average American overlooked the significance of Yeltsin's unplanned stopover as well as his subsequent public remarks about the quantity and quality of food he found there. It was, after all, only a local market—there were literally tens of thousands of them in the United States. Even small towns had one or two supermarkets.

From Yeltsin's perspective, this was outrageous. Soviet citizens had suffered for decades to build the military and nuclear forces Soviet leaders considered essential to their security. The Soviet people had also subsidized client regimes across the Third World, from Cuba to Angola to Vietnam. Finally, they had suffered tens of thousands of casualties in the failed war in Afghanistan. What did they have to show for all of this? The Soviet Union could not even feed itself and depended on grain imports from the West. When oil prices were high, the Soviet Union could afford its imports of food and high-tech equipment, but once petroleum prices collapsed in 1986, Moscow was reliant on Western banks for hard-currency loans and credits.[7]

After General Secretary Mikhail Gorbachev took power, he realized that the current system was unsustainable and sought to rescue communism through reforms affecting many sectors of Soviet society. Because defense spending was growing out of control, Gorbachev wanted the Soviet military to adopt a "defensive" framework that eschewed violent "class struggle," while he wound down costly foreign adventures such as the Afghanistan War and negotiated arms-control agreements with West.[8] Ordinary Soviet citizens may not have fully understood how much they were spending on nuclear weapons, but they well knew that many shelves in their stores were bare. The discrepancies between Soviet pretensions and reality gave Yeltsin an opportunity to undercut Gorbachev. Yeltsin had once been a protégé of Gorbachev but had broken with him over the slow pace of reform. When Yeltsin broadcast the images of a fully stocked supermarket in Clear Lake on Soviet television, he was sending a shocking message about the failures of communism as an economic system and the costs of maintaining an empire.

Yeltsin's intent was not to replay the famous 1959 "Kitchen Debate" between Vice President Richard Nixon and Soviet premier Nikita Khrushchev. At that time, Soviet visitors had gawked at the conveniences afforded middle-class American housewives, but Khrushchev had conceded nothing to Nixon and extolled the Soviet system. Three decades later, the story was different. Yeltsin was attempting to manipulate political outcomes in the Soviet Union through the medium of the American media. He needed public support to chip away at the Soviet empire, especially in Eastern Europe. This expensive set of satellite countries existed only to provide defense in depth against the armies of the North Atlantic Treaty Organization (NATO). Gorbachev recognized the burden of Soviet military expenditures, but until 1989 he was unwilling to relinquish the Soviet empire. Yeltsin had no such reservations because he wanted to focus on the development of Russia and worried that Gorbachev would rally opposition in Soviet institutions. Yeltsin's campaign would finally succeed in 1991 when the Soviet Union was dissolved.[9]

In the United States, a few people understood the purpose of Yeltsin's visit to Clear Lake. A number of submariners were probably among them. Why? Since the beginning of the Cold War, that small group had access to highly classified and unvarnished intelligence gathered during patrols off the Soviet coast.[10] Because their mission involved reading the Soviets' mail, the submariners knew better than most that conditions in the Soviet Union were getting truly desperate.[11]

Submariners also knew that coercion was becoming a less effective tool of control for the regime. A few weeks after Yeltsin's visit, a second critical event occurred—the Berlin Wall fell on November 9, 1989. Remarkably, there was no Soviet reaction. Why did the Soviets simply stand aside while their most loyal client regime was overwhelmed by popular unrest? In 1956 and 1968 Moscow had sent tanks into the streets of Budapest and Prague. This time the Soviet Army stayed in its barracks.[12] What was happening?

During the subsequent Malta Conference between Gorbachev and President George H. W. Bush aboard the flagship of the Soviet Mediterranean Fleet, the Soviets announced they were finished with Cold War competition. On December 3, 1989, Gorbachev's senior military adviser, Marshal Sergei Akhromeyev, prepared for Bush a one-page pictorial that showed the Soviet Union surrounded by US naval forces.[13] Two years before, Akhromeyev had presented a similar "letter" to senior US military officials to highlight the aggressive posture of US forces against the Soviet Union. Now, however, Gorbachev's accompanying words, according to Vice Adm. J. D. Williams (a submariner then serving as the commander of Sixth Fleet) were "We have read every one of your submarine messages for ten years and have been unable to find or kill even one of them [the US submarines]. We quit."[14]

Despite Yeltsin's visit to the Texas supermarket, the fall of the Berlin Wall, and the revelations from the Malta meeting, many Americans—particularly if they were not members of the Bush administration and dealing with Soviets directly—still struggled to grasp the immensity of the changes unfolding before them.[15] The Cold War had gone on for two generations. After almost fifty years, it was impossible for many in the national-security community to contemplate a life beyond the comfortable certainties of bipolarity.

Following the collapse of the Soviet Union in December 1991, many US officials were content to rest on their laurels or speculate about how to establish American hegemony indefinitely.[16] Kelso was an outlier. He realized that the military was in a new race to adapt to the new world. If the Soviet Union was no longer a threat and China remained a land power in Asia, the United States would require a very different Navy.[17] But time was of the essence. Hanging over everyone's head was the certainty of future budget cuts to fund a "peace dividend."[18]

Just as after 1945, many military leaders refused to acknowledge what was happening. Some members of the Bush administration, most notably Secretary of Defense Dick Cheney and JCS chairman Colin Powell, acknowledged, with varying levels of enthusiasm, that US military forces would have to shrink, if only to get ahead of those arguing for even deeper cuts.[19] Powell, in fact, articulated sweeping reductions in force levels—the so-called base force—of up to 25 percent from Cold War levels.[20] Kelso's predecessor, Adm. Carlisle Trost, opposed Powell, but Kelso saw the writing on the wall.[21] He also recognized that the Navy had an opportunity to get ahead of the process:

> [It] was my perception and my belief that there was no way that the Navy or any of the armed forces were going to remain at the same size they have been maintained over the period of the time of the Cold War, and frankly I did not believe one could make a case for them to remain at that size. . . . There were those who did not agree. . . . They wanted to hold on to a larger Navy, believing the country would continue to deploy forces as we had done before. . . . My view was that it would not happen that way; that such a stance would likely accelerate the freefall.[22]

THE KELSO ALTERNATIVE

We should not assume the challenge confronting Kelso was identical to the one the Navy had faced after World War II or even to the problems Elmo Zumwalt had dealt with after the Vietnam War.[23] There was no need to modify the fleet to accommodate major technological changes. Race relations within the Navy were much improved, although gender relations still needed major work.[24] In the realm of strategy and budgets, however, the task confronting Kelso and the other service chiefs was similar to what their predecessors had confronted after World War II and Vietnam. Simply put, the world was changing, and the Navy needed to alter course on its own before someone else seized the helm.

The challenges for the Navy were both intellectual and practical. Solving them required a ruthless calculation of assets and liabilities rather than an accommodation clouded by sentiment and tradition. The admirals had to answer the same set of questions that had bedeviled every generation of naval leaders since Mahan. What was the future role of the Navy? How would it contribute to the national welfare? What physical and human assets were required? What capabilities had to be discarded to preserve the Navy's qualitative and technological edge?

Change is potentially more contentious during a period of austerity, so the sooner the Navy started, the better the chances for success. The team Kelso designated to lead the effort recognized it was vital to start before Congress turned off the money spigot. Once the White House or Congress demanded economies, there would be an overwhelming temptation to adopt across-the-board cuts to preserve internal harmony among the services and within each service. Such an approach might be good for the military's morale in the short run, but it carried long-term risks. Most notably, as Arleigh Burke recognized in the 1950s, compromising or logrolling defers or avoids making hard choices about what will be necessary moving forward.

In these circumstances, it is always easier to stand pat. Immediately after the Cold War ended, the Air Force and Army avoided many hard choices. The two services made changes but not enough, especially in terms of acquisitions and infrastructure. Both services largely retained their Cold War infrastructure and kept investing huge sums to develop weapons designed to fight the Soviet Army in Europe, such as the stealthy F-22 fighter, the Crusader self-propelled howitzer, and the Comanche attack helicopter.[25]

The Navy chose a different path. Understanding why requires knowing how its leaders perceived what was happening in the world. Fortunately, there is a record of how Kelso approached the problems confronting the Navy, and it provides many useful insights that national-security leaders may wish to apply in the future.

It starts with an obscure office in the Pentagon. Just as in 1949, when the Revolt of the Admirals was coordinated not from the CNO's office but rather from the then captain Burke's OP-23, the Navy's pivot to the post–Cold War world was led from a small but powerful office that took all the inputs from its various components of the Navy and assembled them into what was known as the program objective memorandum (POM).[26] Today that office is known as N80, the Programming Division of the Directorate for the Integration of Capabilities and Resources, but back in the 1980s it was called OP-80 and led by the OP-08 (a three-star deputy CNO and the former OP-090).[27]

Since McNamara, the POM has been the building block of the budget process. Each service and defense agency has a POM, which is a five-year plan for how it plans to translate its Defense Planning Guidance or Service Program Guidance—both of which are derived from the National Security Strategy, the National Defense Strategy, and the National Military Strategy—into reality. The comptroller for the secretary of defense resolves conflicts among the services and puts everything together into a single document, which the OSD then uses for its budget submission to the White House.[28]

There are some fundamental differences among how the Navy and Marine Corps and the other two services construct their portion of the POM. In the Navy, each component's inputs are balanced against the other inputs at the Pentagon and may be modified or eliminated depending on how OPNAV (OP-80) assesses that the assignment of dollars will affect the Navy's overall capabilities and priorities. Contrary to this approach, the Army and Air Force assume that the component commanders can and have performed that rationalization. At the Pentagon, therefore, the two services generally accept the decisions made by individual headquarters and tabulate the various inputs when building their POMs.[29] Unlike the Navy, the Army and Air Force have no central authority to ensure that their POM's components are integrated horizontally and vertically.

Because of this role in constructing the POM, OP-80 therefore had extraordinary influence. This document is the lever by which CNOs put their stamp on the service. Old timers at the Pentagon often speak nostalgically about the reorganizations that periodically rippled through OPNAV as various factions fought over control of different aspects of its mission. OP-80, however, was never reorganized, only renamed. It was and arguably remains the source of the CNO's power. The intricacies of the "how" are beyond the scope of this book. The key fact is that Kelso's ability to reshape the Navy arose from the fact that the Navy's POM was prepared centrally, under his control, a few doors away from his own office.[30]

In the late 1980s, OP-80 had a staff of about thirty people, mainly officers who represented each of the Navy's communities. A two-star admiral ran the office and was advised by a senior career member of the Senior Executive Service (SES). A one-star rear admiral served as the deputy, while a post-major-command captain managed the "bullpen" (the designation applied to the open space where most officers' desks were located).[31]

The officers who staffed the desks in OP-80 were responsible for "selling" the needs of their community to their peers in the bullpen. These men generally held the rank of commander and were handpicked for the assignment, which meant they were up-and-comers in their communities.

In years past, during POM development, the heads of the Navy's warfare communities (aviation, surface warfare, and submarines), support areas (logistics, etc.), and all the other "claimants" sent their program requests to OP-80.[32] There they were combined and cross-checked against various algorithms written to reflect past experience and any new guidance from the CNO.

For example, an algorithm might be used to calculate the monthly repair costs for a fighter airplane that flies thirty hours a month and had been in service from six to eight years. The algorithm may show that maintenance costs increase when the airplane is in its twelfth to fourteenth year of service or flies more than forty hours a month. If one of these new conditions applied and the unit servicing a hundred of those airplanes did not revise its budget submittal, OP-80 would ask questions. As an example of a common sleight-of-hand, a field unit might submit a lower budget request for older aircraft by claiming it had a new plan for improved maintenance. The resulting fiscal savings were often a pretext to divert funds to a senior officer's pet project. So, whenever a suspicious budget request arrived, a red flag would go up for the appropriate bullpen officer.

After the bullpen officers investigated and reconciled the various program requests against one another and the CNO's goals, they were also assembling the POM. They then briefed the final product in one or two well-attended meetings that always included the CNO, the commandant of the Marine Corps, and both the secretary and undersecretary of the Navy.

Because there were tens of thousands of choices affecting hundreds of thousands of items in every POM, for decades the process had been conducted in great secrecy. There was a fear that nothing would get done if every budget request was subject to "reclamas," which is the Pentagon term for "But did you think about this?"[33] In case the reclamas did not have the desired effect, there was the inevitable follow-up of "You may have considered that, but I now have someone even more senior who wishes to complain." Consequently, there was a gentleman's agreement within OP-80 that no one discussed what went on inside the bullpen with outsiders. The one exception was if the CNO or N-8 (the vice admiral to whom OP-80 reported) wanted the information shared, in which case bullpen members were the authorized "leak channel." One study aptly labeled the whole process as "competition, expert analyst intervention, imposed integration & opaque high-level decision(s)."[34]

This opaque process created a fair bit of controversy across the Department of the Navy (recall that the Navy supports the Marines in many areas). There was a great deal of suspicion that the favored communities—specifically the flyboys, the "bubble-heads" (submariners), "body merchants" (anyone involved in personnel), and, of course, the Marines—were somehow hiding the true cost of their pet projects and slipping those burdens onto the unsuspecting backs of the rest of the Navy. The director of OP-80 worried that the kinds of changes the Navy needed with the end of the Cold War would be impossible unless everyone's cards were on the table and face up. He therefore decided it was time to make the POM process transparent and collaborative.

This approach would complement Kelso's emphasis on total quality leadership (TQL). Once in office, Kelso would put a great deal of his prestige behind this concept, which was adapted from William Edwards Deming's management principles.[35] Kelso explained, "I wanted a process by which the senior leaders had to get involved from the beginning and become a part of the detailed planning. It should be their plan. I wanted it to be their plan. I wanted the admirals of all warfare disciplines to have to work with and listen to the problems of the entire Navy."[36]

THE KELSO PROCESS

A few months before Kelso became CNO, Rear Adm. Dave Oliver, who was then serving as the head of OP-80, set up a forum of Navy admirals and Marine generals to receive a set of independent briefings to establish a common base of knowledge among Navy and Marine leaders and then expand these briefings to cover current issues affecting the two services. By educating leaders about the state of the world, the flag officers could subsequently make informed decisions about the factors involved in a POM for a postwar Navy. A similar series of meetings had proved useful to Zumwalt two decades earlier when he was CNO. The forum would even meet in the same Pentagon room (4D710) that Zumwalt had used for such meetings.

Setting up such a forum sounds easy, but it was not. It was vital that each of the invited thirty-five admirals and generals attend every meeting. Otherwise, when meetings became contentious, as they surely would, there would be a temptation for a key member to avoid a gathering or send a powerless subordinate who lacked decision authority to sit in their stead. Accordingly, the forum's leaders established some ground rules. Meetings started at 5:30 a.m. so that no one could claim that they had a scheduling conflict or a meeting with a superior. No attendance substitutes were permitted, and no minutes were published. This meant that affected parties had to attend to know what happened. The lack of minutes also allowed people to speak freely without fear of reprisal.

Among the questions to be addressed:

- What was happening with the United States' peer competitors?
- How long was the current geopolitical situation likely to persist?
- Were there historical parallels that might guide the Navy's thinking?
- Should the Navy expect funding levels to change drastically?

The forum began by commissioning independent studies from three civilians who were hopefully immune from pressure within the Navy or the OSD to come up with a particular answer:

- Jacques Gansler, the senior vice president of The Analytic Sciences Corporation (today TASC), who seven years later became undersecretary of defense for acquisition for President Bill Clinton
- Dov Zakheim, the CEO of the analytic firm System Planning Corporation, who a decade later became the Pentagon comptroller for President George W. Bush
- Phil Odeen, who was then the managing partner of the accounting firm Coopers & Lybrand and subsequently became CEO of BDM and then chairman of TRW, two technical services firms that were also major defense contractors

These men were among the most respected defense analysts in the United States. Contracts were also awarded to two federally funded research and development centers: the Institute for Defense Analyses (IDA) and the aforementioned CNA. It is important to note that the Navy was not asking for recommendations but rather for data to reach its own conclusions.

Figure 4.1 was developed during these briefings and shows defense funding in constant dollars. Some people who saw it thought it indicated a base level of public support for defense and that spending rose above it during periods of tension. Others disagreed—they saw only periodic spikes

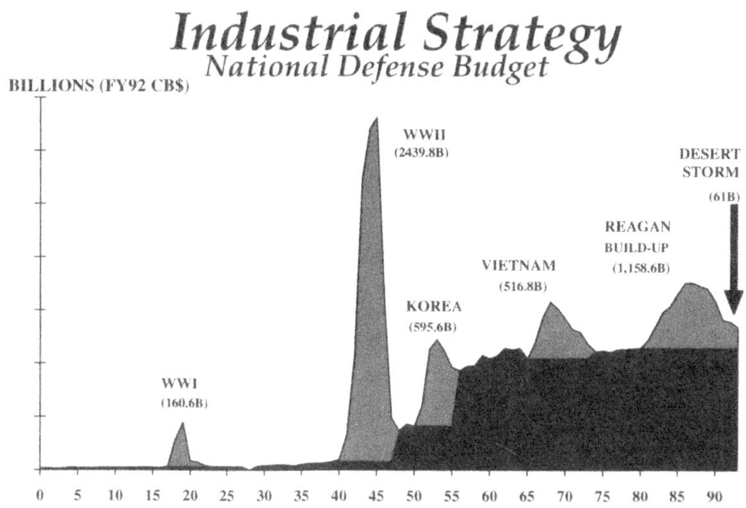

Figure 4.1 Industrial Strategy: National Defense Budget

Source: Office of the Chief of Naval Operations, OP-80 (Navy Programming and Planning), 1991. Original in Dave Oliver's possession.

and declines. Nevertheless, by the end of the briefings, the entire "Breakfast Club" had reached the following conclusions:

1. Defense spending would decrease.
2. Probably no peer competitor would arise for the next twenty to thirty years—with the caveat that a determined enemy could become a threat within as little as a decade.

These findings bear a superficial resemblance to the "Ten-Year Rule" that Britain adopted in 1919. Updated annually, the ruled shaped defense expenditures on the assumption that the country would not fight any major wars for the next ten years.[37] Critics of the rule claimed that it left Britain unprepared for World War II.[38]

This is not a useful analogy for understanding either British decision-making after World War I or the Kelso process. First, the British rule was abandoned in 1932—a year *before* Adolf Hitler took power in Germany—so it can hardly be the sole reason why Britain was unprepared for war in 1939. Second, critics overlook the precarious nature of the British economy after

World War I, which left the country with high unemployment, inflation, and budget and trade deficits. British officials of the time considered a healthy economy to be the "fourth arm" of defense alongside the army, navy, and air force. A strong economy, they reckoned, would allow Britain to borrow cheaply to fund a protracted war, which officials hoped would deter aggressor nations.[39] How exactly would an economic collapse in the 1920s exacerbated by high defense spending, when no great-power adversary existed, have served the cause of containing fascism in the 1930s?

Finally, the men and women of the naval Breakfast Club were not creating a postwar grand strategy to last for all time.[40] Rather, they were making tough decisions about the structure of the Navy based on an unsentimental assessment of the budgetary outlook after the Cold War. They brought their collective military wisdom to bear on one question above all others: Was the Navy's force structure, both current and planned—the one that so many exceptional individuals had spent forty years optimizing for the Cold War—still appropriate? If not, maintaining or moderately downsizing the Cold War force would hamstring future leaders by saddling them with expensive and obsolete infrastructure and systems while starving the services' critical R & D elements.

Figure 4.2 was probably the most critical one in the presentations the supporting staff developed for the club. It showed that Congress, as a whole, was not influenced by the arguments each service deployed to claim it was more deserving of funding than the others. This implied that when the axe fell, it would land on everyone's neck.

Given Congress's preference to provide each service with a consistent share of the overall defense budget, the Breakfast Club decided that, when cuts came, the Navy and Marines should not waste time trying to steal from the other services. They should instead focus their energies on preserving core capabilities for the future.

While this might seem like a minor decision or just basic policy, for the Breakfast Club it was a monumental step. It was telegraphing that the wider Navy community (including the Marines) was not going to waste time solving problems at each other's expense or that of the Air Force and the Army. For people raised on the hearty diet of interservice rivalry, this was not an easy decision to make. Many members of the club still remembered hearing about the Revolt of the Admirals, even if their personal knowledge of the specifics was hazy or biased.

As we explained at the end of chapter 1, perhaps the worst legacy of the "revolt" was inculcating a degree of smugness among naval officers that they did not have to explain themselves to outsiders. McNamara and the

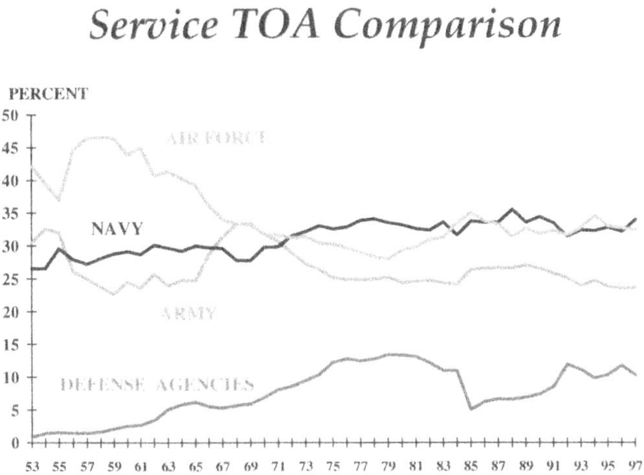

Figure 4.2 Service Total Obligatory Authority Comparison

Source: Office of the Chief of Naval Operations, OP-80 (Navy Programming and Planning), 1991. Original in Dave Oliver's possession.

challenges of the 1970s (the fallout from Vietnam and the postwar budget cuts) had shaken that confidence, but it had rebounded following Ronald Reagan's election in 1980. His administration pushed through major increases in defense spending. Reagan was no longer in office by the time Kelso took over, but many naval officers still believed the Navy was living a charmed existence thanks to John Lehman, whom nearly everyone considered the most effective Navy secretary since Forrestal.[41]

Lehman was a charismatic advocate for the Navy and made many important changes to how it operated, such as engineering Rickover's ouster, but we should not exaggerate his accomplishments. Despite temporarily arresting the decrease in ship numbers, apart from a brief funding bump at the start of the Reagan administration, even Lehman admitted that the Navy's share of the defense budget relative to the other services and the Department of Defense during his tenure had declined.[42]

Another one of Lehman's initiatives had been to raise the public profile of the Navy, but it was unclear how well he had succeeded. The leaders of the Breakfast Club understood that few people outside of the Beltway could distinguish among the different service uniforms and ranks, much less master esoteric subjects such as the services' roles, missions, and functions. Ordinary people were, in fact, completely uninterested in interservice "food fights." They paid their taxes and expected the military professionals to do their best with a minimum of fuss or waste. For uniformed men and women who had devoted their lives to military service and served in unhospitable or dangerous locations, the public's indifference was difficult to fathom. To disabuse club members of any notion that the public was deeply engaged with the Navy's mission, however, one morning, a member of the club (Oliver) read aloud from an article mentioning how in Kansas City most viewers of *Top Gun*—a movie about naval aviators—considered the film a "terrific Air Force recruitment movie."

Having achieved consensus on the immediate fiscal outlook, the organizers of the morning briefings decided that the best way to proceed was to examine relevant programs in front of all thirty-five admirals and generals attending—a number that constituted a quarter of the total in the Navy and Marine Corps and represented every community. Within the Navy, the sacred cows of the post–Cold War period—the expensive items everyone wanted to examine—were aviation, submarines, and personnel. In addition, the admirals had questions about the number and cost of the Navy's bases.

PUTTING THE NAVY ON A FIRM FOUNDATION

The first problem facing the Breakfast Club was getting rid of costly, unnecessary Cold War weapon systems. Specifically, Navy was designing an unaffordable airplane—the A-12—under a flawed contract structure to do an unnecessary job (stealth penetration of Soviet airspace). It was also building a prohibitively expensive nuclear-powered attack submarine (the *Seawolf* class) when there were no competitors above or below the waves. Interestingly enough, there did not appear to be any immediate issues within the surface-warfare community, with the exception of liquidating the remains of the nuclear-powered surface fleet that Rickover had championed over Zumwalt's opposition. In fact, the new *Arleigh Burke* destroyers were exceptional anti-air-warfare and sea-control ships—albeit a tad expensive for the post–Cold War world.

Some dilemmas proved easier to solve than expected. The *Seawolf* was designed for the Cold War. It could close on the Soviet coast undetected and shower the enemy with a barrage of cruise missiles launched from its torpedo tubes. Each submarine could, theoretically, deliver the same firepower as a strike from a carrier's air wing. Was such capability still necessary? Vice Adm. Dan Cooper (the "submarine czar"—OP-02) tackled the issue by forming a group to study the development of a littoral submarine, which would still have many of the same state-of-the-art capabilities as the *Seawolf* but at a significantly lower cost.[43]

Cooper's group concluded that if the submarine community continued to build the *Seawolf* boats, the whole Navy would suffer. The Soviets understood that quantity sometimes has a quality all its own, particularly as a deterrent. The *Seawolf* boats were, conversely, soaking up a disproportionate amount of the shipbuilding budget, which hobbled the entire fleet. Besides impairing the construction of surface ships, the group believed that building the *Seawolf* would prevent the submarine community from devoting sufficient resources to R & D to react to the next generation's peer threat. The submarine force, to its credit, recognized these issues on its own as well as the need to find a replacement.

In preparation for his 1992 State of the Union speech, President George H. W. Bush announced he was canceling the *Seawolf* and replacing it with a new, less expensive submarine. The latter eventually became the *Virginia* class.[44] After some congressional pushback to ease the disruption at the Electric Boat shipyard in Groton, Connecticut, the government capped production of the *Seawolf* class to three boats instead of the planned twenty-nine. Electric Boat would then shift to production of the *Virginia* class.

In firepower and performance, the *Virginia*-class submarines were less capable than the *Seawolf* submarines they were replacing, but the benefits to the Navy outweighed the drawbacks. The service had ended the Cold War with thirty-two SLBM submarines and ninety-three attack submarines.[45] This might seem like a large fleet but not compared to the Cold War challenge. Considering that only one-third of these boats were normally on patrol at any given time, if hostilities began, there were never enough attack submarines to fulfill all of their tasks, such as hunting down the more than three hundred Soviet submarines.[46]

The problem was now reversed. In a post–Cold War world without a peer competitor, the Navy could not afford to maintain the number of submarines the United States had already built. But no matter what the circumstances, submarines were still the United States' first line of defense, and the Navy needed its boats to remain state-of-the-art. It therefore made sense to scrap the older attack boats to afford at least twenty-five newer submarines on each coast. As for the strategic submarine component (the Trident-armed boats), the Navy would make any decisions regarding these force levels in concert with the Air Force and the Joint Staff.

The size of the attack-submarine force was not based on maintenance requirements, ocean size, or particular deployment patterns. The Navy believed the greatest two dangers to this force were lagging behind the technology curve and losing the so-called Medal of Honor edge. Submarine crews had been ineffectual in the Pacific during the first year of the war against Japan until the Navy fixed its faulty torpedoes and found commanders with sufficient skills and aggressiveness.[47] Kelso knew he needed sufficient submariners, especially officers, so that the Navy had enough numbers to replace subpar skippers during any future conflict.[48] If the country decided to ramp up submarine production to meet a new threat, Cooper's committee decided that a force of fifty boats would provide a sufficient technical, research, and professional base. The results of this change in submarine strategy were included in the budget President Bush submitted to Congress in January 1991.

Another group of flag officers were working a similar problem in aviation. Vice Adm. John "Spider" Lockhart, the commander of Naval Air Systems Command (NAVAIR), labeled their problem the "shadows on the ramp." He was referring here to the venerable practice of keeping old planes in reserve as replacements or for spare parts, the cost of which was limiting his ability to maintain the more modern aircraft currently in service. During the Cold War, the Navy had accumulated one-third more airplanes than needed to fulfill carrier and training requirements. Many of these were older planes that had been held in reserve in the event of war, since the Navy worried that the defense industry could not respond quickly enough to replace early losses.

While it may appear counterintuitive, as with automobiles the less a plane is used, the more expensive it becomes to maintain.[49] In the post–Cold War, the old planes were soaking up maintenance dollars but providing no return. Using scarce funds to maintain nonflying airplanes consequently reduced the full-mission capability rates on the fifteen hundred planes in service. According to Vice Adm. Joseph Dyer (who succeeded Lockhart at NAVAIR), "investment in nonproductive capital would be better deployed in better utilization and modernization."[50]

Industry had developed new manufacturing methods since World War II. Within the field of aviation, airplane construction techniques had altered so that it made it unnecessary for NAVAIR to retain tens of thousands of reserve aircraft. Concurrently, changes in precision-part manufacturing and numerical machining, combined with revolutions in information technology and air transport, had greatly simplified logistics. Spare parts could now be available worldwide in hours rather than in days, weeks, or months. These advances permitted the Defense Logistics Agency and the services to reduce their costs by eliminating many storage areas and revising their purchasing requirements.

To the surprise of many who did not attend the early morning meetings, the aviation working group agreed to reduce the aircraft inventory by thousands. Each plane that was scrapped, sold, or sent to the boneyard saved the Navy millions each year. So much for the problem of the shadows on the ramp—they were merely an appetizer for the other savings to come.

KICKING THE HABIT OF LONG-RANGE STRIKE

An aviation problem that proved far more difficult to fix was the ill-starred A-12.[51] Development flaws had multiplied and drawn external scrutiny. Fortunately, the same group that studied the shadows issue had been working the A-12 problem for several months.[52] This aircraft was supposed to replace the Navy's long-range, carrier-strike workhorse, the A-6 Intruder. Secretary of the Navy John Lehman, who signed off on the A-12, was a Naval Reserve bombardier/navigator qualified in A-6s.[53] He disliked the A-6's potential replacement, the F/A-18 (Hornet), which was unsuited for long-range bombing missions because of its inadequate fuel capacity and bomb load.[54] Lehman wanted a new long-range strike aircraft so the Navy could compete with the Air Force.[55]

In 1988 one of Lehman's successors awarded McDonnell Douglas and General Dynamics a contract to develop the stealth airplane that would eventually be designated the A-12.[56] It was a fixed-price contract of $4.4 billion to build twelve prototypes, with the Navy and contractors splitting any cost overruns up to $4.8 billion.

From the first day of the initial decision, two cracks appeared in the A-12 program's foundation. One was fiscal. A fixed-price contract is one where the contractor receives a specific amount, as opposed to cost-plus, where they get a certain percentage beyond their costs. This contracting model has proven destructive when developing a radically new concept.[57] A fixed-price contract may be a useful device under which to produce established technologies but is inappropriate for unproven designs or those requiring significant modifications (which entails renegotiating the contract as requirements, costs, and other factors change).[58]

The A-12 was to be the first carrier-based stealth strike aircraft, which was the very definition of an unproven technology. Consequently, the contract placed excessive risk onto the contractor.[59] Enforcing the contract would have resulted in the collapse of both companies, with negative consequences for the entire defense industrial base.

General Dynamics had never built a stealth airplane, and $5 billion was a fraction of the funds necessary to develop the A-12.[60] The Air Force had spent more than $50 billion to build its B-2 Spirit stealth bomber, which was a less complicated platform.[61] The contractors probably believed that the Navy would pick up the costs once the program progressed beyond a certain point.[62] Until then, it was essential for the contractors to preserve the legal and public fiction that the program was making progress because the total contract, if the plane proved successful, was potentially worth $100 billion (for one thousand planes).

The second problem was conceptual. The chief of naval aviation, Vice Adm. Dick Dunleavy (OP-05), had announced that the A-12 was the Navy's "only hope" of acquiring the capacity for a "deep-strike mission" (the modern incarnation of "strategic bombing" or "deep interdiction") to preserve its position vis-à-vis the Air Force.[63] That deeply held belief made it difficult for the aviation community to cut its losses. After the immolation of Adm. Louis Denfeld's career following the Revolt of the Admirals, CNOs had stopped advocating for naval participation in strategic bombing. CNO James Holloway had even reorganized the fleet into "battle groups" in 1977 explicitly to project Army and Marine forces ashore and protect the immediate vicinity.[64] Unfortunately, a segment of the naval aviation community had not given up the chimera of strategic bombing—it was still fighting the same battles of the 1940s, even after the Soviet Union had collapsed—and that steadfast resolve led directly to the A-12 disaster.

Considering the circumstances, both the contractor and those individuals in the naval aviation community who supported strategic bombing had reasons to cover up any missteps. The A-12 began as a questionable concept, migrated to a contracting mistake, and quickly became a development disaster. Within a year, investigators determined that the plane was already overweight, behind schedule, and half a billion dollars over budget.[65] Why this happened made sense only if one understood high-tech acquisition.

The only companies that had any experience with stealth were Lockheed (the F-117 Nighthawk) and Northrop (the B-2 bomber). Neither was interested in disclosing their development costs (much higher than advertised) that were hidden within the Air Force's "black budget."[66] Because both of these stealth programs belonged to the Air Force and because the Air Force considered itself in competition with naval aviation, the Air Force had no intention of sharing with the Navy any information about stealth knowledge, especially its high costs. At the same time, Lockheed and Northrop were not about to share trade secrets with competitors (General Dynamics and McDonnell Douglas) that had a contract to design a Navy plane.

Because it was its job, OP-80 ferreted out some numbers and also did some new parametric analysis.[67] Perhaps because it had members with personal ties to the A-12 program office, OP-80 also heard rumors of hidden cost overruns before almost anyone else. It also learned that the historically superb NAVAIR accounting shop had used a flawed assumption that had underestimated the cost of the A-12 by a factor of at least three. NAVAIR had assessed the A-12's costs using algorithms that relied on estimates that were based on dollars per pound of titanium. It had thus computed the A-12's flyaway cost at about $90 million.[68] The problem with these calculations was that stealth aircraft were not built solely from titanium but also required load-bearing, radar-absorbing materials. Such exotic materials required brand-new (i.e., expensive) designs that were both stable and airworthy. These were exponentially more expensive than titanium, a light and extremely durable metal that was then state-of-the-art in aircraft, missile, spacecraft, and even submarine design.[69]

Even after spending tens of billions of development dollars, the B-2 was still costing the Air Force a billion dollars per plane.[70] Meanwhile, the Navy and Marine Corps needed 845 A-12s to replace their A-6s, and these planes had to operate from an unforgiving carrier environment. As the TFX/F-111 example showed, because of the problem of corrosion at sea and the stresses imposed by the catapults and arresting wires, naval aircraft have requirements different from those of ground-based planes and therefore require specific modifications. In addition, because a carrier is rolling and moving with the sea and the wind, when landing on a carrier, a Navy pilot must maintain a constant descent rate of five hundred feet per minute onto a steel ship, as compared to an Air Force pilot who flares their aircraft to reduce speed immediately before touchdown. Carrier landings are therefore best understood as controlled crashes at the end of each flight. Any airplane that hopes to still be stealthy after several landings must have stealth capability inherent in its design rather than as the result of delicate plastic overlays or items that must constantly be measured to see if they still work. For these reasons, to anyone other than those blindly trying to compete with the Air Force, it was obvious that the Navy could not build and maintain a fleet of A-12 airplanes at an affordable cost.

Besides the technical and cost issues, the most important aspect of the A-12 issue—the one that had been causing the Navy headaches since the Revolt of the Admirals—was this: Why was the Navy still trying to duplicate the Air Force's long-range strike mission when that particular mission was of questionable value? What was the point, after all, of wasting scarce naval sorties destroying economic and logistical hubs? Or destroying supplies that were days or weeks away from the battlefield—assuming the conflict even lasted that long? To any solder who, while under enemy fire, looked up to find the skies empty of friendly aircraft, these were not abstract questions.

Leave aside the issue of whether precision strike was effective. With the Cold War over, how important to the Navy was the capability to launch intermittent long-range strikes from carriers? Was it as critical as maintaining a continuous air umbrella over amphibious-landing areas or carrier-strike groups? Was it as important as using aircraft to provide close air support to troops on the ground? For how much longer could the Navy ignore geography and the fact that carrier-launched planes were best suited to provide a continuous air umbrella in regions of the world where the United States lacked land bases?

Stepping away from questions of tactics and operations, why was the Navy ignoring the technological changes in guidance, geolocation, and lethality that were every day making unmanned missiles—the TERCOM-enabled Tomahawks we introduced in chapter 3, for instance—more competitive with long-range manned-aircraft strikes? Finally, what was the purpose of naval airpower? Was it supposed to compete with the Air Force or provide a different set of capabilities? If it was the latter, was the A-12 debacle going to be a missed opportunity to improve the carrier air wing?[71] NAVAIR already had another, less expensive airplane ready to be developed that would give the Navy a multipurpose successor to the F/A-18 C/D and the A-6. It was becoming more and more evident that every airplane in theater needed the flexibility to adapt to whatever its mission required. Although the plane on the drawing board—the F/A-18 E/F Super Hornet—had a similar name and appearance as the Hornet, in fact, the Super Hornet would be a radically different airplane, with a much larger airframe and an ability to do the multiple missions of air defense, close air support, and strike.

The F/A-18 E/F (the "E" was the single-seat variant, and the "F" a twin-seater) would not be a stealth aircraft, but the Breakfast Club had concluded that existing stealth technology was unsuitable to the carrier environment and that the Navy did not need stealth for the immediate post–Cold War world. By contrast, although the Super Hornet was not necessarily cutting edge, it was based on a proven technology that could satisfy the Navy's requirements for now and the immediate future. Here, at last, was an opportunity to break the deep-strike addiction that had haunted the Navy since the 1940s.

All of these issues were items of discussion during the first few months of the early morning flag and general officer meetings concerning the Navy's programs. These were often emotional events, but the participants slowly made progress. Gradually the majority of flag officers agreed to dump the A-12. Nevertheless, the head of NAVAIR was still a supporter of the A-12, and, unlike with the *Seawolf* submarine, the CNO could not decide on his own to scrap the airplane. It had too many supporters outside the Navy, so he would need help.

It is unclear what exactly went on in Secretary of Defense Dick Cheney's office on January 5, 1991, when the A-12 was terminated, but it is not important for our story.[72] Contrary to news reports that the Navy was unprepared for the A-12's cancellation, after Cheney made his decision, the Navy took immediate action.[73] The same afternoon, the aforementioned John Lockhart brought forward a plan to use the money remaining in the A-12 budget lines ($5 billion) to develop the F/A-18 E/F Super Hornet. The Navy assigned that plane a name that was virtually identical to that of its predecessor, the Hornet, to defuse congressional objections and bypass certain formal steps in the acquisition process.[74]

The A-12 decision, following the resolution of other pressing issues, was the climax of the Navy's transition to the post–Cold War world. The emotions aroused by walking away from the deep-strike capability traumatized the naval aviation community. Fortunately, officers from other communities placed immense pressure on aviators not to put the interests of the aviation community over the entire service. It is proof that the services can police themselves effectively and make hard choices about the future allocation of resources to manage new geopolitical or even fiscal environments.

HUMAN AND PHYSICAL INFRASTRUCTURE

Besides the future of the aviation and submarine communities, the third major issue concerning the future of the Navy was personnel. The problem was deceptively simple—the Navy had too many people. It also was continually underestimating just how expensive they were. Every command liked having its "own people" it could order around. Sailors only seemed inexpensive because commands did not have to pay their full costs. While sailors might cost nothing to the local command, for the Navy as a whole they were in fact very expensive to recruit, train, and care for during and after their service. Since commands never considered the total fiscal burdens, individual managers used sailors to do work that could have been contracted out and accomplished much less expensively.

What seemed like a simple case of underestimating liabilities turned out to be much more complex.[75] The failures did not end at the local commands either. No one in the Navy factored in the total (life-cycle) costs of their labor inputs. For example, the Navy did not consider the retirement cost of its sailors. These unfunded liabilities were covered by the Treasury to the tune of $88 billion in FY 2021. Furthermore, the Department of Defense was not directly responsible for the full cost of medical care as a great deal of it was funded by the Veterans Administration.[76] The cost of retirement pay and veterans' health care are significant. As of FY 2017, the unfunded liabilities for military retirements was $768 billion and those of retiree health care were $156 billion plus the cost of all Department of Defense–funded benefits. If these indirect personnel costs were included in the annual defense budget today, they would bring the total annual defense bill well over $1 trillion. Unfortunately, few uniformed officers understood the full costs of military personnel.

Consequently, sailors were treated as nearly free commodities. There were all sorts of contests to boost recruitment despite the fact that every single new sailor was essentially an expensive, long-term obligation that, unlike a ship or airplane, could not be retired early and written off if the Navy suddenly calculated it had too many. Once inducted, new "hires" required a steady financial commitment—training, salaries, allowances, housing, health care, and so on—that could last for years, decades, even lifetimes.

The Breakfast Club meetings spent many hours discussing this issue and commissioned studies to find areas where the Navy could trim its rolls. The participants sparred frequently with Vice Adm. Mike Boorda, then head of BUPERS.[77] Every time the participants of the meetings decided to reduce the number of sailors, Boorda would raise recruiting goals, until Kelso finally overruled him and mandated cuts of over one hundred thousand. Boorda lost this battle but would continue the war when he replaced Kelso as CNO in 1994.[78]

When the Navy delivered its POM to Cheney in November 1991, the choices it had made reflected its intent to adapt to the post–Cold War world. The Navy had done this without specific direction from Congress, the president, the secretary of defense, the secretary of the Navy, or the chairman of the JCS. Bureaucratically speaking, it was one of the Navy's finest moments—but few noticed. As Kelso later lamented, he had tried to draw public attention to the fact that the Navy was being proactive in tackling the problems it expected.[79] In 1990, at the start of his tour as CNO, he coauthored a paper with the Marines—*The Way Ahead*—to publicize the thinking of the Department of the Navy, but publication was delayed and the pamphlet had little impact.[80]

Kelso even tried to help the other services. He asked the chiefs of the Army and Air Force if they would like a briefing about the assumptions the

Navy had made regarding the post–Cold War period, the methods it had used to build consensus, and how it had modified its POM. Both service chiefs declined. He then offered to have OP-80 brief them not in the Pentagon but privately at their "quarters" so they had deniability. Again, they declined.

The final issue the Navy had to consider was bases and physical infrastructure. It was important to recognize that all of the money the government set aside for defense was fungible. For example, a dollar used to pay for heating a guard shack at the lone gate on an isolated base could be redirected to repair an airplane if the base were closed. Before that could happen, however, Congress needed to give the Navy the necessary legal wherewithal. Fortunately, this was an era during which Congress did a great deal to assist the Defense Department in rationalizing its overhead despite the knowledge that there was no political upside for members whose states or districts lost bases.

Following the work of Chairman Powell concerning the post–Cold War base force, the George H. W. Bush administration informed Congress that future defense budgets assumed a reduction in force structure of 25 percent.[81] The Base Realignment and Closure (BRAC) process was Congress's response to an argument that had been ongoing for several decades about the excessive size of the US continental base infrastructure. Congress had concluded the services could not afford to maintain their existing infrastructure and continue to modernize within a constrained budgetary framework.[82]

To give a sense of the problem, by the end of the Cold War, the Air Force had more than four hundred bases in the United States, and the Navy more than two hundred. Meeting the challenge of the moment and choosing to ignore members' self-interest, in 1990 Congress gave the services the power to close excess bases with limited political interference.[83] The services thereupon began compiling an extensive database of all of their facilities and evaluating their future utility.

The military services are immense organizations that use large land spaces as bases and depots and have extensive human and capital infrastructure. The changes the Navy was contemplating meant that some of the current sites were no longer needed, while a few new facilities might be necessary. The Navy needed to start immediately, taking advantage of the BRAC to redirect the savings into force structure, modernization, readiness, and maintenance. Consequently, Kelso detailed a team of Navy officers and civilians to come up with a list of bases that were no longer delivering a "core capability."[84] Kelso assigned the task to Oliver, who leveraged the contacts and insights he gained from the Breakfast Club meetings.

Even something as simple as closing obsolete or redundant bases is not straightforward. For example, one must have the funds to pay for environmental remediation before returning the property to the original owners or selling it to the public. Nevertheless, the Navy could no longer ignore this issue. If Navy leaders chose to retain unnecessary bases (the politically easier path), they would leave to their successors the task of dealing with a bloated, underfunded, and crumbling infrastructure. This was a situation that called for leadership—not the physical sort of bravery we normally associate with the military—but moral courage in the face of unpalatable political choices.

With the end of the Cold War, the Navy no longer needed all of its bases. In some cases, the tasks they had performed had changed or the specific platforms they had hosted had disappeared. In others, there was civilian encroachment that impeded military functions.[85] For example, the fields around the Marine Air Station at El Toro (near Irvine, California) were no longer filled with lima beans as when the base was built. Now the installation closely abutted houses and schools. This placed playgrounds directly under aircraft landing patterns, heightening the danger of deadly accidents. If El Toro closed, however, the Marines would need another base for their helicopters. There was no obvious solution, as there was insufficient land available in Southern California. Since the Marines at El Toro primarily flew short-range helicopters that needed to marry up with Navy ships homeported at San Diego, the best option was for the Marines to move to Miramar. Unfortunately, that was also the Navy's most modern and desirable air station. (Miramar was located in San Diego—a large city with numerous amenities, including a vibrant night life, which was nirvana for the Navy pilots stationed there.)

If the Marines got Miramar, the Navy would have to move to Lemoore, California, a little desert town (population fourteen thousand) with two great runways and not much else. That was a nonstarter for Navy pilots. The reader should not forget that although the Navy and Marine Corps are both part of the Department of the Navy, there is ample competition between the two sister services. Nevertheless, after senior Navy and Marine senior officers thought about the possible future warfighting scenarios, they decided to move the Marines to Miramar and most of the Navy pilots to Lemoore.[86] This was a terribly unpopular move in the Navy, but it was done for the good of the country.[87]

The base closures or realignments affected the entire country. On the East Coast, it was impossible for the thousands of enlisted men and women who worked for BUPERS in Arlington, Virginia, to find affordable housing without a commute of several hours. Therefore, the most powerful of the old Navy bureaus—the one that controls promotions and billeting—was relocated away from where most admirals lived to Millington, Tennessee, to improve the living conditions of the junior enlisted. At the same time,

NAVAIR moved out of Crystal City to Patuxent River, Maryland, and the Naval Sea Systems Command (NAVSEA) left its offices in the same office complex as NAVAIR for spare buildings in the Washington Navy Yard in the District of Columbia. The Navy Yard had been surrounded for years by dilapidated buildings and urban blight. The Navy expected that the contractors dependent on business from NAVSEA would make the necessary investments to revitalize the area in the vicinity of the Navy Yard.

Not every service used the BRAC as an impetus for making painful choices. One problem of change that many secretaries of defense face is the problem of a "golden child"—a military officer who considers themselves or their service above the priorities of the administration or the direction of Congress. In the 1950s Arleigh Burke was a repeat offender, but in the 1990s it was Gen. Ronald Yates, the commander of Air Force Systems Command from 1990 to 1992 and Air Force Materiel Command from 1992 to 1995.

Since the processes for repairing airplanes are similar, the Navy, Marines, and Air Force decided to evaluate together their bases that repaired and maintained planes, using a common standard. Each of these services also employed or contracted for the same expensive maintenance personnel and, before the post–Cold War drawdown, had more maintenance bases than they needed. Accordingly, the Navy and the Air Force agreed to do a joint maintenance base review. The goal was to decide which facilities in the continental United States were the most capable, which could be consolidated, and which could be closed. After months of work, Yates wrecked the process by inverting the value of the Air Force's five repair bases (depots). He designated the Air Force's least capable bases—Kelly (San Antonio, Texas), Hill (Ogden, Utah), and McClellan (Sacramento, California)—as its most valuable and labeled its largest and most modern bases in Georgia and Oklahoma (Robins and Tinker—incidentally, the bases with the strongest political support in the Senate, which ensured they would not be closed) as the Air Force's least valuable repair bases. As Yates put it during a press conference, forcing him to close any of his bases was like "asking me to choose between my children, and I won't do that."[88]

This was a deliberate effort to sabotage the BRAC process. It is remarkable that no senior Air Force officer or political appointee in the Air Force or the OSD challenged him. Their silence squandered the political bravery of Congress and left a mess for the next administration. Nevertheless, the Navy and Marine Corps went on to implement the base changes they had themselves determined during the 1993 BRAC. The Air Force, by contrast, made fewer base closures than the other services, to the point that its physical infrastructure by 1998 was 24 percent larger than necessary and, combined with grueling operations in the Persian Gulf, hindered modernization of that service.[89]

In a sense, the behavior of the Air Force was understandable if less than commendable. If the end of the Cold War was insufficient to induce the president, the secretary of defense, or Congress to mandate changes in defense spending and priorities, why should any service take responsibility? Without leadership, external or internal, the Air Force and even the Army to a lesser extent were determined to hold tightly to the past and ignore any uncertainty about the future. This effectively meant preserving their Cold War structure—adapting the circumstances to the means available rather than vice versa.[90] Within a very few years they would come to regret their choice. By 1995 *Air Force Magazine* was bemoaning that the service "will purchase no bombers and no fighters for the first time in its forty-eight year history" and was "presently on a 560-year replacement cycle."[91]

In contrast, realizing that there was no pressing threat on the high seas after the Cold War, the Navy freed up assets to focus on the littorals—the shallow waters lapping on the shores next to developing nations where it was most likely that future conflicts might brew and involve or threaten American interests. The Air Force ended up using advanced, fifth-generation fighters to drop ordnance on lightly armed insurgents in the Middle East after 9/11. Similarly, the Army continued preparing for a Soviet attack through the Fulda Gap by investing in new howitzers and attack helicopters until both of these programs were canceled by Secretary Donald Rumsfeld. We will never know what the Army and the Air Force might have chosen to invest in if they had freed up dollars that were locked into Cold War items. We can only imagine what flexibility those decisions might have afforded those two services during the global war on terrorism.

SUMMARY

Frank Kelso did not have Arleigh Burke's wartime reputation, nor did he possess the personal political skills and connections of David McDonald or Elmo Zumwalt. In fact, Kelso's reputation never recovered from the Tailhook scandal, and he would retire early as CNO.[92] That scandal has sadly overshadowed his remarkable accomplishments as CNO.

Kelso succeeded where many before him had failed because he had access to insights his predecessors would have paid a fortune to duplicate by virtue of his membership in the submarine community, which had been reading the Soviet Union's mail for years. Consequently, unlike many of his peers in the Navy or the broader national-security community, Kelso knew the Soviets were finished well before the Cold War officially ended and that the Navy had to change along with the rest of the world. Because Kelso was at ease with himself, he empowered his subordinate flags to work together to develop a consensus plan for the Navy in the post–Cold War world. In contrast to Zumwalt's reforms, Kelso's reliance on transparent and inclusive process encouraged the rest of the Navy leadership to participate, make necessary compromises, and, most important, abide by them. Kelso did not always get complete accord, but he did obtain sufficient informed consent to recast the Navy and refocus it on the challenges it would face in the next century.

NOTES

1. E.g., see Frank Carlucci, "No Time to Change U.S. Defense Policy," *New York Times*, January 27, 1989; and John Lehman, *Oceans Ventured: Winning the Cold War at Sea* (New York: Norton, 2018), 241–43.
2. Albert Wohlstetter, "The Delicate Balance of Terror," *Foreign Affairs* (January 1959): 211–34.
3. Scott Sagan, "SIOP-62: The Nuclear War Plan Briefing to President Kennedy," *International Security* 12, no. 1 (1987): 22–51.
4. David Minton and Alfred Berzin, *From Opposite Sides of the Periscope: The Trail Is On* (Bloomington, IL: Archway, 2018); John Craven, *The Silent War: The Cold War Battle beneath the Sea* (New York: Simon & Schuster, 2001).
5. The sites of the largest Soviet submarine bases on the Atlantic and the Pacific.
6. Craig Hlavaty, "When Boris Yeltsin Went Grocery Shopping in Clear Lake," *Houston Chronicle*, January 31, 2018, https://www.houstonchronicle.com/neighborhood/bayarea/news/article/When-Boris-Yeltsin-went-grocery-shopping-in-Clear-5759129.php.
7. Yegor Gaidar, *Collapse of an Empire: Lessons for Modern Russia* (Washington, DC: Brookings Institution Press, 2007), summarized in "The Soviet Collapse: Grain and Oil," American Enterprise Institute for Public Policy Research, April 2007, https://www.aei.org/wp-content/uploads/2011/10/20070419_Gaidar.pdf.
8. William Odom, *The Collapse of the Soviet Military* (New Haven, CT: Yale University Press, 1998), 88ff.; Odd Arne Westad, *The Global Cold War* (Cambridge: Cambridge University Press, 2005), 364ff.
9. Jack Anderson and Michael Binstein, "Yeltsin-Gorbachev Feud Still Festering," *Washington Post*, October 8, 1992; Michael McFaul, "Yeltsin's Legacy," *Wilson Quarterly* 24, no. 2 (2000): 42–47, 50–58; Mackenzie Knorr, "Why Did Russia Let the Republics Go? Revisiting the Fall of the USSR," Wilson Center, n.d., https://www.wilsoncenter.org/publication/why-did-russia-let-the-republics-go-revisiting-the-fall-the-ussr; Strobe Talbott, "The Man Who Lost an Empire," *New York Review of Books*, December 21, 2017, https://www.nybooks.com/articles/2017/12/21/mikhail-gorbachev-man-who-lost-empire/.
10. Sherry Sontag and Christopher Drew, *Blind Man's Bluff: The Untold Story of American Submarine Espionage* (New York: Public Affairs, 1998).

11. For the economic situation in the Soviet Union, see Bradford Johnson, *Quality of Life in the Soviet Union: A Conference Report* (New York: Research Foundation of the City University of New York, 1984); Jonas Christiansen, "Back in the USSR: What Life Was like in the Soviet Union," Adam Smith Institute, n.d., https://www.adamsmith.org/research/back-in-the-ussr; Mark Harrison, "The Soviet Economy, 1917–1991: Its Life and Afterlife," *Independent Review* 22, no. 2 (2017), https://www.independent.org/pdf/tir/tir_22_2_06_harrison.pdf.
12. As of 1990, 380,000 Soviet troops were stationed in East Germany, along with support personnel and dependents. There were also thousands of armored vehicles, artillery pieces, and aircraft (both fixed-wing and rotary). Serge Schmemann, "Soviet Troops in Germany Become Army of Refugees," *New York Times*, December 17, 1990; Rick Atkinson, "Russian Troops Leave Germany," *Washington Post*, September 1, 1994.
13. Dave Oliver, *Against the Tide: Rickover's Leadership Principles and the Rise of the Nuclear Navy* (Annapolis, MD: Naval Institute Press, 2014), 137.
14. Lehman, *Oceans*, 235–38, 256–57. The Soviets had stolen US submarine codes through the efforts of the Walker spy ring. Pete Early, *Family of Spies: Inside the John Walker Spy Ring* (New York: Bantam, 1988).
15. Hal Brands, *Making the Unipolar Moment: U.S. Foreign Policy and the Rise of the Post–Cold War Order* (Ithaca, NY: Cornell University Press, 2016), 274ff.
16. Patrick Turner, "U.S. Strategy Plan Calls for Insuring No Rivals Develop," *New York Times*, March 8, 1992; James Mann, *Rise of the Vulcans: The History of Bush's War Cabinet* (Penguin: New York, 2004), 198ff.; William Burr, ed., "'Prevent the Reemergence of a New Rival': The Making of the Cheney Regional Defense Strategy, 1991–1992," NSA Electronic Briefing Book 245, February 26, 2008, https://nsarchive2.gwu.edu/nukevault/ebb245/; Alexandra Homolar, "How to Last Alone at the Top: US Strategic Planning for the Unipolar Era," *Journal of Strategic Studies* 34, no. 2 (2011): 189–217; Hal Brands, "Choosing Primacy: U.S. Strategy and Global Order at the Dawn of the Post–Cold War Era," *Texas National Security Review* 1, no. 2 (2018), https://tnsr.org/2018/02/choosing-primacy-u-s-strategy-global-order-dawn-post-cold-war-era-2/.
17. Frank B. Kelso, *The Reminiscences of Admiral Frank B. Kelso II, U.S. Navy (Retired)* (Annapolis, MD: US Naval Institute, 2009), 570–74.
18. Seymour Melman, "The Peace Dividend: What to Do with the Cold War Money," *New York Times*, December 17, 1989; David Rosenbaum, "Peace Dividend: A Dream for Every Dollar," *New York Times*, February 18, 1990; Ronald Fraser, "What Is a Peace Dividend?," *New York Times*, April 24, 1990; Ann Markusen, "Department of the Peace Dividend," *New York Times*, May 18, 1992.
19. Eric Schmitt, "A New Battle Is Ahead for Powell: The Budget," *New York Times*, January 17, 1992.
20. Lorna Jaffe, "The Development of the Base Force, 1989–1992," Joint History Office, Office of the Chairman of the Joint Chiefs of Staff, July 1993, https://www.jcs.mil/Portals/36/Documents/History/Monographs/Base_Force.pdf, summarized in "The Base Force," *Air Force Magazine*, December 2000, https://www.airforcemag.com/PDF/MagazineArchive/Documents/2000/December%202000/1200base.pdf; Eric V. Larson, David T. Orletsky, and Kristin Leuschner, *Defense Planning in a Decade of Change* (Washington, DC: RAND Corp., 2001): 5–39.
21. B. H. Friedman, "The Navy after the Cold War: Progress without Revolution," in *US Military Innovation since the Cold War: Creation without Destruction*, ed. Harvey Sapolsky (London: Routledge, 2009), 78–79.

22. Kelso, *Reminiscences*, 669–70. See also Thomas Hone and Curtis Utz, *History of the Office of the Chief of Naval Operations, 1915–2015* (Washington, DC: NHHC, 2015), 378ff.
23. While the United States had a smaller Navy in the 1980s than after Vietnam, its ships and aircraft were generally newer, larger, and better maintained. Kelso, *Reminiscences*, 668–70.
24. The major problems within the Navy that Kelso did not appreciate were the culture of alcoholism in the aviation community and the slow integration of women into the Navy's ranks. These problems collided at the September 1991 Tailhook Convention. Kelso probably did not understand the depth of the alcohol problem in the air community because the submarine community had already dealt with it. Adm. Bud Kauderer had tackled the issue in the Pacific Submarine Force in 1983 by relieving a number of alcoholic commanding officers and chief petty officers. He had followed up with similar measures when he became commander of Atlantic Submarine Forces. Kelso, *Reminiscences*, 587, 726, 730; Hone, *OPNAV*, 385–88.
25. The last two programs were canceled a decade later, while Secretary of Defense Robert Gates limited acquisition of the F-22 to a mere 187 operational planes. "Air Force F-22 Fighter Program," Congressional Research Service, July 11, 2013, https://www.everycrsreport.com/files/20130711_RL31673_c70b986e6de321f9f00ccbb5173d56d3fc781d1a.pdf. See also Mike Benitez, "Out of Time: Do Not Revive the F-22," War on the Rocks, May 4, 2016, https://warontherocks.com/2016/05/out-of-time-do-not-revive-the-f-22/.
26. The following discussion draws from Irv Blickstein, *Navy Planning, Programming, Budgeting, and Execution: A Reference Guide for Senior Leaders, Managers and Action Officers* (Santa Monica, CA: RAND Corp., 2016).
27. Hone, *OPNAV*, 583; Peter Swartz and Michael Markowitz, *Organizing OPNAV (1970–2009)*, Center for Naval Analyses (January 2010): https://www.cna.org/cna_files/pdf/D0020997.A5.pdf, 35ff.
28. For details, see *Defense Primer: Future Years Defense Program (FYDP)* (Washington, DC: Congressional Research Service, 2018); *Defense Primer: Planning, Programming, Budgeting and Execution Process (PPBE)* (Washington, DC: Congressional Research Service, 2016); and "Program Objective Memorandum (POM)," AcqNotes, May 30, 2021, https://acqnotes.com/acqnote/acquisitions/program-objective-memorandum-pom.
29. See, e.g., Headquarters, USAF, *Planning Programming, Budgeting and Execution System Training Program: Reference Manual* (Washington, DC: USAF Directorate of Programs, 2016), https://afacpo.com/AQDocs/PPBE.pdf, esp. 37ff.
30. For a more detailed overview of the bureaucratic wrangling among the programmers (OP-80), systems analysts, and strategists, see Dmitry Filipoff, "Irv Blickstein on Programming the POM and Strategizing the Budget," Center for Maritime and International Security, March 26, 2021, https://cimsec.org/irv-blickstein-on-programming-the-pom-and-strategizing-the-budget/; and Dimitry Filipoff, "A Conversation with Trip Barber on Fleet Design, Budget Analysis, and Future Warfighting," Center for Maritime and International Security, February 18, 2020, https://cimsec.org/a-conversation-with-trip-barber-on-fleet-design-budget-analysis-and-future-warfighting/.
31. In the Navy, surface-warfare officers (commanders and captains) have two command tours. During the first, they serve initially as an executive officer before being "fleeted up" to command. If they are successful in their first command tour, they will be eligible for major command. Assuming they commanded a destroyer in their first tour, during their major command tour they might command a destroyer squadron (DESRON).

The other branches (aviation or submarine) have slightly different arrangements but still select officers for two command tours.

32. Claimants were the other parts of the Navy that were responsible for their own budgets.
33. Reclamas are how the services formally object to the decisions of the secretary of defense during the budgeting process.
34. Swartz and Markowitz, *Organizing*, 58.
35. Kelso, *Reminiscences*, 574–82; Hone, *OPNAV*, 380–81. Deming was a statistician, business professor, and consultant who pioneered the notion that focusing on quality would enhance profitability by reducing marginal costs and increasing productivity and sales. Shunned in the United States, these ideas proved immensely influential in Japan during the period of postwar reconstruction after 1945. See David Halberstam, *The Reckoning* (New York: William Morrow, 1986), 301–18; Rafael Aguayo, *Dr. Deming: The American Who Taught the Japanese about Quality* (New York: Simon & Schuster, 1990); and Andrea Gabor, *The Man Who Discovered Quality: How W. Edwards Deming Brought the Quality Revolution to America* (New York: Times Books, 1990).
36. Kelso, *Reminiscences*, 576. For additional discussion of the Navy's use of TQL, see A. Houston and S. L. Dockstadter, "A Total Quality Management Process Improvement Model," Navy Personnel Research and Development Center, 1987, https://apps.dtic.mil/dtic/tr/fulltext/u2/a202154.pdf.
37. For the genesis of the term and its various meanings, see John Ferris, "Treasury Control, the Ten Year Rule and British Service Policies, 1919–1924," *Historical Journal* 30, no. 4 (1987): 859–83.
38. See, e.g., Peter Silverman, "The Ten Year Rule," *RUSI Journal* 116, no. 661 (1971): 42–45.
39. G. C. Peden, *Arms, Economics and British Strategy: From Dreadnoughts to Hydrogen Bombs* (Cambridge: Cambridge University Press, 2007), 98ff.; Steven Lobell, "Britain's Grand Strategy during the 1930s," in *The Challenge of Grand Strategy: The Great Powers and the Broken Balance between the World Wars*, ed. Jeffry W. Taliaferro, Norrin M. Ripsman, and Steven E. Lobell (Cambridge: Cambridge University Press, 2012), 167.
40. Despite the early hour, no one served food at these meetings. Nevertheless, coffee cups with the label of "Breakfast Club" did appear and were sold at various Arlington and McLean yard sales for several years.
41. Dmitry Filipoff, "Reagan-Era Navy Secretary John Lehman on Naval Recapitalization," Center for International Maritime Security, February 8, 2017, https://cimsec.org/30911-2/.
42. John Lehman, *Command of the Seas* (New York: Scribner, 1988),148; Richard Halloran, "Navy Chief Says Lehman Was Not 'Balanced,'" *New York Times*, April 30, 1987. See also Hone, *OPNAV*, 345.
43. Six submarine commanders and a civilian from CNA studied the issue under the direction of Rear Adm. Dave Oliver. Each of the officers had just completed their command tour at sea, and later in their careers each of them would become an admiral. The group found an empty room in the Pentagon and met for two weeks. Oliver briefed Cooper and then the staff of Adm. Bruce Demars of NAVSEA 08 (the nuclear safety section). Demars was the successor (once removed) to Rickover. His team did not have an engineering plant design in hand that would fit a smaller hull and was not enthusiastic about the project, but the submarine's overall design was not its decision.
44. "SSN-21 Seawolf-class," Federation of American Scientists, May 9, 2000, https://fas.org/man/dod-101/sys/ship/ssn-21.htm.

45. Peter Swartz with Karin Duggan, *The U.S. Navy in the World (1981–1990): Context for U.S. Navy Capstone Strategies and Concepts* (Alexandria, VA: Center for Naval Analyses, 2011), 59.
46. Joel Holwitt, "Sub vs. Sub: ASW Lessons from the Cold War," *Proceedings* 145, no. 10 (October 2019), https://www.usni.org/magazines/proceedings/2019/october/sub-vs-sub-asw-lessons-cold-war.
47. Eliot Cohen and John Gooch, *Military Misfortunes: The Anatomy of Failure in War* (New York: Free Press, 1990), 59–94; Clay Blair, *Silent Victory: The U.S. Submarine War against Japan* (Philadelphia: Lippincott, 1974); Michael Hennelly, "Fire One, Fire Ten: Implications of the Torpedo Scandal of World War II," Strategy Bridge, February 8, 2018, https://thestrategybridge.org/the-bridge/2018/2/8/fire-one-fire-ten-implications-of-the-torpedo-scandal-of-world-war-ii.
48. Kelso, *Reminiscences*, 592–93.
49. A complicated platform needs to be operated often so that small discrepancies can be fixed as they occur. If left idle, it may develop several problems that produce a catastrophic negative feedback loop.
50. Joseph Dyer to Dave Oliver, email, March 30, 2020.
51. There are two well-known books regarding the A-12: James Burton's *The Pentagon Wars: Reformers Challenge the Old Guard* (Annapolis, MD: Naval Institute Press, 1993), 213ff.; and James Stevenson's *The $5 Billion Misunderstanding: The Collapse of the Navy's A-12 Stealth Bomber Program* (Annapolis, MD: Naval Institute Press, 2001). Both accounts have valuable details and rightfully stress the flawed fixed-price contract as the root cause of the debacle, but their authors lacked access to the inner circles of the Navy during the periods when the key A-12 decisions occurred.
52. For a brief overview of this escapade, see George Wilson and Peter Carlson, "Stealth Albatross," *Washington Post*, October 29, 1995.
53. Bill Keller, "The Navy's Brash Leader," *New York Times*, December 15, 1985.
54. Gregory Vistica, *Fall from Glory. The Men Who Sank the U.S. Navy* (New York: Simon & Schuster, 1995), 201ff.
55. It is unclear whether Lehman supported the A-12 or went along with it to get funding for new A-6s. Hone, *OPNAV*, 372, 388–89.
56. A stealth platform minimizes the reflection of electromagnetic energy from searching radars and also hides its infrared signatures. Stealth aircraft are constructed from exotic, expensive materials and can only be flown using complicated software.
57. Richard Stevenson, "Are the Pentagon's Cuts Leaving Defense Thin?," *New York Times*, January 13, 1991; David Frick, "Risk in Fixed-Price Contracts," *Defense AT&L*, November/December 2013, 55–57. One of the most famous examples of the hidden costs of fixed-price contracts was the 2011 Refueling Tanker Aircraft competition between Boeing and Airbus. Boeing won the contract with a less capable aircraft by promising to absorb the extra costs. When Boeing could not deliver a successful replacement on time, the Air Force incurred billions in extra costs to keep the old refueling fleet flying for years longer than planned. Frank Kendall, "KC-46 Tanker Problems Call for a Rethink of Fixed-Price Development Programs," *Forbes*, March 31, 2020, https://www.forbes.com/sites/frankkendall/2020/03/31/should-the-kc-46-tanker-have-been-a-fixed-price-development-program-maybe-not/#7ae252d173fe.
58. There is an excellent summary of the strengths and weaknesses of the various sorts of defense contracts (fixed-price, cost-plus, and incentive) in Lehman, *Command*, 201ff.,

431–33. Lehman extolled fixed-price contracts during his tenure, but he became a critic of them after leaving the Navy Department. Dimitry Filipoff, "Reagan-ERA Navy Secretary John Lehman on Naval Recapitalization," Center for International Maritime Security, February 8, 2017, http://cimsec.org/30911-2/30911.

59. The contractor has no choice but to compete for such contracts. They know the terms are impossible to meet, but there are a limited number of big contracts, and the contractor has to stay in business. McDonnell Douglas was so weakened by the contract's cancellation that it was purchased by Boeing. Boeing and General Dynamics subsequently waged an extended legal campaign against the US government to recoup their losses. In this case, the A-12 contractors stalled the case legally in the courts for thirty years and recouped some losses. When the case finally ended in 2014, the Navy received $400 million worth of aircraft and services from the contractors. "Government and Contractors Seek to End Long-Running 'A-12' Litigation," Department of Justice, January 23, 2014, https://www.justice.gov/opa/pr/government-and-contractors-seek-end-long-running-12-litigation; Andrea Shalal-Esa, "Boeing, General Dynamics Reach $400 Million A-12 Settlement with U.S. Navy," Reuters, January 23, 2014, https://www.reuters.com/article/us-boeing-generaldynamics-settlement/boeing-general-dynamics-reach-400-million-a-12-settlement-with-u-s-navy-idUSBREA0M22820140124.

60. During the meeting when Lehman made the decision to proceed with the A-12, the Navy assumed that the two companies that had developed stealth technology for the Air Force (Lockheed and Northrop) would cooperate with General Dynamics, thus sparing the latter billions in startup costs. Was it even remotely reasonable for the Navy's contracting officer to expect private companies to share trade secrets with a competitor?

61. Peter Westwick, *Stealth: The Secret Contest to Invent Invisible Aircraft* (Oxford: Oxford University Press, 2020), 183.

62. Hone, *OPNAV*, 389.

63. Telcon between Rear Adm. Riley Mixson, former chief of naval aviation (and Dunleavy's deputy), and Dave Oliver, November 1, 2020. Mixson relieved Dunleavy after the A-12 was canceled and was instrumental in building support for the adoption of the F/A-18 E/F.

64. Hone, *OPNAV*, 313–14.

65. According to two separate reviews, one by the Navy comptroller and the other by the OSD. US Congress, Committee on Armed Services, Investigations Subcommittee, *A-12 Acquisition, Hearings*, 102d Cong., 1st Sess. (Washington, DC: GPO, 1992), 5.

66. The Air Force budget is divided between the "blue" and "black" portions. The former concerns normal expenditures, while the latter is blacked out in most documents and funds a variety of classified programs as well as a portion of the Intelligence Community's budget. Partisans of the Air Force complain that this practice inflates that service's relative share of the defense budget. Mackenie Eaglen, "Time to Get the Black out of the Blue," RealClear Defense, June 13, 2018, https://www.realcleardefense.com/articles/2018/06/13/time_to_get_the_black_out_of_the_blue_113532.html; Mackenzie Eaglen, "Is the Army Richest Service? Navy? Air Force?," Breaking Defense, February 5, 2020, https://breakingdefense.com/2020/02/is-army-richest-service-navy-air-force-aeis-eaglen-peels-back-budget-onion/; Amy McCullough, "The Budget and the Truth," *Air Force Magazine*, April 1, 2020, https://www.airforcemag.com/article/the-budget-and-the-truth/.

67. Parametric analysis is how a model behaves as you vary one or more of its input parameters. In this case, one member of the bullpen did a paper that showed how aircraft development costs had differed over the past thirty years depending on aircraft type.

A fighter was much more expensive to develop than an attack aircraft, which was in turn more expensive than a cargo aircraft. This data alone made the old A-12 estimates problematic.

68. The flyaway cost is the cost of a single aircraft and does not include the R & D or tooling costs. If used improperly, it can obscure the full cost of a weapon. Dan Grazier, "Selective Arithmetic to Hide the F-35's True Costs," Project on Government Oversight, October 21, 2019, https://www.pogo.org/analysis/2020/10/selective-arithmetic-to-hide-the-f-35s-true-costs/.
69. Andrew Kramer, "Titanium Fills Vital Role for Boeing and Russia," *New York Times*, July 5, 2013.
70. The current figure is $2.1 billion per plane, including retrofitting, and $135,000 per hour of flight time. Laura Thompson, "The Ten Most Expensive Military Aircraft Ever Built," Air Force Technology, May 30, 2019, https://www.airforce-technology.com/features/most-expensive-military-aircraft/.
71. An air wing can be modified depending on the mission but is often built today around four squadrons of fighter or strike F/A-18s, a squadron of electronic jamming aircraft, another of surveillance aircraft, and other of helicopters, as well as some logistical support aircraft. The A-12s were intended to replace a squadron or two of attack airplanes.
72. There is a useful summary of the bureaucratic maneuvering in David Montgomery, "How the A-12 Went Down," *Air Force Magazine*, April 1, 1991, https://www.airforcemag.com/article/0491navy/.
73. Eric Schmitt, "A-12 Decision Starts Scramble for Alternatives," *New York Times*, January 9, 1991.
74. Hone, *OPNAV*, 392–95. This decision had its share of critics. See James Stevenson, *The Pentagon Paradox: The Development of the F-18 Hornet* (Annapolis, MD: Naval Institute Press, 1993), 305ff.
75. The figures in this paragraph come from Todd Harrison and Seamus Daniels, *Analysis of the FY 2020 Budget and Its Implications for FY 2021 and Beyond* (Washington, DC: Center for Strategic & International Studies, 2020), https://csis-website-prod.s3.amazonaws.com/s3fs-public/publication/HarrisonDaniels_FY20DBA_v4.pdf?FA48YSbbC3Vj.aH7pKhpdIbU56OQ9QUZ.
76. This is an irresponsible way to do accounting, but such examples abound across the government. E.g., as the former director of Washington Headquarters Services, David Cooke, told Dave Oliver, because the White House is powered from a Pentagon substation, its electrical costs are hidden inside a Department of Defense facility budget, which makes it impossible to track the White House's electrical usage.
77. Kelso, *Reminiscences*, 589.
78. Kelso, 699. This seems too high because Boorda continued to slow-roll every attempt to reduce personnel.
79. Kelso, 668–72.
80. Kelso, 669; Hone, *OPNAV*, 378–79.
81. Frederick Shaw, *Locating Air Force Base Sites: History's Legacy* (Washington, DC: Air Force History and Museums Program, 2004), 160.
82. There were multiple rounds of the BRAC until 2005. The resulting closures were so politically painful that Congress has not repeated the process since then, despite the urging of the Pentagon that 20 percent of its physical infrastructure is superfluous. Christopher Mann, "Base Closure and Realignment (BRAC): Background and Issues for

Congress," Congressional Research Service, April 25, 2019, https://www.everycrsreport.com/reports/R45705.html; Ferderico Bartels, "A New Defense Strategy Requires a New Round of BRAC," *Strategic Studies Quarterly* 13, no. 3 (2019): 73–92; Jon Harper, "Is BRAC Worth a Political 'Food Fight'?," *National Defense*, May 24, 2021, https://www.nationaldefensemagazine.org/articles/2021/5/24/is-brac-worth-a-political-food-fight.

83. Michael Gordon, "Despite War, Pentagon Plans Big Buts," *New York Times*, February 3, 1991, https://www.nytimes.com/1991/02/03/us/despite-war-pentagon-plans-big-cuts.html?searchResultPosition=97; "FY 2020 Budget Estimates: DoD Base Realignment and Closure," Department of Defense, March 2019, https://comptroller.defense.gov/Portals/45/Documents/defbudget/fy2020/budget_justification/pdfs/05_BRAC/BRAC_Exec_Sum_J-Book_FINAL.pdf.
84. Hone, *OPNAV*, 394–95.
85. Lehman wanted to disperse part of the Navy into smaller ports (the Strategic Homeporting Initiative/Plan) to build political support in Congress for his shipbuilding plans (the "600-ship Navy"), but this was a political maneuver that distracted the service from more pressing tasks. US Senate, Committee on Armed Services, Subcommittee on Military Construction, *Strategic Homeporting Initiative, Hearing*, 99th Cong., 2d Sess. (Washington, DC: GPO, 1986); GAO, "Statement of Bill W. Thurman, Deputy Director, National Security and International Affairs Division, before the Committee on Armed Services Subcommittee on Military Installations and Facilities, House of Representatives, on the Navy's Strategic Homeporting Plan," February 26, 1986, https://www.gao.gov/assets/110/101243.pdf; GAO, *Navy Homeports: Expanding Structure Unnecessary and Costly*, GAO/NISAD-91-158, June 1991, https://www.gao.gov/assets/160/150619.pdf.
86. Lemoore became a "master jet base"—the homeport of several carrier-based squadrons. Other units originally based at Miramar, such as the Naval Fighter Weapons School (TOPGUN), moved to Fallon, Nevada, which is currently the Navy's primary facility for training aviators in air-to-air and air-to-ground combat.
87. "Though Disappointed, Many Know Consolidating Is Smart," *Virginian-Pilot*, March 1, 1995.
88. Matthew Brown, "General Won't Speculate on Depot Closures," *Deseret News*, March 24, 1993, https://www.deseret.com/1993/3/24/19038539/general-won-t-speculate-on-depot-closures. See also Genevieve Anton and Jeff Thomas, "The Politics of Base Closures," in *American Defense Policy*, ed. Peter Hayes (Baltimore: Johns Hopkins University Press, 1997), 241.
89. For the Air Force's side of the story, see Otto Kreisher, "The Base Closure Flop," *Air Force Magazine*, July 1998, https://www.airforcemag.com/PDF/MagazineArchive/Documents/1998/July%201998/0798brac.pdf.
90. The Air Force insisted on buying the B-2 and funding the F-22 even after the Soviet Union's air defenses had collapsed. Eric Schmitt, "General Sees No Hint of New Soviet Air Shield," *New York Times*, October 10, 1991.
91. John Tirpak, "The Air Force Heads for a Stable Landing," *Air Force Magazine*, July 1995, 32–37 (quotation from p. 34).
92. John Cushman, "Adm. Frank B. Kelso Dies at 79; Tied to Tailhook Scandal," *New York Times*, June 28, 2013.

PART II

WHAT IS TO BE DONE AND BY WHOM?

CHAPTER 5

Political Appointees

Our system of government puts civilians in charge of the Department of Defense and of each service. These political appointees have tremendous responsibilities. They are answerable for enforcing the president's vision as well as coordinating the response to oversight from the legislative branch. Their remit extends well beyond the confines of the Pentagon to include the many Department of Defense subagencies and support of the combatant commands.[1] Robert McNamara argued that these men and women were *leaders* with the responsibility of stimulating new ideas within the Pentagon.[2] While many political appointees have proven to be extraordinary stewards of the public trust, not all of them have lived up to McNamara's standard. Experience has demonstrated time and time again that political appointees are unlikely to succeed at unilaterally imposing sweeping and long-standing change on the Department of Defense.

This chapter focuses attention on officials who fill the executive ranks of the OSD and the services. These are extraordinary people. Most candidates for these jobs have more than just "potential"—nearly all have already made their mark in the world before they even set foot in the Pentagon. Most take significant pay cuts to work longer hours.[3]

What do these political appointees bring to the table that the career civil servants in the Pentagon do not already possess? In addition to valuable personal ties with other appointees in an administration, sometimes including the occupant of the White House, political appointees often bring valuable perspectives shaped by their life experience beyond the Beltway. Because they are usually outsiders, they do not automatically share the same bias and parochialism of people who have spent their entire careers within the Pentagon. Nevertheless, no matter how impressive their résumé, few secretaries of defense, service secretaries, or key members of their staffs have been able to lead, direct, encourage, cajole, or threaten the military into moving quickly or very far without its consent, particularly on what the uniformed military considers its bread and butter, such as specific weapons platforms or force structure.[4]

Why? The military, like any large social organization, is a complex, sprawling entity that does not welcome outsiders. Concurrently, most defense appointees simply do not know enough about the organization they oversee—not just its tasks but also its culture, which in turn informs military norms (implicit or explicit) and values. Unsettling as the concept may be in a liberal democracy, the only group that does understand the requirements, interrelationships, and levers of power are the officers who effectively run those services—the O-5s and O-6s (commanders and captains in the Navy and lieutenant colonels and colonels in the other services) who constitute the bulk of the key staffs and the admirals and generals who manage the service components or commands.

Second, the very structure of large bureaucracies, which the Pentagon surely qualifies as, resists change. Many parts of each service are so complex that individual officers spend their formative years learning just one sector.[5] It is important that each service has experts who are masters of their craft—who understand the complexities of their weapon systems, of potential alternatives, and the overarching environment. In the Navy, it takes roughly ten to twenty years of experience at sea to become a capable submariner, aviator, or ship driver. That expertise is difficult to acquire in peacetime and even more costly to learn in combat. These subject-matter experts are the same people the service would like to promote and eventually run the service. They are the officers who best understand what military capabilities their service can bring to bear on problems both large and small.

Being raised within one sector of one service, typically with minimal contact with other communities or services, much less the civilian world, leaves the majority of these officers—even those fortunate enough later to be chosen to wear stars on their uniform—often unaware of key developments or considerations outside of their own organization. It is tempting to conclude that their very professionalism is an obstacle to any reform agenda. At the same time, however, these are the same men and women who best understand their services. How can someone accomplish anything without them? To paraphrase the catch-22 that so frustrated Capt. John Yossarian, military leaders' inside knowledge makes them indispensable partners to any secretary of defense who wishes to implement lasting changes, but that same knowledge also enables these same officers to be the greatest obstacle.

When administrations use their statutory power to impose their defense preferences—well-meaning though they may be and perhaps through no fault of their own—the results have been disappointing. As we discussed in chapter 1, following World War II President Harry Truman and Secretary of Defense Louis Johnson went along with the Army and the Air Force and bet the security of the United States on "strategic bombing" and newfangled atomic weapons. The Korean War made a mockery of their assumptions. Fortunately, the Navy retained sufficient capability after its postwar budget cuts and there was no rival naval power to challenge the United States when it became necessary to assist beleaguered US and South Korean forces.[6] McNamara's centralization of power within the OSD created new problems as quickly as it solved others. In the process of imposing the OSD's control over acquisition, procurement, budgeting, and strategy while breaking the services' stranglehold over these realms, McNamara too often disparaged the value of professional military judgment on technical matters where the military's expertise eclipsed his own. This led, among other things, to expending enormous resources on a failed airplane—the TFX.

More recently, President George W. Bush and Donald Rumsfeld led the United States into a war with Iraq with a troop force that was large enough to overrun the country but too small to occupy it safely—a fact that Gen. Eric Shinseki, the chief of staff of the Army, publicly identified before the war. Rumsfeld had feuded with the Army over force size since he had assumed office and was convinced that his "light footprint" approach that "worked" in Afghanistan would also succeed in Iraq.[7]

As the acting undersecretary of defense for acquisition, Dave Oliver had a bird's-eye view of the debate between Rumsfeld and Shinseki over the troop numbers needed in Iraq. Later, in 2003, Oliver served as a member of the Coalition Provisional Authority (CPA). He saw why, due to the shortage of troops in Iraq, the US Army was forced to defend itself from static rather than dynamic positions. He observed how once an Army unit had established a position and set up a defensive perimeter, the insurgents' clock began ticking. It was only a matter of hours before they discovered a weakness in the Americans' perimeter. Moreover, static defense meant ceding control of the civilian population outside of the position to the insurgents.

A shortage of troops also meant there were not enough soldiers to guard burn pits, protect oil pipelines, or prevent the stripping of copper from power lines. The burn pits provided explosives for the roadside bombs that would maim US soldiers, the pipelines were essential for the one export vital to rebuilding Iraq, and the rolling blackouts from the sabotaged electrical lines telegraphed American weakness. Worst of all for the soldiers on the ground, the Army could not guarantee responsive support to units under fire. This shortcoming applied across the board. It was as true for Army personnel serving at checkpoints as for those on resupply sorties. It was also true for troops facing a crowd of Iraqis. As a consequence, some Army officers acted with a lack of restraint that produced unnecessary incidents and further alienated the civilian population. Yet, despite the negative consequences of these missing American troops, the George W. Bush administration was never willing to admit it had underestimated the number of troops necessary to occupy Iraq.

An inability to plan for or address an insurgency was not Rumsfeld's only similarity with McNamara. Rumsfeld was also determined to impose change on the Department of Defense. "Transformation" was the word du jour, and in practice it meant slashing administrative bloat and embracing the information-technology revolution to create a smaller, nimbler, more lethal military. There was much that was laudable about Rumsfeld's agenda, if not necessarily his means. Shinseki and the rest of the Army's old guard were not always right. For example, the general's support for the Cold War–era mobile howitzer (Crusader) was misplaced since it was ill-adapted to the kinds of low-intensity conflicts the United States was waging, impeded jointness by discouraging cooperation with the Air Force in terms of tactical air support, and clashed with Rumsfeld's intent to create a nimbler force.[8] Rumsfeld correctly challenged the military's spending priorities, but when President George W. Bush decided to invade Iraq, his secretary of defense was slow to pivot his attention to the war. Instead, he continued to worry about altering how the Pentagon operated and relegated oversight of problems in Iraq to Deputy Secretary Paul Wolfowitz, who was unsuited for such a role.[9]

Historian Andrew Bacevich offered an appraisal of McNamara's and Rumsfeld's leadership: "Both McNamara and Rumsfeld subscribed to a common proposition: They confused the management of the Pentagon with the management of war. They assumed that taming the former put you in a position to control the latter. Both were disastrously wrong, although others end up paying for the consequences of their errors."[10]

Bacevich was alluding to their botched wars, but he assumed that both men were successful in their management efforts until their military fortunes changed. Our chapter 2 suggests that is not the case—that McNamara's problems predated the Vietnam War and that his efforts were meeting unrelenting opposition even before military setbacks tarnished his image. Accordingly, there must be some broad factors transcending specific administrations that impair the effectiveness of political appointees.

CONSTRAINTS ON CIVILIAN LEADERSHIP

Our analysis suggests four reasons why political appointees find it challenging to impose constructive change on the Department of Defense: the scale of the challenge, the absence of subject-matter expertise among political appointees, a dearth of organizational skills, and a lack of leadership skills.

Regarding the first factor, consider the sheer numbers involved. An average administration sends fewer than four hundred political appointees into the Department of Defense. These include about sixty who require Senate confirmation (secretaries, undersecretaries, and assistant secretaries), 120 noncareer SESs (usually deputy assistant secretaries), and 250 Schedule C employees. The latter group most often fill a wide variety of lower-level positions, ranging from office directors and chiefs of staff to secretaries or administrative assistants.[11]

Consider the few senior political appointees. These are the individuals who support the secretary of defense and other senior decision-makers in developing and carrying out national military strategy in concert with senior military officers and civil servants. The secretary of defense gets a dozen and a half political appointees who require Senate confirmation. The more senior of the secretary's staff also receive another two dozen SESs and a number of Schedule C appointments.[12] The service secretaries have smaller staffs. Each have eight or nine political appointees requiring Senate confirmation and two to three dozen SESs.

How much impact do political appointees have? It is completely dependent on their personality, professional network, and relationship with the secretary of defense. Each official works within the world's largest office building.[13] The Pentagon held twenty-five thousand people before any of these appointees arrived.[14] The new arrivals are therefore relatively small in number. They might soon become swamped by their jobs, or they could take charge—it all depends on their character and the circumstances. The people already at work in the Pentagon (whether military or civilians) are not armed to the teeth, ready to fight in distant lands, but instead—like their comrades across the national capital area—they are public servants (bureaucrats) with years of education and training in their specialty. They customarily work long hours to keep their small segment of responsibility tuned up and running.

Few people beyond the Beltway appreciate how much these career public servants across the entire federal bureaucracy are doing each day or how their actions affect the daily lives of Americans. Let us provide a sense by using one military service as an example. The Navy currently has nearly six hundred thousand employees: 340,000 regular enlisted and officers, 59,000 reservists, and 195,000 civilians.[15] This means that when every new president is sworn in and a few dozen new appointees come aboard, they will find hundreds of thousands of uniformed and civilian public servants already hard at work fulfilling the roles, functions, and missions of the Navy.

It is unreasonable to expect many incoming appointees to have an in-depth understanding of what these sailors and civilians are doing. Some appointees may not have the slightest idea of what would happen if even a portion of these public servants, civilian and military, should stop working for as much as a few hours.

Incoming political appointees will soon find out that all of these people are necessary. The "warriors" in the Navy have been trying to increase the ratio of tooth-to-tail (combat troops versus everyone else [e.g., logistics, headquarters staff, and contractors]) since the days of John Paul Jones, and they have failed time and time again. During World War I, the American Expeditionary Force in Europe had a tooth-to-tail ratio of two combat soldiers for every support person. By World War II, the tables had turned—now the ratio in the European Theater of Operations for Army divisions was 1.6 support personnel for every combat soldier, which was also the case in Korea and Vietnam. The gap widened considerably during the first Gulf War—3.3 support personnel per combat soldier—but declined slightly during Operation Iraqi Freedom to 2.5 support personnel for every combat soldier. Overall, from 1945 to 2007, the Army's tooth-to-tail ratio averaged 1:2, with logistics occupying a larger share of force strength than combat units.[16] This pattern is repeated across the services. A 2008 study by the Defense Business Board concluded that 42 percent of the Pentagon's annual spending was devoted to its "tail," with growth rates of 5 percent in personnel and 9 percent in management.[17]

The reason the warriors have failed to cut this tail is that the tail is indispensable for modern warfare. The services require hundreds of thousands of support personnel precisely because our military is so complex. This was why McNamara instituted the PPBS and program management in the first place—because the services did not know or were not considering the full cost and complexity of maintaining the weapon systems they were buying. An airplane or a helicopter is not just its pilot, crew, and airframe. There are the many systems and weapons it carries. There are the myriad processes supporting different programs to facilitate logistics, train people, and integrate data networks. The cost and maintenance of different strike platforms also encompass the training of everyone who maintains that platform, the infrastructure involved in deploying it, the spare parts it will require every year, and the training for the personnel who are going to install those millions of parts. Finally, all of this capability needs to exist worldwide and operate relatively swiftly because, quite often, people's lives are at risk.

Someone has to understand how all of this interrelates. The needs of systems must correlate with those of the young people—many with nothing more than a high-school education—who will be recruited to be part of this team. Let us not forget the outsiders who are nonetheless indispensable—for example, the oil companies that will refine the special fuels and lubricants the military needs and the defense industrial base that supports the personnel and equipment. This process involves contracts, algorithms, software, warehouses, and specifications that, when printed out, result in a stack of paper taller than an NBA player.

Additionally, no appointee, no matter their past experience, has the knowledge and experience to change a particular program without risking serious damage that could ripple across the defense enterprise. Of course, a particular program might well need to be changed or even terminated, but the people involved in the program day to day need to be involved to avoid undue waste or loss of efficiency.

From where does this dearth of knowledge spring? Since the draft was terminated in 1973, fewer and fewer political appointees have firsthand experience of how the military operates. We do not mean knowledge of national security so much as the culture and realities of military life, which range from the monotonous to the terrifying. The closest many civilian leaders have gotten to planning and applying military power is writing an op-ed or making a PowerPoint slide deck. Even retired military officers who may now be serving as political appointees are years, or even decades, removed from the day-to-day experiences of the vast majority of service personnel.

If the political-appointment process works, individuals who held junior-level positions in earlier administrations are among the strongest candidates for the senior positions when their political party again gains the White House. Those junior positions were often in the same organizational units (a service or a functional unit like, say, finance), which means they will bring that knowledge to their next job. The details of daily operations may have changed since they were last in an appointed position, but their knowledge of how the system works will still be relevant.

At the same time, myriad factors work against accumulating too much experience. Academics, for instance, may spend years studying national security or regional affairs, but universities will not permit them to abandon their scholastic duties for longer than two years and still retain tenure. For a number of similar reasons in other professions, not to mention the stress of the jobs, the average time in office for a political appointee in the OSD is less than two years (roughly the same as the average across the federal government).[18]

Absent specific knowledge or prior experience, good appointees approach their jobs with the expertise they bring with them from civilian life—as a politician, academic, or business person—but rarely as a military professional. That works in most of federal bureaucracy *except* the Pentagon. There the political appointee is generally assigned supervisory authority over one or more generals or admirals. Each person they supervise has an infinitely greater expertise in military affairs than the appointee.

If the latter chooses to interpret their writ as second-guessing every decision the generals or admirals make, their tour will be fraught with difficulty.[19] These officers represent the best and worst about military professionals. Every flag officer has a great deal of military experience, often acquired firsthand, with which to develop requirements and evaluate new or existing weapon systems or paths of action. Many military systems are the product of several failures and a long development process. Senior officers have observed these failures in the acquisition process or in the field. Consequently, they are reluctant to give up the tried and true, even if it has a few warts. In other words, they are, by virtue of their profession experience, "small *c*" conservatives.

Alongside their undeniable tactical, operational, and leadership skills, there are also some mismatches or shortcomings that can lead to problems with the political leadership. It is the rare flag or general officer who, like Adm. David McDonald, has acquired a great deal of experience interacting with Congress, either political party, the media, or industry (unless they have served in their service's acquisition corps). These officers seldom have a network of political friends in either party or have any idea of the myriad informal relationships that exist in the civilian world.[20] Military officers yearn for clear lines of authority that do not exist in the political world and can resent political appointees for not respecting process or structure. Finally, according to surveys of military officers recently promoted to flag rank, most of the services select—intentionally or not—senior leaders who are indifferent to professional education and strategic analysis, prefer hierarchy, and are reluctant to express criticism before superiors.[21]

These mismatches all contribute to communication difficulties. One person does not hear what the other believes they are clearly saying. In addition, everyone brings to their job not only their prior belief systems and assumptions but also their past experiences. The Navy once received a female senior appointee who was breaking the proverbial "glass ceiling." Unbeknownst to anyone but her closest friends, several years earlier her husband had been selected for promotion to brigadier general in the Army, but at the time his service only promoted to general officer married men whose spouses did not have careers. She was a bright, motivated woman who was at the very top of her peer group. She had refused to give up her career, and the Army rescinded her husband's promotion.

The aforementioned woman was now assigned to supervise a service that not only had no female flag officers but also a reputation for sexual harassment. (The Tailhook scandal had occurred a couple of years before.) How might this particular appointee have felt about the notion she should defer to Navy admirals and Marine generals? Unsurprisingly, her relationship with her uniformed counterparts was frequently strained. Whatever the reasons why it goes awry, communication—ideally built on a foundation of trust and mutual respect—is critical, as each group needs one another. The political appointee needs the military's expertise to fulfill the president's or Congress's wishes, while the military requires the legitimacy of the appointees as well as the broad perspective they bring to understanding war as a sociopolitical rather than a purely technical phenomenon.

Finally, there is the issue of different skill sets. Appointees tend to be people who came from positions that they can leave or rejoin without excessive penalties. That is to say, most walked away from a career in the civilian world in which there were not thousands of people dependent on them, or they were members of professions to which they could return, or they had the skills to build a new career after leaving appointed service. These attributes tend to describe attorneys, academics, financiers, entrepreneurs, and politicians (including their senior staff).

Again, these people are almost uniformly bright and hardworking. But few of them have ever managed large staffs. Even fewer have managed immense, diverse bureaucracies. Not many have served in jobs that teach and emphasize teamwork or leadership. Knowing how to manage yourself and others are skills that are essential in military organizations. Likewise, few military leaders have much time or patience for the blood sport of partisan politics, which is utterly antithetical to their professional ethos. Consequently, even exceptional civilians assigned to political roles in the Pentagon sometimes find these assignments challenging, and they are often particularly ill-equipped to direct major changes.

For all of the reasons we have outlined—the scale of the challenge, a lack of subject-matter expertise, the dearth of the necessary organizational skills, and the extraordinary leadership challenges—appointees in the Pentagon are dependent on both the uniformed personnel and career civilians. As an added complication, while those staff who are assigned to the appointee are loyal, they are also dependent on their service rather than the appointee for their advancement. The service chiefs control the officer talent pool, the promotion system, and assignments (billeting). This process is the lifeblood of each service, and every officer knows their career depends on it.

SOLVING PROBLEMS WITH A MEAT AXE VERSUS A SCALPEL

Programs and agendas rarely succeed without the right mix of people. Any arrangement that ignores this reality is likely doomed, as happened to the acquisition system following the passage of the Goldwater-Nichols Act of 1986. This legislation increased the power of the chairman and streamlined communication among the president and the military commanders in theater by removing the service chiefs from the chain of command.

The bill also implemented several recommendations of the previous years' Packard Commission. Fiscal hawks in Congress had pressured the Reagan administration to create a commission to address the very public scandal of simple tools such as hammers, toilet seats, and coffeemakers costing the Pentagon hundreds, sometimes thousands of dollars per unit.[22] It subsequently turned out that many of the prices quoted were inflated due to federal accounting practices and that the military was not actually paying vendors hundreds of dollars for a hammer.[23] Still, there were a number of legitimate criticisms that the acquisition system was discouraging competition and not delivering the Pentagon weapons and parts at a reasonable cost.[24] These concerns were behind the formation of the Packard Commission (led by the aforementioned David Packard). The commission's remit extended to all manner of "issues surrounding defense management and organization" and complemented the ongoing work of the Senate Armed Services Committee, where Sen. Barry Goldwater and Sen. Sam Nunn had been preparing sweeping proposals for defense reorganization since 1982.[25]

Packard had been intimately involved in reforming defense management since his time as Melvin Laird's deputy. The "P" in HP (Hewlett-Packard), Packard was one of many appointees from the business world who believed that the government should learn from private industry. He was not the first to be disappointed, for as we will explain in chapter 7, while private industry can serve as a source of innovation for the Pentagon, leaders cannot "manage" national defense in the same way as a private firm. While serving as Laird's deputy from 1969 to 1971, Packard had recommended the services follow commonsense acquisition principles such as adopting better cost estimates, risk analysis, and testing before starting production of any weapon system.[26]

A decade later, the Packard Commission concluded that experts from private industry should oversee the Pentagon acquisition process. The intent was to ensure that the Pentagon benefited from the best practices in private industry. The commission also recommended adoption of two-year defense budgets and five-year defense plans, increasing the power of the JCS chairman, greater legal scrutiny of contractors, and streamlining the acquisition process by enhancing the OSD's power relative to the services.[27] This last point was an important departure from Packard's thinking during his tenure at the Pentagon, when he had supported (perhaps as a reaction against McNamara's policies) the services having control of their own acquisitions with only limited OSD oversight. Many of the commission's recommendations were similar to the Senate Armed Services Committee's thinking at the time, and the committee rolled them into several pieces of legislation.[28]

Most of the attention lavished on Goldwater-Nichols has focused on the law's efforts to enhance civilian control of the military and promote "jointness" by increasing the power of the JCS chairman and combatant commanders at the expense of the service chiefs.[29] Navy officers, for instance, claim the reforms gutted the Navy's cadre of strategists by dispersing them throughout the joint bureaucracy and discouraged bright officers from taking jobs at OPNAV. The act certainly eliminated any vestiges of the service chiefs' operational responsibilities.[30]

The Navy experienced its own particular problems in this area even before the Goldwater-Nichols acquisition changes. In 1985 Secretary of the Navy John Lehman dissolved the Naval Material Command, which handled all of naval acquisition, dispersing its responsibilities across several of the systems commands. Perhaps because they oversee two services (the Navy and the Marine Corps), Navy secretaries have historically enjoyed greater political freedom than their Army and Air Force counterparts. Lehman exploited this luxury to its utmost—for example, by publicly opposing the Goldwater-Nichols legislation.[31] Within the Navy itself, he was frustrated by the slow pace of the naval bureaucracy and wanted to centralize control over procurement. His actions yielded mixed results for the naval acquisition process.[32]

Unfortunately, for two reasons, Goldwater-Nichols did not prove much of an improvement.[33] One was a problem that could not have been foreseen and had to do with the political appointees. The law established five positions: an acquisition executive (chief) in each service who would report to the undersecretary and the principal deputy undersecretary for acquisition in the OSD. These officeholders would all ideally have previous industry experience and assist the services in efficiently buying weapons, parts, and services. Unfortunately, over the following decades, it often proved challenging to fill these jobs with qualified people. The reasons were financial and personal. Men and women with desired industry qualifications were paid well, at the height of their earning power, and had enormous respect and power within their industry. Why should such qualified people take government jobs when officials such as Secretary Lehman (who enjoyed privileged access to the president) promised to bypass acquisition officials if they ever disagreed with any of their decisions?[34] Thus, the key billets often went empty for long periods of time or were occupied by less qualified individuals and occasionally even crooks.

Using the Navy as an example, its chief acquisition officer is currently the assistant secretary of the Navy for research, development, and acquisition. During the thirty years that Goldwater-Nichols required this billet to be filled with a business executive, this goal was met only for thirteen—and that includes the tenure of Melvyn Paisley, who spent some of those years committing crimes that earned him a conviction for bribery and several years in prison. For another six years, the job was held by individuals whose primary qualification was that they had been senior congressional staffers. For nine years, the billet was held by a longtime employee of the Navy who had no previous industry or commercial experience. Meanwhile, in the Air Force, there were many years during which its chief acquisition billet went unfilled, especially after Principal Deputy Undersecretary Darleen Druyun (the number-two acquisition official in the Air Force, a senior civil servant with no prior private business experience) went to prison in 2004 for assisting Boeing in a bid to lease aerial-refueling tankers to the Air Force.[35]

The second great flaw with the legislation was elementary and should have been foreseen. The act separated responsibility for accomplishing the task from the responsibility for assigning the talent to perform the task. Specifically, it separated the requirements process (what systems were supposed to do)—which was still dominated by the services—from acquisition. After the legislation was written, a political appointee had the burden for acquisition, but the service chiefs were left with the responsibility for assigning officers to fill acquisition positions. The chiefs, perhaps resenting the loss of their earlier responsibilities, made the job of the OSD acquisition "czar" tougher by not detailing their best officers to acquisition jobs. Whatever the reason, too often the officers they did assign lacked sufficient knowledge or experience to serve as effective program managers. Meanwhile, the rotational system and relatively low pay of the military compared to industry encouraged the few exceptional officers to retire and join the private sector.[36]

For decades, a great number of people labored hard to make the flawed Goldwater-Nichols system work, but it proved impossible.[37] Billions of lost dollars and a hundred studies later, the acquisition process was no better than before the legislation of the 1980s. Starting in 2015 Congress turned back the clock by transferring responsibility for acquisition back to the service chiefs.[38] Responsibility was now realigned back with the authority to assign personnel talent. If the chiefs wanted the system to work, they had the authority to make it so—but also the responsibility if it did not. The OSD has continued this process of delegating acquisition authority downward right up to the present day by granting the heads of Pentagon agencies and combatant commanders the right to enter into prototyping agreements.[39]

Goldwater-Nichols is an example of what happens when Congress tries to do too much—fix the chain of command *and* acquisition—too quickly. What happened is yet another real-life example of the law of unintended consequences. Trying to fix acquisition created a new set of problems, to the point where the only option was to return to the status quo. We discuss Congress's shortcomings in the next chapter, but the whole episode further demonstrates the fact that no public official, no matter how broad their remit or perspective, can manage defense on their own because of the complexity of the task. Fortunately, they have staffs of hundreds—perhaps thousands—of career civilians and military feeding them information and alert to their bidding. Those staffs expect to be led and managed, which presents another challenge for political appointees.

Running a large bureaucracy requires a special set of skills. The leader cannot become overwhelmed by the task. They cannot obsess about minutiae. Large organizations, even government bureaucracies, are not all the same. For example, embassies are organized to gather and process information to inform decision-makers. The State Department reflects that modus operandi. The Pentagon, by contrast, is designed to act. As the individual responsible for placing political appointees in the Pentagon during the Clinton administration explained, "the military's culture gives the Pentagon a different decision process than other organizations. It's clear the focus is on doing something and then doing an after-action [report] on it. It's a culture that has little patience for a long, drawn-out decision process. Successful incoming political appointees need to recognize that."[40]

The executive skills to operate in this culture are second nature to the generals and admirals who rise to the top of their services. They simply would not hold such rank unless they were action and decision oriented. Not every senior political appointee, however, comes from a background that develops the same attributes. Offsetting this disadvantage, however, political appointees often bring their own unique skills.

Since the creation in 1973 of an all-volunteer force, the US military has been losing the contact it had with the rest of the United States.[41] Each year, there are fewer people in our country who have experienced a boot camp, deployed overseas, or just spent several months getting to know men and women who decided "they might as well stay in the service."[42] One of the few benefits of our recent decades of military misadventures has been the increase in the number of people who have direct or indirect experience of military life, many of whom are now entering the ranks of public service, either as civil servants or elected officials at all levels of government.[43]

For those who have never served in uniform, each cycle of Pentagon appointments is among the few instances where citizens can serve side by side with the military before returning to civilian life. These appointees gain invaluable experience, not as veterans but as civilians who can speak from firsthand experience about the quality of military personnel, comment on their attitudes, and make informed judgments about the strengths or shortcomings of the military as an institution or the utility of force.

We should also not forget the qualifications political appointees bring to defense, which makes them both a source of change within the Pentagon and invaluable partners for like-minded military professionals. First, as we have already mentioned, the civilian appointee often has relationships with counterparts elsewhere in the Pentagon or in the other federal agencies, if not the White House. Another good place to have contacts is in Congress, which guards its appropriations and authorization powers jealously and must be accommodated if the appointee wants to do their job smoothly.

Second, perhaps bizarrely to outside observers, military officers often actually pride themselves on their lack of political acumen. They understand that the nation expects them to be nonpartisan and are comfortable standing above party politics. A minority are more alert, however, since they understand they can hardly shun politics altogether when war is fundamentally a political act. Fortunately, political appointees are often experts in this area, which means they can make vital contributions to decisions at the highest levels of war, such as strategy. Similarly, the appointee usually has precisely the sorts of political, professional, and intellectual connections that most officers lack. They are therefore invaluable in directing or guiding their service, agency, or department's strategy for getting the necessary authorizations and funding.

Political appointees also often bring a lifetime of experience from a much different environment to the Pentagon. Having the appointee inside the organization makes it more difficult for the services to ignore their experience and suggestions. The appointee's hiring can, assuming they have the right temperament and come into office under propitious circumstances, enable new ideas to gain a hearing. At a minimum, these individuals provide a set of fresh eyes for the problems their segment of the defense team is experiencing.

SUMMARY

The track record of political appointees since 1947 has at best been mixed. The military is not some underperforming company that can be turned around on a dime by management consultants. Despite their occasional successes, therefore, we should not exaggerate the capacity of civilian outsiders to impose change. Avoiding unnecessary friction requires collaboration among the civilians, with their outside perspective, and the military, with their practical skills and mastery at navigating the immense military bureaucracy.

The point of this chapter was to emphasize the realities involved in managing the Department of Defense without undermining the importance of the principle of civilian control of the military. The Pentagon operates with a delicate balance among political appointees, career civil servants, and the uniformed military—the epitome of a three-legged stool. Civilian political appointees do not have the depth of understanding and experience of their military counterparts. Additionally, due to the limited numbers of appointees, no administration can accurately assess the situation, much less direct the course of events except through collaboration with the military services and the civilian workforce that supports the both of them.

NOTES

1. Bradley Peniston, "Explainer: What Is the Pentagon's Fourth Estate?," Defense One, February 6, 2020, https://www.defenseone.com/threats/2020/02/what-pentagons-fourth-estate/162939/.
2. Robert McNamara, *The Essence of Security: Reflections in Office* (New York: Harper & Row, 1968), 87–88; Thomas Hone and Curtis Utz, *History of the Office of the Chief of Naval Operations, 1915–2015* (Washington, DC: NHHC, 2015), 246.
3. Since 1971 the Presidential Personnel Office (PPO) has been responsible for recruiting and vetting candidates for the roughly four thousand federal jobs that each administration can fill. A well-functioning PPO is essential to a president's ability to find and place people who will implement their agenda through management of the federal bureaucracy. Every major cabinet department and federal agency (except independent regulatory commissions) has a White House liaison (WHL). The WHL serves, by agreement of the president and the relevant cabinet secretary, as an extension of the PPO. The WHL must ensure that each appointed position is filled with individuals committed to the president's goals but also competent to occupy their post. Among the people or institutions that influence the appointment of executive branch personnel, Congress—especially the Senate, with its confirmation powers—is particularly important. James Bailey (former associate director of the PPO for President Clinton from 1993 to 1994) to Dave Oliver, email, September 7, 2020.

4. Many works on Pentagon reform focus on making the Department of Defense bureaucracy operate efficiently. Peter Levine, *Defense Management Reform: How to Make the Pentagon Work Better and Cost Less* (Stanford, CA: Stanford University Press, 2020). Matters such as contracting and personnel are, of course, vital matters, but we should not confuse *what* the Pentagon does with *how* it does it.
5. There are many military sectors. Speaking just of primary combat elements, in the Army there are infantry, artillery, armor, rotary aviation, engineers, and special operations forces (e.g., Rangers, Delta Force, and Special Forces). The Navy warfighting communities (the "unrestricted" lines) are aviation, surface warfare, submarines, and special warfare (e.g., SEALs and Explosive Ordnance Disposal). The Air Force is divided by the demands of the airplanes flown and whether the missions are tactical or "strategic." In the Marine Corps, the core is the infantry, with every other community occupying a distinctly subordinate role.
6. Edward Marolda, ed., *The United States Navy in the Korean War* (Annapolis, MD: Naval Institute Press, 2007), esp. chaps. 1–2; "History of U.S. Naval Operations: Korea," NHHC, June 2000, https://www.history.navy.mil/research/library/online-reading-room/title-list-alphabetically/h/history-us-naval-operations-korea.html.
7. Matthew Engel, "Scorned General's Tactics Proved Right," *The Guardian*, March 28, 2003, https://www.theguardian.com/world/2003/mar/29/iraq.usa; Michael O'Hanlon, "History Will Credit Shinseki," Brookings Institution, June 19, 2003, https://www.brookings.edu/opinions/history-will-credit-shinseki/; Nicolaus Mills, "The General Who Understood Iraq from the Start," *Dissent*, April 25, 2008, https://www.dissentmagazine.org/online_articles/the-general-who-understood-iraq-from-the-start.
8. "Rumsfeld Dumps Crusader, Defends Decision," CNN, May 9, 2002, https://www.cnn.com/2002/ALLPOLITICS/05/08/rumsfeld.crusader/index.html; Eric Schmitt, "$11 Billion Artillery System Is Dead, Officials Say," *New York Times*, May 7, 2002. See also "Scott Shuger, "Outgunned: What the Crusader Cancellation Really Means to the Army," Slate, May 23, 2002, https://slate.com/news-and-politics/2002/05/what-the-crusader-cancellation-really-means-to-the-army.html; "Rumsfeld Pulls Plug on Big Gun," *Wired*, May 8, 2002, https://www.wired.com/2002/05/rumsfeld-pulls-plug-on-big-gun/.
9. H. D. S. Greenway, "The Problem That Is Wolfowitz," *New York Times*, April 17, 2007. Rumsfeld's second tenure at the Pentagon is still waiting for a scholarly study based on declassified records. For hints as to the scope of Rumsfeld's reform agenda, see Ivan Eland, "Rumsfeld vs. the Pentagon," Cato Institute, April 11, 2001, https://www.cato.org/publications/commentary/rumsfeld-vs-pentagon; Rumsfeld to de Leon, "Pentagon Bureaucracy," April 10, 2001, NSA Electronic Briefing Book 615, https://nsarchive.gwu.edu/briefing-book/foia/2018-01-24/rumsfeld-snowflakes-come-cold; Rumsfeld to de Leon, "Blechman Letter," April 17, 2001, NSA Electronic Briefing Book 615; Rumsfeld to White, "Battlefield of the Future," June 23, 2001, Rumsfeld Papers, https://papers.rumsfeld.com/; Rumsfeld, "The DoD Challenge" June 25, 2001, Rumsfeld Papers; Rumsfeld, "Goals," July 17, 2001, NSA Electronic Briefing Book 615; Rumsfeld to Di Rita, "Thornberry Article," August 18, 2001, NSA Electronic Briefing Book 615; Rumsfeld to Bush and Cheney, "Waste to Warfighting," September 2001, Rumsfeld Papers; Rumsfeld to Wolfowitz, Zakheim, and White, "Providing to States," October 8, 2001, NSA Electronic Briefing Book 615; Donald Rumsfeld, "Transforming the Military," *Foreign Affairs* (May/June 2002); Donald Rumsfeld, *Known and Unknown: A Memoir* (New York: Sentinel, 2011), 279–81, 291–304, 331–33; Paul Light, "Rumsfeld's Revolution at Defense," Brookings

Institution, July 1, 2005, https://www.brookings.edu/research/rumsfelds-revolution-at-defense/; Peter Boyer, "Downfall: How Donald Rumsfeld Reformed the Army and Lost Iraq," *New Yorker*, November 13, 2006, https://www.newyorker.com/magazine/2006/11/20/downfall-2; and Robert Kaplan, "What Rumsfeld Got Right," *Atlantic Monthly*, July/August 2008, https://www.theatlantic.com/magazine/archive/2008/07/what-rumsfeld-got-right/306870/.

10. Andrew Bacevich, "Field Marshal McNamara," *National Interest*, May/June 2007, 82.
11. OSD, Directorate for Organizational Policy and Decision Support, *Organization and Management of the Department of Defense, Resource Guide v 3.2* (Washington, DC: OSD, 2019), https://fas.org/irp/agency/dod/org-man.pdf.
12. Scott Maucione, "Pentagon Staff Size Takes More Flak from Experts," Federal News Network, December 8, 2015, https://federalnewsnetwork.com/defense/2015/12/pentagon-staff-size-takes-slack-experts/.
13. Michaila Hancock, "Pentagon: The World's Largest Office Building—in Infographics," *Architects Journal*, August 27, 2015, https://www.architectsjournal.co.uk/news/pentagon-the-worlds-largest-office-building-in-infographics#:~:text=The%20Pentagon%2C%20the%20USA's%20Headquarters,State%20Building%20in%20New%20York.
14. To make matters more complicated, while there are three service departments, there are also eight uniformed services, including the six military services.
15. Mark Cancian, *U.S. Military Forces in FY 2020: Navy*, Center for Strategic & International Studies, October 3, 2019, https://www.csis.org/analysis/us-military-forces-fy-2020-navy.
16. John McGrath, *The Other End of the Spear: The Tooth-to-Tail Ratio (T3R) in Modern Military Operations* (Fort Leavenworth, KS: Combat Studies Institute Press, 2007), https://www.armyupress.army.mil/Portals/7/combat-studies-institute/csi-books/mcgrath_op23.pdf.
17. Defense Business Board, "Review of Tooth-to-Tail," Report FY08-2 (April 2008), https://dbb.defense.gov/Portals/35/Documents/Reports/2008/FY08-2_Tooth_To_Tail_Analysis_2008-4.pdf. Established in 2001, the Defense Business Board provides the secretary and deputy secretary of defense with independent advice, reflecting its members' private-sector perspective, on best practices in business that can be applied in the Pentagon. The board consists of approximately twenty business executives.
18. Cheryl Marcum, ed., *Department of Defense Political Appointments, Positions and Process* (Washington, DC: RAND Corp., 2001), 16n16.
19. Much of the discussion that follows draws from Dave Oliver, *Making It in Washington: An Essential Guide for Political Appointees* (Victoria, BC: Trafford, 2002).
20. This is obviously a generalized statement. Besides McDonald, Adm. Mike Boorda (Kelso's successor as CNO) also had close relationships on Capitol Hill. The Marine Corps, which has long felt its existence to be under threat, has made a determined effort to place officers in congressional liaison billets. Harvey M. Sapolsky, Eugene Gholz, and Caitlin Talmadge, *US Defense Politics: The Origins of Security Policy* (London: Routledge, 2013), 110–29.
21. Kimberly Jackson, Katherine L. Kidder, Sean Mann, William H. Waggy II, and Natasha Lander, and S. Rebecca Zimmerman, *Raising the Flag: Implications of U.S. Military Approaches to General and Flag Officer Development* (Washington, DC: RAND Corp., 2020).
22. Jack Smith, "$37 Screws, a $7,622 Coffee Maker, $640 Toilet Seats; Suppliers to Our Military Just Won't Be Oversold," *Los Angeles Times*, July 30, 1986; William Hartung,

"Only the Pentagon Could Spend $640 on a Toilet Seat," *The Nation*, April 11, 2016, https://www.thenation.com/article/archive/only-the-pentagon-could-spend-640-on-a-toilet-seat/.

23. James Barron, "High Cost of Military Parts," *New York Times*, September 1, 1983; Sydney Freedberg, "The Myth of the $600 Hammer," *Government Executive*, December 7, 1998, https://www.govexec.com/federal-news/1998/12/the-myth-of-the-600-hammer/5271/.
24. Steven Roberts, "The Provocative Saga of the $400 Hammer," *New York Times*, June 13, 1984.
25. James Locher, *Victory on the Potomac: The Goldwater-Nichols Act Unifies the Pentagon* (College Station: Texas A&M University Press, 2002), 277ff.
26. Ronald Fox, *Defense Acquisition Reform, 1960–2009: An Elusive Goal* (Washington, DC: Center for Military History, 2011), 43–79.
27. President's Blue Ribbon Commission on Defense Management, *A Quest for Excellence: Final Report to the President* (Washington, DC: 1986); Fox, *Reform*, 125–50.
28. Locher, *Victory*, 391ff.
29. Locher, 437ff.; Hone, *OPNAV*, 365ff.
30. Steven Wills, "The Effect of the Goldwater-Nichols Act of 1986 on Naval Strategy, 1987–1994," *Naval War College Review* 69, no. 2 (2016): 21–40.
31. Locher, *Victory*, 252ff.
32. George Wilson, "Navy Secretary Declares War on Bureaucracy," *Washington Post*, April 5, 1985, https://www.washingtonpost.com/archive/politics/1985/04/05/navy-secretary-declares-war-on-bureaucracy/2421f832-a6cd-4fd6-846f-672c40ea04dd/; William Rempel, "Lehman Aide Was Strengthened: Procurement Reform May Have Led Way to Scandal," *Los Angeles Times*, June 29, 1988, https://www.latimes.com/archives/la-xpm-1988-06-20-mn-3515-story.htmll; Hone, *OPNAV*, 339–42.
33. The following discussion draws heavily from Charles P. Nemfakos, Irv Blickstein, Aine Seitz McCarthy, and Jerry M. Sollinger, *The Perfect Storm: The Goldwater-Nichols Act and Its Effect on Navy Acquisition* (Washington, DC: RAND Corp., 2010), https://www.rand.org/content/dam/rand/pubs/occasional_papers/2010/RAND_OP308.pdf.
34. Fox, *Reform*, 142ff.; Hone, *OPNAV*, 369ff.
35. Boeing's CFO also went to prison and the secretary of the Air Force had to resign. John Tirpak, "Tanker Twilight Zone," *Air Force Magazine*, February 1, 2004, https://www.airforcemag.com/article/0204tanker/; Leslie Wayne, "Air Force at Unease in the Capital," *New York Times*, December 16, 2004; "The Boeing Tanker Case," Compendium of Arms Trade Corruption, n.d., World Peace Foundation, https://sites.tufts.edu/corruptarmsdeals/the-boeing-tanker-case/.
36. Fox, *Reform*, 189ff.
37. Fox, 151ff.
38. Sydney Freedberg, "'If We Fail, Fire Us': CSA Gen. Milley on Acquisition Changes," Breaking Defense, October 8, 2015, https://breakingdefense.com/2015/10/if-we-fail-fire-us-csa-gen-milley-on-acquisition-changes/; "Defense Acquisition Reform: Background, Analysis, and Issues for Congress," Congressional Research Service, May 23, 2014, https://www.everycrsreport.com/reports/R43566.html; Heidi Peters, "Acquisition Reform in the FY2016-FY2018 National Defense Authorization Acts (NDAAs)," Congressional Research Service, January 19, 2018, https://www.everycrsreport.com/reports/R45068.html#_Toc504570767.

39. Lauren Williams, "DOD Cuts Red Tape to Support Fast Prototyping," FCW, April 10, 2020, https://fcw.com/articles/2020/04/10/dod-ota-lord-prototype.aspx.
40. Elizabeth Bailey (WHL in the OSD during the second Clinton administration) to Dave Oliver, email, September 7, 2020.
41. This was a development critics of the all-volunteer force warned of in the 1970s. James Fallows, *National Defense* (New York: Random House, 1981).
42. As of 2017, less than 8 percent of the total US population were veterans. Jennifer Schultz, "Veterans by the Numbers," National Conference of State Legislators, November 10, 2017), https://www.ncsl.org/blog/2017/11/10/veterans-by-the-numbers.aspx; Kristen Bialik, "The Changing Face of America's Veteran Population," Pew Research Center, November 10, 2017, https://www.pewresearch.org/fact-tank/2017/11/10/the-changing-face-of-americas-veteran-population/.
43. Tim Johnson and Dalton Conley, "Civilian Public Sector Employment as a Long-Run Outcome of Military Conscription," *Proceedings of the National Academy of Sciences of the United States of America* 116, no. 43 (2019): 21456–62; Leo Shane, "Will the Number of Veterans in Congress Rise Next Year?," *Military Times*, October 19, 2018, https://www.militarytimes.com/news/pentagon-congress/2018/10/19/will-the-number-of-veterans-in-congress-rise-next-year/; Leo Shane, "Hundreds of Veterans Are Winning Elections—at the State Level," *Military Times*, April 17, 2016, https://www.militarytimes.com/news/2016/04/17/hundreds-of-veterans-are-winning-elections-at-the-state-level/; "Veterans in Public Office," American Enterprise Institute, November 10, 2015, https://www.aei.org/politics-and-public-opinion/veterans-in-public-office/; "Serving after Serving: Veterans in State Public Office," American Enterprise Institute, April 12, 2016, https://www.aei.org/politics-and-public-opinion/serving-after-serving-veterans-in-state-public-office/.

CHAPTER 6

Congress

Congress plays a vital role in shaping, if not necessarily controlling, US national security. Even if presidents since Franklin Roosevelt have loved to style themselves as the "commander in chief," it is worth noting two facts. First, the president's authority is over the Army and Navy—not the nation as a whole (article II, section 2 of the US Constitution). Second, while there is a separation of powers among the three branches of government, the notion that they are coequal is a myth. In fact, the structure of the Constitution and the intentions of its framers (as evidenced by *The Federalist Papers,* among other sources) indicate that the legislature was supposed to be the preeminent branch.[1]

As we have seen on occasion, Congress has ample authority to check any "imperial presidency." Perusal of the Constitution reveals that whereas the executive branch (article II) comprises four sections, the legislative branch (article I) has ten sections, including the all-important power of the purse (section 8). Article I also tasks Congress to provide for "the common Defense." The president would have nothing to command if Congress did not appropriate the money for the services, which Congress must do at least once every two years.

This constitutional provision on timeliness and the good will of patriots have thus far kept the United States from suffering the same fate as Germany. In the 1860s Germany (or, more specifically, Prussia) went down the road of autocracy and dictatorship when Otto von Bismarck defied the liberal Prussian legislature by appropriating money for the army using previous years' budgets. Once the executive has untrammeled authority over the armed forces, it is hard to make the claim that the country still has a federal system of government, much less a liberal democratic one.[2]

Since the founding of the republic, Congress has enjoyed immense power over the operations of the federal government, especially national defense. That power has only grown over time, even if it has diffused somewhat through the subsequent creation of separate appropriations and authorization processes and the proliferation of committees and subcommittee with oversight over defense.[3] Today the responsibility for funding and oversight of defense is divided between two committees in both the House of Representatives and the Senate: armed services committees that evaluate the president's budget submission and "authorize" the creation or maintenance of specific defense programs and defense appropriations subcommittees that provide the legal budget authority for executive agencies to incur previously authorized financial obligations (agreements that yield outlays from goods to labor).[4]

Those committees are full of hardworking, often exceptional employees who understand where power exists in the US political system—namely, the budget but also through the confirmation of senior officials—and they often use their influence to extract concessions from the executive branch or the services. Does that mean that a determined Congress is actually capable of managing the Pentagon?

Despite the skill of individual legislators, the record would suggest no. In practical terms, Congress suffers several major handicaps and has, in the last few decades, made its job more difficult by reducing the size and quality of its staff. Beyond specific groups such as the Senate Armed Services Committee, any semblance of a bipartisan approach to national security has evaporated. Finally, there is the low esteem of Congress in the eyes of the public. All of these factors put the legislative branch at a significant disadvantage in national-strategy affairs with the executive branch. Nevertheless, whether or not Congress can successfully drive changes in national security, it must be included in the process because of its powerful ability to frustrate positive actions and because individual legislators can, in fact, offer meaningful insights to those responsible for executive action.

LEARNING FROM THE BEST

One fall 2003 afternoon in Alaska, near the middle of the Kenai River, while working as a defense industry executive, Dave Oliver attended a master class in intelligence affairs. He was seated alongside Sen. Ted Stevens—who at that time had represented Alaska in the Senate for almost thirty-five years—in a four-man boat motoring slowly upstream just ahead of the returning run of Coho salmon.[5] Oliver and Stevens were the first to catch the limit, and thankfully the senator caught the largest salmon by far. Oliver had no issues to raise that day and was making conversation when he mentioned that his spouse, who was serving as the general counsel for the Naval Criminal Investigative Service, was working the Aldrich Ames case.[6] The subject caught the senator's interest, and for the next several hours, while the other two men in the boat continued to cast, drink beer, and exaggerate about the fish they had almost hooked, Stevens shared his wisdom about intelligence matters.

Stevens had learned an immense amount in the Senate. His comments that day were a compelling demonstration of the depth and breadth of knowledge that a member of Congress can possess on specific national questions. Among members of Congress, there were and are a few diamonds with a sophisticated understanding of national security. Stevens was one of them, like Carl Vinson, Richard Russell, Barry Goldwater, Sam Nunn, John McCain, Jack Murtha, Carl Levin, Ike Skelton, and Jack Reed, but such legislators are not the norm.

At the other end of the spectrum was Rep. Randy Cunningham. Cunningham claimed wide-ranging expertise in national security by virtue of his perch on the House Armed Services Committee as well as his service in the Navy during the Vietnam War.[7] Neither Cunningham's skills as a pilot nor his physical courage were ever in doubt—only his honor and decency. The same year as the Kenai boat trip with Stevens, Cunningham pleaded guilty to bribery, fraud, and tax evasion. Among other transgressions, he had pressured OSD personnel to arrange sweetheart deals for a contractor who had bribed the congressman.[8] When Cunningham went to prison, he took with him a plausible claim to be the most incompetent member of Congress.

Stevens and Cunningham may well have been the alpha and omega of Congress with respect to defense matters; most legislators fall somewhere in the middle. Leaving aside the pervasive denigration of government service since at least the 1980s, which affects the quality of people who run for office and win election, it is unreasonable to expect members not on the national-security committees (armed services, intelligence, and foreign affairs) to fall on Stevens's end of the spectrum.[9] The business of governing is extraordinarily complex, and mastering the complexity of the defense enterprise is taxing even for the sharpest minds.[10]

Because of the many competing demands for their attention, the majority of senators and representatives focus on defense matters that have a direct relevance to their constituents. If a substantial number of constituents are affected by a particular issue, their member of Congress often seeks assignments on the committees and subcommittees that have oversight over those interests. In the case of members seeking spots on the armed services committees, often their state or district is home to shipyards, repair depots, bases, or factories manufacturing military products. Serving on a committee does not, however, instantly make one an expert on the issue.

For those members who choose to become involved in a defense issue, they cannot rely on their staff to fight their battles.[11] These staffs are swamped with constituent affairs, and some have in recent years offloaded some of the workload on the Congressional Research Service (CRS). Long considered Congress's internal think tank, the overstretched and underresourced CRS today spends so much of its time responding to constituent inquiries that it has little bandwidth left to do serious analytic work.

The CRS's burden is aggravated by the fact that many congressional staffers are underpaid and overworked, and they rarely stay in their jobs for long.[12] High turnover prevents these staffers, including those attached to congressional committees, from building subject-matter expertise equivalent to that in the executive branch, with the CRS serving as a "training and orientation organization." Consequently, if a lone member wishes to legislate on defense issues without the services or the OSD providing the necessary military or civilian expertise, that legislator has to rely on lobbyists.

As one CRS staffer complained, partisanship and political gridlock have made nearly everything controversial. Today even facts are up for debate on Capitol Hill, and therefore the CRS must always use "flat" language, discriminating only in the issues it chooses to review, not in its findings or conclusions.[13] Sadly, it also appears that there is an unspoken rule within the CRS that it will not publish reports critical of the priorities of congressional leaders, who control its budget.[14]

WHAT CONGRESS CAN AND CANNOT DO

Congress has the power to make any change it desires, but it is generally starved for knowledge. As is true with the political appointees who serve within the Pentagon, it is exceedingly difficult for a member to make changes in defense and at the same time avoid collateral damage. To use a term popular on Capitol Hill, it is easier to swing a "meat axe" than wield a surgical scalpel, as occurred in 2013 when Congress imposed across-the-board cuts to federal spending after failing to reach an agreement concerning taxes and spending.[15]

Experience has shown that Congress can cut or "plus-up" a program, but members are seldom if ever able to make fine-tuned adjustments. Because there are too many moving parts in Pentagon or service programs, it is very difficult for the men and women on Capitol Hill to reach across the Potomac River with a "five-mile screwdriver." Instead, legislators need to convince the OSD or the relevant service of the need for each specific change. If the men and women "in the arena," as Theodore Roosevelt might have put it, are not convinced there is a problem or a viable solution, reform efforts often bog down.

It is not difficult to understand why a specific legislator's knowledge of defense matters might be limited. Leaving aside the dearth of technical expertise among legislators, very few of them—18 percent in 2019—have any personal military experience.[16] Moreover, even those who served usually did so at junior or mid-range (tactical or operational) levels and have little familiarity with questions of higher strategy, not to mention technical issues such as budgeting or acquisitions.[17] At the same time, there are always other issues competing for each member's attention—not the least of which is the pressure to fundraise for reelection. Gone are the days when a man like Carl Vinson, representing a landlocked, rural district in Georgia, could afford to become an expert on naval affairs, even though that issue had no direct relevance to his constituents. Vinson had that luxury because he was a Democrat running in the "solid South" and did not have to bother with fundraising. His successors are usually not so fortunate.[18]

Most of what individual legislators know today about defense issues is invariably tied to the interests of their constituents, who make their views known through lobbyists. While many consider these lobbyists to be a problem, simply eliminating them would create a new set of headaches. Since 1995, when the new Republican majority under Speaker Newt Gingrich reduced congressional staffs by 40 percent, cutting many irreplaceable permanent employees of various committees, it is difficult to imagine how individual members can keep up to date on issues without the (obviously self-interested) assistance of lobbyists.[19]

Finally, Congress has to confront the same problem any administration faces: the sheer complexity of defense. There are 535 members of Congress: 100 senators and 435 representatives. These men and women are responsible for the full spectrum of issues that affect a country of 331 million Americans with a GDP of $20 trillion. By contrast, within the US military, nine hundred generals and admirals aided by roughly ten thousand colonels and Navy captains are responsible for 1.3 million active-duty service personnel (plus another 865,000 reservists) and a significant portion of the $700 billion Pentagon budget. (Since the 1960s, Department of Defense agencies, including the combatant commands and members of the Intelligence Community, have claimed a growing percentage share of the total budget even as the services' nominal budgets have increased.)[20]

It is simply impossible for members of Congress to comprehend all facets of a complex program unless the relevant service assists. And if no general or admiral understands the entirety of defense after more than forty years of service, how can a member of Congress, even one with an extraordinary staff and unconcerned with reelection, hope to keep pace? There simply is not enough time in the day to attend to all of the vital matters that cross a legislator's desk. That is why elected officials, even in a democratic society, must rely on the advice of experts. In the case of military affairs, that means the people in whom the country has invested so much to master the art of war.[21]

In years past, Americans worried that if the military became too influential within the corridors of power, the "specialists in violence" would gradually replace the "specialists in bargaining" (politicians) and create an authoritarian state.[22] We must always guard against such an eventuality, but if the COVID-19 pandemic has taught us anything, it is the need for experts to enlighten policymakers. Experts should not direct a liberal democracy, but there is no functioning society without their assistance. No one can develop expertise without time and resources to focus on a particular skill set. This is not a luxury the average lawmaker possesses.

CULTURE CLASH

Another reason why it is so difficult for Congress to understand the military is the cultural differences between the two bodies. As with political appointees, this is not intended as criticism. Organizations develop different cultures to achieve their specific goals, but that can create a scope for misunderstandings, mischief, and disaster.

To illustrate, after the United States invaded Iraq in 2003, the deputy secretary of defense asked Dave Oliver (as a consequence of his experience in the American defense industry) to go to Baghdad to manage restarting Iraq's economy.[23] The situation in Iraq was volatile, although no one yet knew how bad it could get. After Oliver arrived in early June 2003, all of the US Treasury representatives left on the next flight, having decided (quite reasonably) that getting shot at or blown up was not in their job descriptions.

The next day, Peter McPherson, the president of Michigan State University, who was in Iraq serving temporarily as the director of economic policy for the Office of Reconstruction and Humanitarian Assistance (which shortly became the Coalition Provisional Authority), assigned Oliver responsibility for the Ministry of Finance and then added the Ministry of Planning for good measure. These were two of the twenty-eight ministries reporting to Amb. Paul "Jerry" Bremer, who led the CPA after Jay Garner's ouster in April.

Many, if not most, of the senior people working for Bremer in the Baghdad Palace were from the State Department. Because of the dominance of diplomats within the CPA, even though Bremer reported to the secretary of defense and was collocated with the military commander (Lt. Gen. Ricardo Sanchez), the organizational structure Bremer created mimicked that of an embassy. Consequently, the CPA focused on receiving and processing information, and its executive capabilities suffered. To make matters worse, the environment in Iraq was spartan—intermittent to nonexistent electricity, limited water, and high heat—with the added excitement of unexpected gunfire and explosions. Military training helps people prepare for just this sort of environment, but of the three hundred individuals in the CPA (including the representatives from the United Kingdom and Australia), fewer than a dozen had any military experience.

Had the military or retired military officials staffed the CPA, it would have been organized and operated differently. A military organization places a premium on rapid adaptation during combat and the structured flow of information and procedures to facilitate "taking necessary action." During the wasted months of the early occupation of Iraq, even as the world briefly marveled at the apparent success of the United States in quickly subduing Afghanistan and Iraq, it was clear to those few CPA officials with military experience that life in Iraq was not returning to normal nearly fast enough.

In Baghdad the power was still out, people were pilfering money from the new government, and the wrong people (political exiles with little domestic support) were flowing back into the country to run it. Despite the increasing violence and loss of life, many officials in Baghdad and Washington were relieved when Saddam Hussein was captured in December 2003, which optimists hoped would end the incipient insurgency. In fact, Iraq was already past the tipping point and headed downhill.

Congress and the military have similarly different ways of approaching the world. Few people join either institution without a deep commitment to public service, but that is where the similarities end. It would be inaccurate to claim that the differences among them are analogous to the dichotomy Plato identified in his *Symposium* between *logos* (reason) and *eros* (passion—not sexual desire but rather the impulse to achieve greatness). There is plenty of reason and passion—some may term it patriotism—to be found in both institutions. Unlike the military, however, legislators thread the needle between reason and passion with the "countervailing" power of *interest* (i.e., staying in office), which keeps passion from overwhelming reason.[24]

No one can deny that Congress works with words, emotions, and interests. Legislators may rely on the power of the purse, but they also rely on guiding, shaping, and reflecting public opinion. There is not a high barrier to entry to (or exit from) Congress. There is a popular saying among politicos that "Washington is Hollywood for ugly people."[25] This is cruel, but it captures some essential truths about American political life. For one thing, there are no qualifications beyond the constitutional age limits. Even the seniority system in Congress seldom rivals the twenty-five years of experience the youngest army general possesses.[26] (Yet there are still people crying out for congressional term limits—as if less experienced legislators will somehow be wiser.[27])

For another, the absence of strong third parties as in other mature democracies means that members are less answerable to their party leaders than they are to activists who vote in primaries or donors who fund primary or general elections. Accordingly, members are, in the delicate words of the CRS, best described as "political entrepreneurs," who focus on their individual self-interest rather than that of the collective, which also means that they are keenly attuned to the demands of their constituents, particularly the most influential or best funded.[28]

The fear of losing their jobs keeps legislators attentive to the needs of their constituents, but whether this produces the optimal outcomes for national defense is debatable. Representatives and senators usually have good judgment—how else would they have gotten elected and reelected? They also often have good ideas—after all, why enter public service if not to effect change? They generally make good decisions on issues before them as long as the issue at hand does not directly harm a constituent's interests, which seems to be rather the point of representative government.

That said, there is little incentive in Congress toward long-term planning.[29] An individual in an elected office does not want to be found to be in error or on the wrong side of an issue. Because members are more likely to be punished for acting rather than not, members tend to be very risk-averse and, if permitted, will avoid taking clear positions and defer making decisions until the last possible moment (to better judge the political winds).

This is all in complete contradiction to how the military operates. There is a very high barrier to entry for a Navy captain or Army colonel. Not only have such officers devoted twenty years of their life to their profession, but their service has also invested millions of dollars in that person's development. Every officer or even a noncommissioned officer also has to learn how to think and act quickly. As Arleigh Burke remarked during the height of the fighting in the Pacific during World War II, "the difference between a good officer and poor one is about ten seconds."[30]

Because some of those decisions—taken as they are in the heat of the moment—will inevitably be wrong, analysts can learn a lot about an organization by how it deals with failure. If there are high penalties for small errors, leaders will be cautious and search for scapegoats. This attitude will proliferate throughout the ranks and leave good people in body bags, since military professionalism cannot thrive in an atmosphere of cronyism or backstabbing.[31]

Despite all of its many, many failings, the gold standard of learning from tactical and operational mistakes was the German Army before 1945. The worst thing a German officer could claim in an after-action report was that his unit had performed flawlessly. Instead, officers were encouraged to identify shortcomings and methods of overcoming them in future.[32] This is a tough standard to emulate. Ideally, the US military would balance someone's errors against their body of work and promise. If they fall short, their service either fires or reassigns them, or it accepts the mistake as the cost of doing business and moves on. There are only a very few classes of mistake that are inexcusable, and good officers can be salvaged even after conspicuous failures.[33] Legislators in a democratic society simply cannot operate on a similar standard because they are responsible to voters rather than any single institution.

SUMMARY

Congress has many of the same advantages and even more of the same disadvantages as political appointees. There are members of Congress and their staff who have a rich understanding of the essence of many if not all aspects of US power. Even more important, legislators sign all checks issued by Uncle Sam, which totals roughly one-third of the US GDP. Consequently, lawmakers know that their actions will have ramifications for the entire economy and that they are responsible for allocating scarce resources among competing national interests, public and private.

Through the power of the purse and subpoena, there are few checks on the power of Congress over defense, and there is certainly no lack of interest by members if a defense matter affects their constituents. In practice, however, extraordinary staff reductions in 1995 and a dearth of legislators with firsthand experience of or deep familiarity with military or national-security affairs limit Congress's ability to do more than tinker at the edges of the defense enterprise.

NOTES

1. Garry Wills, "The Framers' Answers to Three Myths about Impeachment," *New York Review of Books*, December 3, 2019, https://www.nybooks.com/daily/2019/12/03/the-framers-answers-to-three-myths-about-impeachment/; Kevin R. Kosar, Paul Glastris, Lee Drutman, Jonathan Rauch, Molly Reynolds, and Yuval Levin, *Restoring Congress as the First Branch*, R Street Policy Study 50, 2016, https://www.rstreet.org/wp-content/uploads/2016/01/RSTREET50.pdf. For an alternative perspective, see John Lehman, *Making War: The 200-Year Old Battle between the President and Congress over How America Goes to War* (New York: Scribner's, 1992), 57ff.
2. Gordon Craig, *The Politics of the Prussian Army, 1640–1945* (Oxford: Clarendon, 1955), 136ff.
3. For a critical perspective on this development, see Lehman, *Making War*, 241ff.
4. To make matters even more complicated, the funds that Congress provides have different, circumscribed periods of availability. If an agency fails to spend its appropriated money in time, it cannot use those funds to incur new obligations. "Financial Management: Authorization/Appropriation," AcqNotes, n.d., https://acqnotes.com/acqnote/careerfields/authorization-appropriations; US Senate Committee on Appropriations, "Budget Process: Authorization vs Appropriation," n.d., https://www.appropriations.senate.gov/about/budget-process; Corporate Office Properties Trust, *The Annual Defense Budget Process* (January 2020), https://s23.q4cdn.com/233908562/files/doc_downloads/irw/COPT_Research/Annual-Defence-Budget-Process.pdf.
5. He would serve until 2009 and died the following year in a plane crash.
6. Ames was a particularly destructive Soviet/Russian mole in the CIA. Tim Weiner, David Johnston, and Neil A. Lewis, *Betrayal: The Story of Aldrich Ames, an American Spy* (New York: Random House, 1995).
7. He was the only US Navy pilot to achieve the status of "ace" (five confirmed kills of enemy aircraft) during the Vietnam War.
8. Dave Oliver testified against Cunningham at his trial.
9. Dan Balz, "Crisis Exposes How American Has Hollowed Out Its Government," *Washington Post*, May 16, 2020, https://www.washingtonpost.com/graphics/2020/politics/government-hollowed-out-weaknesses/. President Reagan memorably remarked, "The nine most terrifying words in the English language are: I'm from the Government, and I'm here to help." Reagan Quotes and Speeches, August 12, 1986, https://www.reaganfoundation.org/ronald-reagan/reagan-quotes-speeches/news-conference-1/. More broadly, see Hedrick Smith, "Reagan's Effort to Change the Course of Government," *New York Times*, October 23, 1984, https://www.nytimes.com/1984/10/23/us/reagan-s-effort-to-change-course-of-government.htm. Arguably, the process started in the 1970s with public disillusionment rising during the Vietnam War, the Watergate Crisis, and stagflation arising from the 1973 oil shock. Judith Stein, *Pivotal Decade: How the United States Traded Factories for Finance in the Seventies* (New Haven, CT: Yale University Press, 2011).
10. Besides the sources cited below, the following chapter draws from Christian Brose, *The Kill Chain: Defending America in the Future of High-Tech Warfare* (New York: Hachette, 2020), chap. 11.

11. Daniel Schuman, "Keeping Congress Competent: Staff Pay, Turnover, and What It Means for Democracy," Sunlight Foundation, December 21, 2010, https://sunlightfoundation.com/2010/12/21/keeping-congress-competent-staff-pay-turnover-and-what-it-means-for-democracy/.
12. Casey Burgat, "Congressional Staff Turnover Isn't Usually a Problem. But When It Is, It's Bad," *Washington Post*, July 31, 2018, https://www.washingtonpost.com/news/posteverything/wp/2018/07/31/congressional-staff-turnover-isnt-usually-a-problem-but-when-it-is-its-bad/; Casey Burgat, "How Do Congressional Committee Staff Turnover Rates Compare to Personal Staff Turnover?," LegBranch.com, May 10, 2018, https://www.legbranch.org/2018-5-9-how-do-congressional-committee-staff-turnover-rates-compare-to-personal-staff-turnover/; Katherine Tully-McManus, "Congress Wakes Up to Its Staff Retention Problems after Covid, Bomb Threats and Riots," *Politico*, September 10, 2021, https://www.politico.com/news/2021/09/10/congress-staff-retention-problems-510879.
13. Discussion by Dave Oliver with a senior CRS official, September 7, 2021.
14. Kevin Kosar, "The Atrophying of the Congressional Research Service's Role in Supporting Committee Oversight," *Wayne Law Review* 64 (2018): 149–62, summarized in "Why I Quit the Congressional Research Service," *Washington Monthly*, January/February 2015, https://washingtonmonthly.com/magazine/janfeb-2015/why-i-quit-the-congressional-research-service/.
15. Paul Shinkman, "Budget Armageddon: DoD Prepares for Congressional 'Meat Axe,'" *U.S. News & World Report*, January 10, 2013, https://www.usnews.com/news/articles/2013/01/10/budget-armageddon-dod-prepares-for-congress-meat-axe.
16. Leo Shane, "Veterans in the 116th Congress, by the Numbers," *Military Times*, November 20, 2018, https://www.militarytimes.com/news/pentagon-congress/2018/11/21/veterans-in-the-116th-congress-by-the-numbers/.
17. Few military officers over the course of their training develop expertise in the highest levels of strategy and resource allocation. This has been a problem since the 1960s, at least. Alain Enthoven, *How Much Is Enough? Shaping the Defense Program, 1961–1969* (Santa Monica, CA: RAND Corp., 2005), 88ff.
18. James Cook, *Carl Vinson: Patriarch of the Armed Forces* (Macon, GA: Mercer University Press, 2004).
19. Lee Drutman, "Why Congress Relies on Lobbyists Instead of Thinking for Itself," *The Atlantic*, March 10, 2015, https://www.theatlantic.com/politics/archive/2015/03/when-congress-cant-think-for-itself-it-turns-to-lobbyists/387295/; Philip Wallach, "Congress Rebuked but Not Reimagined," Law & Liberty, January 15, 2020, https://lawliberty.org/congress-rebuked-but-not-reimagined/; Nicholas Thompson, "Gingrich Said to Be Pro-Science but Anti-Expertise," Office of Technology Assessment Archive, January 31, 2012, https://ota.fas.org/2012/01/31/gingrich-said-to-decimate-congressional-expertise/.
20. K. K. Rebecca Lai, Troy Griggs, Max Fisher, and Audrey Carlsen, "Is America's Military Big Enough?," *New York Times*, March 22, 2017; "General and Flag Officers in the U.S. Armed Forces: Background and Considerations for Congress," CRS, February 1, 2019, https://fas.org/sgp/crs/natsec/R44389.pdf; figures on ranks taken from Statista.com.
21. Thomas Nichols, *The Death of Expertise: The Campaign against Established Knowledge and Why It Matters* (Oxford: Oxford University Press, 2017), 219.

22. Harold Lasswell, "The Garrison State," *American Journal of Sociology* 46, no. 4 (1941): 455–68.
23. This discussion draws from the Oliver's recollections and the following sources: Dave Oliver, "Restarting the Economy in Iraq," November 2003, https://oversight.house.gov/sites/democrats.oversight.house.gov/files/documents/20070206180618-70251.pdf; Nora Bensahel, *After Saddam: Prewar Planning and the Occupation of Iraq* (Washington, DC: RAND Corp., 2008), https://www.rand.org/content/dam/rand/pubs/monographs/2008/RAND_MG642.pdf (esp. 53ff., 197); Special Inspector General for Iraqi Reconstruction, *Hard Lessons: The Iraq Reconstruction Experience* (Washington, DC: GPO, 2009), 84, 99, 101; James D. Savage, *Iraq's Budget as a Source of Political Stability*, Special Report 328 (Washington, DC: United States Institute of Peace, March 2013, https://www.usip.org/sites/default/files/SR328-Iraqs%20Budget%20as%20a%20Source%20of%20Political%20Stability.pdf; and James D. Savage, *Reconstructing Iraq's Budgetary Institutions: Coalition State Building after Saddam* (Cambridge: Cambridge University Press, 2013), 76ff.
24. Albert Hirschman, *The Passions and the Interests: Political Arguments for Capitalism before Its Triumph* (Princeton, NJ: Princeton University Press, 1977), 20ff.
25. "That line, or a variation thereof, was first used by Paul Begala [an aide to Bill Clinton] in the 1980s. Begala says he might have heard it in a bar. Which is where most truths about Washington and Hollywood originate." Roger Simon, "Washington Is Hollywood for the Ugly," *Politico*, April 29, 2014, https://www.politico.com/story/2014/04/white-house-correspondents-dinner-roger-simon-106118.
26. The problem is worse for the Republican Party, which has a six-year term limit for holding the chair of a House committee. Zachary Goldstein, "Early Retirements: The Debate over Committee Leader Term Limits," Solve with National Journal, December 18, 2019, https://solve.nationaljournal.com/early-retirements-the-debate-over-committee-leader-term-limits/.
27. Casey Burgat, "Five Reasons to Oppose Congressional Term Limits," Brookings Institution, January 18, 2018, https://www.brookings.edu/blog/fixgov/2018/01/18/five-reasons-to-oppose-congressional-term-limits/; Jessie Bur, "Congressional Term Limits: Countering Power Abuse or Counterproductive," *Federal Times*, June 19, 2019, https://www.federaltimes.com/federal-oversight/congress/2019/06/19/congressional-term-limits-countering-power-or-counterproductive/. The argument for term limits disparages the value of expertise: "In practice, voters seem no better served by a 30-year legislator than by a 30-year staffer, since both tend to represent the political culture, influential interests, and the entrenched state more than anything approaching the public interest." Doug Bandow, "How to Term-Limit Congress," Cato Institute, January 29, 2019, https://www.cato.org/publications/commentary/how-term-limit-congress.
28. "The Congressional Research Service and the American Legislative Process," CRS, April 12, 2011, https://crsreports.congress.gov/product/pdf/RL/RL33471.
29. The impulse to develop such competence—usually in the executive branch—briefly flourished during the New Deal before expiring quietly in the 1970s. Otis Graham, *Toward a Planned Society: From Roosevelt to Nixon* (Oxford: Oxford University Press, 1974).
30. William Daly, "Ten Seconds to Live or Die," *Proceedings* 144 (December 2018), https://www.usni.org/magazines/proceedings/2018/december/ten-seconds-live-or-die.

31. Caitlin Talmadge, *The Dictator's Army: Battlefield Effectiveness in Authoritarian Regimes* (Ithaca, NY: Cornell University Press, 2015).
32. Williamson Murray, "The German Response to Victory in Poland: A Case Study in Professionalism," *Armed Forces & Society* 7, no. 2 (1981): 285–98.
33. Thomas Ricks, *The Generals: Military Command from World War II to Today* (New York: Penguin, 2013).

CHAPTER 7

Private Industry

There is a widespread belief that the Department of Defense would benefit if only it adopted practices from private industry. Because of the growing role of information technology in national defense, people often urge leveraging insights from Silicon Valley.[1] As one "Big Tech" CEO boasted—apparently without irony—to a combatant commander, "If I got under your tent for a day, I could solve most of your problems."[2] Coincident with these beliefs is the idea that the CEOs of the major companies, notably defense and aerospace firms, can bring a great deal to the table, especially in terms of understanding program management and industry incentives. In 2018 one defense executive nearly became secretary of defense (Patrick Shanahan of Boeing). And let us not forget the other distinguished executives who have served as secretaries in the past: Charles Wilson (General Electric), Robert McNamara (Ford), and Donald Rumsfeld (Searle).[3]

Is this faith in the wisdom of the private sector warranted? Let us start by examining the second proposition, which, on its face, appears quite rational. The men and women at the helm of the major defense companies are all accomplished and politically astute.[4] They have a wide range of professional acquaintances (since they do business worldwide) along with a profound knowledge of the challenges confronting the defense sector. They are responsible for maintaining a working relationship with their customers in the Pentagon as well as elected, appointed, and career officials in the White House and on Capitol Hill.

This competence and the semblance of indispensability brings multiple rewards to these individuals and hence to their companies. The rewards are not simply financial—a critical intangible benefit is access. Access provides invaluable market information not only as to what their customers (the Pentagon and the services) will want but also how much the potential customers may be willing to pay. Access also delivers psychic rewards. CEOs, defense or otherwise, become known commodities and are often consulted, formally or informally, by executive and legislative leaders on all manner of issues, including national security.

The influence of the defense industry—contractors—on the Pentagon and the services is often overestimated by outside observers. This is understandable. To begin with, compared to the other players in the defense world such as the executive or legislative branches, the defense industry on the face of it looks much like the services. Its workforce includes large numbers of people with STEM degrees, and many actually have prior military service. As a consequence, the employees in the defense sector understand the jargon of their customers, unlike civilians who frequently flounder in a sea of acronyms when they first approach the world of the Department of Defense. Because of these common backgrounds, defense contractors are at least familiar with the services, their history, and their needs. They are much more so than any commercial firm trying to break into the defense market. There are, however, two key areas of difference between defense contractors and the military: motivation and culture (norms and values). Understanding these differences is essential to recognizing the limitation of importing a private-sector mindset into defense.

INSTITUTIONAL CULTURES AND MOTIVATIONS

When people join the US government, they take an oath to protect their nation against all enemies, foreign and domestic. To fulfill their pledge, some service members, diplomats, and intelligence officers work in dangerous environments, usually not of their own choice, often displaced from their families. The military expects the rank-and-file to answer each call, only considering what is in the best interests of the nation. This sense of being part of a tradition of service is not just a recruiting slogan.

When Dave Oliver was a political appointee in the Pentagon, several Army officers served rotations as his aides. Each of them had experienced very different career trajectories, but they all shared one characteristic. All had at least once occupied a billet that traced its lineage back more than two hundred years to the Revolutionary War. Each officer who served in that billet had visited the gravesite of the Continental Army officer who had first filled that billet. The officers never advertised their undertakings, but such a pilgrimage was integral to their service culture.

It is a misnomer to speak of a single, monolithic "US military culture." As we have seen, the services each have a specific set of norms and values arising from its particular history, they operate primarily in distinct domains, and they execute force very differently.[5] One thing that binds all of the services, however, is the importance of integrity. It is a touchstone of military life. Integrity is central to many other fields and professions (even if the definitions vary), but this is not always true in business.[6]

While it is possible for firms to learn and use US military jargon, no matter how many former service members a company employs, it has sometimes proven very difficult for commercial firms to capture the services' ethos. For example, while Boeing is a remarkable company and has an extraordinary relationship with the US government going back almost a century, its ethical lapses have, at times, virtually destroyed its relationship with the Pentagon.[7]

The cultural differences between government and private industry go beyond individual failings. Fundamentally, private industry, whether it is the defense sector, Big Tech, or any commercial firm, has a completely different value framework ("incentive structure" as economists might phrase it) than the military. To begin with, as MBA students have learned for decades, the foremost duty of the leadership of any publicly traded firm is to maximize shareholder value. This means taking every legal action to increase profits and returning those profits to shareholders in the form of higher share prices and dividends.

This idea, immortalized by the conservative economist Milton Friedman in 1970, says nothing about benefits to the firm's workers, its customers, or the communities it serves.[8] Most important from our perspective, it says nothing about the country that establishes and maintains the rule of law that protects the firm. On the list of a firm's priorities, according to Friedman, loyalty to the United States does not exist. It is neither above nor below shareholder value. It is not interspersed among the interests of executives, employees, and customers. It simply is not there.

If executives care about things such as "social responsibility," Friedman said they should worry about it in own spare time, using their own money, rather than that of their firm's owners (shareholders). For the most part, American executives have followed his lead. Consider the example of Lee Raymond, the former CEO of Exxon. When asked by another executive why Exxon did not build more refineries in the United States to enhance US security, Raymond responded, "I'm not a U.S. company, and I don't make decisions based on what's good for the U.S."[9]

Under Raymond or Friedman's logic, the overriding goal of any public company (meaning those whose shares are traded publicly) is to maximize the monetary benefits for shareholders. If the company can do so by, say, investing in R & D or building new infrastructure or hiring more workers, then it should prove it by completing a variety of complicated calculations (net present value, the time value of money, etc.) demonstrating that the long-term return on investment for shareholders is greater than the short-term gain achieved through, say, higher dividend payments.

That is how it works in textbooks, but in real life it is not so clear-cut.[10] For example, since the executives running the company are human, unless the board is more involved and aggressive than average, corporate executives may undertake actions that maximize executive compensation. Remember, in most major American corporations, the senior executives receive the bulk of their compensation not from their salary but from stock options and bonuses.[11] Ultimately, it is fair to say that maximizing shareholder return privileges short-term returns, which—whatever its shortcomings as a business model—is also antithetical with the military preference for planning.[12]

The gulf between the motivations of the military and private industry is unbridgeable in a capitalist society. Some years ago, when Oliver was the principal deputy undersecretary of defense for acquisition, he had a discussion with the CEO of General Dynamics, Nicholas Chabraja. Oliver went to Chabraja's office to seek his support on an issue. Both men had been present during a discussion with the Army over a proposed change in the Army's logistics policy. There were millions of dollars of savings available, but the Army, for reasons that escaped Oliver, was digging in its heels against the change.

Chabraja understood the facts yet had remained silent during the meeting. Oliver traveled to visit him at the headquarters of General Dynamics, nestled in the Northern Virginia suburbs. He was curious to find out why exactly Chabraja had not spoken up. If he had, his words might have tipped the scales, as the Army was the largest customer of General Dynamics. Army leaders knew and respected Chabraja.

Chabraja admitted that he agreed with Oliver that the Army was wasting money. But he added that, as the CEO of General Dynamics, his primary responsibility was to his shareholders, then to his employees, and finally to his family. He had realized early in the meeting that the Army was not interested in change, and Chabraja figured the Army would resent anyone siding with the OSD to force the Army to take this step. As Chabraja saw things, it was not the responsibility of General Dynamics or any other private company to assume risk to help the government to become more efficient.

As this anecdote demonstrates, the motivations of private industry are irreconcilable with those of government organizations. Governments can and do promote their industries at home and abroad because they are acting in the national interest rather than a specific sector of the economy, but we cannot expect private firms to put the collective good over their own well-being. Private firms can and should focus on their long-term well-being—that is why capitalist economies, where private markets comprising individuals or firms allocate capital based on price signals, are so dynamic and successful. But success in the business world is measured differently than in the realm of government, and expecting otherwise is futile.

In principle, this incompatibility in motivations will endure indefinitely and applies to all private firms, whether they are members of Big Tech or the major defense contractors. The question for this chapter is not whether private industry can provide good ideas (it has and will do that, as we shall see) but whether the private sector can *lead* or even inspire change. Our answer is that this is impossible to count on because it would require industry to act in a manner contrary its interests. Asking business people to take actions that irritate their customers and cost their shareholders money—even for the sake of Uncle Sam—is a tough sell even in wartime. It is virtually impossible in the absence of a conflict, when publicly traded companies are under immense pressure to maximize returns either for shareholders or immediate stakeholders such as their employees. To make matters worse, even when companies—for whatever reason—do put the public interest above their own, sometimes government is unable or unwilling to take advantage of their industry's generosity, as the following case study demonstrates.

SAVING MONEY IS NOT ENOUGH

John Hamre was one of the most capable political appointees who has ever served in the Department of Defense. In the late 1990s, he wanted the services to consider the insights private firms had acquired over the last decade to see if any were applicable to the Pentagon. Hamre had a great deal of power as the deputy secretary of defense, but he also had all of the other necessary attributes to be a success. Besides being intelligent, he was soft-spoken, charming, and very knowledgeable, having served as the senior staff member for the Senate Armed Services Committee for years.[13] Hamre probably understood the ins and outs of defense as well as any political appointee before or since.

One day Hamre decided, like many before him, that it was time to enlist private industry in reducing waste at the Pentagon. This was no publicity ploy. His plan featured none of the gimmicks that lesser politicians use to pretend they are doing something. There was to be no grand announcement, followed by press releases, the establishment of a team with goals, briefings, more fanfare, and an out-briefing. Instead, Hamre intended to invest his own time and prestige into making this effort work.

He had his staff plan a dinner with a very specific guest list. He wanted the chairman or CEO of the dozen largest defense companies to attend. He also invited the vice chairman of the Joint Chiefs (who approved all weapon system requirements) as well as the senior staffers of both the House and Senate Appropriations Committees (the individuals on the Hill who were instrumental to getting anything funded). Hamre's staff then juggled the dinner date so that all of these people could attend.

Hamre began the dinner with a soliloquy on the dramatic defense budget cuts he predicted in the near future. He then spoke on the consequential need for reform, particularly in the area of acquisition. Finally, Hamre asked—pleaded, in fact—each of the assembled defense executives to go back to their companies and return to him with policy changes that would save the Pentagon money.

Such was the reputation, eloquence, and charm of Hamre that within a couple of weeks each company put forward a list of several items that it believed were costing the government money for no good reason. The companies provided solid recommendations. That each of the defense companies was so accommodating came as quite the surprise to some members of Hamre's staff. Perhaps the private executives figured it was more important to appear reasonable to a senior civilian leader before any general bloodletting began than to continue cultivating the hidebound services. Perhaps Hamre could do the seemingly impossible. Who knows? Whatever the reason, the lists they provided were genuine.

Time for a very short digression. An unnecessary military "requirement" is so terribly expensive because it bites at least twice and sometimes three times. Here is an example. Let us assume that company A makes a radio for the Army that meets the fifteen requirements the Army has stated, but three of those "requirements" are actually not vital. Whether or not those last three are truly necessary is irrelevant—once those "requirements" are on the list, the Army will pay for the development of their technical solution. Not only that, the Army will continue to pay for the added costs for any additional material, assembly, and testing for those three requirements for all the years the Army buys that radio.

These extra development costs and the higher prices are the first bite. What about the second? Let us say that company B has a radio that is three times better in the twelve ways that really matter to Army operators and is available at a lower price, but it cannot meet one of those three unnecessary "requirements." Unless hell freezes over, company B will never be able to sell its radio to the Army. For company A, that is the second bite, because those three worthless requirements provide company A with a terrific barrier to competition.

The third bite, like the first, works against the US government, for the auditing system the government forces on all companies that sell to it makes it impossible for company A to sell its radio at a competitive price on the commercial market. Company A therefore has lower sales and higher overhead costs, for which it is entitled to additional compensation from the government.[14] In other words, it gets paid for being less efficient and receives extra margin on top for this inefficiency.

With this understanding, it was not in the best interest of the defense company representatives attending Hamre's dinner to provide the deputy secretary with what he was requesting. Whether it was due to Hamre's charm or their own patriotism, those CEOs subsequently acted against their corporate interest. The recommendations they provided could have saved the government several billion dollars a year in today's dollars. The next step was to have these lists evaluated by the services. When swarms of officials examined the lists, they confirmed that each company had been making substantial money, quite legally, from these excessive requirements.

One item provides the general tenor of the list. At the time, General Electric (GE) had commercial and military customers for the same type of jet engine, the F110 (used in high-end fighters such as the F-15 Strike Eagle and the F-16 Fighting Falcon).[15] All of the engines were built in the same plant in Lynn, Massachusetts. Because of the onerous government requirements for shipping military packages, GE had to maintain two completely separate manufacturing lines inside its factory. The costs of the duplicate military line, all of which GE was legally passing on to the government with a markup, were considerable, and the company recommended closing the government-only line.

Hamre and his team appreciated these kinds of arguments. In addition to the military paying more than commercial customers for the same goods, the Air Force was getting worse service. If an engine was destined for a commercial or foreign government customer, GE had to deliver the engine undamaged and install it on wing anywhere in the world. If not, GE owed the customer a replacement engine and paid the customer for any lost revenue that airplane would be generating until a replacement arrived and was installed.

On the other hand, if the engine was for the US Air Force, under Department of Defense regulations all the manufacturer had to do was package it in accordance with the latest military instructions. The government was then responsible for transportation. When the engine arrived at its destination, Uncle Sam was still responsible for installation. If the engine was damaged in transit, under the contract with the Air Force, it was then shipped at the military's expense back to GE's warehouse in Massachusetts. It then was up to the Air Force to come up with the money to repair the engine or purchase a new one. All this time, the airplane missing an engine sat idle. To make matters worse, the defense engine-packaging standards had not been updated in years, were inferior to existing commercial packaging requirements, and nearly required an advanced degree to decipher.

Given these two vastly different incentive structures, GE made sure that the packaging for commercial customers met the very highest standards and included the newest innovations to prevent damage during transportation. Not surprisingly, the packaging for the Air Force met the contract specifications and nothing more.

As icing on the cake, at the moment when this issue came to the OSD's attention, it just so happened that the Air Force was complaining it had an airplane out of action in Bahrain. The replacement engines for that airplane (the same F110 engines we are discussing) had been damaged in transit because of inferior packaging. The Air Force claimed it did not have enough money to afford the repairs and therefore was requesting that the OSD forward an emergency supplemental request to Congress. GE's suggestion to eliminate the duplicate production line (that the Air Force was paying for) was a remarkable opportunity for the Air Force to reduce future costs and increase readiness simply by modifying an outmoded method of doing business.

These were exactly the sort of changes that had gone out for review by the services and the Joint Staff. And now, along with the request for extra funding for a new engine, all of the responses had arrived. Unfortunately, it was a clean sweep. Every suggestion the companies had recommended was rejected for one or more specious reasons.

In the case of the GE engine-packing example, although the immediate savings of this change would accrue to the Air Force, all the services agreed that no change was preferable. Each service had its own internal logic for its opposition. In the case of the Army, the Department of Defense packing school was located on an Army base, so the Army appeared worried that any reduction in the use of its archaic standards might lead eventually to the school's closure and a reduction in the size of an Army command. The Marines and the Navy had no particular stake in the issue but also seemed to have no interest in implementing any changes in acquisition practices. Finally, although the Air Force would save millions of dollars, it went along with the other two services (a fine example of logrolling) to avoid antagonizing either.

At the end of the review, not one service or agency could imagine anything better than the status quo even when every proposed change reflected lessons private industry had learned at great expense. To add insult to injury, the Army indicated it would request that Congress expand the Army's Tri-Service School of Military Packaging Technology at Maryland's Aberdeen Proving Ground to install a Packaging Hall of Fame, and the Air Force had the gall to insist it still needed the extra money to repair the engines for its inoperative plane in Bahrain. The whole episode was yet another demonstration of the axiom that the only thing worse than too much interservice rivalry is too little.

A combined effort by political appointees, senior congressional staffers, and the defense industry to adopt best practices from private industry in just one narrow area of the Department of Defense—logistics and support (i.e., buying, providing, moving stuff around)—had produced nothing. Thus ended another effort to introduce change from the private sector into the Department of Defense.

One might reasonably argue that Pentagon leaders have not cast their net widely enough beyond the defense contractors. The latter's dependence on contracts from a government that is seemingly indifferent to missed deadlines and cost overruns has made them anything but lean, efficient engines of capitalism. This argument looks superficially compelling but falls apart under closer scrutiny after considering the immense barriers to entry that nontraditional defense companies face if they do decide to compete for defense contracts.

THE ISOLATION OF THE US DEFENSE INDUSTRY

While there are many companies in the United States or allied/partner nations that would theoretically love to compete for defense contracts, it has historically been incredibly difficult for new firms to enter this market, and it is getting even more difficult. Contractors can, indeed, make money, but they must also deal with the problems of a monopsony—essentially a market that has a single buyer, in this case the US government. In the golden age of "heroic" defense capitalism, men such as Hyman Rickover and Bernard Schriever (whose Air Force team developed the first ICBMs) could operate with virtually no oversight and unlimited budgets thanks to their direct reporting relationship with President Eisenhower.[16] The government was also far more willing to tolerate the existence of "black box" projects such as Polaris.[17]

Today there is far less tolerance for waste, fraud, and abuse, which means that oversight is continuous and extensive. Furthermore, the government is an incredibly fickle customer. Defense agencies think nothing of overloading new platforms with exotic technologies ("gold-plating"), imposing excessive regulations, frequently modifying requirements, and suddenly changing spending plans depending on new political priorities. Then there is the vaunted "Valley of Death"—the immense lag time between developing a weapon and getting it designated as a "program of record" (i.e., going into production)—which disadvantages new, cash-poor firms.[18] As if that were not enough, contractors must also ensure they have the backing of key legislators, which means conducting business on the basis of political rather than purely economic considerations.[19] Not surprisingly, fewer and fewer companies are willing to bear the risk of competing for defense contracts. While there were 46,180 "prime vendors" serving the Defense Department in FY 2020, that number had declined by one-third during the previous decade, and today a mere five companies account for half of all defense contracts by value.[20]

Beyond limiting competition, the many obstacles entailed by government contracts have also isolated the Pentagon from the skills and insights of the rest of the nation. Consider the difficulty in recruiting top-notch scientific talent. In 1987 the Naval Research Laboratory (a part of the Office of Naval Research) held a dinner featuring seven Nobel laureates who were working or had worked at the laboratory. Since 1946 the Navy had supported the work of fifty-nine Nobel laureates.[21] Today, one cannot find enough Nobel laureates working for the Defense Department to fill a small table in the Pentagon's cafeteria.[22]

The growing separation of the US commercial and defense industries is no secret.[23] The very fact that the Department of Defense draws such a large percentage of its products from only one rather insular segment of American industry—a sector that many suspect is the least-innovative portion and thus unprepared to support a nimbler military—is a problem that has vexed many presidents and secretaries of defense.[24]

The biggest drawback of the small size of the US defense industry is that it lacks all of the benefits of competition, which is the surest way to ensure that the Department of Defense will get value for its money. Literally no one in government has all the knowledge necessary to write specifications so precise and so absent of loopholes that they do not need the "invisible hand" of competition/self-interest to get their needs satisfied at the least cost. The larger the pool of competing firms, the better the odds that someone will come up with a new and better way to solve problems.[25] When it comes to major defense contractors—often referred to as prime contractors because they subcontract a great deal of their work—the pool is not very deep and may be stagnant.[26] From 2001 to 2016, 80 percent of the new firms that entered the market for government contracts went out of business.[27]

Over the years, many people have tilted at this particular windmill. In particular, they have tried to increase the number of firms competing for defense dollars. Unfortunately, commercial companies cannot accept the basic contracting premise that Congress has established requiring companies doing government work to have noncommercial accounting systems. Even though $19 trillion of business is done annually in the United States under the Uniform Commercial Code, Congress requires a completely different set of contracting rules (Defense Federal Acquisition Rules) for the $700 billion worth of work done by the defense industry. Commercial companies cannot afford to operate two different accounting systems within the same company, and the government-mandated one is unnecessarily expensive for commercial work. The government-mandated system requires different deductible items and reporting methods, and it provides nothing of commercial value. Plus, there is the real risk that if a firm adopts two sets of accounting standards, it will unnecessarily burden business lines on the commercial side of business.

Congress took its latest run at this in the 2016 National Defense Authorization Act. The legislation established an Advisory Panel on Standardizing and Codifying Acquisition Regulations (the 809 Panel). This group of sixteen experts met from August 2016 to July 2019 and reported its findings. Congress passed many of their recommendations, but it appears that the basic problem—that most of American industry is shut out from the defense market—remains.[28]

It is worth recalling at this point how the US defense industry developed. The industry today bears all of the hallmarks of an oligopoly, but that is not the result of any "conspiracy" by the firms involved. Rather, it arose from a deliberate government policy after World War II. At that time, the US government took a series of conscious decisions to rely on private firms, instead of the government arsenals, to develop and produce weapons. The arsenals had a distinguished history, particularly when it came to innovation. For example, the Harpers Ferry Armory in West Virginia had pioneered the development of standardized parts—the basis of mass production.[29]

The reliance on private firms arose not from any belief that the private sector was inherently more "efficient" than government. Rather, officials wanted to prevent the rise of a large national-security interest group that would meddle with the civilian economy or claim a disproportionate share of defense dollars. The decision-makers preferred, therefore, to rely on a decentralized archipelago of defense firms for R & D and production that could, theoretically, be checked by a vigilant Congress.[30] This was an enlightened decision designed to protect American liberties, but it also required an active oversight by Congress, which has not happened, and perhaps the preservation of some government arsenals that could undertake the sorts of R & D that private firms did not consider immediately profitable.

The collaboration among private and public interests during the Cold War yielded some tremendous gains. Many of the country's greatest minds had worked for the government during World War II, and the partnership continued even after these remarkable individuals returned to the private sector. Not surprisingly, many continued their exploration of the atom and the challenges that nuclear weapons posed. And while the government got out of the business of producing weapons after the war, it—specifically the military—spared no expense to promote work related to national security.

The Pentagon has, at least since the 1970s, accounted for roughly half of all government research spending, although total R & D spending (including for defense) has declined in real terms in recent years.[31] It is still orders of magnitude higher than any other nation of the Organisation for Economic Co-operation and Development, but China is catching up.[32] The Internet was an inadvertent development from a system that encouraged subsequent innovations such as the Global Positioning System and perhaps the most important technological development supported by the government—the ballistic missile—whose technological spin-offs enabled everything from soda cans and WD-40 to touch-screen technology.[33]

The engineering talent that had been working on grand challenges such as the Manhattan Project during World War II and the Army-supported program at Bell Telephone Laboratories to create miniature, mass-produced transistors immediately afterward came swarming out of laboratories and universities eager to build new companies or technologies.[34] They established enclaves in areas such as Silicon Valley, and the American economy prospered as a result.

The success of today's giant technology firms was enabled by decades of public support, much of which was funded from the Pentagon.[35] We say this not to claim that military spending is always good for the economy—the evidence is mixed—only to state a historical truth.[36] This sort of honesty is vital at a time when employees of many technology firms today are reluctant for ideological, ethical, and even commercial reasons to work on national-security projects (recall the aforementioned Valley of Death).[37] This is unfortunate considering the new technologies and processes that these technology firms are developing.[38] The Pentagon needs all our Silicon Valleys, yet there are a variety of factors driving them apart at a time when the demands of US national security call for closer integration.[39]

The significant differences in motivation and culture between government and private industry make it inappropriate to expect private industry to lead changes in defense. This is true as much for the relatively small defense industry as for any other segment of US industry. That is not to say that the Pentagon should not look for ideas from private industry but that change will come only as a result of a political and bureaucratic process involving Congress, the administration, and senior officers within the services.

SUMMARY

One cannot expect profit-making firms, even those that live and die by defense contracts, to act against their self-interest by shouldering the responsibility for terminating bad programs or redirecting resources to higher-priority endeavors. These are all fundamentally political questions, which means they are the responsibility of government officials, not the private sector. By contrast, private firms cannot act against their self-interest when they have a financial stake in preserving existing approaches that generate healthy profits for executives, wages of employees, and returns for investors—even if those practices are demonstrably inefficient. Sometimes private firms will surprise you, but expecting it to happen routinely in a capitalist system that privileges the interests of shareholders over stakeholders is simply a bridge too far.

NOTES

1. Mahlon Apgar and John Keane, "New Business with the New Military," *Harvard Business Review*, September 1, 2004, https://hbsp.harvard.edu/product/R0409B-HCB-ENG; Fred Kaplan, "The Pentagon's Innovation Experiment," *MIT Technology Review*, December 19, 2016, https://www.technologyreview.com/2016/12/19/155246/the-pentagons-innovation-experiment/; Mark Wallace, "The U.S. Air Force Learned to Code—and Saved the Pentagon Millions," *Fast Company*, July 5, 2018, https://www.fastcompany.com/40588729/the-air-force-learned-to-code-and-saved-the-pentagon-millions; Chris Dougherty, "Want an Agile Pentagon? Don't Go Chasing 'Waterfalls,'" *Defense One*, March 22, 2021, https://www.defenseone.com/ideas/2021/03/want-agile-pentagon-dont-go-chasing-waterfalls/172835/. Big Tech commonly refers to the five largest US information-technology companies: Amazon, Apple, Alphabet (Google), Facebook, and Microsoft.

2. Jonathan Wong, "Why You Can't Call in an Air Strike with an iPhone," War on the Rocks, July 2, 2020, https://warontherocks.com/2020/07/why-you-cant-call-in-an-air-strike-with-an-iphone/.
3. Michael Krepon, "The Business of Running the Pentagon: Shanahan's Abilities May Not Determine His Success," *Forbes*, January 8, 2019, https://www.forbes.com/sites/michaelkrepon/2019/01/08/the-business-of-running-the-pentagon-shanahans-abilities-may-not-determine-his-success/?sh=7d0509d68b79. We are excluding the many lawyers or investment bankers from this list.
4. As of 2021, the Big Five primary contractors by revenue (all American) were Lockheed Martin, Raytheon, Boeing, Northrop Grumman, and General Dynamics. The revenues of the next largest US firm, L3 Harris Technologies (number 9 worldwide) were roughly half those of the smallest of the Big Five, General Dynamics ($14.9 billion vs. $29.8 billion). "Top 100 for 2021," *Defense News*, n.d., https://people.defensenews.com/top-100/.
5. Although somewhat dated, a good description of each service's culture is Carl Builder, *The Masks of War: American Military Styles in Strategy and Analysis* (Baltimore: Johns Hopkins University Press, 1989).
6. Andrew Bartlett and David Preston, "Can Ethical Behavior Really Exist in Business?," *Journal of Business Ethics* 23, no. 2 (2000): 199–209.
7. We mentioned the scandal regarding Air Force tankers in chapter 5, but there were others. See Irwin Ross, "Inside the Biggest Pentagon Scam," *Fortune*, January 1993, https://money.cnn.com/magazines/fortune/fortune_archive/1993/01/11/77357/index.htm.
8. Milton Friedman, "A Friedman Doctrine: The Social Responsibility of Business Is to Increase Its Profits," *New York Times*, September 1, 1970; Kurt Andersen, "How Liberals Opened the Door to Libertarian Economics," *New York Times*, September 11, 2020.
9. Steve Coll, *Private Empire: ExxonMobil and American Power* (New York: Penguin, 2012), 71.
10. Steve Denning, "The 'Pernicious Nonsense' of Maximizing Shareholder Value," *Forbes*, April 27, 2017, https://www.forbes.com/sites/stevedenning/2017/04/27/harvard-business-review-the-pernicious-nonsense-of-maximizing-shareholder-value/#36fef41971f0.
11. Steven Clifford, "How Companies Actually Decide What to Pay CEOs," *The Atlantic*, June 24, 2017, https://www.theatlantic.com/business/archive/2017/06/how-companies-decide-ceo-pay/530127/; Lawrence Mishel and Julia Wolfe, "CEO Compensation Has Grown 940% since 1978," Economic Policy Institute, August 14, 2019, https://www.epi.org/publication/ceo-compensation-2018/.
12. Steve Denning, "Making Sense of the Shareholder Value: 'The World's Dumbest Idea,'" *Forbes*, July 17, 2017, https://www.forbes.com/sites/stevedenning/2017/07/17/making-sense-of-shareholder-value-the-worlds-dumbest-idea/#3e7b37742a7e.
13. By convention, the deputy secretary of defense usually handles the administration of the Department of Defense (including budgetary affairs), while the secretary is responsible for policy, strategy, and military operations.
14. For a discussion of how ineffective many think the efforts to bypass these basic congressional barriers are, see Michael Fischetti, "The Challenges Facing 'Non-traditional' Contractors," *Defense Acquisition*, March/April 2020, https://contractingacademy.gatech.edu/2020/04/10/15587/.
15. "The F110 Engine," General Electric Aviation, n.d., https://www.geaviation.com/military/engines/f110-engine.

16. Christian Brose, *The Kill Chain: Defending America in the Future of High-Tech Warfare* (New York: Hachette, 2020), chap. 3.
17. Donald MacKenzie and Graham Spinardi, "The Shaping of Nuclear Weapon System Technology: US Fleet Ballistic Missile Guidance and Navigation: II: 'Going for Broke'—The Path to Trident II," *Social Studies of Science* 18 (1988): 611ff.
18. Matthew Steckman and Megan Milam, "DOD Valley of Death: Closing the Two Year Gap," Anduril Industries blog, January 23, 2021, https://medium.com/anduril-blog/dod-valley-of-death-closing-the-two-year-gap-758907be9b9f.
19. Harvey Sapolsky, "Defense Industrial Policy Myths Debunked," *National Defense* 96, no. 699 (February 2012): 20–21; Gilbert Diaz, "The Shrinking Private Supplier Base and Acquisition Reform," *Defense Acquisition Magazine*, May 12, 2020, https://www.dau.edu/library/defense-atl/blog/The-Shrinking-Private-Supplier-Base-and-Acquisition-Reform.
20. Mark Thompson, "The Incredible Shrinking Defense Industry," Project on Government Oversight, August 1, 2019, https://www.pogo.org/analysis/2019/08/the-incredibly-shrinking-defense-industry/; Travis Tritten and Paul Murphy, "Fewer Defense Companies in Military Spending Boom Raise Alarms," Bloomberg Government, March 8, 2021, https://about.bgov.com/news/fewer-defense-companies-in-military-spending-boom-raise-alarms/.
21. Binyamin Applebaum, "A Shrinking Military Budget May Take Neighbors with It," *New York Times*, January 6, 2012, https://www.nytimes.com/2012/01/07/us/a-hidden-cost-of-military-cuts-could-be-invention-and-its-industries.html?hp.
22. Hard numbers are difficult to find, but there is a slackening pace in recent years among Nobel laureates supported by the current Office of Naval Research. "All ONR-Sponsored Nobel Laureates," Office of Naval Research, n.d., https://www.onr.navy.mil/en/About-ONR/History/Nobels. See also "DOE Nobel Laureates," Department of Energy, n.d., https://science.osti.gov/About/Honors-and-Awards/DOE-Nobel-Laureates; "The Federal Government: A Nobel Profession: A Report on the Path-breaking Nobel Laureates in Government, 1901–2002," Partnership for Public Service, December 2002, https://ourpublicservice.org/wp-content/uploads/2002/12/193690852dfe6b696a3d8216af41ee89-1414079066.pdf; and "The Nobel Prize and RAND," RAND Corp., n.d., https://www.rand.org/about/history/nobel.html.
23. Jacques Gansler, *Democracy's Arsenal: Creating a Twenty-First-Century Defense Industry* (Cambridge, MA: MIT Press, 2011), 39.
24. E.g., see Ashton B. Carter, *Inside the Five-Sided Box: Lessons from a Lifetime of Leadership in the Pentagon* (New York: Dutton, 2019), 326–30.
25. Jacques S. Gansler, William Lucyshyn, and Michael Arendt, *Competition in Defense Acquisitions* (College Park: Center for Public Policy and Private Enterprise, School of Public Policy, University of Maryland, 2009), https://apps.dtic.mil/dtic/tr/fulltext/u2/a529406.pdf.
26. "Defense Primer: Department of Defense Contractors," Congressional Research Service, January 31, 2020, https://fas.org/sgp/crs/natsec/IF10600.pdf.
27. Brose, *Kill Chain*, chap. 3.
28. Joe Dyer (former commander of NAVAIR and CEO of iRobot) and Charlie Williams (former director of Defense Contract Management Agency) to Dave Oliver, email, April 28, 2021. Dyer and Williams were both members of the 809 Panel.
29. Merritt Roe Smith, *Harpers Ferry Armory and the New Technology: The Challenge of Change* (Ithaca, NY: Cornell University Press, 1977).

30. Aaron Friedberg, "Why Didn't the United States Become a Garrison State?," *International Security* 16, no. 4 (1992): 136ff. Aaron L. Friedberg, *In the Shadow of the Garrison State: America's Anti-Statism and Its Cold War Grand Strategy* (Princeton, NJ: Princeton University Press, 2000), 9ff., 245ff.
31. American Association for the Advancement of Science, "Historical Trends in Federal R&D," n.d., https://www.aaas.org/programs/r-d-budget-and-policy/historical-trends-federal-rd.
32. "Government Expenditures on Defense Research and Development by the United States and Other OECD Countries: Fact Sheet," Congressional Research Service, January 28, 2020, https://fas.org/sgp/crs/natsec/R45441.pdf; Patrick Turner, "US Defense R&D Funding Falls as China's Keeps Growing," *Defense One*, February 10, 2020, https://www.defenseone.com/technology/2020/02/us-defense-rd-funding-falls-chinas-keeps-growing/163021/.
33. Contrary to popular mythology, the Internet was not designed to enable communication in the event of a nuclear war. How could it once scientists understood the effects of electromagnetic pulse (EMP) waves? Rather, it was actually an outgrowth of congressionally mandated requirements that various government and private labs develop a standardized method of communicating with one another. "Brief History of the Internet," Internet Society, 1997, https://www.internetsociety.org/wp-content/uploads/2017/09/ISOC-History-of-the-Internet_1997.pdf; Roy Rosenzweig, "Wizards, Bureaucrats, Warriors and Hackers: Writing the History of the Internet," *American Historical Review* 103, no. 5 (1998), https://rrchnm.org/essay/wizards-bureaucrats-warriors-hackers-writing-the-history-of-the-internet/; Gordon Crovitz, "Who Really Invented the Internet," *Wall Street Journal*, July 22, 2012; Ian Peter, "Myth #15: The Internet Was Invented by the Pentagon and Designed to Survive a Nuclear Attack," Internet Governance Forum Berlin, 2019, https://www.internetmythen.de/en/?mythen=myth-15-the-internet-was-invented-by-the-pentagon-and-designed-to-survive-a-nuclear-attack; Cade Metz, "Paul Baran, the Link between Nuclear War and the Internet," *Wired*, September 4, 2012, https://www.wired.co.uk/article/h-bomb-and-the-internet; Margaret O'Mara, *The Code: Silicon Valley and the Remaking of America* (New York: Penguin, 2020); Arthur L. Norberg, Judy E. O'Neill, and Kerry J. Freedman, *Transforming Computer Technology: Information Processing for the Pentagon, 1962–1986* (Baltimore: Johns Hopkins University Press, 2000); Janet Abbate, *Inventing the Internet* (Cambridge, MA: MIT Press, 2000).
34. Thomas Misa, "Military Needs, Commercial Realities, and the Development of the Transistor, 1948–1958," in *Military Enterprise and Technological Change: Perspectives on the American Experience*, ed. Merritt Roe Smith (Cambridge, MA: MIT Press, 1985), 253–87.
35. Vernon Rattan, *Is War Necessary for Economic Growth? Military Procurement and Technology Development* (Oxford: Oxford University Press, 2006).
36. Institute for Economics & Peace (IEP), *Economic Consequences of War on the U.S. Economy* (Sydney: IEP, 2015), https://www.economicsandpeace.org/wp-content/uploads/2015/06/The-Economic-Consequences-of-War-on-US-Economy_0.pdf.
37. Brose, *Kill Chain*, chap. 5. See also James Joyner and Matthew Burns, "The Pentagon Is Flubbing Its Pitch to Silicon Valley," *Defense One*, May 1, 2019, https://www.defenseone.com/ideas/2019/05/pentagon-flubbing-its-pitch-silicon-valley/156641/; Aaron Mehta, "Cultural Divide: Can the Pentagon Crack Silicon Valley?," *Defense News*, July 28, 2019, https://www.defensenews.com/pentagon/2019/01/28

/cultural-divide-can-the-pentagon-crack-silicon-valley/; Kelsey Atherton, "Can the Pentagon Sell Silicon Valley on AI as Ethical War?," *C[4]ISRNET*, April 25, 2019, https://www.c4isrnet.com/unmanned/2019/04/26/can-the-pentagon-sell-silicon-valley-on-ai-as-ethical-war/; Zachary Fryer-Biggs, "The Pentagon Tries to Win Hearts and Minds in Silicon Valley," Center for Public Integrity, December 21, 2018, https://publicintegrity.org/national-security/the-pentagon-tries-to-win-hearts-and-minds-in-silicon-valley/; Catherine Aiken and Margarita Konaev, "Are AI Professionals Actually Unwilling to Work for the Pentagon?," *Defense One*, November 30, 2020, https://www.defenseone.com/ideas/2020/11/are-ai-professionals-actually-unwilling-work-pentagon/170359/.

38. Sarah Feldman, "Private Sector Outspends Defense Contractors in R&D," Statista, October 1, 2019, https://www.statista.com/chart/19515/defense-spending-research-development/.
39. Rachel Olney, "The Rift between Silicon Valley and the Pentagon Is Economic, Not Moral," War on the Rocks, January 28, 2019, https://warontherocks.com/2019/01/the-rift-between-silicon-valley-and-the-pentagon-is-economic-not-moral/. For the problems with just one service (the Navy), see John Kroger, "Esper's Fantasy Fleet," *Defense One*, October 13, 2020, https://www.defenseone.com/ideas/2020/10/espers-fantasy-fleet/169179/.

CHAPTER 8

Achieving Change

The individuals appointed to serve as stewards of our Department of Defense, our secretaries of defense, have, as a group, long shared a concern about how the United States' military edge might evaporate. Even after the Cold War ended, when American power seemed unassailable, Secretaries Les Aspin, William Perry, William Cohen, and Donald Rumsfeld still devoted a great deal of thought to how to avoid being surprised by a peer or near-peer adversary. Their thinking depended, in turn, on the insights of their closest advisers, most of whom are unknown to the public and even most historians.

One of the most important of these advisers was Andrew Marshall, who came to the Pentagon during the lowest ebb of the United States in the Cold War. During his long career, which outlasted the Soviet Union and saw the rise of the United States' current great-power rival, China, Marshall studied how technological and organizational changes had revolutionized warfare during previous eras, thereby shifting the balance of military power. Often these changes appeared obvious in hindsight, but at the time many militaries failed to appreciate their significance in real time. Marshall was particularly interested in the German practice of blitzkrieg during World War II, but there are many examples from US history that can inform officials and educated citizens, such as the introduction of the repeating rifle, nuclear-powered submarines, and remotely piloted vehicles (RPVs—drones in common parlance).

New weapon systems sometimes have the potential to revolutionize existing methods of warfighting, yet the military establishments of the time often resist or soft-pedal their adoption.[1] Since many of these military-technological revolutions have already received extensive scholarly attention, we will focus on the understudied history of the RPV.

RPVs proved essential in the wars the United States fought after 9/11, yet the story of their development and integration within the US military is consistent with the history of many other transformational weapons—specifically, that the relevant service (in this case, the Air Force) opposed adopting them. That hostility did not relent even after RPVs had proven their worth during the Kosovo War of 1999. This chapter will explain why RPVs were developed, why they engendered so much military opposition, and how a group of senior political appointees finally overcame the Air Force's obstruction.

REVOLUTIONS IN MILITARY AFFAIRS

Nobody likes to hear information that contradicts their most cherished beliefs, yet somehow, even though his job was to question military dogma, Andrew Marshall survived—indeed thrived—for four decades as a Pentagon iconoclast. The small organization he founded and led, the Office of Net Assessment (ONA), was established within the OSD in 1973, and it still exists under his handpicked successor.[2]

Marshall retired from the ONA in 2015 and died four years later at the ripe age of ninety-seven. Cynics said Marshall lasted as long as he did because he kept his office small so that he was not a target for budget hawks. Those who knew him best believed it was because his advice was always fresh and innovative. He also had a talent for melting into the woodwork. The German general Alfred von Schlieffen admonished his elite general staff officers "to be more than you seem."[3] Marshall lived by that credo. At one of his birthdays, one of his best friends, James March, said, "Very few smart people can tolerate anonymity, but Andy can."[4]

Marshall obviously did not lack for intelligence, but bright minds are neither rare in Washington nor a guarantee of success. Perhaps more important, Marshall also valued scholarship, and he used his patronage to create a large formal and informal network of acolytes throughout the national-security community. In that sense, Marshall was replicating his personal experience, albeit on a larger scale. Long before he arrived at the five-sided puzzle palace, Marshall had worked at the RAND Corporation with a number of prominent thinkers, including such luminaries as the nuclear strategists Herman Kahn, Albert Wohlstetter, and Bernard Brodie as well as Charles Hitch, who reorganized the Pentagon's budget process for Secretary McNamara. Marshall's experiences in that freewheeling atmosphere of ideas in turn shaped how he operated for the rest of his life.[5]

When President Richard Nixon tapped one of those RAND intellectuals, James Schlesinger, to be his third secretary of defense in the spring of 1973, Schlesinger took his old RAND friend, Marshall, from Kissinger's NSC, where Marshall had tried, without much success, to establish a net assessment office.[6] From his first day in the Pentagon, Marshall was intrigued by the question of why militaries have difficulty recognizing and adapting to major technological or doctrinal changes in warfare.

He was not the only one thinking along such lines. Starting in the 1970s, Soviet analysts surmised that the United States' deployment of precision-guided munitions presaged a "military-technical revolution" that might upend the conventional military balance. Marshall picked up on the term, which he rebranded as the "revolution in military affairs" (RMA). He also sponsored extensive historical research by scholars who embedded the RMA within the wider framework of "military revolutions" whose political, social, technological, and economic effects produced RMAs at the tactical and operational levels of war.[7]

What else did Marshall learn from his researches? He observed that few military leaders appreciated when their key assumptions were shifting like sand beneath their feet. Even fewer understood that a problem existed. Successful militaries were often prone to excessive optimism, as they relied on earlier assumptions that had previously served them well. Military history was littered with examples of such complacency and often with disastrous consequences. First in many people's minds was the swift collapse in May and June 1940 of France, which on paper possessed Europe's finest army.

Most often, it took a terrible battlefield defeat, even the loss of a war or revolution, to shake the mental cobwebs that afflicted military leaders, as it had with the French Army after 1789 and the German Army after 1918. Defeat was frequently the tonic for improved military performance, but could the United States afford to take such a risk in the atomic age, when a lost conflict might end with a nuclear holocaust? Marshall's overriding mission was to ensure that Americans would recognize when the ground was shifting beneath their feet. He did so by analyzing both military history and the contemporary environment. The latter led him to developing net assessments of the military balance among the United States and its potential adversaries.[8] This exercise gave him insights into comparative strengths and weaknesses that were otherwise inaccessible through conventional analysis and allowed him to develop competitive strategies that exploited any asymmetries in relative power or capabilities, which in turn allowed the United States to adopt strategies that imposed disproportionate costs on its adversaries.[9]

For example, during the late 1970s, Marshall championed the B-1 bomber not because he was enamored of strategic bombing but because it was more expensive for the Soviets to develop and deploy an integrated air-defense system than it was for the United States to field a bomber force. Similarly, Marshall urged the US Navy to continue investing in quieting its submarines because this would impose immense and disproportionate costs on the Soviet Union. The submarines of the Soviet Navy were much louder than their American counterparts, which means the Soviets had further to go to catch up technologically. Moreover, even if they did quiet their submarines, the costs to them would be greater than to the US Navy because submarines made up a much larger proportion of the Soviet fleet.[10]

Marshall was always thinking about the challenge that was over the horizon rather than the problem in the headlines. For example, in the 1970s, fifteen years before the fall of the Berlin Wall, Marshall abandoned the Soviet Union as the pressing issue and began to study China. Marshall was also loath to engage in public arguments. He was not interested in being known as the first person to have a new slant on an old problem. Heeding the old dictum of New York City planner Robert Moses that "you can get an awful lot of good done if you're willing to let someone else take the credit for it," Marshall was content to advance the intellectual process.[11]

During our discussion of the RMA, we noted that Marshall's preferred strategy was to fund studies on issues he considered important to accumulate data, even if the findings contradicted his own beliefs.[12] As mentioned before, one historical phenomenon that intrigued him was blitzkrieg. According to the traditional "bean-counting" approach to military assessment, the Allies should have handily defeated the Germans in 1940 since they had major qualitative and quantitative hardware advantages on both land and in the air, not to mention richer economies. Nevertheless, the Germans had triumphed, which meant that just tallying tanks and aircraft was inadequate for explaining the outcome of the 1940 campaign.[13]

Before 1939, the German Army was not the only military thinking about how to take advantage of the motorization of warfare—indeed, the Germans' early tanks were noticeably inferior to those of the British and French. The German approach nonetheless became the template for combined operations in the twentieth century after the German Army defeated France in six weeks. Marshall wanted to know how Germany had developed blitzkrieg and, more important, how the United States could avoid playing the role of the French in the future.

The Germans' success arose, in part, from their inspired decision to marry two established technologies—the tank, first used in combat by the

British in 1916, and the wireless radio, an idea made practical by the Italian Guglielmo Marconi twenty years before World War I began. What was "new" about blitzkrieg was therefore not its platforms (the ingredients) but rather how they were arranged (the recipe). Unlike the tank-heavy units divisions the British and French fielded in 1940, the Germans established balanced divisions comprising armor, artillery, and mobile infantry along with embedded forward air controllers to leverage close air support.

This novel application of emerging technologies was grafted onto a longstanding commitment within the German Army (dating back to Frederick the Great) for aggressive action, concentration against the enemy's center of gravity, and individual initiative. The result was ground forces with extraordinary mobility and lethality that ran circles around their more numerous and better-equipped adversaries until 1943.[14] The Germans, thankfully, lost World War II, but despite their immense material inferiority, their warfighting skills (along with some good luck before 1941) allowed them to overrun Europe from the Atlantic coast to the gates of Moscow before being battered into submission by an overwhelming preponderance of Allied forces.[15]

The study of blitzkrieg in the United States, with its emphasis on the importance of military innovation and "mission command" as the recipe for operational excellence, has yielded mixed results.[16] On the one hand, it has contributed to a distortion of the historical record, minimizing the German Army's brutality, and an unhealthy obsession with operational "art" and technological dominance to compensate for strategic poverty.[17] On the other, the study of blitzkrieg has encouraged the United States and other militaries to jettison top-down models of leadership and build forces that are, theoretically at least, more flexible and attuned to coping with the challenges of fog and friction in war.[18]

Marshall's acolytes blazed a new path that transformed the study of war in the Anglo-American world. Once the value of this sort of history was rooted in the minds of American national-security professionals, it was clear that there were other episodes deserving of attention.

THE COMPLEXITY OF ADOPTING TRANSFORMATIONAL SYSTEMS

One particularly American story was that of the repeating rifle, which emerged after a technological discovery was married with an innovative process. The discovery was that brass had the right flexibility and strength to be crimped around the lead bullet to make a cartridge. The process breakthrough was precision manufacturing, first developed at the government arsenal at Harpers Ferry. This latter change presaged the many innovations pioneered at other government arsenals and laboratories in the twentieth century.[19]

The first repeating rifles (i.e., capable of more than one shot per reload) were the seven-shot Spencers introduced to the battlefield by individual soldiers of the Union Army at Gettysburg in 1863. Some fifteen-round Henrys also saw limited action later in the war.[20] The results during the Civil War may not have proven much, but these firearms were truly revolutionary. They enabled soldiers to shoot multiple times before pausing to reload and eventually to fire from a prone position. But the full effect was still to come. First, the country needed a manufacturing and logistical base capable of sustaining mass armies fielding such weapons.

During the 1860s in the United States, the repeating rifle's introduction was constrained not only by the relatively small size of the New England manufacturing base but also by the greater demands the higher ammunition expenditure placed on the US logistical network. This, in turn, magnified the centrality of the railroad in supporting large numbers of troops in the field. The region that had both the necessary industrial base and railway infrastructure was Western Europe. There the combination of repeating-weapons production, trains to overcome the constraints of time and space, and mass armies raised through conscription produced a decisive effect during the Wars of German Unification from 1864 to 1871.[21]

Back in the United States, after the post–Civil War Army demobilized, repeating rifles compensated for the dearth of manpower. While the United States fought no extended ground campaigns until World War I, fire superiority still proved invaluable even during the protracted, low-intensity campaigns to "pacify" the Native American tribes and repress insurgents in the Philippines and across Latin America. But why is any of this relevant to this book?

As Marshall and the secretaries of defense he supported recognized, problems arise when the prevailing military culture ignores or downplays a possible transformation. Prior to the introduction of repeating, breech-loading rifles, soldiers were equipped with muskets (some rifled but mostly smoothbore until the nineteenth century). Because these muskets were muzzle loaders, soldiers had to go through a lengthy muzzle-loading process. Eighteenth- and nineteenth-century muskets were far less complex than the flintlocks and matchlocks of earlier periods, but the rate of fire was only marginally better.

Accordingly, despite such weapons' lethality, attacking soldiers had one important advantage—the abysmal accuracy of smoothbore weapons limited their effective range to under 150 yards. Until the middle of the nineteenth century, disciplined troops could close this distance while the defender was reloading. Of course, if infantry weapons could deliver accurate rifle fire beyond three rounds a minute, then centuries of infantry tactics would become obsolete. The deployment of rifles such as the Springfield by the Union Army solved the problem of range but not the slow rate of fire, and the muzzle-loading mechanism still left soldiers exposed to enemy fire. Once breech-loading rifles such as the Sharps and the Henrys appeared on the battlefields of North America (and Dreyse needle-guns and chassepots in Europe), it should have been obvious that charges across open terrain without extensive artillery support was now suicidal.[22]

Yet, when World War I began, more than fifty years after the first use of the repeating rifles, all of the major armies of the world still conducted massed infantry attacks. They persisted despite observations from conflicts such as the Russo-Japanese War of 1904–5, when Russian barbed wire, high explosives, and indirect artillery fire frustrated repeated Japanese assaults on Port Arthur for months.[23] Why had European and US militaries not heeded these warnings? Well, for a variety of reasons, not the least of which was the widespread belief (from Europe to Japan) that martial vigor—what we might call the results of training and patriotism today—could triumph over an enemy's technological advantages.[24]

We are far removed from the pathologies of the nineteenth-century world, but the US military services still retain strong cultures that divide them as corporate institutions while distinguishing them from their civilian counterparts. Military norms and practices may seem bizarre, even archaic, to outsiders. When one serves in uniform, however, it soon becomes clear that there are plenty of valid reasons why military cultures persist. For one thing, they assist recruits in adjusting to and accepting danger as well as dealing with the emotions that accompany fear and hardship (both physical and emotional).

Military culture arises to help uniformed personnel cope with the peculiar (and dangerous) nature of their jobs and tasks. They assure those individuals that the travails they confront, while extraordinary, can be surmounted through discipline and that their emotional reactions, while natural, need not hinder them from performing their duty under terrific stress. Perhaps ironically, that same culture, by stressing regimentation and discipline, may also stifle innovation. The closest analogy is that of window shades. The lower one pulls a shade, the less glare from the sun, and the easier it is for the people working inside. The farther the shade is pulled down, however, the more outside events pass unseen. As an institutional culture becomes stronger, it is equivalent to pulling the shades even lower.

The great military historian Michael Howard once observed that the sheer complexity of running a modern army often distracts leaders from reflecting on "what it is run *for*."[25] Fretting about how every development in warfare might render an existing training practice, organization, or equipment obsolete is a recipe for paralysis. It is only natural, therefore, that leaders might, on occasion, pull down their figurative shades to focus on the task at hand. Alas, the very tool that helps people better adjust encourages, within the military, a tendency to "prepare for the last war."

INSTANCES OF SUCCESSFUL ADAPTATION

There are some surprising exceptions to this pattern, but they are definitely not the norm. Consider the US Navy's submarine community during World War II. To avoid the threat of "friendly fire" in the Atlantic and harass the Japanese advance in the Pacific after much of the Pacific Fleet was lost or damaged during the attack on Pearl Harbor, the Navy transferred all of its submarines to the Pacific.[26] These boats could be spared from the Atlantic because submarines were ineffective in protecting the convoys carrying troops and equipment to Britain. These were not the submarines we think of today. Their electric batteries provided limited speed and endurance while underwater. Accordingly, they spent most of their time on the surface, relying on diesel engines for propulsion and submerging only to approach, evade, or attack the enemy.

Although classified as warships, World War II–era submarines were quite fragile. Their thin hulls could not withstand even the smallest round from a destroyer's gun, and their long periods on the surface made them vulnerable to air attack. That said, merchant ships were sitting ducks for any submarine that could find them. Although there was never any formal Navy directive to refocus US submarines against Japanese merchant ships or a coherent plan to derange the Japanese war economy, over the course of eighteen months the submarine community adapted to its new (and technically illegal under international *and* US law) "unrestricted" campaign against all Japanese ships, civilian or military. The initial results were disappointing, but once the submariners developed new tactics, and the Navy fixed its faulty torpedoes and replaced ineffective skippers (30 percent were sacked in 1942 alone), they devastated the Japanese economy to an extent that American analysts did not appreciate until after the war.[27]

The submariners' success came at a price: 16 percent of the officers and 13 percent of the enlisted became casualties.[28] Although few in number, US submariners received a disproportionate number of the Medals of Honor awarded to Navy personnel during the war—seven out of forty-seven.[29] These numbers are important for our purposes because the submarine force was challenged immediately after the war to accept new technology (nuclear power) and dramatically change how it operated. This process was difficult for such a decorated force. Some of the officers who had performed so well in World War II proved ill-suited for the new nuclear submarine force. Nevertheless, while the rest of the postwar Navy was built along the lines of the fleet that destroyed the Japanese Navy—with the carrier strike group as its core—the submarine community had to chart a new path.

The Soviet Union would not be deterred simply by threatening its sea lines of communication. The submarine force therefore had to find new ways to contribute to US national security. It may come as a shock that the US submarine force today is not designed to hunt enemy merchant ships. Even if it wanted to, there are more targets than torpedoes. Instead, the submarine force is designed to fulfill missions that are largely divorced from its historical experience: provide credible nuclear deterrence, hunt enemy submarines, collect intelligence either through signals intercepts or the deployment of special operations forces, and sweep the seas of any enemy surface combatants that threaten US interests.

This sort of rupture with history was extraordinary even within the US Navy. The example of the Polaris missile is instructive here. When the OSD adopted the Polaris over a mobile Minuteman concept, the Navy insisted that it should not bear the cost alone since that would upset the balance of funds between the major communities within the service (surface warfare, aviation, and submarines), cutting into the resources available for ships and planes. With OSD funds not forthcoming, the Navy considered putting the Polaris on cruisers (large surface ships), which would have been foolish on multiple levels. It made no sense to mix conventional and strategic forces because ordinary battle damage would jeopardize US nuclear forces. Additionally, equipping cruisers cost just as much as building submarines, but the Navy threatened to choose this path because it was a reason to build more surface ships that could also perform existing (conventional) roles and missions. There was no strong Navy interest in developing a new set of limited (strategic) capabilities.[30]

The other option was submarines, but putting the Polaris missile system aboard them would require that community to adopt increased levels of control and safety. There would be no room for the kind of swashbuckling behavior that had earned those seven Medals of Honor during World War II. So how did the submarine force make a clean break with its past? Well, even before the development of the Polaris, Arleigh Burke and President Dwight Eisenhower supported Hyman Rickover's plans to build the world's first nuclear-powered submarine. Rickover's brainchild, USS *Nautilus*, proved to be so successful that succeeding presidents and Congresses funded additional nuclear submarines as fast as American shipyards could weld steel together, including forty-one submarines armed with SLBMs from 1958 to 1962.

What is most remarkable, perhaps, is that the Navy managed to develop the Polaris following the Korean War when its budgets were almost flat.[31] Since World War II, in fact, the Navy had accorded ballistic missile development a low priority. Consequently, when money again became relatively tight after Korea, the Navy partnered with the Army (on paper) to develop a ballistic missile—the Jupiter. Since that weapon was unsuitable for use on submarines (its liquid fuel had a worrying tendency to ignite), the Navy then supported the Air Force in the JCS to strip the Army of its role in ballistic missile development. These bureaucratic maneuvers permitted the Navy to move forward with its own program, a solid-fueled missile appropriate for shipboard use—the Polaris.[32]

The Navy did not get a significant financial bump to pay for the development of this new strategic missile force, costing over $10 billion from FY 1956 to FY 1967. Granted, Navy budgets from 1958 to 1964 were, on average, 13 percent higher than during 1953–57, but real growth relative to the overall increase in the defense budget was only 5 percent. Moreover, roughly one quarter of the Navy's cumulative increases from FY 1956 to FY 1967 went to ballistic missile programs. The Air Force set aside a similar proportion, but its basic budget increase was *twice* as large as the Navy's ($86 billion versus $42 billion). The Navy's new nuclear submarine force was built at the expense of the Navy's conventional capabilities, specifically through deferred maintenance on existing assets and reduced investment in future weapon systems (such as cancellation of the Regulus II cruise missile). By 1961–62, the Polaris was consuming *half* of the Navy's shipbuilding budget and roughly 14 percent of its total budget.[33]

The Navy justified the Polaris for a number of reasons. Married with a submarine, the Polaris missile force was invulnerable, and the United States could, theoretically, wipe out the Soviet Union with a fleet of twenty-nine submarines at sea even if the Soviets destroyed the rest of the US strategic force. The Polaris's cost was also limited since it was primarily a deterrent and retaliatory weapon (i.e., countervalue, as evidenced by its modest accuracy compared to today's Trident missiles—the D-5—with its "hard-target" kill capability). The Polaris was required, therefore, only in finite numbers as opposed to the Air Force's open-ended counterforce structure.[34] Still, because the Navy had to pay for the Polaris out of its own hide, it budgeted enough for only three new ballistic missile submarines in FY 1961 and FY 1962 and (wishfully) insisted that the other services should share some of the cost.[35]

If the Polaris were not already sufficiently threatening to the other communities of the Navy (from which the great majority of its admirals rose), Rickover also dragooned many of the Navy's most talented officers into "his" submarines, where they promptly disappeared from sight of the rest of the Navy.[36] Submarine security requirements were so stringent that nonsubmariner flag officers were never fully briefed on the submarine community's accomplishments.[37] All of this produced an environment of intraservice mistrust that would remain for decades. The Navy, unlike the other services, is a multidomain force, providing US leaders with power projection, sea control, presence, expeditionary warfare, and sea-based deterrence capabilities. Not all Navy platforms or components can perform all of these roles.[38]

Nevertheless, a great power—particularly a maritime nation like the United States or Britain before it—needs a range of proficiencies. It is therefore the responsibility of Navy admirals not simply to lead this force but also to weld the disparate elements into a cohesive whole.[39] To that end, the admirals commanding the various US fleets believed they should know about everything occurring in their theaters. This was no longer possible as the submarine community grew in size and developed an independent set of strategic and intelligence-gathering missions.[40] The existence of secret submarine operations beyond the admirals' control therefore created enormous resentment outside of the submarine community.

In the years after USS *Nautilus* went to sea, the balance of power between the Navy's communities dramatically shifted. The surface-warfare and aviation communities continued to press for strike groups built around supercarriers. These were the most visible elements of US naval power, but they no longer controlled the sea domain. Along the littorals, large ships remained at the mercy of humble mines, while on the high seas the submarine threat was growing. US submarines and mines had brought Japan to its knees in 1944–45 without the need for a single American to set foot on the home islands until after Japan's surrender.

Submarine technology also moved by leaps and bounds after World War II, first through the deployment of advanced diesel-electric submarines that could operate underwater for long periods of time and then the construction of nuclear-powered submarines with even greater speed and range.[41] Anyone who served on submarines during the Cold War understood the stealth and lethality of nuclear-powered submarines. Unfortunately, due to the security restrictions, this was often not evident even to the rest of the Navy. Consequently, when senior Navy leaders proposed changes to the US war plan in the 1980s as part of the Maritime Strategy championed by

Secretary of the Navy John Lehman, they initially underestimated the lethality of modern submarines.

How could they commit such a blunder? Some context is necessary. The Maritime Strategy flowed from the work of CNO Thomas Hayward and others in the late 1970s. Hayward, in particular, was furious that, under the Carter administration's war plans against the Soviet Union, the Navy had no offensive role—it was limited largely to defensive operations such as protecting convoys. By contrast, the Maritime Strategy called for a quick force-projection move against the Soviet Union in both the Arctic and Pacific theaters in the event of hostilities, to include the destruction of Soviet SLBM submarines operating in their polar bastions.[42]

Besides undermining the foundations of deterrence by eliminating the Soviets' second-strike capability, thereby increasing the possibility of "inadvertent escalation" of conventional conflict into a nuclear war, the Maritime Strategy would have run headfirst into the sharp end of the spear of Soviet naval capabilities. The Soviets built their Navy around their submarine force, not to threaten US supply lines but rather to deny the United States control of specific areas such as Soviet submarine bastions in the Arctic and marginal seas (maritime areas partially enclosed by bodies of land) in the Barents Sea and the Sea of Okhotsk rather than the broad commons. Accordingly, the Soviet submarine force would be lying in wait in precisely those areas the Maritime Strategy was targeting.[43]

The strategy was not simply a warfighting guide—it was also a political document because it provided the rationale for Lehman's demands for a "600-ship" Navy.[44] (The Maritime Strategy was not acknowledged publicly until 1986, several years after the Reagan administration's initial request for a six-hundred-ship Navy, but the existence of the former was implicit in the latter.[45]) Leaving aside the financial and resource demands, because the Maritime Strategy did not take into account certain operational realities, it would have been a disaster if the United States had ever used it as originally conceived.[46] Fortunately, the responsible fleet commanders identified its flaws, and after an exercise at sea demonstrated the validity of their fears, the war plan was revised to make the Navy's initial actions less aggressive. These changes failed to convert all of the critics, who remained doubtful that the Navy could eliminate the Soviet submarine threat before penetrating the Soviet bastions. Fortunately, the United States never had to find out which side was correct.[47]

Despite this quiet drama, some of the Navy still had difficulty coming to grips with the concept that nuclear submarines were truly revolutionary and that they had to abandon some assumptions about naval warfare. Some might argue that there are groups in the Navy today that remain equally stubborn in the face of potentially transformative emerging technologies.[48]

THE TORTURED HISTORY OF RPVS

Another service that was equally resistant to transformative technologies was the Air Force in its hostility to RPVs—specifically the Global Hawk, a high-altitude surveillance drone, and the Predator, a relatively short-range platform. Developing these platforms proved to be less challenging technically than bureaucratically. Although they provided valuable new capabilities, getting the Air Force to accept them proved to be exceedingly difficult. This was not because the Air Force had any particular hostility to new technologies. The Air Force was, in fact, the first service to field combat RPVs, during the Vietnam War. Indeed, the Air Force's history with RPVs compares favorably with that of the Navy, whose record with new technologies such as radio or even RPVs is no better or even worse than the Air Force's.[49]

Still, the Air Force had "abdicated" its development of RPVs in the mid-1970s to focus its resources on its manned programs that enabled deep penetration of the Soviet Union. With resources again scarce following the end of the Cold War, the service would no doubt protect its manned programs.[50] Fortunately, many high-ranking OSD officials had expected the Air Force's response. Exploring how they managed to overcome bureaucratic resistance from the Air Force is an illustrative case study that has great importance for the future of the Defense Department.

The Predator has a radius of four hundred miles and can loiter for fourteen hours at altitudes up to twenty-five thousand feet.[51] While the Predator does not place a pilot at risk, it duplicates the intelligence, surveillance, and reconnaissance (ISR) capabilities of many piloted aircraft because it carries many of the same sensor pods. The major new capability Predator provides is continuous presence over a selected portion of the battlefield since the Air Force no longer has to worry about pilot safety or fatigue. While the Predator carries only a fixed sensor package and can surveil only a limited sector, its capabilities are still invaluable.

Global Hawk is a different bird.[52] It was designed to remain aloft for even longer periods—the original proposal to industry from the Defense Advanced Research Projects Agency (DARPA) suggested as long as a week. Accordingly, Global Hawk has extraordinarily long wings, a thin body, and flies at high altitudes (sixty thousand feet). It can readily surveil an area the size of South Korea in one mission in a single day.[53] Nothing else in the US arsenal can provide the same capabilities as the Global Hawk. As an added benefit to many, since DARPA (a defense-wide agency rather than one specific to a service) developed it, Global Hawk was not subject to disputes over which service or community controlled it or to which it could provide real-time communications and data. The downside at the onset was that it threatened an existing aircraft community that had no other mission (the U-2) and also could perform some missions better than the existing (and expensive) satellites in the space and intelligence communities.

Satellites that travel in low earth orbit (LEO—250,000 to 300,000 feet above the surface) avoid the dangerous belts of radiation that encircle the earth. Physics makes LEO satellites wonderful surveillance assets because of their multiple daily orbits over large swaths of the planet's surface. Because they are so low, however, LEO satellites are subject to the drag of the atmosphere, and they must continually be boosted upward. Also, their sensors can sample only one particular area for a few seconds during each orbital pass.

It is possible to damage one of these satellites with a laser or a missile, but doing so requires advanced technology available to few nations, and since basic physics will show the location of the platform that performed the hostile act, retaliation is possible. Finally, satellites may be expensive, but it is not technically difficult to replace them once a nation has the capacity to build and launch satellites in the first place.

The U-2 spy plane had some of the same characteristics of LEO satellites but more flexibility. The U-2 is not subject to the laws of orbital physics, so it can view specific areas at desirable times. For safety, the U-2, like a LEO satellite, relies on its altitude (seventy thousand feet or higher) and high speed to keep it safe. As with satellites, the U-2's sensors can sample the earth's surface only along a relatively straight path. Also, like satellites, a U-2 can be knocked down, but the mathematics of intercept are not simple. Unlike satellites, however, the U-2 requires skilled pilots with extraordinary physical and mental stamina.

Satellites and U-2s are superb ISR assets, but neither satisfies the need for what is called "persistent" ISR. U-2s risk their pilots' lives, and expensive satellites require an immense infrastructure to build, launch, and control them. Satellites and U-2s are also expensive platforms, ever in short supply, and for commanders in the field, their use often seems to be prioritized elsewhere.

Many Army, Navy, and Marine commanders would have traded every billion-dollar satellite in the sky for one cheap ISR asset under their control. They were not interested in everything that was being done across the electromagnetic spectrum—just what was happening in their specific area of operations. Operational commanders dreaded waking up to find that their surveillance had been turned off the previous night because some GS-9 at an Air Force base on the other side of the world had decided that the field commander's needs fell below the "cut line" of missions deserving of support.

If persistent ISR was expensive and demand exceeded the supply, the obvious solution was to develop cost-effective means of providing it. One inexpensive option was blimps, which had hunted German submarines during both world wars. When Dave Oliver returned from Seventh Fleet to the Pentagon in 1986, Lehman made him the manager for the blimp-ISR program. A direct reporting relationship between the secretary of the Navy and a one-star admiral was highly unusual, particularly since NAVAIR fell under the jurisdiction of a three-star aviator admiral, while Oliver was supposed to be working for a three-star surface-warfare admiral in the Pentagon doing warfare planning. Recall the military's love of hierarchy and clear lines of authority.

In addition, Oliver was an odd choice for program manager. He had no prior experience in acquisition. He was not a member of one of the baronial "bureaus" or systems commands that have run the Navy since time immemorial. Not only was he not an aviator, but he had never even flown in a blimp. It turned out that the blimp program had caught Lehman's interest. The blimp promised to carry a huge sensor load, to stay aloft for a week or more (compared to four or five hours for most fixed-wing airplanes), and to be relatively inexpensive. But the secretary was meeting resistance from the aviation community. A platform that promised to be cheap and effective should have sailed through the acquisition process—but this one did not.

Navy officers observe strict pecking orders based on the status or difficulty of their jobs. For example, it requires greater hand-eye coordination to land a jet-powered aircraft on a moving ship at sea than it does to land a propeller-driven aircraft on land. It also takes superior skills to serve as a tactical officer aboard a destroyer than just about any role aboard an amphibious-assault vessel. And so forth and so on. The point is, status is important in any organization. One of the other factors that affects that pecking order in the military is speed—faster is better. Blimps were not going to land upon or gather around a carrier, and they flew at about forty miles an hour. Blimps thus were, by the Navy's own definition, the lowest of the low, alongside minesweepers.

Nevertheless, NAVAIR, like the entire Navy, got its marching orders from its secretary, and the naval-aviation engineering community put together a request for proposal (RFP) to industry. (These documents are how the government communicates its requirements to prospective contractors.[54]) It delivered the many-hundred-page draft RFP to the Pentagon for approval one afternoon the Wednesday before Thanksgiving. Because of some congressional limitations on the money it appropriated for that purpose, the proposal had to be released to industry by the following Monday.

The Navy captain who delivered the proposal wanted it signed immediately so that it could be published. Rear Adm. Oliver, the recipient, declined. There was no way he was going to sign off on something he had not read. So, his staff divided the proposal into sections and began poring through it. What they found in the fine print defied common sense. For example, the blimp was *required* to use explosive hydrogen rather than the readily available and inert helium. It was as if NAVAIR considered the *Hindenburg* as a role model rather than a warning.

Within hours, Oliver's staff was ready to discuss its sections of the proposal. Oliver began making calls to his friends in the aviation community requesting additional technical assistance. Late Friday night, he went down the Pentagon corridor to speak to Secretary Lehman with a list of the ten most egregious items in the proposal. The first three are summarized as follows:

1. The blimp would be filled with hydrogen. This would make it incredibly dangerous to its crew even during routine operations. Since there was no factory in the United States that manufactured hydrogen, a plant to produce it would have to be constructed *and then, by the state law of the known competitors, dismantled* after the hydrogen was manufactured. (Note that helium, such as that used in the Goodyear Blimp, is abundant in the United States.) The cost of building and then dismantling the hydrogen facility was to be tacked onto the blimp's program cost.
2. By specification, all solid components in the blimp were to be made from cast iron rather than aluminum, titanium, plastic, or any other light material. Cast iron's weight (think of frying skillets) required a larger and more expensive blimp to generate sufficient lift to get it aloft. At the same time, the unnecessary weight would limit the blimp's ISR payload.
3. The blimp was required to have a workout room for pilots to use between their shifts. The pilots supposedly needed it to maintain their muscle tone during blimp missions lasting a week or more. The proposal also required the use of dead weights in the workout room rather than lighter resistance or elliptical gear.

The rest of the list had to do with other poor design specifics. Several senior aviators, when asked for their opinion, were unanimous in concluding that these items reduced airworthiness. After a while, Oliver's team even heard rumors that the vice admiral in charge of NAVAIR had received a letter from senior members of his staff detailing many specific problems and urging him not to forward the proposal without corrections. The admiral had apparently filed this report in his desk without taking any action.

Lehman signed a letter to NAVAIR listing its proposed blimp's flaws and sent Oliver off to NAVAIR's headquarters in Crystal City to deliver it. When he arrived, the commanding admiral did not even bother to read the letter. Instead, he leaned back in his chair, folded his hands, and began a long soliloquy about how the Navy had gotten rid of blimps after World War II because they were too big and slow. As long as he was in charge of NAVAIR, the Navy was never, ever going back to blimps.

As the minutes of contentious board meetings often record, "a discussion ensued." Ultimately, NAVAIR could not ignore a signed letter from the secretary of the Navy. Accordingly, the chief of NAVAIR promised that his staff would rewrite the blimp proposal over Christmas. He thus made sure that the proposal would not see the light of day until well into the New Year (1987). Three things happened over the next few months that ensured the project would fail: Lehman retired, Oliver rotated to a new job back out in the fleet, and the company that eventually won the blimp-ISR contract suffered a fire that burned down its enormous blimp hangar, which was virtually irreplaceable because of the immense cost to replace it.

The project was dead. The NAVAIR admiral had won.

Before all of these unpleasant events came to pass, on one summer day over the Maryland countryside, Oliver flew in a blimp (courtesy of Goodyear) for the first time. While admiring the pastoral scene below, he noted the lack of noise from the small engine and how simple the controls would be to automate. During those several hours aloft, he calculated that the platform's payload could be increased by a factor of ten to thirty if the weight of the crew-safety equipment was removed. Lehman's instincts about blimps had been on the mark—they would have been an invaluable ISR asset but were rejected because the Navy was not prepared to accept a change that ran so contrary to its values. A decade later, several civilian officials would strive to ensure that the same fate did not befall RPVs.

In the Air Force, the service with the primary responsibility for airborne reconnaissance, pilots were fighting RPVs for the same reason naval aviators opposed blimps. When Robert Gates, then director of Central Intelligence, tried to partner with the Air Force in 1992 in developing RPVs because of their potentially remarkable ISR capabilities, the Air Force service brushed him off with the excuse that "people join the Air Force to fly airplanes and drones had no pilots."[55] Unlike with the blimps, in the case of RPVs, political appointees were more persistent in their advocacy and ultimately more successful.

President Bill Clinton's second secretary of defense, William Perry, was convinced that RPVs were a technology deserving of special support. He also believed that his personal advocacy was essential to overcoming the Air Force's resistance. Perry was assisted by Larry Lynn (the head of DARPA) and Paul Kaminski (the undersecretary of defense for acquisition and technology). DARPA was just the sort of agency to back this effort. Back in the 1970s, to counteract the Soviets' supposed conventional military superiority in Europe, DARPA had supported the development of "disruptive" technologies such as stealth aircraft and stand-off precision-strike weapons at the prompting of the then secretary of defense Harold Brown and his undersecretary for research and engineering, Perry.[56] Two decades later, Perry, Lynn, and Kaminski were convinced that RPV technology was sufficiently mature to become operational. According to Lynn,

> The history of the UAVs [unmanned aerial vehicles] is one of cultural anathema, not technological.[57] UAVs were built when I was invited to come to DARPA back in the '70s—this was, like 1972. . . . [The] real problem with all of these has been no user really wanted them. And so, unconstrained people at ARPA [Advanced Research Projects Agency—renamed DARPA in 1972]—scientists, not generally military, though some military people—could easily look at these and say, "There's got to be some value in being able to sit over the enemy at a thousand feet and see what he's doing." The military had a lot of difficulty doing that. They preferred to go in a helicopter or a manned airplane. So there was the cultural acceptance issue.[58]

To build the Air Force's acceptance of this new technology, Lynn drafted Air Force major general Kenneth Israel as one of his program managers. From 1995 to 1998, Israel's office was known as the Defense Airborne Reconnaissance Office (DARO).[59] Israel organized DARPA's RPV programs into three different types of capabilities and conducted competitions among private firms to find the best designs. The competitions were enormously successful. The Predator, built by General Atomics, won the competition for medium-altitude and -range platform, and Ryan Aerospace's Global Hawk triumphed in the long-range, high-altitude category. There was no then affordable product in the third category—stealth.

Field commanders were overjoyed at finally having persistent, low-cost ISR support. These platforms would not just deliver a badly needed capability, but also, since DARPA did not report to the Air Force, the Navy and Army could get ISR for their own needs without jumping through unnecessary Air Force hoops.

The Air Force liked its administrative hoops and loved its monopoly over ISR. It convinced Congress to write into law that DARO assets be returned to the Air Force. As soon as they were, the Air Force forced Israel to retire and omitted the Predator and Global Hawk from its next budget. The stated reason was that both programs were not yet ready. There is no way of knowing how long the Air Force might have buried RPVs, but—inconveniently—a war broke out in Kosovo. At the time, President Clinton was trying to walk a fine line of preventing the genocide of Kosovar Albanians by Serbian paramilitary forces without deploying US ground troops. From March to June 1999, the United States and its NATO allies bombed Serbia and Serbian forces in Kosovo. During this conflict, the United States threw everything in its arsenal at the Serbs, including Tomahawk missiles launched from Navy ships and precision-guided munitions ("smart bombs") dropped by F-117s, B-52s, and even stealth B-2s flying thirty-hour missions from Whiteman Air Force Base in Missouri.[60]

Despite this wealth of airpower, without boots on the ground or continuous ISR, the US campaign was ineffective. The Serbs were skilled at camouflage and rarely exposed themselves to NATO attack. Serbia did not have much of an air force, but its antiaircraft arsenal made low-flying missions too dangerous, even knocking down a stealth aircraft, and increased the consumption of smart bombs, whose accuracy was often limited by fog. US weapons sometimes killed refugees, journalists, and other innocents, but they rarely destroyed their intended military targets.[61] The collateral civilian deaths were especially embarrassing since the campaign was supposed to be a humanitarian mission that would end ethnic cleansing. The air campaign shambled along until an enlisted RPV "pilot" located back in the United States at Indian Springs Air Force Base (later renamed Creech) near Las Vegas who was remotely operating a Predator noticed a concentration of Serbian troops in Kosovo in a clearing. From halfway around the world, he redirected a B-52 from a planned bombing run to a mission that killed enough Serbian soldiers to change some minds in Belgrade.[62]

During the war, Secretary of Defense William Cohen had believed his military commanders' assurances that air strikes were destroying half of Serbia's artillery and about one-third of each class of armored vehicles. At the war's end, the numbers of successful strikes began shrinking dramatically. For example, now the US military claimed to have destroyed only ninety-three of the one thousand Serbian tanks. In the months that followed, NATO investigators could locate only twenty-six wreckages.[63] Nor did the campaign do lasting damage to Serbia's military capabilities. When arms-control investigators compared Serbia's inventories for 1999 and 2000, they found that the total number of tanks had decreased during the war by only nine.[64]

With official figures under fire, Cohen asked Oliver, his principal deputy undersecretary for acquisition, along with two Air Force generals, to conduct an informal review of the conflict. These three men were not interested in the question of how much Serbian hardware had been blown to bits. It was obvious that the enemy had done a good job of hiding its assets and that the United States, even with complete control of the air, had not quickly overwhelmed a relatively small and contained enemy. Arguing over exact numbers was best left to bureaucrats and journalists.[65] Oliver's group had to answer the more important question of what could have been done better.

It soon became apparent that the RPVs, along with their persistent ISR capability, had not been well integrated into the campaign plan. Ever since the Cold War, the Air Force has structured its wartime operations around complex air tasking orders that specified what every plane in the theater was doing, right down to the precise ordnance they should carry. This was to deconflict the air space, prioritize targeting, and minimize the risk of friendly fire or collisions. Navy and Marine pilots complained that the Air Force system was too prescriptive and also unresponsive to the demands of close air support.[66] In the case of unmanned aircraft over Kosovo, since there were no provisions for including RPVs in the air plan, the Air Force had flown them at different altitudes from the manned airplanes from the Air Force, Navy, and Marines, which were doing "real" work. Yet, despite all of this planning, it was only through a combination of chance and personal initiative that a lone Predator pilot contacted a B-52 on its way to the theater, redirected it to the target, and singlehandedly changed the course of the Kosovo War.

To strike targets more effectively, US forces needed the kind of persistent ISR that RPVs provided. The average combatant is not the most dispassionate observer of events. When the shooting starts, adrenaline levels rise, which helps to overcome fear but historically has also contributed to exaggerated mission-kill claims. The United States had invested all sorts of camera and recording systems to overcome this problem. The US military collects as much data as possible about what happens during air combat, but the action is taking place under fire at hundreds of miles per hour.

Predators and Global Hawks, whose computer brains contained no adrenaline and suffered from no distractions, had none of the drawbacks of human operators in combat. Instead, RPVs would have allowed US forces to evaluate the situation just before, during, and immediately after a strike. Just as important, a third party—someone who was not emotionally involved in the strike as a participant or planner and may be thousands of miles away—can immediately perform a battle-damage assessment, which was essential to providing field commanders with an accurate assessment of the situation. Not surprisingly, the official British study of the campaign concluded that in the future NATO forces required better ISR, precision targeting, and battle-damage assessment.[67]

Before briefing Cohen on the results of the review, Oliver decided to visit the RPV base at Indian Springs as well as the two facilities manufacturing RPVs, both of which were located near San Diego. In Las Vegas, he met the Air Force general who commanded both of the bases at Indian Springs and Nellis Air Force Base. There were fighter squadrons at Nellis, but they had not seen combat during the recent war. Oliver and the general then trekked to Indian Springs, which was almost an hour's drive away. It was miserably hot in the Las Vegas area, but the general assured his VIP guests that he had modified a van with dual air-conditioning units to make the trip more comfortable.

Indian Springs had directed all of the Predators during the Kosovo conflict. Every Air Force Predator pilot was stationed there. Oliver wanted to get a feel for the place, the morale of the crews, and how they performed different sorts of missions. The general commanding the base was of little help—he admitted that this was his *first* visit to Indian Springs. He asked Oliver to award the medal Cohen had authorized for the airman who had been so crucial to the success of the Kosovo bombing campaign.

Oliver found the conditions at Indian Springs disappointing. The airmen complained how uncomfortable their hour-long daily bus ride was to and from their government housing in Las Vegas. Apparently, the air-conditioning unit on their bus had been missing for weeks. On the way back to Las Vegas, the base commander admitted that he had removed the air-conditioning unit from the Indian Springs bus to ensure his VIP van was always ready. Despite having an annual budget of several hundreds of millions of dollars, he believed he could find money *next month* to fix the air conditioning for the RPV operators. He was careful to assure Oliver, however, that the real pilots at Nellis were comfortable. As further evidence of just how difficult it is to change a service's culture, the conditions for the RPV operators at Indian Springs/Creech remained substandard and, despite the increased RPV use with 9/11, did not improve until Secretary Gates finally took action a decade later.[68]

Oliver then flew to San Diego to tour the General Atomics facility and observe the flight of a Predator. After his visit, he concluded the Predator was ready for deployment. He spent the next day at Ryan Aerospace, thirty miles away, where they were building the Global Hawk. As he stood in the twilight, watching a unit taxi down the runway, the chairman and CEO of Northrop Grumman, Kent Kresa, drove up out of the desert and got out of his limousine.[69] Kresa had heard through the grapevine that Oliver was in the area. Without any preamble, Kresa asked, "What do you think?" Since Ryan Aerospace was a one-product company, Oliver knew exactly what Kresa meant. He replied along the lines of "I think it is exactly what DOD needs. I think Bob Mitchell [Ryan Aerospace's CEO] is brilliant, but Ryan has fewer employees than the Air Force typically puts into managing a single program. To be successful, Ryan is going to have to hire some solid program management types to survive knocking heads with the Air Force. I also suspect they need more depth in engineering."

The Global Hawk had by now reached the end of the runway and turned into the wind. Kent was attentively watching the aircraft and did not look away from it as he spoke. "The Northrop Grumman Board just gave me approval to buy Ryan. I'm going to leave Bob in charge and provide him the engineering support he doesn't have. Now all you have to do is convince the Air Force to buy Global Hawk."

The RPV seemed to take forever to turn ninety degrees. Finally, it began to roll forward. Then it picked up speed as it crabbed a bit into the crosswind. The two men watched the long wings lift like gull feathers and pull the long thin body soundlessly into the sky. The Global Hawk would return the day after tomorrow. Kent got back into the rear seat of his limousine and drove away into the dark.

Oliver returned to the Pentagon and set to work. How could he encourage the Air Force to accept RPVs? A year previously, Secretary Cohen had sent a signed directive to every official in the OSD who reported to him directly (plus the secretaries and chiefs of each of the services) stating that RPVs were a transformational technology and that the entire Pentagon should support them. Cohen's predecessor, Perry, had pushed a similar message. Still, despite years of pressure from two secretaries of defense, the Air Force had not budged in its opposition to RPVs, and yet again RPVs were still not in the Air Force's latest budget submission.

Oliver had just inspected both industrial bases and concluded they could support full-scale production. He had also calculated the cost savings from removing human pilots from ISR vehicles. Finally, the United States had just gone through a war during which inaccurate aerial bombing had killed hundreds of innocents while expending large amounts of munitions and money torching haystacks. The country could not afford such setbacks in the future, either militarily or morally.

The Air Force was, if anything, going backward. It had seized bureaucratic control of the RPV program from DARPA, a move that outside observers suspected was done only to keep the RPVs out of production. Optimists contended otherwise: maybe the Air Force was preparing to do the right thing and the RPVs would be included in the next Air Force budget. Time would soon tell which side was correct.

In late 1999 the Air Force submitted its FY 2001 budget request to the OSD. At that moment, the F-22 Raptor was the Air Force's focus, and there had been a great deal of controversy surrounding it. Everyone in Washington knew the Air Force was doing its best to cover the F-22's warts, having already devoted billions to the program. In that same budget request, the service again failed to include funding for either the Global Hawk or the Predator. This was despite the fact that only a few months before, the Air Force's deputy chief for operations admitted to the HASC that the B-2s needed the assistance of RPVs to achieve their "impressive" results during the war—11 percent of targets destroyed by only 1 percent of the sorties.[70]

The Air Force might have again succeeded in stalling RPVs, but it had made a costly mistake. The team putting together the Air Force budget for the F-22 had failed to add to the program nearly a hundred million dollars to cover a mandatory cost-of-living adjustment. Consequently, the Air Force's priority program was not correctly funded.

These things sometimes happen during the hectic process of completing budget submissions. Resolving them is why political appointees build up relationships with other appointees across the Pentagon (as we mentioned in chapter 5), so that when someone makes such an error, they can walk into a colleague's office and say, "Listen, I made a $92 million mistake. Can you cover the deficit?" With the right relationships, there is always money to plug "small" holes.

But an oversight such as this was also an opportunity. It was a rock that might serve as the fulcrum upon which a reformer might place a lever. The Air Force chief of staff and the secretary of the Air Force had already signed their flawed budget, certifying it was accurate. This meant the F-22 program was, to use both a legal term and a term of art, "improperly funded." There had been a great deal of bad press about such programs in the past, when the services had understated costs to shield problems from discovery. To discourage this, Congress had given two political appointees the authority to cancel any program that was not "fully funded"—the undersecretary for acquisition and his principal deputy (Oliver).

Threatening to cancel a program was a dangerous political move. Technically, any decision to terminate an improperly funded program was not subject to review by either the secretary of defense or the president. Congress had deliberately set it up in that manner to preserve the integrity of the acquisition process from political meddling.

In reality, no political appointee could have survived the fallout from such an action without the backing of their bosses. The F-22 simply had too many political and industrial friends. But that did not mean the program was bulletproof. Many people questioned the need in the post–Cold War world for what was essentially a single-mission fighter.[71] The program also had its problems. In fact, the Air Force had recently, and very publicly, fired the two generals who had been serving as the program manager and deputy program manager. The Air Force was not interested in more bad F-22 publicity. Further revelations about improper funding, while small in the grand scheme of things, might have proven fatal to the beleaguered stealth airplane.[72]

If change ever were to come about, this was the moment. If everyone drew lines in the sand—that is, if the Air Force demanded that the OSD provide the missing cash but refused to budge on RPVs, while Oliver pushed for cancellation—there would be blood on the floor.

After a day or so of posturing, the Air Force backed down. The Air Force chief of staff and the secretary of the Air Force both agreed to give public speeches about the importance of RPVs to the Air Force's future. After they did so, they signed a revised Air Force budget that included funding for the Predator and Global Hawk programs for the first time.

Two years later, after George W. Bush was sworn into office, the new president appointed Donald Rumsfeld to his second tour as secretary of defense. On his first day, the new secretary called a staff meeting for the half dozen people reporting directly to him, one of whom was Oliver, the only holdover from the previous administration. Rumsfeld did not mince words: "I want to be a transformational secretary. I know I need to protect Global Hawk. Now tell me what the other equivalent programs are." He was as his good as his word. A month later, he signed off on a memorandum approving production of the Global Hawk, which complemented his "priority of developing leap ahead technologies." Rumsfeld's closest aide, Chris Williams, later blessed the proposal by scribbling the following memo to Rumsfeld: "Global Hawk is an important program. Dave Oliver has scrubbed the program hard + well, and all agree it is ready to move forward."[73]

The casual reader might think that the Global Hawk story is one with a happy ending, in which the plucky underdogs came out ahead. That is not the way things work in the Pentagon. In hindsight, it is remarkable that Global Hawk went into production despite the opposition of the Air Force. If that service had listed its top programs in 2000, the Global Hawk would not have made the list. The global war on terrorism spurred the growth of unmanned systems to roughly 5 percent of the Air Force's aircraft inventory (fifty-five hundred as of FY 2020), but that appears to be the peak.[74]

In its FY 2021 budget submission, the Air Force eliminated a portion of its Global Hawk inventory and refused to procure any new unmanned aircraft but continued to fund the very costly manned U-2 program. Theoretically, these cuts required a number of senior military and civilian officials to certify that the Air Force's decision was consistent with US national security, but HASC staffers marking the defense bill commented that "right now none of those conditions have been met to give us any sort of peace of mind that the Air Force's fiscal year 2021 . . . is with acceptable risk."[75] Nevertheless, in its FY 2022 submission, the Air Force continued its divestment of thirty Global Hawks and planned to purchase only manned aircraft.[76]

Each of the services likes to have absolute control over its budget and is accustomed to horse-trading to protect its interests. The hard facts of life inside the Beltway are that in return for the Air Force promising not to attack some specific Navy, Army, and Marine programs, the other service chiefs keep their reservations about Air Force priorities quiet (again, more "log-rolling"). Defending the interests of the *entire* Department of Defense is usually the responsibility of the secretary of defense, but that does not mean the OSD has the power to make it happen quickly.

Getting the Global Hawk into production over Air Force opposition took the concerted efforts of three secretaries of defense, numerous senior officials, and at least one titan of industry. Only then was it possible to strong-arm the Air Force into accepting a technology that saved many American lives. As an Air Force–sponsored study later conceded, "[there] remains little doubt that the services, like all organizations, will not change without an external catalyst." The same study, however, complained that "external containment of the prime implementers disassociates the services, dampens internal change processes, and ultimately hinders weapon system innovation."[77] In other words, outsiders might have forced the Air Force to use RPVs, but that did not mean the Air Force had to like them. Despite RPVs' many successes after 2001, the Air Force continued to drag its heels in expanding its RPV capability to the detriment of what the uniformed military considered its more valuable programs, while simultaneously insisting that the Air Force control all RPV operations, much as it did with traditional ISR platforms.[78]

SUMMARY

Transformation, the revolution in military affairs, or whatever term is current is critical to maintaining the qualitative military advantage of the United States. At the same time, it should be recognized that many transformational technologies and concepts have faced varying degrees of resistance, ranging from indifference to outright rejection. Nevertheless, once accepted, such technologies changed decades or even centuries of warfighting thinking and practice. Of course, it is necessary for professionals to be attentive to new technologies and concepts, but that is also insufficient because good ideas do not speak for themselves. Unfortunately, as historical experience has repeatedly demonstrated, the transformational qualities of any particular weapon or doctrine do not by themselves guarantee that a military will embrace them. Turning the military into partners rather than adversaries when it comes to such changes will be the focus of our concluding chapter.

NOTES

1. A summary of this chapter appeared in Dave Oliver and Anand Toprani, "Why Is Technological Change in the Military So Messy?," *RUSI Newsbrief* 41, no. 4 (May 2021), https://rusi.org/publication/rusi-newsbrief/why-technological-change-military-so-messy.
2. "Office of Net Assessment (ONA)," US Department of Defense, n.d., https://www.defense.gov/Our-Story/Office-of-the-Secretary-of-Defense/Office-of-Net-Assessment/. For details about Marshall's life and work, we have relied on the excellent biography of Marshall by two of his acolytes: Andrew Krepinevich and Barry Watts, *The Last Warrior: Andrew Marshall and the Shaping of Modern American Defense Strategy* (New York: Basic Books, 2015).
3. David Zabecki, *Chief of Staff: World War II to Korea and Vietnam* (Annapolis, MD: Naval Institute Press, 2008), 40. There is some confusion as to the author of this quote—Schlieffen or Helmuth von Moltke the Elder.
4. Krepinevich, *Warrior*, 195.
5. John Schutte, *Casting Net Assessment: Andrew W. Marshall and the Epistemic Community of the Cold War* (Maxwell AFB, AL: Air University Press, 2015), https://media.defense.gov/2017/Nov/21/2001847253/-1/-1/0/DP_0016_SCHUTTE_CASTING_NET_ASSESSMENT.PDF.

6. Jerry Hendrix, "Just Andy Marshall," *National Review*, April 17, 2019, https://www.nationalreview.com/2019/04/remembering-andrew-marshall/. Schlesinger was never supposed to be the secretary of defense. Following his reelection, Nixon had appointed Schlesinger as director of Central Intelligence, with the express purpose of "shaking up" Langley through job cuts targeting the agency's highest ranks. "Conversation between President Nixon and the President's Assistant for National Security Affairs (Kissinger)," February 27, 1973, Department of State, https://history.state.gov/historicaldocuments/frus1969-76v38p2/d2. The sudden resignation of Richard Kleindienst as attorney general in April 1973 as a result of the Watergate scandal forced Nixon to engineer a cabinet shuffle. Elliot Richardson, who was Nixon's handpicked replacement for Melvin Laird, moved from the Pentagon to the Department of Justice, while Schlesinger went from Langley to the Pentagon and William Colby took over at Langley. "Richardson Draft Surprises Pentagon," *New York Times*, May 1973.
7. Williamson Murray and MacGregor Knox, "Thinking about Revolutions in Warfare," in *The Dynamics of Military Revolution, 1300–2050*, ed. Williamson Murray and MacGregor Knox (Cambridge: Cambridge University Press, 2001), 1–14.
8. Andrew Marshall, "The Origins of Net Assessment," and James Roche and Thomas Mahnken, "What Is Net Assessment?," in *Net Assessment and Military Strategy: Retrospective and Prospective Essays*, ed. Thomas Mahnken (Amherst, NY: Cambria, 2020); Mie Augier, "Thinking about War and Peace: Andrew Marshall and the Early Development of the Intellectual Foundations for Net Assessment," *Comparative Strategy* 32 (2013): 1–17.
9. Barry Watts, "Net Assessment in the Era of Superpower Competition," in Mahnken, *Net Assessment*, 57ff.
10. Krepinevich and Watts, *Last Warrior*, x, 122–25, 130–32, 167.
11. Robert Caro, *The Power Broker: Robert Moses and the Fall of New York* (New York: Knopf, 1974), 315.
12. "Military Operations Research Society (MORS) Oral History Project Interview of Andrew W. Marshall," *Military Operations Research* 20, no. 1 (2015): 77. Among the most influential publications ONA sponsored were multinational studies of "military effectiveness" by leading scholars of military history. Allan R. Millett and Williamson Murray, ed. *Military Effectiveness*, vol. 1, *The First World War* (Cambridge: Cambridge University Press, 2010), xiii–xiv, xvi. For an example of an ONA study that contradicted Marshall's views, see William Burr and Svetlana Savranskaya, eds., "Previously Classified Interviews with Former Soviet Officials Reveal U.S. Strategic Intelligence Failure over Decades," NSA, Electronic Briefing Book 285, September 11, 2009, https://nsarchive2.gwu.edu/nukevault/ebb285/.
13. Krepinevich and Watts, *Last Warrior*, 65, 144–47.
14. The literature on blitzkrieg is immense. See, for a start, Gerhard Gross, *The Myth and Reality of German Warfare: Operational Thinking from Moltke the Elder to Heusinger* (Lexington: University Press of Kentucky, 2017); James Corum, *The Roots of Blitzkrieg: Hans von Seeckt and German Military Reform* (Lawrence: University Press of Kansas, 1992); Robert Citino, *The German Way of War: From the Thirty Years' War to the Third Reich* (Lawrence: University Press of Kansas, 2012); Williamson Murray, "Germany Army Doctrine, 1918–1939, and the Post-1945 Theory of 'Blitzkrieg Strategy,'" in *German Nationalism and the European Response, 1890–1945*, ed. Carole Fink, Isabel V. Hull, and MacGregor Knox (Norman: University of Oklahoma Press, 1985), 71–94.

15. R. J. Overy, *Why the Allies Won* (New York: Norton, 1995); Phillips Payson O'Brien, *How the War Was Won: Air-Sea Power and Allied Victory in World War II* (Cambridge: Cambridge University Press, 2019); John Ellis, *Brute Force: Allied Strategy and Tactics in the Second World War* (London: Andre Deutsch, 1991). The importance of luck in Germany's shocking defeat of France is now historical fact. See Karl-Heinz Frieser, *The Blitzkrieg Legend: The 1940 Campaign in the West* (Annapolis, MD: Naval Institute Press, 2013); Robert Doughty, "Myth of the Blitzkrieg," in *Challenging the United States Symmetrically and Asymmetrically*, ed. Lloyd Matthews (Carlisle Barracks: US Army War College, 1998), 57–79; Williamson Murray, "May 1940: Contingency and Fragility of the German RMA," in Murray and Knox, *Dynamics*, 154–74.
16. Rolf Hobson, "Blitzkrieg, the Revolution in Military Affairs and Defense Intellectuals," *Journal of Strategic Studies* 33, no. 4 (2010): 625–43.
17. Justin Kelly and Mike Brennan, "How Operational Art Devoured Strategy," Strategic Studies Institute, September 2009, https://publications.armywarcollege.edu/pubs/2027.pdf.
18. Eitan Shamir, *Transforming Command: The Pursuit of Mission Command in the U.S., British, and Israeli Armies* (Stanford, CA: Stanford University Press, 2011).
19. Joseph Bilby, *A Revolution in Arms: A History of the First Repeating Rifles* (Yardley, PA: Westholme, 2005).
20. Thomas Lecaque, "The Guns That Almost Won the West: Repeating Weapons and the American Western Frontier," *Apprentice Historian* 14 (2008): 35–52.
21. Dennis Showalter, *Railroads and Rifles: Soldiers, Technology and the Unification of Germany* (Hamden, CT: Archon, 1975).
22. Compare chapters 2 and 3 of John Keegan, *The Mask of Command* (New York: Penguin, 1988).
23. Jonathan Bailey, "Military History and the Pathology of Lessons Learned: the Russo-Japanese War, a Case Study," in *The Past as Prologue: The Importance of History to the Military Profession*, ed. Williamson Murray and Richard Hart Sinnreich (Cambridge: Cambridge University Press, 2006), 170–94.
24. Michael Howard, "Men against Fire: Expectations of War in 1914," *International Security* 9, no. 1 (1984): 41–57; Michael Howard, "Men against Fire: The Doctrine of the Offensive in 1914," in *Makers of Modern Strategy from Machiavelli to the Nuclear Age*, ed. Peter Paret (Princeton, NJ: Princeton University Press, 1986), 510–26.
25. Michael Howard, "The Use and Abuse of Military History," *Parameters* 11, no. 1 (1981): 21.
26. To get a sense of how much submariners feared attacks from friendly aircraft and ships, consult the Harry Gilmour series of novels by David Black.
27. Stephen Peter Rosen, *Winning the Next War: Innovation and the Modern Military* (Ithaca, NY: Cornell University Press, 1991), 130–47; Frank Hoffman, *Mars Adapting: Military Change during War* (Annapolis, MD: Naval Institute Press, 2021), chap. 3; Joel Holwitt, *"Execute against Japan": The U.S. Decision to Conduct Unrestricted Warfare* (College Station: Texas A&M University Press, 2013). For the effects on the Japanese economy, see Lance Davis and Stanley Engerman, *Naval Blockades in Peace and War: An Economic History since 1750* (Cambridge: Cambridge University Press, 2006), 321–82. The many problems with American magnetic and acoustic torpedoes, as well as efforts to rectify them, are described in Clay Blair, *Silent Victory: The U.S. Submarine War against Japan* (Philadelphia: Lippincott, 1976); Michael Hennelly, "Fire One, Fire Ten: Implications

of the Torpedo Scandal of World War II," Strategy Bridge, February 8, 2018, https://thestrategybridge.org/the-bridge/2018/2/8/fire-one-fire-ten-implications-of-the-torpedo-scandal-of-world-war-ii; and Robert Gannon, *Hellions of the Deep: The Development of American Torpedoes in World War II* (University Park: Pennsylvania State University Press, 1996).

28. Naval History Division, *United States Submarine Losses, World War II* (Washington, DC: Office of the Chief of Naval Operations, 1963), https://www.history.navy.mil/research/library/online-reading-room/title-list-alphabetically/u/united-states-submarine-losses.html.
29. In 1945 there were 232 submarines in the 6,748-ship Navy. "US Ship Force Levels," NHHC, November 17, 2017, https://www.history.navy.mil/research/histories/ship-histories/us-ship-force-levels.html. Submarine warfare was even more deadly in the Atlantic—casualty rates among German submariners exceeded 70 percent. Ernest Imhoff, "How the Hunters Were Hunted Down," *Baltimore Sun*, June 2, 1999, https://www.baltimoresun.com/news/bs-xpm-1999-06-02-9906020125-story.html.
30. Enthoven oral history, JFKL.
31. The following discussion draws from Harvey Sapolsky, "The U.S. Navy's Fleet Ballistic Missile Program and Finite Deterrence," in *Getting MAD: Nuclear Mutual Assured Destruction, Its Origins and Practice*, ed. Henry Sokolski (Carlisle, PA: Strategic Studies Institute, US Army War College, 2004), 123–35; Donald MacKenzie and Graham Spinardi, "The Shaping of Nuclear Weapon System Technology: US Fleet Ballistic Missile Guidance and Navigation; I—From Polaris to Poseidon," *Social Studies of Science* 18 (1988): 424–39. See also Elliott Converse, *Rearming for the Cold War, 1945–1960* (Washington, DC: OSD Historical Office, 2012), 394–95, 522ff.
32. Appendix B, Russell interview.
33. Harvey Sapolsky, *The Polaris System Development: Bureaucratic and Programmatic Success in Government* (Cambridge, MA: Harvard University Press, 1972), 160ff.; Eric Labs, "Finding Funding for the New Boomer," *Proceedings* 141 (February 2015): 66–67; Eric Labs to Dave Oliver, email, August 26, 2021.
34. In nuclear strategy, "countervalue" means the targeting of enemy's cities, civilian population, and economy. It is primarily designed to deter an adversary by imposing immense human costs in retaliation for any attack. "Counterforce," by contrast, focuses on targeting of an opponent's military infrastructure, including its nuclear forces and command and control. It is therefore a preemptive strategy that is supposed to hinder an opponent's ability to utilize their own nuclear forces.
35. Alain Enthoven, *How Much Is Enough? Shaping the Defense Program, 1961–1969* (Santa Monica, CA: RAND Corp., 2005), 16–17, 92–93.
36. James Sagerholm, "The Great Draft of 1963," *Submarine Review*, January 12, 2011, 25–28.
37. William R. Smedberg III, *Reminiscences of Vice Admiral William R. Smedberg III, U.S. Navy (Retired)* (Annapolis, MD: US Naval Institute, 1979).
38. Peter Swartz, "American Naval Policy, Strategy, Plans and Operations in the Second Decade of the Twenty-First Century," Center for Naval Analyses, January 2017, https://www.cna.org/cna_files/pdf/DOP-2017-U-014741-Final.pdf.
39. Edward Rhodes, "Do Bureaucratic Politics Matter? Some Disconfirming Findings from the Case of the U.S. Navy," *World Politics* 47, no. 1 (1994): 1–41.
40. The submarine force at the end of the Cold War totaled around 140 boats (out of a US fleet of over 500 combatants), and submarines still account for roughly one-quarter of

the fleet today (about seventy out of less than three hundred vessels). "US Ship Force Levels."

41. Owen Cote, *The Third Battle: Innovation in the U.S. Navy's Silent Cold War Struggle with Soviet Submarines*, Newport Paper 16 (Newport, RI: Naval War College, 2003), https://digital-commons.usnwc.edu/cgi/viewcontent.cgi?article=1015&context=newport-papers.
42. The best summaries of the Maritime Strategy are Christopher Ford and David Rosenberg, "The Naval Intelligence Underpinnings of Reagan's Maritime Strategy," *Journal of Strategic Studies* 28, no. 2 (2005): 379–409; and John Hattendorf, *The Evolution of the U.S. Navy's Maritime Strategy, 1977–1986* (Newport, RI: Naval War College, 2004), https://digital-commons.usnwc.edu/cgi/viewcontent.cgi?article=1018&context=newport-papers. See also Thomas Hone and Curtis Utz, *History of the Office of the Chief of Naval Operations, 1915–2015* (Washington, DC: NHHC, 2015), 316–17, 319–20, 329ff.; Dmitry Filipoff, "Secretary John Lehman on Strategic Credibility and Leveraging Command of the Seas," Center for International Maritime Security, March 22, 2021, https://cimsec.org/secretary-john-lehman-on-strategic-credibility-and-leveraging-command-of-the-seas/; Dmitry Filipoff, "Peter Swartz on Defining the Maritime Strategy," Center for International Maritime Security, March 22, 2021, https://cimsec.org/peter-swartz-on-defining-the-maritime-strategy/; and John Lehman, "Getting Back on Top: How to Rebuild the Navy," *Proceedings* 148/1/1,427 (January 2022).
43. For the risk of "inadvertent escalation," see Barry Posen, *Inadvertent Escalation: Conventional War and Nuclear Risks* (Ithaca, NY: Cornell University Press, 1991); and Dmitry Filipof, "Barry Posen on Risking Escalation and Scrutinizing Plans," Center for International Maritime Security, March 25, 2021, https://cimsec.org/barry-posen-on-risking-escalation-and-scrutinizing-plans/. For excellent discussions of Soviet naval strategy, see N. Bradford Dismukes, *Hidden in Plain Sight: CNA and the Soviet Navy* (Arlington, VA: Center for Naval Analyses, 2018); and Dmitry Filipoff, "Dismukes on the Soviet Navy and Attacking Ballistic Missile Nuclear Submarines," Center for International Maritime Security, March 4, 2021, https://cimsec.org/brad-dismukes-on-the-soviet-navy-and-attacking-ballistic-missile-nuclear-submarines/.
44. John Lehman, "The 600-Ship Navy," *Proceedings*, January 1986, https://www.usni.org/magazines/proceedings/1986/january-supplement/600-ship-navy; Tim Ahern, "Lehman Says 600-Ship Navy Is Affordable," Associated Press, September 10, 1985.
45. The strategy went through several iterations. See John B. Hattendorf and Peter M. Swartz, eds., *U.S. Naval Strategy in the 1980s*, Newport Paper 33 (Newport, RI: Naval War College, 2008), https://digital-commons.usnwc.edu/cgi/viewcontent.cgi?article=1032&context=newport-papers.
46. For questions about affordability, see Congressional Budget Office, *Future Requirements for the 600-Ship Navy* (Washington, DC: CBO, 1985), https://www.cbo.gov/sites/default/files/99th-congress-1985-1986/reports/1985_09_futurebudget requirements.pdf.
47. Dave Oliver, *A Navy Admiral's Bronze Rules: Managing Risk and Leadership* (Annapolis, MD: Naval Institute Press, 2021), 86; Bernard Trainor, "Lehman's Sea-War Strategy Is Alive, but for How Long?," *New York Times*, March 23, 1987.
48. John Kroger, "The US Navy Has Drifted Badly off Course," *Defense One*, September 21, 2020), https://www.defenseone.com/ideas/2020/09/navy-has-drifted-badly-course/168632/.

49. See, e.g., Susan Douglas, "Technological Innovation and Organizational Change: The Navy's Adoption of Radio, 1899–1919," in *Military Enterprise and Technological Change*, ed. Merritt Roe Smith (Cambridge, MA: MIT Press, 1985), 117–73.
50. Thomas Ehrhard, *Air Force UAVs: The Secret History* (Arlington, VA: Mitchell Institute Press, 2010), 35ff.
51. Later the Air Force would increase the size of the Predator and add more armament. This new platform was designated the Reaper. "Predator RQ-1/MQ-1/MQ-9 Reaper," Air Force Technology, n.d., https://www.airforce-technology.com/projects/predator-uav/.
52. Perhaps the best history of LEO surveillance, the U-2, and the birth of the Global Hawk is Rick Thomas, *Global Hawk: The Story and Shadow of America's Controversial Drone* (self-pub., 2015). The equivalent work for the Predator/Reaper is Richard Whittle, *Predator: The Secret Origin of the Drone Revolution* (New York: Picador, 2014). Unfortunately, neither work examines the bureaucratic and emotional struggle between the innovators supporting these new technologies and the leadership of the relevant military services, which (unlike those at the lower ranks) was nearly always bitterly opposed to such changes.
53. "Global Hawk," Northrop Grumman, n.d., https://www.northropgrumman.com/what-we-do/air/globalhawk/.
54. Federal Acquisition Regulation: Part 15—Contracting by Negotiation, Acquisition.gov, https://www.acquisition.gov/far/part-15.
55. Robert Gates, *Duty: Memoirs of a Secretary at War* (New York: Knopf, 2014), 128.
56. Richard H. Van Atta and Michael J. Lippitz with Jasper C. Lupo, Rob Mahoney, and Jack H. Nunn, *Transformation and Transition: DARPA's Role in Fostering an Emerging Revolution in Military Affairs, Volume 1; Overall Assessment* (Arlington, VA: Institute for Defense Analyses, 2003).
57. All RPVs are UAVs, but not all UAVs are RPVs, such as those that operate autonomous of human control.
58. Interview with Larry Lynn, December 8, 2006, https://www.esd.whs.mil/Portals/54/Documents/FOID/Reading%20Room/DARPA/15-F-0751_DARPA_Director_Larry_Lynn.pdf.
59. John David Blom, *Unmanned Aerial Systems: A Historical Perspective* (Fort Leavenworth, KS: Combat Studies Institute Press, 2010), 81ff.
60. Chris Hellman, "Lessons of Kosovo: More B-2 Bombers?," *Weekly Defense Monitor* 3, no. 24 (June 24, 1999).
61. Richard Norton-Taylor, "How the Serb Army Escaped Nato," *The Guardian*, May 8, 2000, https://www.theguardian.com/world/2000/mar/09/balkans1.
62. Ultimately, airpower was more useful in creating political momentum within Belgrade to accept terms than degrading Serbia's military capabilities. Stephen Hosmer, *Why Milosevic Decided to Settle When He Did* (Washington, DC: RAND Corp., 2001, https://www.rand.org/content/dam/rand/pubs/monograph_reports/2001/MR1351.pdf.
63. Joseph Fitchett, "But Command Still Defends the Air War: NATO Lowers Its Tally of Tanks Hit in Kosovo," *New York Times*, September 17, 1999.
64. Bruce Nardulli, *Disjointed War: Military Operations in Kosovo, 1999* (Washington, DC: RAND Corp., 2002), https://www.rand.org/content/dam/rand/pubs/monograph_reports/2007/MR1406.pdf, 55.
65. Compare John Barry, "The Kosovo Cover-Up," *Newsweek*, May 14, 2000, https://www.newsweek.com/kosovo-cover-160273, with Stephen Aubin, "*Newsweek* and the 14

Tanks," *Air Force Magazine*, July 1, 2000, https://www.airforcemag.com/article/0700newsweek/.

66. Benjamin Lambeth, *Combat Pair: The Evolution of Air Force-Navy Integration in Strike Warfare* (Washington, DC: RAND Corp., 2007), esp. 5–12, 33ff.
67. Andrew Martin, "Revisiting the Lessons of Operation Allied Force," Air Power Australia Analyses, June 14, 2009, http://www.ausairpower.net/APA-2009-04.html.
68. Gates, *Duty*, 131.
69. Kresa had been the director of DARPA's Tactical Technology Office during the development of RPVs. HASC, *Hearings on Military Posture and H.R. 3689 (H.R. 6674)*, 94th Cong., 1st Sess. (Washington, DC: GPO, 1975), 3971. He was then the chairman of Northrop Grumman from 1990 to 2003 and of General Motors for a period after the financial crisis of 2008.
70. Hearing before the Military Procurement Subcommittee of the HASC, "Performance of the B-2 Bomber in the Kosovo Air Campaign," 106th Cong., 1st Sess., June 30, 1999, http://commdocs.house.gov/committees/security/has181200.000/has181200_0f.htm.
71. For reasons beyond the scope of this book, the consensus at that time was that future warplanes needed to be multirole—able to deliver weapons on the ground as well as shoot down other aircraft. In 2002 the F-22 was rebranded, on the fly, as the F/A-22 (the *A* is for "attack") with a decidedly modest weapons-delivery capability. See John Tirpak, "The F-22 Out Front," *Air Force Magazine*, August 1, 1998, https://www.airforcemag.com/article/0898raptor/; and "F-22A Raptor Advanced Tactical Fighter," Air Force Technology, n.d., https://www.airforce-technology.com/projects/f22a-raptor/.
72. Michael O'Hanlon, "The Plane Truth: Fewer F-22s Mean a Stronger National Defense," Brookings Institution, September 1, 1999, https://www.brookings.edu/research/the-plane-truth-fewer-f-22s-mean-a-stronger-national-defense/.
73. Oliver to Rumsfeld, "Global Hawk Approval to Energy Engineering and Manufacturing Development (EMD) and Initial Production," February 28, 2001, Rumsfeld Papers, https://papers.rumsfeld.com/.
74. Mark Cancian, "U.S. Military Forces in FY 2021: Air Force," Center for Strategic & International Studies, December 2020, https://csis-website-prod.s3.amazonaws.com/s3fs-public/publication/201203_Cancian_FY2021_AirForce.pdf; John Venable, "An Assessment of U.S. Military Power: U.S. Air Force," Heritage Foundation, November 17, 2020, https://www.heritage.org/2021-index-us-military-strength/assessment-us-military-power/us-air-force.
75. Valerie Insinna and David Larter, "House Lawmakers Put Limits on the Air Force's Planned Global Hawk Divestment," *Defense News*, June 22, 2020, https://www.defensenews.com/air/2020/06/22/house-lawmakers-pput-limi_-the-air-forces-planned-global-hawk-divestment/#.Xvl1oZEwpgo.email.
76. Sadly, the other services were equally reluctant to purchase RPVs. Mark Cancian, "The Five Surprises in Pentagon's 2022 Budget," Breaking Defense, June 10, 2021, https://breakingdefense.com/2021/06/the-five-surprises-in-pentagons-2022-budget/.
77. Ehrhard, *Secret History*, 57.
78. Gates, *Duty*, 128ff.

CONCLUSIONS AND RECOMMENDATIONS

Complaining about Pentagon waste and inefficiency is a favorite pastime of national-security professionals. There are, indeed, grounds for criticism. Nevertheless, throughout American history, it has been extraordinarily difficult, if not impossible, for outsiders to implement major changes to the defense enterprise. Political appointees, Congress, and private industry officials all have demonstrated shortcomings (several in common) that can hinder them from mandating change.

Perhaps the key shortcoming is that no outside organization or person brings sufficient stand-alone qualifications to push through alterations and ensure they take root. This gulf in knowledge and experience between civilian and military institutions has always been present, and it has widened since the advent of the all-volunteer force in 1973. Today few civilian reformers or political appointees have the necessary subject-matter expertise, appropriate career experiences, and deep understanding of the culture of the organizations they might wish to reshape.

In contrast, US military leaders—specifically the admirals and generals perched atop each service—have spent their entire professional lives steeped in their service's culture. They are experts in a wide variety of arcane military affairs and know how to locate within their organizations individuals who have the necessary expertise for particular tasks. Externally mandated change can seldom proceed without these officers' support, but the sledding will be tough and success dependent on unique circumstances. When there is a requirement to transform defense to adapt to changing circumstances or technological advances, even when admirals and generals are part of the problem, they nevertheless need to be part of the solution.

A strong military with a qualitative edge over its adversaries is essential to the United States. Military power is not the only instrument of national power and may not even be the most important.[1] Nevertheless, a strong military is still an indispensable tool for US leaders to promote peace and prosperity. Preserving this advantage has never been easy, especially when changing circumstances at home, abroad, and in the nature of warfare are washing over societies. Unfortunately, the professional soldier cannot overnight discard the habits of thought and action acquired over a lifetime of training or combat. Nor, absent exceptional circumstances, can (or should) the military, like any other complex bureaucracy, abruptly change course. This often frustrates outsiders, to whom the military's professional conservatism may appear to be obscurantism.[2]

Such complaints have merit. Just as other sectors of the United States must change and adapt, so, too, must the military. Military officers and analysts may realize something is happening but not know what to do in response.[3] When a conflict ends, public attention shifts funds away from the military, and the services either adapt or conform to a solution that reflects the fiscal reality.

One plausible argument against change warns that if an organization acts, any movement it takes implies that yet more change is possible. If it is acceptable to shift one brick, then why not another and yet another? Where and when do you stop? How do you measure success short of victory or defeat in a major war? That is why militaries so stubbornly defend their numbers of squadrons or ships or brigades. Every time a military or service chief accepts a specific change, they worry whether doing so weakens their ability to resist further cuts.

What critics frequently underestimate are the many practical problems and significant disruption that accompany major changes. Many problems exist just because the United States has a comparatively large military, national bureaucracy, and defense industry. Nothing is simple or straightforward in this world, including introducing revolutionary weapons into the force. There is a need to design, test, and manufacture the new equipment; to arrange for logistical and maintenance support; and, finally, to outfit every unit (and perhaps key allies). In addition, new equipment inevitably means development and training with different tactics—some that may not be immediately obvious—with possibly deadly consequences if important steps are overlooked or skipped. At the same time, new equipment brings the accompanying requirement that units be trained to think differently—to understand how the new concept or equipment affects tactics and operations with comrades and allies.[4]

Imposing *lasting* change on a complex, sprawling, and proud (some might say stubborn) institution such as the Department of Defense is a challenging process, and it is not a surprise that people seek shortcuts. Swift change, even in the face of determined opposition, is possible, as Secretary Robert McNamara proved in the OSD and Adm. Elmo Zumwalt did for the Navy. Both of those men's efforts also demonstrated the extraordinary dangers of shortcuts. Once they were gone, their foes rolled back many of their advances, often using only the flimsiest of excuses. Just as good ideas do not speak for themselves, they also cannot take root and flourish without an inclusive process to consider and implement them.

ONE PROCESS FOR RESHAPING THE DEPARTMENT OF DEFENSE

When it comes time to rebalance, reshape, or significantly change the Department of Defense, it is unwise and even dangerous to initiate such efforts with a set of preconceived answers. There are always a number of "experts" of any philosophical stripe willing, if not eager, to provide the president or secretary of defense with an opinion or a full program for reconstructing national defense. Reformers would be wise to avoid relying on any single silver bullet. Ideas do not stand or fall on their intellectual merit alone, and people must look beyond mere utility and consider both their feasibility and the challenges arising from long-term implementation. The best way to consider a problem and enduring solutions is through a process that empowers interested stakeholders and encourages them to make necessary sacrifices or compromises.

Our emphasis on process may seem perverse considering the scale of the challenges the United States faces. While it would be foolish not to recognize that at any time there will always be specific issues that are more "front and center" than others—today it is China for some, climate change for others—it is important that no proposal come before the president or the secretary of defense until after it has been subjected to the white-hot crucible of the process.

A good model is the process (described in chapter 4) that Adm. Frank Kelso used to reposition the Navy after the Cold War ended. That process built upon lessons that Navy officers had learned from previous efforts.[5] The first step was establishing the team that would oversee the process. There are three keys: the leadership, the individuals assigned to the team, and their focus. The leadership for such a task must have the appropriate prestige and authority to impose, if necessary, their will on recalcitrant institutions or individuals. That means appointing both political appointees and military leaders (admirals and generals). Both groups must be relatively senior and reflect the equities of all major stakeholders (most of all, the services), their goal being to achieve consensus and address real-world demands. Most important, while the participants should reflect a diversity of viewpoints, their primary obligation must be achieving solutions rather than representing parochial concerns.

The secretary of defense or president may find it necessary to override one or more objectors—for example, a service or a particularly well-connected senior leader—and their particular hobbyhorses (or "rice bowls" in Pentagon parlance), but they should not do so without first making an honest effort to consider all various alternatives. Because of the scale and complexity of the issues at hand, there will be months of briefings, research, debate, and exploration of alternatives. No one will leave the experience entirely happy. The answers to some key issues—changes in the method of delivery of firepower and consequently which platforms to maintain or scrap, for instance—will doubtless provoke criticism from discontented parties. We should not, however, fear such an outcome. The Kelso process suggests that if senior military and civilian officials have access to the same data and if they believe the exercise has been transparent and fair, a majority will accept sacrifices in the interest of building consensus.

To be successful, the group must have the right sort of dynamics. Policymakers must identify participants early and ensure they are committed to seeing the process through its conclusion. Individuals are not interchangeable. One three-star admiral who has commanded a fleet is not identical to another fleet commander even if their biographies appear identical to an outsider. The process requires the group possess a common knowledge base and set of assumptions on all of the relevant topics as well as an appreciation of each other and their personal expertise. Simply swapping one participant for another because it is more convenient ignores the essence of what is required for this sort of process to succeed.

Such group also has to be sufficiently broad so as to include professionals who possess expertise across the entire spectrum of missions that the Department of Defense performs beyond simply warfighting—logistics, personnel, medical, and so on—to ensure that less glamorous communities have adequate representation. There is no place here for the legions of hangers-on who proliferate merely to take notes. Rather, the group has to be sufficiently self-contained so that its members can build a sense of community.

Just as important as who is in the group is who is not. It is critical that leaders—whether from the White House, the OSD, Congress, or the services—not permit even one "larger-than-life" military personality, no matter how well-connected or articulate, to escape the scrutiny of their peers. There will always be officers like these, and because they are often legends within their community or service, they are difficult to ignore, but the success of the rebalancing process depends on it.

Senior officers will work for the common, interservice good only if the less enlightened or selfish among them are forced to participate as equals and not permitted to hold privileged positions. Every successful process prohibits "free riding."[6] If not, a perverse incentive system will take root. If each service or component is not subject to equal review and accountability, a service chief has no reason to participate in good faith—much less to forgo the traditional logrolling approach.

Free riders are a danger to any effort to reshape or rebalance national defense. In chapter 4, we noted an example from the 1990s after Congress had provided bipartisan approval of four rounds of base closures to permit the services to adjust to lower post–Cold War budgets. It was an extraordinary effort because Congress empowered senior military officers in each service to take appropriate action and leave the political fallout to the legislators. Congress put its faith in the integrity of the services, but unfortunately not all of the services rose to the challenge. While many superfluous bases were closed or consolidated, the Department of Defense's collective performance was suboptimal, as evidenced by the fact that one-fifth of the Pentagon's facilities infrastructure is redundant, even assuming a larger force.[7] In the case of the Air Force, that number is perhaps as high as one-third thanks to the efforts of just one misguided general.[8]

Some previous Defense Department–wide efforts have fallen short because the secretary did not appreciate that cynics, the selfish, and "golden boys" exist even at the very highest levels of the US military. This is not the same thing as assuming that the military leadership is composed of venal, self-serving individuals—an attitude that colored the recollections of men such as McNamara. That said, if even a few generals or admirals on the review panel confuse their service interest with the national interest, it will jeopardize the department-wide goals. Accordingly, civilian leaders ought to consider the following whenever they are crafting a future process:

- Military officers believe in their services. Each joined when they were young and grew up within their service. Many have risked their lives for the principles their service represents. They know, appreciate, and care about their peers. They have spent their professional lives sacrificing for their country, and they know what they have done has value, tangible or otherwise. The downside, unfortunately, is that because of the complexity of their jobs, even after tours in joint-duty assignments or attendance at war colleges, military officers often lack a comprehensive understanding of how their sibling services operate or how civilian departments support national security.
- Given their background, it is easy for service members to believe that defense dollars are best spent on their service and that during periods

of belt-tightening, if hard choices are necessary, their service should suffer less, relative to the others. These beliefs are often reinforced by the civilians who are assigned to political roles within the services, either as career civil servants or political appointees, some of whom may be retired service members or alternatively have been quickly "captured" by their service.[9]

- Interservice competition has more benefits than drawbacks. Unseemly as service infighting may appear to outsiders, competition over ideas and resources can spur innovation and progress. Competition also provides political appointees with insights they never would otherwise gain. Enforced unanimity, on the other hand, as Arleigh Burke and others have warned, is likely to result in wasteful logrolling that does not make the most efficient use of national resources.
- Extensive oversight by Congress and other agencies over Pentagon purchases is such that companies doing business with the military must undertake protective measures that provide little, if any, value in terms of cost savings and impose onerous "belt-and-suspenders" (i.e., excessively conservative) barriers to entry into the defense market for domestic and foreign commercial firms that can provide superior products. This essentially divides the American economy into a vibrant, innovative, and competitive $20 trillion commercial economy and an oligopolistic $700 billion defense industry that is primarily responsible for providing the material requirements of national defense.[10] As a result, because the defense industry is more and more isolated from civilian industry and because the government acquisition process is so ploddingly slow, the Department of Defense often is unaware or unable to capitalize on the advances occurring in the private sector. This perennial problem always deserves study.
- The services seldom adequately account for the life-cycle costs of programs.[11] One reason why is the services' excessive optimism about their ability to control long-term development and production costs, but they also do not include the full costs of military personnel.[12] Military personnel costs not included in the defense budget—mainly pensions and health care for veterans—are equivalent to over 40 percent of recent defense budgets.[13] This issue also deserves continuous scrutiny.
- The services do not routinely review the marginal utility or opportunity costs of the missions they already perform. They do not, except under duress, consider canceling current or old capabilities when adding new ones. There are examples in every service. It is as if a

homeowner hoarded every possession in the attic rather than putting useless items on the curb for Goodwill.
- Finally, "black" programs do not get nearly the same routine scrutiny as ordinary defense expenditures. These are projects where the details and funding levels are highly classified and blacked out of all publicly released documents. Access to the classified documents is restricted to those holding an SCI (sensitive compartmented information) clearance and being "read into" the relevant program.[14]

After the formation of any group charged with reshaping the Pentagon, the first part of any successful process is one that establishes a common base of knowledge and operating assumptions. In the case of a wholescale rebalancing of Pentagon priorities and budget allocation, the group must achieve consensus on two issues at the outset: one is the future trajectory of the US economy and government spending; the other is the international-threat environment.

To obtain adequate data to make informed assumptions about these factors, the group should commission multiple studies of the same subject from the think tanks allied with each of the services (e.g., the Center for Naval Analyses for the Navy, RAND for the Air Force, and the Institute for Defense Analyses for the Army) to give each service confidence in the data if not necessarily the interpretation. For those who would question such a duplicative effort, it is worth bearing in mind that penny-pinching in analysis rarely leads to cost-effective outcomes.

No process to change something as complex as the Pentagon and its priorities is ever simple. Any analysis should begin by considering whether there are new or unusual circumstances since the last major review that should reframe the participants' thinking. It is also important to note that the review should neither begin nor end with major defense acquisition programs (MDAPs).[15] While MDAPs are the focus of much attention inside the Beltway, the review should instead start with ideas and principles, not specific programs.

Since the last major defense realignment at the end of the Cold War, many new technologies, firms, and industries outside of the defense industrial base have arisen, while others have fallen. Defense leaders must ask how these developments affect their world. They must also consider what factors are contributing to the chasm between public- and private-sector performance in areas of mutual interest, from acquisitions, to information technology, to logistics, and beyond.

Defense leaders should also reexamine the regulatory and political burdens that have emerged and grown between the Pentagon and private industry. Improvements here will significantly enhance warfighting capacity while simultaneously yielding major cost savings that can be invested elsewhere, but they will be politically fraught—hence the need for active military support to ease any qualms about reducing oversight, particularly among legislators. Finally, because military leaders are often reluctant to embrace technological change, there needs to be time to review the pace and direction of contemporary technological development so that leaders can make informed decisions about what matters and what does not.

There are a number of past models for the process.

One possibility is the "Night Court" established by Mark Esper when he was secretary of the Army. This process redirected roughly $33 billion within the Army to meet the objectives identified in the 2018 National Defense Strategy.[16] Unfortunately, Esper never had the opportunity to implement his program when he became defense secretary, so it is unclear how well it would have worked in a larger context.

Another alternative is Gates's review of the Pentagon's FY 2010 budget submission. This effort yielded major changes and savings (roughly $330 billion in lifetime costs), but it did not address the preliminary framing issues we listed. Rather, it began by focusing on specific MDAPs rather than the larger trends and had least one other shortcoming. Gates not only led the process, which included a handful of top political appointees plus the JCS chairman and his deputy; he also directed it by identifying all major changes and cuts beforehand and then presented them to the service chiefs for debate.[17]

Vital to any effective defense-wide review is a process in which each player focuses on what they specifically bring to the table. The secretary of defense and other political appointees have gravitas to lead the process and enforce its decisions. They can also interject new perspectives and should be better attuned to the wider political context domestically and internationally. Senior military and civilian personnel in the Defense Department also bring irreplaceable knowledge to the table. Although it is tempting and certainly much easier when the secretary makes decisions after consulting with trusted staff members and presents them to the service chiefs, that approach fails to incorporate the expertise the military and civil service counterparts can bring, no matter how much time is permitted for subsequent debate. Military expertise can play a constructive role only if senior military leaders actively participate from the outset in the review.

During a comprehensive review, all programs, including those that are highly classified, require review so that the participants are comfortable that no one is hiding anything from legitimate scrutiny. Since all of these subjects will require careful study, discussion, and numerous side meetings to resolve factual, analytic, and even emotional disputes, it would be wise to avoid overloading the participants, who are also performing their "day jobs." Experience suggests that more than two or three briefings a week would be excessive since further discussions will almost certainly become necessary to address follow-up questions or resolve major disputes that threaten to derail the entire process.

The aforementioned process will probably last a minimum of nine months and as much as two years. To achieve full value, it should start well in advance of the budget cycle in which relevant programs must be established, modified, or canceled (the Pentagon begins each budget process two years before it will take effect), leaving the appropriate time for consultation with Congress and other relevant stakeholders.

Reformers often believe that many senior officers would much rather close their eyes than confront the necessity for change. While these officers are imperfect, they have devoted their lives to serving the nation, have considerable irreplaceable expertise, and deserve to be convinced rather than directed. Most senior officers will cooperate and even become allies if treated with respect. Hopefully, only a few of the old guard will be irreconcilable.[18] There is simply no viable alternative to cooperation among civilians and military leaders or among the services. Unilateral actions may satisfy the public's desire for "dynamic" leadership to cut through red tape or "put the military in their place," but history has shown such a strategy to be counterproductive. Considering the stakes, we ignore these hard-won insights at our peril.

NOTES

1. Michael Dennis and Anand Toprani, "An Alternative/Alternate History of the U.S. Response to COVID-19," Strategy Bridge, June 23, 2020, https://thestrategybridge.org/the-bridge/2020/6/23/an-alternativealternate-history-of-the-us-response-to-covid-19; George Packer, "We Are Living in a Failed State," *The Atlantic*, June 2020, https://www.theatlantic.com/magazine/archive/2020/06/underlying-conditions/610261/.
2. David Sanger, "Pentagon Is Clinging to Aging Technologies, House Panel Warns," *New York Times*, September 29, 2020.
3. William Fuller, "What Is a Military Lesson?," in *Strategic Logic and Political Rationality: Essays in Honor of Michael I. Handel*, ed. Bradford Lee and Karl Walling (London: Frank Cass, 2003), 38–59.
4. Jamie Morin and Bill LaPlante, "What We Don't Know about Military Innovation," *Defense One*, October 20, 2020, https://www.defenseone.com/ideas/2020/10/what-we-dont-know-about-military-innovation/169398/.
5. There is a summary of what follows in Dave Oliver and Anand Toprani, "The 2018 Strategy Is Unworkable. We Need a Fundamental Defense Rethink," *Defense One*, May 13,

2021, https://www.defenseone.com/ideas/2021/05/2018-strategy-unworkable-we-need-fundamental-defense-rethink/173954/.

6. The free-riding problem—that it is "rational" for individuals to defect from a group when their individual gains outweigh their negligible contributions—was developed by laissez-faire opponents of state economic planning during and after the 1930s. Most defenses of interservice rivalry stress the benefits arising from competition but do not grapple with the consequences of individual defections thwarting collective action. For the origins of free riding, see Richard Tuck, *Free Riding* (Cambridge, MA: Harvard University Press, 2008), esp. 205–15.
7. Jared Serbu, "DoD Says It Has 19 Percent More Facilities than It Needs, Even Assuming a Larger Military," Federal News Network, October 18, 2017, https://federalnewsnetwork.com/defense/2017/10/dod-says-it-has-19-percent-more-facilities-than-it-needs-even-assuming-a-larger-military/.
8. Adam Hebert, "Too Many Bases, Not Enough Air Force," *Air Force Magazine,* May 24, 2016, https://www.airforcemag.com/article/too-many-bases-not-enough-air-force/.
9. This is the military variant of the wider problem of "*regulatory capture* . . . the result or process by which regulation, in law or application, is consistently directed away from the public interest towards the interests of the regulated industry, by the intent and action of the industry, itself." Daniel Carpenter and David Moss, eds., *Preventing Regulatory Capture: Special Interest and How to Limit It* (Cambridge: Cambridge University Press, 2014), 13 (emphasis in the original).
10. See chapter 7.
11. Mark V. Arena, Robert S. Leonard, Sheila E. Murray, and Obaid Younossi, *Historical Cost Growth of Completed Weapon Programs* (Santa Monica, CA: RAND Corp., 2006); Joseph G. Bolten, Robert S. Leonard, Mark V. Arena, Obaid Younossi, and Jerry M. Sollinger, *Sources of Weapon System Cost Growth: Analysis of 35 Major Defense Acquisition Programs* (Santa Monica, CA: RAND Corp., 2008); Mark Cancian, "Cost Growth: Perception and Reality," *Defense Acquisition Review Journal* 17, no. 3 (2010): 389–403; William O'Neil, "Cost Growth in Major Defense Acquisition: Is There a Problem? Is There a Solution," *Defense Acquisition Review Journal* 18, no. 3 (2011): 277–94; "DOD Weapon System Acquisition," Government Accountability Office, n.d., https://www.gao.gov/highrisk/dod_weapon_systems/why_did_study.
12. "Requiring the Use of Fully Burdened and Life Cycle Personnel Costs for All Components in Total Force Analysis and for Budgetary Purposes: Update Report to the Secretary of Defense," Reserve Forces Policy Board, September 10, 2019, https://rfpb.defense.gov/Portals/67/Final%202019%20Fully%20Burdened%20Life%20Cycle%20Cost%20Methodology%20Report%20Update%2010%20SEP%202019_1.pdf.
13. Lawrence Korb, "The Pentagon's Fiscal Year 2021 Budget More than Meets U.S. National Security Needs," Center for American Progress, May 6, 2020, https://www.americanprogress.org/issues/security/reports/2020/05/06/484620/pentagons-fiscal-year-2021-budget-meets-u-s-national-security-needs/.
14. Black programs can be quite large. They were once reserved for intelligence programs that were considered so sensitive that even the knowledge that the program existed could harm the national interest. The first such program was Project Corona—the construction and deployment of the first generation of imaging satellites that spied on the Soviet Union starting in the 1960s. Jeffrey Richelson, ed., *Secrecy and U.S. Satellite Reconnaissance, 1958–1976,* NSA, Electronic Briefing Book 225, July 13, 2007, https://nsarchive2

.gwu.edu/NSAEBB/NSAEBB225/index.htm. Today, there are many programs that fit into the black category. Some programs have migrated "into the black" to avoid the normal review process. This lack of expert review can lead to billion-dollar disasters, such as when the Future Imagery Architecture program was awarded to Boeing instead of the more experienced Lockheed. Philip Taubman, "In Death of Spy Satellite, Lofty Plans and Realistic Bids," *New York Times*, November 11, 2007.

15. MDAPs are the highest level of the Pentagon's three acquisition categories. There are approximately ninety MDAPs at the moment, with a total cost of $70 billion and an average age of fourteen years. "Acquisition Process: Acquisition Category (ACAT)," AcqNotes, n.d., https://acqnotes.com/acqnote/acquisitions/acquisition-category; Office of the Under Secretary of Defense (Comptroller), *Program Acquisition Cost by Weapon System* (Washington, DC: Department of Defense, 2021), https://comptroller.defense.gov/Portals/45/Documents/defbudget/FY2022/FY2022_Weapons.pdf; Eric Lofgren, "Major Defense Programs Are Getting Older and More Expensive," Acquisition Talk, July 21, 2021, https://acquisitiontalk.com/2020/07/major-defense-programs-are-getting-older-and-more-expensive/.
16. Joe Gould, "Esper's Pledge to Trim Pointless Programs Will Test His Political Clout," *Defense News*, August 30, 2019, https://www.defensenews.com/2019/08/30/espers-pledge-to-trim-pointless-programs-will-test-his-political-clout/; Paul McLeary, "Esper Starts Setting Up DoD-Wide 'Night Court,'" Breaking Defense, September 9, 2019, https://breakingdefense.com/2019/09/esper-starts-setting-up-dod-wide-night-court/.
17. Gates, *Duty*, 311ff.
18. There are ways to deal with them. In 1940 Army chief of staff Gen. George Marshall established a committee that forced five hundred superannuated colonels into retirement. Dwight Jon Zimmerman, "Gen. George C. Marshall Eliminates the 'Dead Wood,'" Defense Media Network, September 1, 2015, https://www.defensemedianetwork.com/stories/gen-george-c-marshall-eliminates-dead-wood/. Forty years later, another chief of staff, Gen. Edward "Shy" Meyer, removed twenty generals to end the rot afflicting the post-Vietnam Army. Matt Schudel, "Edward C. Meyer, General Who Revamped Post-Vietnam 'Hollow Army,' Dies at 91," *Washington Post*, October 13, 2020, https://www.washingtonpost.com/local/obituaries/edward-c-meyer-general-who-revamped-post-vietnam-hollow-army-dies-at-91/2020/10/13/141fbc48-0436-11eb-a2db-417cddf4816a_story.html. Zumwalt was more subtle—he squeezed five flag officer annual selection boards into his four years as CNO. He was thereby able to push out of the Navy another twenty-five admirals with racial attitudes he considered unacceptable.

APPENDIX A

Discussion with Adm. Arleigh Burke, USN (Ret.), Chief of Naval Operations, 1955–61

This interview was conducted on May 3, 1974, in Washington, DC, by Lt. Cmdr. Dave Oliver. Admiral Burke approved the final draft, which has been lightly edited for clarity.

OLIVER: An author named Roherty has written about the issue of nuclear power for the CVA-67 and has noted that the problem was that "the Navy did not enter into the fray with its customary assuredness."[1] Is that what you perceived as happening?

BURKE: No. What do you need a carrier for? To provide mobile air power for concentration [of firepower] at a specific point. What do you need to obtain that? You need the aircraft. You need living quarters for the men. You need defensive units to protect you against submarines, and you need some kind of propulsion plant. You don't need nuclear power. You do need all of the rest. Nuclear power is nice, but it costs money. When the question of nuclear power came up again, following the *Enterprise,* I went over to Congress and interviewed a great number of congressmen.[2] I couldn't get sufficient support for the nuclear carrier to enable it to pass, but I thought I could get sufficient support for a conventional one. So, I took what I could get, and I think that it was the proper thing to do.

What so many people don't realize is that the country has a limited amount of money.[3] The amount you spend [on one capability] is absolutely critical. McNamara was wrong on a lot of things, but not on that one. Nuclear power cost a lot of money, which then wasn't available for other things. There are even occasions in which you do not need carriers. There are times in which a conventional submarine will do as good a job as a nuclear one. They are quieter, for instance. But if you have to have just one kind, nuclear submarines are better. The best thing is to have a mix, but Congress would not let me buy any conventional submarines. I would have, but they wouldn't let me.

The basic problem that a CNO has is how to get the maximum combat capability. Some capabilities are necessary, some are good, and some are just nice to have. The question the CNO is always asking himself is, Can I take less and will it serve to accomplish the tasks?

The advances since then in nuclear power have, of course, changed the situation. I, of course, am talking about the increase in core life.[4] At the time, you must remember that in full combat, the ammunition runs out about the same time as the fuel. Not all the time, but sometimes. Since you have to resupply with ammo, you might as well resupply with fuel.

OLIVER: How did you react to Representative [Clarence] Cannon's anticarrier speech in Congress? Was that sentiment widespread?

BURKE: There was some anticarrier sentiment. It was our own fault. We oversold carriers like the Air Force oversold bombers. Carriers can't go everywhere, and they don't last forever. We had zealots that maintained they could, and all this did was irritate the Air Force advocates and others who knew that the carrier wasn't the complete answer every time.

OLIVER: How did you feel McNamara and his immediate staff were oriented on the question of land-based versus sea-based tactical air power when they came into office?

BURKE: They weren't oriented toward anything. They were interested in getting control of the military. They were young. They didn't know their ass from a tin cup about the military, strategy, or world problems. After a while, they learned some of the arguments that were being used [in the Pentagon], and they used the same arguments to try to get control. They wanted simple, single answers. They wanted an answer that couldn't be disproved, so they emphasized the need for a nuclear capability. That would solve everything and was the answer.

Systems analysis was the tool they used to get control. There was such a thing as cost effectiveness long before McNamara. There always had been analysis and particularly so before the McNamara era. The problem with analysis at this time was that he had the power of the computer behind him. He could do a great number of analyses very fast, each time varying the inputs. He could provide rapid comparisons. The problem, of course, was that each time he got garbage out because he put garbage in. The reason it was garbage is because what is needed for defense of the country is only an estimate. It is only a feel that you acquire. You can't analyze or quantify it—it's a feel.

When McNamara came in with his computers, I took a course at IBM so that I could talk with him.[5] I thus was prepared to discuss what was going on. The problem is that the use of analysis is often done cynically. It is done in order to prove something which you have already decided on. It doesn't take anyone too smart to determine that that's not the right way to do something. Look at the DLGN [nuclear-powered guided-missile frigate], which has twin antiair missile launchers and no surface-to-surface [i.e., antiship] missile capability.[6] A high-school boy should be able to see that that's stupid. Look at the ships where we are having mutinies. It doesn't take anyone too smart to, say, look at the other ships. If they are in the same shape, they certainly aren't in any shape to fight. It doesn't take analysis to tell you that.

The Air Force was pushing airpower at McNamara. They either did not have the wisdom nor the integrity, one or the other, to realize that was not the whole answer, that it was wrong. They built up a stock of civilian experts. That was what RAND was, and then several years later we decided to match them [with CNA], and that was a mistake. Now we don't have a code of ethics. We are no longer professional. We are at the mercy of people who do not have responsibility. We are dependent upon tons of paper and analysis, which we can't do, and which produces answers which our decision-makers don't understand. The people who make the decisions do not have the experience in order to make accurate decisions. If the Navy is worth a damn, we should be able to determine our own requirements.

We have lost BUSHIPS, we have lost our intelligence, etc. An example is the surface-to-surface missiles. It was evident ten to fifteen years ago to a high-school boy that we needed surface-to-surface missiles. I started the development of the missile that we're working on today [Harpoon], and it's still four to five years from deployment.[7] Something is wrong with our system. The Soviets have deployed a dozen different kinds. We should have too. Hell, our first one should be obsolete by now. Instead, we don't even have one, and I find out that it is so complicated that it's programmed to operate differently depending upon which ocean it's in. What happens if the ship changes oceans?

The major problem with the system is that we overstudy and overanalyze. I'm against making studies that you don't intend to accept. I have assigned some studies out when I already knew the answers, in order to get some civilians to understand the Navy's problems, but I never encouraged dishonest reports—that is, reports which I intended to discard if they didn't come up with the answers I wanted. You can't have yes-men. You probably won't get in trouble in the first generation, but in the second generation of yes-men you have a group that can't make decisions.

You can't fire people who don't come up with the answers you want. You have to be able to fight honestly. You can't cheat at analysis, even when you know the other side is cheating, and retain your integrity. You may be able to, but others will be misled. I am often amazed at the integrity of civilians. We would like to have Bill Martin on this board I am on.[8] After he retired from the Fed, he said he would have to wait a year, and then after a year he said that he would have to wait a while longer because he had a conflict of interest. And no one suggested that he come anyway because everyone knew that even if he didn't have a conflict, if he thought he did, he did.

I selected my VCNOs [vice chiefs of naval operations] because they were tough. I had a fight with [Jim] Russell every morning of the week. I got a lot of unpleasant advice from him, [at] times when he felt I was wrong. I overrode him lots of times, and also there were lots of times when I didn't do things because he opposed them. I knew we were both dedicated to the same ideal—the security of the country—so I knew there was good reason behind his opposition. You need opposition within an organization. The most damaging thing a subordinate can do is not to tell his boss when he is wrong. The reason for [selecting] a vice chief is because he is loyal to a cause but not the methods.

The hardest thing I have to do is tell my wife when she's wrong. She has ruined many a car engine because she doesn't know how to start it—she always floods it. I should have told her long ago, but it wasn't worth it to me. Now I can't, because she doesn't believe me, but she's still ruining car engines. The problem today is that we don't know the difference between right and wrong with respect to the way of doing things.

You know, McNamara was a quick learner. You had to react immediately. If you didn't nip him in the bud, he was long gone, down whatever lost trail he was chasing. I got to my office about seven. McNamara learned that I did, and he began doing so. I used to go down and see him two or three times a week in order to touch base. I really thought he was quite a fellow at first. Sometimes he would [come] up to my office, and we'd talk.

One day I asked him if I could see an analysis which I was sure he had. He said, "Sure, you can see any analysis I have." I said, "Could I see the analysis that you did on your wife before you married her?" Well, he was furious and turned away and walked off without saying a word. I found out later that when he first went to Michigan [to join Ford], he had been going with a girl, but she got polio and he dumped her because he didn't think she could help him. He really has a swell wife now. I really hit a sore point.[9]

NOTES

1. Ronald Roherty, *Decisions of Robert S. McNamara: A Study in the Role of the Secretary of Defense* (New York: Harper, 1971), 141–42.
2. USS *Enterprise* (CVN-65) was the first nuclear-powered aircraft carrier. The only ship of its class, it was commissioned in 1961 and deactivated in 2017.
3. This was technically true during the Bretton Woods era, when the value of the US dollar was pegged at $35 an ounce. That meant the Federal Reserve could not increase the amount of money in circulation beyond the point where it could defend the gold peg. There was also legislation requiring that the country's gold stock equal at 25 percent of the outstanding paper currency. President Johnson eliminated the gold cover in 1968, and President Nixon ended the government's pledge to other nations' central banks to convert dollars for gold at $35 an ounce in 1971. Joseph Ramage, "The Gold Cover," July 1968, https://fraser.stlouisfed.org/files/docs/publications/frbrichreview/pages/65585_1965-1969.pdf. Burke was probably speaking about political constraints on the size of the defense budget rather than literal limits on the supply of money.
4. The reactors the Navy used had a relatively short life. By the time of this interview, reactors were lasting fifteen years. Soon the newer ones would last thirty before needing to be replaced, which drove down life-cycle costs considerably.
5. Burke's VCNO disagreed about his reasons. See appendix B.
6. "U.S. General Accounting Office Staff Study: DLGN-38 Nuclear Guided Missile Frigate," Department of the Navy, February 1973, https://www.gao.gov/assets/80/78786.pdf.
7. The A/U/RGM-84 Harpoon is an antiship missile originally designed by McDonnell Douglas (which merged with Boeing in 1997) that can be fired from fixed-wing aircraft, submarines, coastal batteries, and surface ships. It entered service in 1977 and remains in use. "Harpoon Missile," US Navy, March 10, 2017, https://www.navy.mil/Resources/Fact-Files/Display-FactFiles/Article/2168358/harpoon-missile/.
8. William McChesney Martin, chairman of the Federal Reserve from 1951 to 1970. Martin was a strong believer in protecting the independence of the Federal Reserve from external interference, and he clashed often with presidents over interest-rate hikes to dampen inflation and promote price stability at the risk of an economic downturn. "The Views of William McChesney Martin," *New York Times*, January 25, 1978; Robert Bremner, *Chairman of the Fed: William McChesney Martin Jr. and the Creation of the American Financial System* (New Haven, CT: Yale University Press, 2004); John Wood, "William McChesney Martin, Jr.: A Reevaluation," *Region Focus*, Winter 2006, 2–7.
9. Burke was mistaken. McNamara and his wife, Margaret Craig, contracted polio after World War II. To pay her medical bills, McNamara decided not to return to Harvard

Business School and sought a position at Ford, even though he confessed that "the happiest time of his life, before he came into government, was when he was teaching at Harvard." Adam Yarmolinsky oral history no. 1, JFKL. See also Michael Beschloss, "Man of Opposites," *Chicago Tribune*, March 14, 1993, https://www.chicagotribune.com/news/ct-xpm-1993-03-14-9303191931-story.html.

APPENDIX B

Discussion with Adm. James Russell, USN (Ret.), Vice Chief of Naval Operations, 1958–61

The interview was conducted on April 30, 1974, in Washington, DC, and on May 2, 1974, at Dulles International Airport by Lt. Cmdr. Dave Oliver. Admiral Russell approved the final draft. This transcript has been lightly edited for clarity.

OLIVER: In discussing the decisions Mr. McNamara made [regarding CVA-67], James Roherty said that "the Navy did not enter into the fray with its customary assuredness.... There was noticeable ambivalence in the Navy attitude toward nuclear propulsion.... The Navy had allowed a doctrinal gap to develop with respect to the utilization of attack carriers."[1]

From a reading of some of the primary-source material, it appeared to me that it may have been more complicated than that. What were your perceptions?

RUSSELL: You have to understand the circumstances. The Navy did not have too good a position with the Secretariat before McNamara. We had a great deal of trouble with Secretary Gates [Thomas S. Gates Jr.]. Two examples are pertinent. Gates was interested in playing down interservice rivalry, and when Admiral [Ruthven] Libby made a speech in San Diego which was purely inflammatory, Gates demanded that Burke fire Libby—that he require Libby to resign immediately.[2] Burke refused and told Gates he was willing to go to the president over it.

The second example occurred over the Single Integrated Operational Plan [SIOP, the targeting plan for the nation's nuclear weapons—B-52s, Minutemen, and Polaris].[3] Burke felt that the whole idea was nothing more than an effort to give the whole strategic package to the Air Force.[4] He went to the president [Dwight Eisenhower] over it, but the president upheld his secretary, so we lost. But Burke insisted that the second-in-command at the JSTPS [Joint Strategic Target Planning Staff] in Omaha [which constructed the SIOP] be a Navy three-star. Furthermore, since the SIOP was computerized, Burke went out and took a course in computers.[5]

Gates was pretty mad at us, and he told McNamara he had to watch those admirals and generals, or they'd run over him.[6] For a man of McNamara's personality, that was all he needed.

We also did not make a good start with the new secretary of the Navy—Secretary [John] Connally. As soon as he was named, Burke invited him to stay at the [Naval] Observatory House [then the CNO's quarters]. The problem is that Burke is not a good host. Connally came up without his wife and was rattling around that house, and Burke forgot about him. Burke gets so involved, he just forgets.[7]

Anyway, I arranged a bachelor party for Secretary Connally and went looking for some good remarks to introduce him with. I found out that very much to his credit, he had been a fighter director aboard a carrier during World War II, and when the action got hot and his congressional friends wanted to bring him back, he refused to go back.[8] I also found out he didn't drink. When I had the party and introduced him, he took my relating of these facts wrong, and when he stood up, he only said, "You have [an] excellent G-2," and sat down. Burke and Russell were in trouble from then on.[9]

To understand the rest of our problems, you have to understand what sort of person McNamara was. He was cold, impersonal, and inconsiderate. For a couple of examples of how he disregarded people, he went mountain climbing in the [Pacific] Northwest and didn't even bother to tell anyone he was coming or that he was there.[10] Later [in 1963], I invited him to stay at my villa in Italy when he was in the area, and he didn't even bother to answer.[11] His secretary came over, and we had a really nice time. McNamara didn't care about anybody!

OLIVER: Was Admiral Burke an effective "politician" for the Navy, or was he somewhat restrained by the events of 1949 after the CNO [Louis Denfeld] had been fired, over the objections of Congress, and Captain Burke had been removed for some time from the promotion list to flag [officer]?

RUSSELL: Burke was a poor speaker. This [actually] helped him on the Hill because of his reputation [as a war hero]. When he searched for a word, everyone was leaning forward trying to help him. He wasn't a particularly good politician. He didn't like to use politics or systems analysis to try to muddy up the waters. He wasn't like Zumwalt—he was reluctant to get in there and lobby and to be "cute" about analysis tricks or congressional ties.

He was not at all inhibited by the events of 1949. I served with him in the Pacific during the war [World War II]. He didn't change. No one thought he was inhibited.

OLIVER: Did you perceive that Secretary McNamara and his immediate staff were particularly pro or con the Air Force or the Navy?

RUSSELL: There is no question about the fact that they favored the Air Force. They understood more about the Air Force. At least they understood about land-based tactical air forces. They didn't understand about how you got the logistics, the petroleum, there. They had this idea about bare base deployment which was half-baked.[12] We had terrible problems trying to educate them. A man named [Herb] Rosenzweig was the man who was in charge of analysis of this, and he didn't understand the use of carriers.[13] We never did succeed in educating him. In fact, he got worse before he left. There was a point in which he was being questioned in Congress, and they got down on him, felt he was misrepresenting various problems, and he really lost emotional control. He was really impossible toward the end.

OLIVER: Do you remember how Admiral Anderson got fired?

RUSSELL: The whole problem was over some testimony before a committee on the Hill. All the members of the secretary of defense's staff were sitting around with sharpened pencils waiting for a copy of his statement, and he told them he didn't have one—he was just going up there to tell the truth [regarding TFX]. Then McNamara sent [Fred] Korth out to the [Naval] Observatory on a Sunday morning to tell Anderson that he was fired. On a Sunday morning, when Anderson was getting ready for an afternoon party for various members of different staffs, Korth came out to tell him he was fired.

Anderson immediately called Kennedy, who didn't know anything about it. Anderson was really deeply hurt. He went in to see McNamara about it the next morning, and McNamara came across his room with his hand out, and Anderson put his hand behind him and said, "No, Mr. Secretary, you have deeply hurt me. I always have believed that a man should be able and required to tell the truth."

Anyway, there was quite some talk about the firing, and McNamara told Kennedy that if the president appointed Anderson to anything in the continental United States, he, McNamara, would resign. So, Kennedy offered Anderson the ambassadorship to Portugal. Anderson asked for forty-eight hours to think it over. Burke advised him not to take it—that it was time to make a stand and not to take anything from them [the Kennedy administration]. But Adm. Claude Ricketts was the VCNO, and he advised Anderson to take it [the job offer] because he could do the country some good as an ambassador. Anderson took Ricketts's advice, and Burke was furious.

I always felt that Korth was instrumental in seeing that the TFX got awarded to [General Dynamics in] Texas. I always felt there was something crooked there. I never did figure out how he got appointed to a position of public trust. He wasn't an honest man. I think Connally just recommended him because he was from Texas. Not even his wife could stand him—she divorced him because he was so obnoxious.

There was no other reason to make that [TFX] decision. I went into McNamara's office with Curtis LeMay, and I told McNamara that a second-rate fighter aircraft was no fighter at all. You can have a second-rate bomber, but what escorts that bomber? McNamara said, "But, Jim, we'll save a billion dollars."

The supersonic capability at low altitudes that the Air Force needed was being compromised in order to reduce the weight to that which could be handled by the carrier catapult gear. As it was, the most optimum catapult that was installed on any carrier would have been the only one capable of launching the aircraft. McNamara didn't understand how difficult it was to achieve a capability to handle the aircraft. He didn't understand what he was doing to the Air Force plane in order to make it meet Navy requirements. I said, "Thank you, Mr. Secretary," and Curtis and I got up to leave. Then Curtis blurted out, "But, Mr. Secretary, if we have to use the same plane, it really should be built to Air Force specifications." That was typical LeMay.

McNamara didn't fire LeMay when he fired Anderson. LeMay had gained too much national support from his performance as head of SAC. He also had an aura about him that made the secretary afraid of him. He had done a good job for them [the Air Force] there, although no one ever thought he was an intellectual heavyweight as chief of staff. Anyway, McNamara called LeMay in his office and talked to him and led him along, telling him how unhappy he was with the job that LeMay was doing, and then at the end he said, "And so, I've decided to ask you to stay on as chief of staff." LeMay went over to the window that looks over the River Entrance [to the Pentagon] and looked out while he composed himself. He was really upset, and then he said, "Thank you, Mr. Secretary, for your confidence," and walked out. He was furious.

McNamara couldn't even use his own staff. You remember "McNamara's Fence" [in Vietnam].[14] He couldn't get his own staff to do it, so he came to me and asked me to evaluate it with General Starbird.[15] The fence was designed to combat infiltration, but the Marines thought it had Maginot Line mentality.[16] You tell the enemy where you are going to stand and fight him. They cleared some areas for the implantation of his devices, but those areas also could serve awfully well as machine-gun sweep/control areas. McNamara came directly to me to ensure that the program was carried out because he couldn't even rely on his own staff.

OLIVER: Did you feel that Admiral Rickover was cooperating with the rest of the Navy on the question of nuclear power for carriers and surface ships? *(Note by Oliver: Although I posed this question at least four times, Russell dodged it. He instead provided insights into his own personal and professional relationship with Rickover.)*

RUSSELL: I remember the first time we met. We had an electrical system [on carriers] in those days that was twelve volts DC, and it was cranky. The first time a new pilot got out on the deck with the wind going over, he'd overprime the engine and run down the battery. Then we'd have to get him off the line and out of the way someway. Well, I figured out that if we ran jumper cables out to the planes, we could get him off no matter how much he overprimed the engine. I figured that if I placed four small motor-generators around the deck, I could make it work.

I talked to the air wing commander and the captain, got in a plane, and went to try to get permission to do so. I went down to the main Navy yard [in Washington] and wandered around trying to find out who was in charge. Finally, I found the officer that was in charge of the Electrical Division, a Lieutenant Rickover. I explained what I wanted to do, and he immediately flew into a rage. He said, "Do you know how much copper that would take? There's not that much copper in the United States," etc. Anyway, he chased me out, and I had to return to the ship from my unsuccessful trip with my tail between my legs.

He was thorough, though. Nothing ever got put on any ship that he personally had not approved.

The second time we met, I was commanding officer of a carrier [USS *Bairoko*] out in the Pacific following World War II, and things were pretty slack—we were making up for the war. I remember setting the course so we would raise Wake Island at dawn, and I got on the MC [microphone] system myself and said, "Now everyone wake up and see the island."

Anyway, in 1947, I got orders to report to Oak Ridge, and would end up being there from 1947 to 1950.[17] When I got there, it was still under Army command. Captain Rickover was there, and I found out that he was the most popular man there. I couldn't believe that this was the same Rickover that I knew. I asked around and found out that he stood number one in his training class and had impressed everyone. He was obsessed with the idea of putting nuclear power on a submarine, and all the scientists there were really impressed with him and were in favor of his efforts.

I remember when *Nautilus* went under the [North] Pole, and we were trying to outdo the Russians' *Sputnik* achievement. Rickover had been against the project from the beginning. When [William] Anderson [the second skipper of the *Nautilus*]—I don't know whether he is Senator or Representative Anderson now—but when he got out from under the pole, we picked him up at sea and flew him into Reykjavík and then to Washington.[18]

Anderson's wife was brought to meet the president, and she didn't know where they [*Nautilus*] had gone, or when they would be back. I was in charge of getting the guests there, and Eisenhower got to worrying about the fact that there might be too many people there. I had already invited CINCLANT [Adm. Jerauld Wright, commander in chief, Atlantic Command], the operational commander. I was hoping he wouldn't want to come, but he accepted. When Gates asked me if we should invite Rickover, I said, "No, he wasn't concerned with operational matters."

Well, the ceremony went off, and Mrs. Anderson was really surprised. The reporters noticed that Rickover wasn't there and went to see him to ask him why he wasn't there. Well, you know Rickover, he wouldn't ever help anybody out. He said, "The sons of bitches didn't invite me."

Well, the next day, there were headlines all over the place. Secretary of Defense Gates had to take the blame to take it off the president, and he wasn't happy. As penance, I had to ride between Commander Anderson and Admiral Rickover in the New York City ticker-tape parade.

Rickover is a remarkable man. I believe all his success is due to his thoroughness. He is tireless and exacting.

Rickover went on a tour of Russia and was invited to tour their nuclear icebreaker in addition to many other areas, and when he came back, I asked him to come over and speak to the officers in OPNAV. He agreed and gave a really good speech. Afterward, he was in my office and looking at me the way he does, and he said, "You know, you can get people to work for you by being nice to them. I never could." I avoided the obvious question as to whether he had ever tried.

Rickover had convinced the Congress that the only thing that was useful was nuclear power. They were even on the point of passing a resolution that all surface ships had to be nuclear powered. Nuclear power was a revolution in submarines but was only another method of propulsion for a surface ship.

OLIVER: How was the feeling in Congress toward the Navy and the carrier?

RUSSELL: There was no question that we had problems. [George] Mahon was even worse than [Clarence] Cannon in many respects.[19] The primary problem we were having in Congress was that they wouldn't vote for the carrier requests unless it was nuclear-powered, and we couldn't get it through the secretary as nuclear-powered. We lost both ways. His [McNamara's] big objection to the nuclear carrier was cost.

OLIVER: Was there any carryover from the Mitchell controversy about carrier vulnerability?

RUSSELL: The Air Force was always sniping. They were a new service, and they didn't have the responsibilities that the other two did. This gave them a great deal more flexibility in establishing various positions.

OLIVER: Vincent Davis credits you as being the "father of the Polaris." Did you feel that the great amount of money being spent for nuclear-powered tactical and strategic submarines detracted from the building-up of tactical [surface] forces, thus leading to block obsolescence?

RUSSELL: Burke used to have a stack of chits on his desk when he was CNO that read, "BLANK is the Inventor of the Polaris."

I was BUAIR [head of the Bureau of Aeronautics] back when BUAIR really had some power.[20] The man who really thought of marrying the submarine and the ballistic missile . . . worked for me.[21] We had an air-breathing missile at that time, but it didn't have sufficient range. So, it was obvious that the solid-propellant ballistic missile was the way to go. I went in to see Charlie Wilson, who was secretary of defense at the time. He said we could do it if we used the Army missile, the Jupiter. Well, the Jupiter was a liquid-propellant missile. Can you imagine loading that extremely noxious nitric oxide on board a submarine? It was an impossible idea. Well, I had some power at the time, so I issued three contracts by myself for the development of a solid-propellant missile.

There was no question that the submarines were expensive and were detracting from the normal building program. We still have the block obsolescence problem. Zumwalt's High-Low mix is probably the worst answer to that.[22]

NOTES

1. James Roherty, *Decisions of Robert S. McNamara: A Study in the Role of the Secretary of Defense* (New York: Harper, 1971), 141–42.
2. Vice Adm. Ruthven E. Libby, commander of the First Fleet from 1958 to 1960.
3. Before the creation of the SIOP in 1960, the services developed their nuclear targeting plans independently. The SIOP was a comprehensive, joint war plan developed under the leadership of Strategic Air Command for the large-scale use of nuclear weapons against the entire communist bloc. William Burr, ed., "The Creation of SIOP-62: More Evidence on the Origins of Overkill," NSA, Electronic Briefing Book 130, July 13, 2004, https://nsarchive2.gwu.edu/NSAEBB/NSAEBB130/.
4. For background, see David Alan Rosenberg, "Origins of Overkill: Nuclear Weapons and American Strategy, 1945–1960," *International Security* 7, no. 4 (1983): 3–71.
5. Russell was contradicting Burke's recollections about why he took the computer course.
6. This was an exaggeration of what transpired. Kennedy had planned to retain Gates to groom Robert Kennedy as his successor. The plan was shelved because it would enhance Gates's political profile as a Republican. McNamara's statements in 1964 that Gates had failed to exercise strong leadership of the services drew a strong public rebuke from Gates. "McNamara Charges Draw Gates Reply," *New York Times*, September 18, 1964; Francis Gavin, "The Myth of Flexible Response: United States Strategy in Europe during the 1960s," *International History Review* 23, no. 4 (2001): 872.
7. Burke believed that he had charmed Connally. Burke oral history, JFKL.
8. Connally served aboard USS *Essex* with future CNO David McDonald.
9. The "2" on any staff is responsible for intelligence gathering and assessment.
10. Russell was born in Washington State and retired there also.
11. In his final assignment, Russell served as commander in chief of Allied Forces Southern Europe—today known as Allied Joint Force Command Naples.
12. "Bare base deployment" referred to the Air Force's capability to build airfields and supporting infrastructure quickly in forward operating zones. Marsha Kwolek, "Bare Base Equipment and Support of the Expeditionary Air Force," Air War College, Air University (2003), https://apps.dtic.mil/sti/pdfs/ADA424751.pdf.
13. Yet another veteran of RAND, Herb Rosenzweig was responsible for tactical air forces in the Office of Systems Analysis. He later had a career within the New York City municipal government. Wolfgang Saxon, "Herb Rosenzweig, 'Whiz Kid' and Welfare Officer, Dies at 64," *New York Times*, August 24, 1994.
14. Officially known as Project Dye Marker but informally as either the "McNamara Fence" or the "McNamara Line," it was actually a complex system of fortifications, sensors, and mines that would run along the Demilitarized Zone between North and South Vietnam. It was supposed to hinder North Vietnamese infiltration of the south. The idea for the barrier came from civilian scientists serving as advisers to the Pentagon but received a

generally negative reaction from the JCS and US commanders. Christopher Twomey, "The McNamara Line and the Turning Point for Civilian Scientist-Advisers in American Defense Policy, 1966–1968," *Minerva* 37, no. 3 (1999): 235–58; Peter Brush, "The Story behind the McNamara Line," May 22, 1997, https://msuweb.montclair.edu/~furrg/pbmcnamara.html; Michael Rühle, "The Rise and the Fall of the 'McNamara Line': Enduring Lessons from the Vietnam War," *Comparative Strategy* 37, no. 5 (2018): 404–13.

15. Alfred Starbird, head of the Defense Information Systems Agency from 1962 to 1967, was selected to oversee construction of the barrier in 1966.
16. The Maginot Line was a series of major French fortifications constructed primarily along France's border with Germany from 1929 to 1938. The line was meant to divert any German attack on France through the Netherlands and Belgium, where it would be halted by French and British motorized and armored divisions. The Germans thwarted the Allies' plans by launching a feint into the Netherlands and Belgium, while the bulk of their armored forces bypassed the Maginot Line by striking through Luxembourg into southern Belgium and then northern France.
17. The Oak Ridge National Laboratory in Tennessee. Russell served with the Atomic Energy Commission and participated in the Sandstone nuclear tests in 1948.
18. Anderson served as the US representative for Tennessee's Sixth District from 1965 to 1973.
19. Mahon was the chairman of House Appropriations Committee from 1964 to 1979. He replaced Cannon, who was the chairman for most of the period from 1941 to 1964.
20. See chapter 1.
21. Individual not identified.
22. See chapter 3.

APPENDIX C

Discussion with Adm. George Anderson, USN (Ret.), Chief of Naval Operations, 1961–63

The interview was conducted on April 22, 1974, in Washington, DC, by Lt. Cmdr. Dave Oliver. This reconstruction was made from Oliver's recollections and notes from the interview. It was provided to Admiral Anderson for his review. Oliver subsequently deleted some comments that the admiral did not want attributed to him. This transcript has been lightly edited for clarity.

OLIVER: What happened with respect to the nuclear power for the CVA-67 controversy?

ANDERSON: The cost for the eight-reactor carrier was excessive—about one and half billion [dollars] and rising. We could get a nonnuclear carrier for $310 million. The lead time on the nuclear carrier was long. In order to get the CV [aircraft carrier], I had to accept a conventionally powered carrier. I sent word to [Admiral Hyman] Rickover that I couldn't justify an eight-reactor carrier and that he should get busy and design a modern plant that would cost less and would be less complicated.

One year later, Rickover came up with a four-reactor carrier. I proposed that we now substitute the four-reactor carrier for the conventionally powered one. McNamara thought I had been conniving behind his back all along (to get the nuclear power plant), so he stuck with his original decision. I had originally agreed to take the conventional power plant, and I stuck with the agreement.

As to which [type of power plant] is cheaper, . . . the long core life and the rising cost of oil, plus the extra storage space for aviation gas, means that over the life of the carrier, nuclear power comes very close to being just as cost-effective as conventional power.[1] In addition to that, the flexibility of being able to operate without the need for a chain of oilers is extremely valuable.

We should build only nuclear-powered carriers. The carrier is freed from logistical constraints. The major escorts also should be nuclear powered. Rickover should concentrate on smaller cores (for surface ships) with bigger outputs [i.e., more megawatts].

Oliver: Was your outlook on the carrier influenced by Chairman [Clarence] Cannon's avowed opposition to the carrier as evidenced by his speeches in the House in 1959?[2]

Anderson: No. I don't recall Cannon's speech.

Oliver: What was the relationship of the Navy with Congress?

Anderson: Rickover had a powerful position with Congress. This infuriated McNamara, but McNamara couldn't get [rid of] Rickover because of his powerful position with Congress. Since he couldn't get Rickover, he went after us [the nonsubmarine portion of the Navy].

Oliver: Did you feel Rickover was cooperating with you and the rest of the Navy?

Anderson: He didn't bother me.

Oliver: Despite McNamara's "revolution," if one looks at the procurement figures for the last years of Eisenhower's reign and the first ones of Kennedy's, the Navy's total percentage of procurement remains about the same.[3] With the building of the increased numbers of Polaris and attack nuclear submarines, it looks as if the submarines were being paid for by the national strategic portion of the budget. Did you think this was true?

Anderson: Polaris was the most forward-looking portion of the strategic forces because of its invulnerability. . . . But it was expensive. We had an understanding that the cost of Polaris would not come out of the tactical Navy's budget. McNamara's talk about money not being a restriction was a lot of hogwash. Money was always a restriction. Polaris and Poseidon both came out of the tactical forces' budget. The problem now is to ensure that Trident doesn't set the tactical forces back again.

Oliver: Did the rapid buildup of the strategic and tactical nuclear submarine force in the Sixties result in there being insufficient funds to build any surface ships for the first five years of McNamara's reign?

Anderson: I think it was the [FY] 1964 budget. We had asked for more nuclear [attack] submarines and the secretary had reduced our request. We had reclaimed the cut, and McNamara had told us, "No." We [the JCS and the secretary] had a meeting down at Palm Beach with the president. The president asked me if I had received enough, and I told him, "No," [and] that there were five items I needed: some more submarines, some money for maintenance, certain aircraft procurement, plus some other things.

I told him I was responsible for the long-term operations of the Navy as well as for the operations today, tomorrow and the day after tomorrow. I told him we never get enough money . . . [, and] we would like professional, experienced naval officers to make the judgment on where to cut. McNamara was irritated because he had previously told the president that we had enough money. Kennedy just smiled. He was backing up his secretary, and that was right.

When I got before Congress that year, Jerry Ford asked me if I had what I needed, and I told him, "No," and told him what I needed. He asked me if I had gone to the secretary of defense and to the president. I told him I had, and he said, "Well, you've done all you could." I reminded him of that just the other day.

OLIVER: When you came into office, what was your order of priorities as to what had to be done? Were you more concerned about the procurement problems of the TFX, V/STOL, surface-to-surface missiles, submarines, [and] the CVA or the CVN?[4]

ANDERSON: I came from my job as COMSIXTHFLEET to relieve Arleigh Burke.[5] I was convinced the first year that my most important job was to make everything work. We were getting extremely poor performance from our guided missiles. I think Burke was right to get them out aboard ship [before they were completely reliable]. The program to fix them up was expensive. The second year, I emphasized the importance of people. I feel this is the most important aspect of the Navy.

We had cut the program of forty-five Polaris submarines to forty-one in order to equalize the distribution of funds throughout the Navy. We couldn't afford a nuclear carrier at that point.

When I became CNO, I had been better prepared than anyone else who had held the job within recent years. I had been a [numbered] fleet commander, had served in both oceans, on the JCS, and in OPNAV. I had a very experienced group of deputies. My people at OP-01, -02, -04, -05, and -06 had all had [command of] fleets. I had Admiral [William] Raborn as my OP-07, which was R & D. I had a wealth of experience. I relied on these people, and I kept in constant contact with the fleet commanders. I didn't rely on a small personal staff as Zumwalt did.

I had good relations with the secretaries of the Navy. Excellent relations with [John] Connally and with [Fred] Korth until the TFX controversy, and Korth was all involved in that one himself.

I had problems with McNamara's staff. As an example, [Alain] Enthoven had a guy working for him who had been in the German air force during the war. His name was Dieter Schwebs, and he couldn't even get a normal security clearance.[6] He spent so much time sending down questions to answer that we couldn't get any other work done.

McNamara was doing so much that he was encroaching on the legal prerogatives of the secretary of the Navy and the CNO.

OLIVER: Was the secretary [of defense] using bureaucratic devices to split up the Navy?

ANDERSON: The Navy was organized as a bilinear organization.[7] This had worked well during World War II. I was not responsible for procurement. The chief of naval material reported directly to the secretary of the Navy, and they [the former] were responsible for procurement problems. I set the requirements. The Army had been monolithic, and they had a great deal more problems during the war than we had with procurement. The Air Force had taken the monolithic structure with them when they split off from the Army. McNamara forced the Navy to reorganize on a monolithic basis. This was a mistake. The Army and Air Force should have adopted the bilinear system.

I am in favor of giving the military more of a voice in the operations and plans side of the military. The CJCS [chairman of the Joint Chiefs of Staff] should be the equivalent of a deputy secretary of defense for operations. The secretary of the Navy should have to cut the mustard as a manager of the procurement problems.

OLIVER: Did you feel that the secretary of defense and his immediate staff were biased because of their background?

ANDERSON: McNamara is a brilliant individual. He has a mind that is statistical. He had two faults. He considered himself infallible, and his judgment was bad.

The Navy's professional talent is based on three factors. The first is the experienced flag officers, the second is the experienced chief petty officers, and the third is the young naval officers, [on] whom we spend a great deal training, educating, [imparting] dedication to duty, and teaching them the can-do spirit. There is always a shortage of ships, aircraft, maintenance money, etc., but these three factors can offset them. This is the way we manage to struggle through. These are the most important factors to maintain in the Navy.

This spirit of importance and dedication is what McNamara did the most to destroy in the Navy. I will never forgive secretaries of the Navy Chaffee and Nitze for bringing in Zumwalt, who got rid of so many experienced officers who could have been of assistance. The secretary of defense and his assistants didn't know anything about the Navy. The only thing they knew anything about was the Air Force.

OLIVER: Did you feel that the old questions about carriers, which had not been settled in 1949 in the Revolt of the Admirals, were still around to haunt you? Did you feel that the Air Force was trying to snipe at you?

ANDERSON: I didn't get involved in interservice rivalry. One of the first things Fred [Korth] brought down to me was word that McNamara expected the Navy to carry the freight in Congress lobbying against the big aircraft—what was it?—the B-70. I told Korth that I wouldn't do it, that I understood the Air Force pretty well, that I knew LeMay, and I wasn't going to do his dirty work for him. We were going to just justify our [budget submissions only]. McNamara was not happy about my refusal.

OLIVER: Did you feel the Navy had so many other problems, like the TFX, that spending chips on the nuclear carrier was not worth it?

ANDERSON: Well, the TFX was another story in itself. McNamara made a snap judgment. He thought he'd make points with the president and the vice president, who was Lyndon Johnson [from Texas, where General Dynamics was located], and he made a mistake. He didn't even read the report [the joint evaluation]. McNamara didn't come back to either the Navy or LeMay to discuss the issue. McNamara put out the word that his decision was to be justified no matter who got hurt if they got in the way. I told everyone in the Navy that this was going to be a big issue and that I wanted everyone to stick to their own area of expertise, to avoid speculation, and to stick to the facts. Korth went into a rage when I refused to follow McNamara's line.

OLIVER: Did you feel McNamara was a good "political animal?"

ANDERSON: No. He told Congress he was going to do one thing at the very time he was doing something exactly opposite.[8]

OLIVER: Well, he was successful for several years, wasn't he?

ANDERSON: Yes.

OLIVER: Did you feel the Navy organized to meet the systems-analysis challenge from the secretary of defense? Did you feel that either of the other services did better? Was that important?

ANDERSON: The Navy had been doing systems analysis for years. We had used the "estimate of the situation" as a basis for reaching a decision. We had the OEG as our evaluation group, and they were very efficient. McNamara may have called it cost-effectiveness, but it was really just the application of operations analysis [research], and we had operations-analysis representatives' teams with all our fleets. We were using cost as an analysis factor.

During the war [World War II], the British did not deploy [a specific type of] airplane. They accepted a slip in operational availability because [their] analysis showed that an alternative airplane would be more effective for the pound [cost]. Operational analysis was not new with McNamara. Cost-effectiveness was just a term. His group of analysis had a tremendous cohesiveness when they arrived due to their common experience of service at RAND.

The Air Force had supported more of the new "Harvard people" who are now being appointed to positions of responsibility, and they had supported more of the East European intellectuals who came to prominence after the 1960s. Most of the latter had very shallow roots in America.

OLIVER: Do you feel that the Navy should rely on contracts with these people rather than on in-house expertise?

ANDERSON: No. We have always had a great number of civilians in business [*sic*] who have Navy experience, such as President Nixon, Vice President Ford, Doug Dillon, etc.[9] We and the Air Force need to have the expertise in-house. We should remain true to our principles.

OLIVER: What are your conclusions about the McNamara era?

ANDERSON: McNamara was the worst thing that could have happened to the country. Zumwalt has increased the deterioration of the Navy. We have too much early selections [for promotion].[10] It takes a great deal of experience to prepare individuals for the responsibility [that] rank brings, particularly captains. One of the worst things I ever had to do was to relieve the skipper of the *Coral Sea*. He was making too many errors; the next one would have been bad for the Navy. I called him directly from the CNO's office, and he said he had been sitting there waiting for my call. He had been early-selected twice and was an excellent officer and would have been a terrific one if he had been permitted the time to mature and gain experience.[11]

Bud [Zumwalt] would have been a good CNO if he had more sea experience. He came in here to take care of all the poor sailors, the Blacks, and he succeeded in undermining the CPOs [chief petty officers, who are] one of those three essential factors in the Navy's success. Then he discarded the flag officers. I never wrote a letter to a flag officer telling him I had no job that he could usefully fill [which Zumwalt had done].

We gave Tom Moorer [CNO immediately before Zumwalt] even more experience than I had. He was CINCPAC and then CINCLANT before he was CNO.[12] I just got through with a study, and do you realize that in Europe all of those flags have practically no sea-command experience at all?

NOTES

1. Oil prices actually fell during the 1960s. The inflation-adjusted (2018 dollars) cost of Arabian Light was less than $20 per barrel by the end of the decade. Following the two energy crises of the 1970s, the Arab oil embargo, and the OPEC price hikes, the posted price had spiked to roughly $110 per barrel by 1980 before declining to around $30 during the third oil shock after 1985.
2. See chapter 1 and appendix A, Burke interview.
3. The Navy's share of total obligatory authority in FY 1961 (the last budget passed during the Eisenhower administration) was just under 29 percent; that of FY 1964 (the last Kennedy budget) was just over 29 percent. "National Defense Budget Estimates for FY 2020," Department of Defense, May 2019, https://comptroller.defense.gov/Portals/45/Documents/defbudget/fy2020/FY20 Green Book.pdf, 95.
4. V/STOL aircraft included the British-designed Harrier, a variant of which was built in the United States and operated by the Marine Corps. A CVA is a carrier that is conventionally powered (i.e., by oil). A CVA is a nuclear-powered carrier.
5. COMSIXTHFLEET: Commander, Sixth Fleet. Anderson's replacement was David McDonald, who subsequently relieved him as CNO.
6. Schwebs was a German PhD physicist who had worked during World War II for the German aircraft manufacturer Henschel, where he served on a team developing one of the first air-to-air missiles (HS-298). After the war, he served as a researcher for the French government and industry, and then he joined the US government in 1953, initially doing tactical studies for the Air Force. He later served in the OSD's Systems Analysis Office and as an assistant director of procurement and systems analysis at the Government Accounting (later Accountability) Office. According to one of his GAO colleagues, Schwebs's greatest flaw was that "he was absolutely too open, too honest, and forthright." Government Accounting Office, *Defense Related Audits, 1937–1975: Interview with Hassell B. Bell, J. Kenneth Fasick, and James H. Hammond* (Washington, DC: GAO, 1989),

https://www.gao.gov/assets/200/194491.pdf, 19. For further details, see US Senate, *Fiscal Year 1975 Authorization for Military Procurement, Research and Development, and Active Duty, Selected Reserve and Civilian Personnel Matters*, 93d Cong., 2d Sess. (Washington, DC: GPO, 1974): 4229–30. Schwebs's "typical Germanic so-called efficiency" earned Anderson's undying scorn after Schwebs produced cost-effectiveness studies critical of carrier-launched tactical aircraft. Walter Poole, "Acquisition in the Department of Defense, 1959–1968: The McNamara Legacy," in *Providing the Means of War: Historical Perspectives on Defense Acquisition, 1945–2000*, ed. Shannon Brown (Washington, DC: Center for Military History, 2003), 90; Anderson oral history, JFKL.

7. Responsibility was divided between the secretary of the Navy (the "producer"), who oversaw administration and procurement, and the chief of naval operations (the "consumer"), who handled operational matters. The Goldwater-Nichols Act ended this arrangement by making the Navy a force "producer" for combatant commands. Robert Gates, "History of the Navy Laboratory System," *International Journal of Naval History* 13, no. 1 (2016), http://www.ijnhonline.org/2016/05/26/history-of-the-navy-laboratory-system/.
8. Contrast this claim with Enthoven's observation of McNamara: "I think that, in the professional range, things that made him happy were when he saw examples of high professional competence[,] when he saw good analysis, clear thinking, [and] honesty. I think one of the things that made him angry and unhappy, was when he saw prejudice or irrationality, unreason, disloyalty." Enthoven oral history, JFKL.
9. Douglas Dillon served as undersecretary of state in the Eisenhower administration and as treasury secretary in the Kennedy and Johnson administrations.
10. Zumwalt had emphasized early promotion for "hot runners." Many of the old guard, led by Anderson, believed this was a mistake.
11. The officer in question was Capt. Robert Elder, who had won two Navy Crosses during World War II. Under his command, the *Coral Sea* ran aground in the waters off Oakland, California, in February 1962. Elder was promptly relieved and soon resigned from the Navy. He went on to have a successful career with Northrop, helping to design the F/A-18.
12. CINCPAC: commander in chief, Pacific Command; CINCLANT: commander in chief, Atlantic Command. Not to be confused with CINCPACFLT: commander in chief, Pacific Fleet; and CINCLANTFLT: commander in chief, Atlantic Fleet.

APPENDIX D

Discussion with Adm. David McDonald, USN (Ret.), Chief of Naval Operations, 1963–67

The interview was conducted on May 2, 1974, in Arlington, Virginia, by Lt. Cmdr. Dave Oliver. This reconstruction was made later that day from his recollections and notes of the interview. The draft was then provided to Admiral McDonald for his review. He requested the deletion of several comments that he did not wish to have attributed to him. This transcript has been lightly edited for clarity.

OLIVER: Do you think the Navy has suffered vis-à-vis the other services by not having enough officers schooled in liberal academic subjects, so that we [the Navy] are not as impressive in the political atmosphere of Washington?

MCDONALD: There is no question about it. Of course, you must remember how this started. In peacetime, we still had our ships and still steamed, so we could conduct all the training that was used in wartime, with the exception of firing the shells, on board the ships at sea. When the First World War was over, the Army couldn't do this. They weren't even mechanized. The only thing they had for their men to do was throw manure and cut grass. So, they established a bunch of schools to occupy their time.

The Air Force was brought up in this atmosphere, and even though they had the planes to look after, they were used to going to [postgraduate] schools. If we send people to schools, we don't have the people to man the ships at sea. However, I bet we have more than four times the percentage of officers in school now than we did in 1922. I never did go to any school except to the National War College. I said why should I go to a school to learn tactics when I'm doing it out here in the ocean?

But there was no question that we were getting licked in the political arena, in the JCS, and the secretary's office [the OSD]. We were not used to fighting the other services—we'd always presented our case [directly] to Congress. As we get more intellectual—better educated, I guess you would say—we need more horse sense. That is what the secretary [McNamara] lacked.

Oliver: Doesn't the fleet still discriminate against officers who receive postgraduate training?

McDonald: Well, yes. I remember when I sat on my last selection board in 1954–55. I didn't think that time in school was worthwhile. If a man's record came up, and he had spent three years in school while he was a commander, that was three years that he wasn't gaining any experience. He didn't have any fitness reports. I don't want some professor telling me who I should promote. But we can't do that anymore. I don't feel that we should emphasize schooling too much, but if you come up with two officers who are equal in all other respects, then maybe the advantage should go to the officer with schooling. If they are equal in all other respects.

Oliver: In a recent book, James Roherty has said that the Navy "did not enter into the fray [about the nuclear carrier in 1962] with its customary assuredness. . . . There was noticeable ambivalence in the Navy attitude toward nuclear propulsion. . . . The Navy had allowed a doctrinal gap to develop with respect to the utilization of attack carriers."[1] Is that the way you saw it?

McDonald: When [Secretary of the Navy Fred] Korth called me over, I didn't know what was going on, but I was suspicious. I never could figure out why George [Anderson] took that ambassador [to Portugal] job. I was really furious. Fred [Korth] asked me if I could take the job [of CNO], and I said, no, I didn't want the job. I already had four stars and wouldn't get any more, and I wanted the job in London.[2] Well, Fred asked me to go sit outside [his office] because he had a couple of things to do and then we'd go down and talk to Bob [McNamara].

We got started down, and he said that Bob was out of town, and that we'd go in and talk to [Roswell] Gilpatric.[3] As soon as we walked in, Gilpatric was walking to me and not me to him. It was obvious that Korth had [already] called him. So, after a while, it became obvious that the president [Kennedy] had already made up his mind, and when I asked Gilpatric that, he said it was true. I told him that I'm not that big a fool [as to defy the president], so I'd take the job.

I looked at my job as one of pouring oil on troubled waters. The Navy and the secretary of defense had gotten so far apart the Navy was not going to get anything. All communications had broken down. I know many people felt I was kowtowing, and they were right. I would have kissed McNamara's ass at high noon if I thought it would help to smooth things over, and there were many times I felt I had. There were lots of times that I didn't agree with him, but I never fought him in public or underhandedly with Congress. The fellow who said he would rather be right than president was never president.

With respect to the carrier [CVN-67], I felt we needed [another] deck. Also, I had never been a rabid supporter of the need for nuclear power for a carrier. If we needed nuclear power, it was for the destroyers. They had to be refueled every day, the carrier only every three to five days. I remember talking in his office with [Sen. John] Pastore, and he said, "Admiral, you are settling for a slice, and we are trying to get a whole loaf."[4] I said, yes, but we're awfully hungry.

I probably never would have made it if it hadn't been for Ike [Isaac] Kidd. He was my aide, and he always said, "Admiral, if you quit, the chances are ninety-nine out of one hundred that your relief will think the same way you do, but he won't have the experience you have in dealing with the current situation." I almost turned in my suit, but I finally didn't.[5] Everyone wondered how I got along with McNamara and Gilpatric and [Secretary of the Navy Paul] Nitze. I didn't agree [with them], but I had made up my mind that I would get along so that the Navy could profit in the end.

Nitze and I discussed that we would have to get along. His aide was Bud [Elmo] Zumwalt, and Bud walked the fine line of not being disloyal to either Nitze or me. Bud was in tight with Nitze. I have never been happier with Barry Goldwater [than] when he refused to permit Nitze to be appointed to ISA the other week.[6] I can't prove it, but I think that Bud would have been back in the Pentagon within a few weeks as a civilian.

I even got along with Alain Enthoven. He was a real intellectual, but I got along with him. He came down to tell me goodbye before I left, and I told him why I had gotten along with him. It was because I knew that he didn't believe in some of those things he had supported. He had been directed to find a way of supporting some decision McNamara wanted to make, and he did so. I don't have any quarrel with a man like that.

The only time that I went to McNamara and said I couldn't support him was over the FDL.[7] The concept was bad—that this ship was going to pull up to a prepared dock and make an unopposed landing. The whole purpose of the idea was to cut down the Army by bringing troops back from Europe. I told Bob that, and he said, "Well, I'll kill it then if you're going to oppose me." I told him that I wasn't going to oppose it, no sir, but I would not support it.

Dick Russell [chairman of the Senate Committee on the Armed Services] and I were from the same small town in Georgia [Winder], probably about six thousand people total, but I never used our friendship.[8] If I couldn't do it above board, I didn't do it. The only time I went to him was when [Hubert] Humphrey was trying to get the CNO's house.[9] Dick didn't know that the bill [authorizing the transfer] was even under consideration, and he told me he'd take care of it. Kidd was doing some things under the table with Congress on the TFX, and I ordered him to stop it when I relieved [Anderson].

McNamara really had us over a barrel. He was trying to reduce the number of carriers to ten or twelve [from fifteen]. We had never had any justification for the number of carriers except that we said that we had to have three for every one deployed, that we needed two for NATO and three for SEATO, so we needed fifteen [in total].[10] We said that for so long everyone believed it, especially our allies. We ended up keeping them deployed so long we ended up wearing down the American bluejacket.[11]

McNamara could cut our legs out from under us. Requirements are a matter of opinion. We are an easy target because it is impossible to prove requirements. You can always change your assumptions—it is only a matter of justifying your opinion.

This is one of the main reasons I disagree with Zumwalt. I have never publicly opposed him. I told him I wouldn't, but change should be gradual. All requirements are essentially a matter of opinion, and if your successor also makes radical changes, then the Navy goes all over the map, zigging and zagging. All changes should be gradual, then if time proves you're going in the right direction, your successor can increase the amount of change.

I believe the time had come for nuclear power, but I also believed that we wouldn't get a nuclear CVA-67 without at least a delay of one year. Actually, we never would have gotten the carrier. If we had made [it] an issue and fought McNamara, he would have delayed the carrier, and we would have had to fight the battle again the next year, and the next year, and the next. Time was important. We needed the carrier. In the end, McNamara went along with me. There was no change in analysis. In addition, it was impossible at the time to advocate the conventional power plant without arguing against nuclear power.

There were a hell of a lot of things on my mind that were more important than the nuclear carrier. Let me give you an example of the need for rapport with the secretary of defense. When it was time to name a new CINCPAC, I was completely outvoted in the JCS.[12] Even the commandant of the Marine Corps voted against me, and he wondered why I didn't support him later. I supported the Corps but not him. Anyway, it was important that the Navy get that job. I didn't think the [Vietnam] war was going to last forever, and when it was over, the other services weren't going to be interested in that area anymore. So, I went to McNamara and told him I wanted Sharp in that job but the rest of the chiefs were voting for the Air Force man.[13] McNamara told me he'd take care of it, and he did so, despite the combined votes of the chiefs. The only problem was that then I owed the son of a bitch a favor.

OLIVER: Did you feel McNamara was using the threat of not building other surface ships to prevent a strong Navy position on the nuclear carrier?

MCDONALD: No. The whole thing was a matter of money. McNamara was a pacifist, you know. He was a perfect schoolteacher. There was a Jekyll and Hyde personality [about him]. We were having him over to dinner, and my wife was scared how she would respond to such a cold fish. I told her she would find him charming.

McNamara was trying to hold the budget down. Johnson didn't want the public to know how much it [the Vietnam War] was costing. He wouldn't let us call up the reserves. McNamara was telling him what Johnson wanted to hear when he told him it could be done out of stockpiles and then rebuilt over a long period. The president was interested in domestic politics and didn't want to be bothered with international affairs. Just like Nixon is the opposite. The president [Johnson] would decide on what he could sell politically for a budget, and it was difficult to argue with a man with his credentials.

It was impossible to tell what the president's policy was or what was McNamara's. I remember in the spring of 1965, when I almost turned in my suit. The chiefs and McNamara had agreed on a policy, and he went to explain it to the president. The next day he came back, and we sat down, and he said now this is what we're going to do. I said, "Wait a minute, Bob, you've got this turned around. We didn't agree on this," and he said, "This is what I've decided." I said, "Why don't you just say that the president didn't buy our plan. I tell my [bureau] heads when someone doesn't buy something, and then I tell them to get out and do it. I don't tell the lieutenant commanders, but I tell my leaders." And Bob sat there and said, "That's not the way I do it." So, it was difficult to assign blame.

You know Johnson was sincere. He had always said that when he got to a position of responsibility, he was going to do something for the poor people, and when he got there he was saddled with that war that he couldn't get out of. In addition, he had a staff that was composed of some Kennedy-philes. They thought that everything Kennedy had done was perfect and that any change was wrong. I would have fired the whole lot of them.

Before we lost him [Johnson], we were down at the ranch a lot. I always sat across from him at the table where we had drinks, and then we would go for a drive in several cars, and I always rode with him, and then we could come back at the big table [of food] they had improvised. Well, we did that once, and the chiefs were standing around talking afterward and getting ready to leave, and Wheeler said that we ought to say goodbye to the president, and I went back and told him goodbye, and he grabbed [me] and leaned over and whispered, "Now, you just don't worry about that carrier, you hear," and I knew that I had won.[14] I went back outside and told the other chiefs, "Well, boys, I won."

OLIVER: How were the Navy's relations with Congress? Did that have an impact upon the carrier?

McDONALD: Well, I never used my relationship with Dick Russell except for that once. John Connally is probably the best friend I ever had in the world. He and I were shipmates during the war.

I didn't use politics the way Zumwalt does—buttonholing people on particular issues and trying to find ways of getting to them. I stopped Kidd from giving Congress info under the table. I said that we'd go up to the [Armed Services] Committee anytime but above board.

Of course, everyone has different methods. I tried to establish a reputation of validity with Congress. They knew I would tell the truth. I was the first CNO to invite visiting CNOs [from abroad] to stay at my house rather than at a hotel. A few weeks after relieving [Anderson], I noticed that a congressman had played football at Michigan, so I called him up and invited him to go with me to the Navy-Michigan football game. He said that unfortunately he always took his eldest sons along with him, so I invited them too. Then Jerry Ford and I went out [to the game], and within a couple of months he and his wife were guests at my house.

We always had some congressmen as guests at all of our social occasions, when just a few couples sat around and talked. And when I went up on the [Capitol] Hill, I had a friend in court, but I didn't discuss specific issues.

Probably the best training I had for the job as CNO was when I was aide to Dan Kimball, and he moved up to be the undersecretary [of the Navy]. He really was [quite] an undersecretary. In England, the military never appear on the Hill, just the civilians. Well, Dan was an old lobbyist, and he loved it. He was really good, [and] he did everything I suggested. I ran the Navy more from his office than I did when I was CNO.

I really got to know quite a few congressmen in that job. Dan was really a diamond in the rough. He drank a lot and ran around a lot, and I had to watch out for him. One thing about congressmen that you have to realize is that the great majority of them are honest patriots doing their job. In some cases, they become convinced that the country is best off with them in office, and they will do things that you and I might not do, but they honestly believe that it is for the good of the country.

OLIVER: Did you feel that McNamara and his staff were initially biased toward the selection of land-based tactical air versus sea-based tactical air because of their backgrounds?

MCDONALD: There was no question about that. In fact, the bias toward the Air Force was shown by the TFX affair. The most critical design parameters were those involved with carrier operations. The several parameters that were most critical should have been selected, and then the plane designed inside the envelope. I have no conflict with the services having the same plane, which is not the optimum design for any one job. I think that it probably would save money. The Navy wasted its time fighting the concept.

I told my people to make it work because it was the only thing we were going to get. I then stayed clear from any knowledge of it because I knew it would fail. If you look at my congressional testimony, I always say, "My technical people tell me it will work, and I believe in them." No one asked me what my seat-of-the-pants evaluation was, and I never volunteered it. You don't realize the bitterness that had been engendered by the TFX fight.

The TFX was more than 50 percent of our problems with McNamara. You don't insult a man's baby daughter. The atmosphere of hatred affected everything else. I supported the TFX in order to get other things and because I knew that if I didn't, we wouldn't get anything else, period.

NOTES

1. James Roherty, *Decisions of Robert McNamara: A Study in the Role of the Secretary of Defense* (Coral Gables, FL: University of Miami Press, 1970), 141–42.
2. Prior to his appointment as CNO, McDonald was serving as commander in chief, US Naval Forces, Europe (CINCUSNAVEUR).

3. The deputy secretary of defense, whose offices are one floor below those of the CNO.
4. Pastore was a senator from Rhode Island from 1950 to 1976 and a chairman of the Joint Atomic Energy Committee. He was also a major supporter of building a nuclear-powered Navy. See Francis Duncan, *Rickover and the Nuclear Navy: The Discipline of Technology* (Annapolis, MD: Naval Institute Press, 1990), 115–46.
5. Naval slang for resigning.
6. ISA: assistant secretary of defense for international security affairs.
7. FDL: fast deployment logistics ship. These ships would transport bulky Army equipment such as tanks, and when combined with prepositioning of supplies and large aircraft to ferry troops, they were meant to increase the mobility of US forces, enabling them to react to crises around the world. Congress canceled the program in 1967. Harold Sutphen, "The Failure of the Fast Deployment Logistics Ship," *Naval War College Review* 23, no. 8 (1970): 69–86; John Jones, "The Birth and Death of the Fast Deployment Logistics Ship (FDLS): A Case Study in Futility," US Army War College, February 28, 1972, https://apps.dtic.mil/dtic/tr/fulltext/u2/764594.pdf.
8. While McDonald's father was a traveling preacher who rotated among several small towns in northeast Georgia, the family lived in Russell's home town of Winder after 1933. David Lamar McDonald, *The Reminiscences of Admiral David Lamar McDonald, U.S. Navy (Retired)* (Annapolis, MD: US Naval Institute, 1976), 337.
9. Hubert Humphrey, vice president from 1965 to 1969. The chief of naval operations had, since 1923, lived in a house (1 Observatory Circle) on the grounds of the Naval Observatory. In 1974 the house became the official residence of the vice president, and the CNO moved to the Washington Navy Yard.
10. SEATO: Southeast Asia Treaty Organization.
11. Slang for an enlisted sailor.
12. CINCPAC: commander in chief, Pacific Command—today the commander of US Indo-Pacific Command.
13. Ulysses S. Grant Sharp, CINCPAC from 1964 to 1968.
14. Earle "Bus" Wheeler, chairman of the JCS from 1964 to 1970.

INDEX

ABOUT THE AUTHORS

REAR ADM. DAVE OLIVER, USN (Ret.), graduated from the United States Naval Academy and American University. During the Cold War he served aboard submarines operating from seven US ports. After spending four years in command of a submarine, Oliver directed the operations of all US and allied attack submarines in the Pacific against the Soviet Union from Yokosuka, Japan.

He then served in various roles as an admiral and as a political appointee for President Bill Clinton and President George W. Bush. Very relevant to this book, Oliver had six tours in various roles in the Pentagon. As a civilian he was also the chief operating officer of EADS in the United States.

Oliver is one of the founding members of the American College of National Security Leaders, an organization with the goal of improving the dialogue between political officials and retired admirals, generals, and ambassadors.

He is the author of three leadership books, *Lead On: A Practical Approach to Leadership* (Novato, CA: Presidio, 1992); *Against the Tide: Admiral Rickover's Leadership Principles and the Rise of the Nuclear Navy* (Annapolis, MD: Naval Institute Press, 2014); and *A Navy Admiral's Bronze Rules: Managing Risk and Leadership* (Annapolis, MD: Naval Institute Press, 2021).

ANAND TOPRANI is an associate professor in the Department of Strategy and Policy at the US Naval War College specializing in diplomatic and military history, energy geopolitics, and political economy. He is a graduate of Cornell, Oxford, and Georgetown Universities and held fellowships at Yale and Harvard as well as from the Smith Richardson and Stanton Foundations. He is the author of *Oil and the Great Powers: Britain and Germany, 1914–1945* (Oxford: Oxford University Press, 2019), which received the 2020 Richard W. Leopold Prize from the Organization of American Historians, and has published articles in numerous scholarly and popular journals.

Toprani previously served as a historian in the US Department of State and an intelligence analyst at US Central Command. He is a term member of the Council on Foreign Relations; a security fellow at the Truman National Security Project; a member of the Planning Board of the City of Newport, Rhode Island; an affiliate of the William R. Rhodes Center for International Economics and Finance at Brown University; and a visiting professor at the Watson Institute for International and Public Affairs at Brown University.